# RUSSIAN FOREIGN POLICY AND THE END OF THE COLD WAR

*This book is dedicated to:*
*Mum and Dad,*
*Veronica and Kate.*

# Russian Foreign Policy and the End of the Cold War

MIKE BOWKER

## Dartmouth

Aldershot • Brookfield USA • Singapore • Sydney

Published by
Dartmouth Publishing Company Limited
Gower House
Croft Road
Aldershot
Hants GU11 3HR
England

Dartmouth Publishing Company
Old Post Road
Brookfield
Vermont 05036
USA

**British Library Cataloguing in Publication Data**
Bowker, Mike
   Russian foreign policy and the end of the Cold War
   1.Gorbachev, M. S. (Mikhail Sergeevich), 1931- - Influence
   2.World politics - 1989- 3.Cold War 4.Soviet Union -
   Foreign relations - 1985-1991 5.Russia (Federation) -
   Foreign relations
   I.Title
   327.4'7

**Library of Congress Cataloging-in-Publication Data**
Bowker, Mike.
      Russian foreign policy and the end of the Cold War / Mike Bowker.
         p.     cm.
      Includes bibliographical references and index.
      ISBN 1-85521-461-X
      1. Soviet Union--Foreign relations--1985-1991. 2. Russia
   (Federation)--Foreign relations. 3. World politics--1989- 4. Cold
   War. I. Title.
   DK510.764.B68     1997
   327.47--dc21                                                           96-39521
                                                                          CIP

ISBN 1 85521 461 X

Printed and bound by Athenaeum Press, Ltd.,
Gateshead, Tyne & Wear.

# CONTENTS

# ACKNOWLEDGEMENTS

So many people have helped over the years, wittingly and unwittingly, in the writing of this book, it is quite impossible to list them all. However, I would like to thank academics and friends in Russia for their patience and time in discussing various issues with me. I would also like to record my gratitude to colleagues in Britain, most notably Michael Cox, Richard Crockatt, Peter Frank, David Mourton, Cameron Ross, Alan Scott, Peter Shearman, Steve Smith and Phil Williams. I also benefited greatly from discussions at the FCO which were organised by David Miller. Thanks are also due to the many journalists on *The Guardian*, *International Herald Tribune* and *Moscow News* whose reports were invariably valuable and insightful.

But I would like to single out two people for particular thanks. First, Michael Innes for the loan of his computer and his generous help in preparing the script for publication. Second, to Veronica, my wife, who has provided much more than the usual tea and sympathy. She helped set up interviews in Russia; she dug out books, articles and documents in Moscow; gave assistance with some of the translations; and also helped prepare the camera-ready copy. Sadly, that still leaves me to take full responsibility for the final text.


Mike Bowker,
Wymondham,
August 1996.

# ABBREVIATIONS AND ACRONYMS

| | |
|---|---|
| ABM | Anti-Ballistic Missile Treaty |
| ACA | Arms Control Association |
| ACV | Armoured Combat Vehicle |
| ANC | African National Congress |
| ASEAN | Association of South-East Nations |
| | |
| BBC | British Broadcasting Corporation |
| BMD | Ballistic Missile Defence |
| | |
| CAP | Common Agricultural Policy |
| CCP | Chinese Communist Party |
| CFE | Conventional Forces in Europe |
| CGDK | Coalition Government of Kampuchea |
| CIS | Commonwealth of Independent States |
| CMEA | Council for Mutual Economic Assistance |
| COCOM | Co-ordinating Committee for Multilateral Export Controls |
| CPD | Congress of People's Deputies |
| CPSU | Communist Party of the Soviet Union |
| CSCE | Conference of Security and Co-operation in Europe (changed to OSCE in January 1995) |
| | |
| DM | Deutsche Mark |
| | |
| EBRD | European Bank of Reconstruction and Development |
| EC | European Community (changed to EU in 1993) |
| EU | European Union (successor to EC) |
| | |
| FAPLA | People's Armed Forces for the Liberation of Angola (Government forces of Angola) |
| FCO | Foreign and Commonwealth Office |
| FMLN | Farabundo Marti National Liberation Front |
| FRG | Federal Republic of Germany (West Germany) |
| | |
| G7 | Group of Seven richest countries |
| GATT | General Agreement on Tariffs and Trade |
| GDP | Gross Domestic Product |

| | |
|---|---|
| GNP | Gross National Product |
| GDR | German Democratic Republic (East Germany) |
| GPALS | Global Protection Against Limited Strikes |
| | |
| IAEA | International Atomic Energy Association |
| ICBM | Intercontinental Ballistic Missile |
| IFOR | Implementation Force (in Bosnia) |
| IISS | International Institute of Strategic Studies |
| IMF | International Monetary Fund |
| INF | Intermediate Nuclear Forces |
| | |
| JNA | Yugoslav National Army |
| | |
| KGB | Komitet gosudarstvenoi bezopastnosti |
| | |
| LDPR | Liberal Democratic Party of Russia |
| | |
| MAD | Mutual Assured Destruction |
| MAS | Mutual Assured Security |
| MBFR | Mutual Balanced Force Reductions |
| MFN | Most Favoured Nation |
| MIRV | Multiple Independently Targetable Re-entry Vehicles |
| MPLA | Movement for the Popular Liberation of Angola |
| MX | Missile Experimental |
| | |
| NAFTA | North American Free Trade Agreement |
| NACC | North Atlantic Co-operation Council |
| NATO | North Atlantic Treaty Organisation |
| NIC | Newly Industrialising Country |
| NJM | New Jewel Movement |
| NPT | Non-Proliferation Treaty |
| | |
| OAS | Organisation of American States |
| OECD | Organisation of Economic Co-operation and Development |
| OSCE | Organisation of Security and Co-operation in Europe (successor to CSCE in January 1995) |
| | |
| PDPA | People's Democratic Party of Afghanistan |
| PFP | Partnership For Peace |
| PLO | Palestinian Liberation Organisation |
| PUWP | Polish United Workers' Party (Communist Party) |
| | |
| RIA | Russian Information Agency |

| SALT | Strategic Arms Limitation Talks |
| SDI | Strategic Defence Initiative (Star Wars) |
| SDIO | Strategic Defence Initiative Organisation |
| SED | Sozialistische Einheitspartei Deutschlands (Communist Party of East Germany) |
| SLBM | Submarine Launched Ballistic Missile |
| START | Strategic Arms Reduction Talks |
| SWAPO | South West African People's Organisation |
| | |
| UN | United Nations |
| UNITA | National Union for the Total Independence of Angola |
| UNO | United National Opposition |
| UNPROFOR | UN Protection Force (in Croatia and Bosnia) |
| UNSCR | UN Security Council Resolution |
| USSR | Union of Soviet Socialist Republics |
| | |
| VOPP | Vance-Owen Peace Plan |
| | |
| WTO | Warsaw Treaty Organisation (Warsaw Pact) |

# INTRODUCTION

The cold war dominated the second half of the twentieth century. It divided the world and legitimised the nuclear arms race. It provided the framework for government decision-making on both sides of the iron curtain throughout the period. By the 1970s, the cold war had lost some of its ideological intensity, but few seemed able to imagine the world without it. Neither side had the strength to contemplate the overthrow of the other in war. Equally, neither side was willing to make significant compromises to bring the cold war to an end. The international status quo appeared frozen by the existence of nuclear weapons and two implacable ideologies.

This all began to change when Mikhail Sergeyevich Gorbachev became General Secretary of the USSR on 11 March 1985. Gorbachev came to power determined to reform the Soviet system. He wanted to humanise the political system and improve economic performance. Gorbachev hoped reform would strengthen communism - initially he had no intention of dismantling it. Thus, Gorbachev wrote in 1987 that the Soviet Union was not interested in becoming capitalist. The aim of perestroika, he said, was more democracy and more socialism (Gorbachev, 1987: 37).

In both domestic and foreign policy, Gorbachev's reform programme went through three distinct phases. The first lasted from 1985 to 1987. In this period, Gorbachev was the most radical member of the politburo. He was not only the instigator but also the leading theoretician of *perestroika* (reconstruction). Compared to what had gone before, Gorbachev's new proposals looked radical, but they did not challenge the fundamentals of the Marxist-Leninist system.

In the second stage, 1988-90, perestroika began to radicalise. Gorbachev emphasised the crisis in the country and the need for change, but increasingly he portrayed himself as a centrist who was attempting to steer a middle course between 'impetuous radicals' and 'over-cautious conservatives'. Gorbachev chose this tactic to obscure the fact that he had actually abandoned reform in favour of what Professor Archie Brown of Oxford University termed 'systemic transformation' (Brown, 1996: 15). Gorbachev, as General Secretary of the CPSU, still claimed to be a communist but his ideas on the nature of Marxism-Leninism had themselves been transformed beyond anything recognisable to any of his predecessors. In this phase, Gorbachev began to attack the basic pillars of Marxist-Leninist ideology. He actively undermined the state-controlled economy through the introduction in January 1988 of *khozraschet* (cost-accounting) which devolved much decision-making power from the central planners to the enterprise director. He also undermined the vanguard role of the party through the introduction of competitive elections and the transfer of executive power from the party to the state.

The result of these innovations, however, was not, as Gorbachev had hoped, a more efficient economy and a more accountable political system. On the contrary, perestroika led to mounting economic crisis, a loss of political authority at the centre and a collapse in Soviet influence around the world. Thus, by late 1989, the process of reform was visibly spinning out of Gorbachev's control. Perestroika had failed in its attempt to create a third way between Western-style capitalism and Soviet-style communism. Instead, from 1990, the country entered the third stage of reform - a time of turmoil and confusion as Gorbachev, for the first time, had to contemplate the end of communism in the USSR. This period ended with the rise of Yeltsin to pre-eminence in 1991, the formal rejection of Marxism-Leninism and the collapse of the Soviet Union as a unified state.

### Gorbachev's New Thinking

In a series of speeches, Gorbachev had stated that his first priority on assuming office was the revival of the domestic economy (see, for example, *Pravda,* 24 February 1989). Later, however, he argued that it was impossible to reform one area of policy in isolation (*Soviet Weekly,* 7 June 1990). Gorbachev, thus, embarked on what Archie Brown has called a 'fourfold transformation' (Brown, 1996: 157). This involved economic reform, democratisation, decentralisation and rapprochement with the West. His new ideas on all these areas will be taken up elsewhere, but here a brief outline will be offered of his thinking on international relations - the main theme of this book.

Gorbachev's ideas on foreign policy developed quickly from the orthodox Marxist-Leninist views expressed in his early speeches (see Gorbachev, 1986) to his more innovatory new thinking outlined in his book, *Perestroika*, first published in 1987. His new thinking had two defining elements. First, it involved an implicit, and at times explicit, rejection of some central planks of Marxist-Leninist doctrine; and second, it embraced many liberal ideas associated with idealist international relations theory (see Shearman, 1993).[1]

The most important break with traditional Marxist-Leninist ideology was Gorbachev's move after 1986 towards a more positive attitude towards capitalism. In an interview, Gorbachev admitted that the Soviet Union had been wrong to predict capitalism's 'early failure' which led to Moscow severely underestimating capitalism's 'ability to adapt and develop in new conditions' (*Soviet News*, 25 January 1989). He acknowledged that Moscow had no monopoly on truth and could learn from other countries and other social systems (Gorbachev, 1987: 152) and, in stark contrast to his predecessors, he also referred favourably to the theory of systemic convergence (Brown, 1996: 224). Gorbachev, therefore, advocated an end to Moscow's self-imposed isolation and encouraged the Soviet Union's integration into the mainstream of international political and economic life (*Pravda*, 8 December 1988).

Gorbachev also began to underplay the militaristic aspects of capitalism which had been at the heart of the Soviet attack on the West. Gorbachev argued that war was no longer inherent in capitalism (Gorbachev, 1987: 147). Evidence for this could be found in countries, such as Japan and the Federal Republic of Germany, which were economically strong without either an extensive military-industrial complex or high levels of defence spending (*Soviet News*, 4 November 1987). The Soviet academic, Georgy Arbatov summed up these views when he said, war was caused not by capitalism, the US or NATO, but by militarism which 'has become a universal threat and danger for all' (*Moscow News*, 25 September 1988).

Gorbachev inferred from this that the class struggle was no longer the central dynamic of international relations (*Soviet News*, 6 July 1988). As a result, Gorbachev argued that peaceful co-existence could govern relations between the two social systems. However, for Gorbachev, peaceful co-existence was not just a breathing space before the onset of war, nor a peaceful interlude before the inevitable victory of communism - as in traditional Leninist theory - but a

---

[1]  Most of idealism's ideas stem from the writings of Immanuel Kant (1950). For a modern reinterpretation, see  David Saunders (1985).

condition which could govern relations between the two opposing social systems over the long-term (*Soviet Weekly*, 4 February 1989).

The influence of liberal idealism to Gorbachev's new thinking could be seen in a number of areas. First, he argued in favour of interdependence and globalism. He believed the world was a single entity which had become uniquely vulnerable in the modern era to the twin threats of nuclear weapons and ecological disaster. Although national and class divisions remained, Gorbachev argued that the world had to unite to deal with such problems. No solutions were possible, he said, unless leaders abandoned their instinctive distrust and showed a greater willingness to co-operate across borders and across the ideological divide (Gorbachev, 1987: 137; and *Pravda*, 8 December 1988).

Second, he argued for greater trust among nations. He rejected the realist idea that peace and stability could be maintained through nuclear deterrence and the continued division of the world into two rival blocs.[2] Instead of building up defences to deter attack, Gorbachev argued that states should remove the original causes of fear and suspicion. Military security should be replaced by political security - in other words, negotiation and diplomacy should replace nuclear brinkmanship. In Gorbachev's idealist world, everybody would benefit as zero-sum games of the cold war were replaced by positive-sum games. A good example of such an arrangement would be disarmament. Not only would arms cuts save both sides considerable sums of money, it would also lessen fear and mistrust and, therefore, greatly reduce the risk of war (*Soviet News*, 1 March 1989). Everyone would benefit.

Third, Gorbachev rejected war as a tool of foreign policy. The maxim of Clausewitz - long favoured in the Soviet Union - that war was the extension of politics by other means, was formally rejected (Gorbachev, 1987: 137). Gorbachev argued that any war between the superpowers, whether conventional or nuclear, would be mutual suicide (Gorbachev, 1987: 141).

Finally, Gorbachev favoured the replacement of militarism and the class struggle by a commitment to international law firmly grounded in a respect for universal human rights. In Gorbachev's vision, the UN would become a proto-world government with the power and the duty to enforce peace and stability. Bloc politics of the cold war era would be replaced by collective security, policed by the Warsaw Pact and NATO (*Pravda*, 8 December 1988).

Gorbachev's ideas could be criticised as naive. They certainly contained

---

2    Realism was the dominant academic theory of International Relations in the West during the cold war period. The main writers have been Carr (1939), Morgenthau (1948) and Waltz (1979). See chapter 13 for further discussion of realism and its normative antecedent, idealism.

many of the flaws of idealism which had been so clearly exposed by leading realist thinkers, such as E. H. Carr (1939) and Hans Morgenthau (1948). Nevertheless, Gorbachev's new thinking challenged orthodoxy both in Washington and Moscow and ultimately, against all expectations, overthrew it. Few had predicted the end of the cold war, even fewer thought it could end without bloodshed. In the past, Soviet leaders had been portrayed as brutal, dogmatic dictators interested only in power. Yet, the Soviet Union took the unusual step of giving up its superpower status without a fight. The reason for this remarkable occurrence is the focus of this book.

## The aims of the book

In trying to understand the shift in Soviet foreign policy, two themes predominate. First, the reasons for change were complex and multifaceted. No single factor, not even the failing Soviet economy, can offer a complete explanation. This does not mean that everything was equally important. Factors varied over time and across issue areas. This is something brought out throughout the book. Second, the book accepts the importance of the domestic in understanding foreign policy changes in the USSR - hence the space allocated to that subject. However, the attempt to determine the relative importance of the internal and external is largely rejected. The two are too closely inter-related, as Gorbachev said, for this to be much more than an academic exercise. Thus, the perceived failure of the Soviet economy was not only a matter of slowing growth rates, but also the growing realisation amongst the Soviet elite that the Soviet economy was performing poorly in international terms.

The central argument of the first chapters on domestic politics is that the reformist wing of the party, led by Mikhail Gorbachev, initiated the process of change. When Gorbachev came to power in 1985, there was pressure from below for reform but not for revolution. The economy was in trouble but not in crisis. The masses were sullen but largely passive. The main constituency for reform came from the growing group of highly educated professionals who felt underpaid and under-valued in a self-proclaimed workers' state. Gorbachev was clearly responding to the demands of this group when he introduced perestroika (see Lewin, 1988: 64). It is, therefore, largely accurate to describe the overthrow of Soviet communism as a bourgeois revolution. In a number of republics, the intellectuals were able to mobilise the masses behind their cause in the name of nationalism. In Russia, however, nationalism was relatively weak and the intellectuals and masses never joined forces against the party and state. As a result, many in Russia regarded the anti-Soviet revolution as both unwanted and the product of alien forces. Inevitably, this had implications when Yeltsin came to power.

In foreign policy, Gorbachev soon came to reject the cold war. During his first twelve months in office, he entered arms control talks with the US, abandoned the Brezhnev Doctrine in Eastern Europe and decided to withdraw from Afghanistan. For reasons outlined in the following chapters, Gorbachev expected that the end of the cold war would enhance rather than diminish Soviet influence in the world. Although he failed in this latter aim, it was important in getting acceptance for his new thinking from the more conservative party ideologues and military officers.

In the West, Gorbachev is treated as a hero. In the Soviet Union his tenure is remembered as one of retreat and humiliation. Instead of reasserting the Soviet Union's place in the world as an acknowledged superpower, new thinking ended up in 1991 with Gorbachev dashing around Western capitals with foreign policy concessions in one hand and a begging bowl in the other.

Boris Yeltsin came to power eager to emphasise the break with the Soviet past. Yeltsin embraced liberal democracy and the market, and argued that Russia and America should become partners rather than enemies. Yeltsin has been largely successful in dismantling the command economy, but the reforms led to economic decline and the impoverishment of large sections of the Russian population. Inevitably, this led to public disillusionment and put further pressure on the nascent democratic structures in Russia. The people voted in 1996 for a continuation of reform, but this does not mean that a transition to a Western-style system is inevitable. On the contrary, Russian history and culture will undoubtedly lead to a highly distinctive post-communist society. Much of Russian politics remains riven by fundamental disputes, not only over the methods of transition, but also over its end goals.

In foreign policy, the honeymoon with the US scarcely lasted a year. Issues which soured the relationship included Russian support for the Serbs in Bosnia, Moscow's more activist policy on the territory of the former Soviet Union, NATO enlargement and Moscow's revived interest in the arms trade. The book argues that the partnership with the West was never likely to last. National interest was always likely to reassert itself after the cold war ended. Nevertheless, the downturn in relations should not solely be attributed to domestic Russian politics and the country's shift towards nationalism. The West also deserves its share of the blame for some ill-considered and insensitive policies.

Yet there has been no return to the cold war, and this is unlikely to happen now that Yeltsin has won a second term as President. Relations between Russia and the West will often be difficult in the future, but there still remain areas - such as nuclear proliferation, trade, and regional stability - where co-operation is both possible and desirable. Cultural and national differences will always exist, but there is no longer a fundamental divide over the ordering principles of international society. To that extent at least, the liberal democratic order has triumphed. This offers the best hope for world peace and stability in the future.

# Chapter One

# GORBACHEV'S POLITICAL REFORM

Western critics of the Soviet Union argued that its political system was totalitarian.[1] Totalitarianism was always better viewed as a theoretical model rather than a description of reality. It gave an impression of total control which never existed in the Soviet Union, even in Stalin's time (see Dunmore, 1980). However, to describe the Soviet Union simply as a dictatorship never seemed enough. Clearly, the Soviet Union was a centralised and repressive state like many others - opposition parties were banned and elections were little more than exercises in mass mobilisation. Yet two factors, above all others, distinguished Soviet communism from other dictatorial systems.

First, the economy was controlled by the state. After Stalin abolished private property and private enterprise in the 1930s, the Soviet citizen became dependent on the state for the most basic means of survival - food, housing, education, health, employment and physical security. Economic control gave the state enormous power over the individual. The post-Stalinist state did not have to arrest or execute its opponents. The fear of losing one's job, being unable to find an apartment, or one's children being denied entry into a school was usually enough to ensure conformity. Not only did Soviet citizens have no means of organising against the state, they had no means of escaping its all-embracing

---

1  The classic text on totalitarianism is by Friedrich and Brzezinski (1956). For a discussion of the various theories and models of the Soviet political system, see Brown (1974).

presence. Big brother was watching.

Second, Marxist-Leninist ideology not only legitimised the dictatorship, it glorified it. The dictatorship of the proletariat was not an unfortunate necessity - a temporary expedient until normality could be restored. It was a necessary prelude to communism - the final stage of societal development. As such, the dictatorship of the proletariat represented progress over 'bourgeois democracy'. Bourgeois democracy was rule by and for the minority capitalist ruling class. The communist dictatorship, on the other hand, was rule by and for the majority working class. Furthermore, the party claimed a monopoly right to rule because it was a vanguard. It was a vanguard in the sense that it was an elite of trained and committed revolutionaries; and also because it was leading the country, in the interests of all, to the long-term goal of communism. Opposition, therefore, was not only illegitimate, it was also, by definition, reactionary (see Lenin, 1902).

The Soviet Union was reformed after Stalin's death in 1953. The political system became more institutionalised. The grotesqueries of the Stalinist personality cult were denounced and the arbitrary nature of terror was abandoned. Rules re-emerged. Life for Soviet citizens became safer and more predictable. It did not, however, become more democratic. The basic pillars of the Soviet dictatorship remained in place. The party retained its monopoly right to rule - indeed, it was formalised in article 6 of Brezhnev's 1977 Constitution. The economy also remained in state hands. Mass, arbitrary terror ended, but more selective terror continued. Perhaps most important of all, Marxist-Leninist ideology remained unchallenged. Indeed, the founder of the Soviet state, Vladimir Ilich Lenin, became an icon - a God-like figure - whose words were quoted in every context and whose physical being was celebrated in endless portraits and statues throughout the country.

When Gorbachev came to power, the Soviet state looked strong and secure; reform almost unimaginable (see Kirkpatrick, 1989). Pressure from below scarcely existed. Strikes and political unrest were rare. Intellectual dissent, which had briefly flowered in the Khrushchev era, was harshly repressed by Brezhnev. According to Roy Medvedev, the socialist dissident writer, only 'several dozen' activists remained at large in the late 1970s (Medvedev, 1980: 146), whilst another few thousand dissidents languished in jail (Reddaway, 1989: 103). It appeared the state retained both the political will and the repressive power to maintain the Soviet system.

Yet what is a strength in one context can become a weakness in another. The Soviet state had enormous power but it was also extremely rigid and inflexible. Civil society was virtually non-existent. The party was a vanguard, therefore, there was no need for the party to consult the people. The party acted in the interests of all, therefore, there was no need for any constitutional constraints on the party and state. Nor any need for institutions or structures to mediate and arbitrate between different groups in society. As a result, the Soviet state had no institutional mechanism to accommodate outside interests. Gradual change could only be generated by the party leadership. The masses could only seek change through rebellion and revolution (see Kennan, 1947: 580).

When Gorbachev came to power, there was little fear of a popular uprising. Yet, despite outward appearances, pressure for change in the Soviet Union was growing. For whilst the political structures of the Soviet Union had remained stuck in the 1930s, society had undergone a social revolution (see Lewin, 1988). The Soviet Union was no longer the illiterate, peasant society which Stalin had known. By the 1980s, it was highly industrialised and predominantly urban. In 1945, 56 million lived in towns; in 1987, it was 180 million, or almost two thirds of the total Soviet population (Smith, 1990: 18). In 1928, barely 5 percent of the population were white collar workers; in 1979, the figure had risen to over 25 percent (Hosking, 1985: 481). It was also a highly educated society. In 1939, only ten percent had secondary education; in 1986, secondary education was virtually universal and 11 percent held a higher degree (Hosking, 1990: 3; Miller, 1993: 29). Soviet society had become more complex and more middle class. It was increasingly difficult to accommodate this growing diversity within a monist political system designed for a different, pre-industrial age.

This is not to say that perestroika in the 1980s was inevitable. Far from it. Brezhnev's party saw little reason to change. The country was stable. The economy was not in crisis. Yet, even then, isolated pockets of reformist opinion did exist. Reformism had first emerged at the top of the party in the 1950s, and although it had been defeated by the Brezhnev counter-revolution, its ideas were submerged rather than eradicated (see Cohen and vanden Heuvel, 1989: 41). The social changes, outlined above in respect to the wider community, also affected the party and views within it. By 1986, 43 percent of party members were white collar workers and 34 percent had higher or incomplete higher education (Sakwa, 1989: 128).

A new generation of party intellectuals had emerged since the war which was increasingly frustrated by the Brezhnev style of leadership (see Hough, 1980). Brezhnev surrounded himself with his old cronies. Critical voices and unwelcome information were firmly kept out. As a Soviet joke had it at the time, Brezhnev simply drew the curtains on his train and pretended it was still moving towards communism.

## Gorbachev's rise to power

Gorbachev was born on 2 March 1931 to a poor peasant family in the small town of Privolnoye in southern Russia, some 125 miles from the regional capital of Stavropol. He was only ten years old when the war started; he was twenty-two when Stalin died. Therefore, Gorbachev grew up under Stalinism, but his political career owed nothing to the man or his policies. Gorbachev was a member of the new political generation and very much a part of the *embourgeoisement* of the CPSU mentioned earlier. Gorbachev held two degrees, in law and agronomy, and his whole career was spent as a 'white collar worker' in the party apparatus. Gorbachev was effectively middle class and he had cultured tastes. He enjoyed reading poetry - the banned poet Boris Pasternak was one of his favourites - and he travelled extensively. His visits to the West, by all accounts, made a deep impression on him (see Brown, 1996: 42-3).

After he received his first degree in law from Moscow State University in 1955, Gorbachev returned to his home region of Stavropol to pursue his political career. His rise was rapid. He was appointed First Secretary of the Stavropol region in 1970 aged thirty-nine, and this gave him the opportunity to meet top political leaders. In 1978, he was duly brought to Moscow as agricultural secretary and in 1980, he was promoted to the politburo. After Brezhnev's death in 1982, the new General Secretary, Yuri Andropov, extended Gorbachev's duties to include overall responsibility for the economy as well as the chairmanship of the parliamentary foreign affairs committee. It was in this latter role that Gorbachev came to Britain in December 1984 and impressed Mrs Thatcher as a new-style Soviet leader (see Thatcher, 1993: 459-463).

When Konstantin Chernenko was appointed as successor to Andropov in February 1984, Gorbachev was informally designated as his deputy. Given Chernenko's age and ill-health, it was clear that his leadership could only be a stop-gap. Conservatives fearing Gorbachev's reformist agenda, mounted a concerted campaign to keep him out of the top office (Gorbachev, 1995a: 263). However, the weakness of the conservative case was evidenced by the paucity of alternative candidates. Grigory Romanov, a member of the politburo and secretariat, looked a potential rival, but he was renowned for corruption and drunkenness. Recognising that he had no chance against Gorbachev, he put his political weight behind another conservative candidate, the Moscow party chief, Viktor Grishin. Grishin, however, was already a septuagenarian in 1985 and few relished the thought of another old man in the Kremlin (Boldin, 1994: 61).

Chernenko's brief and undistinguished time as General Secretary came to an end on 10 March 1985. He was the third General Secretary to die in office in less than three years. It seemed symbolic of the political sclerosis that had afflicted the Soviet Union since the mid-1970s. The politburo met on the evening of Chernenko's death to discuss a successor. Although Gorbachev was clearly the preferred candidate, a final decision was postponed until the following day.

At the subsequent emergency session on 11 March, the Foreign Minister, Andrei Gromyko, opened the debate and was the first to speak in support of Gorbachev's candidature. In traditional Soviet style, the rest of the politburo followed Gromyko's lead and Gorbachev was approved as General Secretary unanimously. A couple of hours later, the decision was confirmed by the Central Committee of the CPSU (Gorbachev, 1995a: 267-9).

What were Gorbachev's aims when he took power? It is difficult to be certain since so many of his statements were ambiguous and even, at times, contradictory. In his 1987 book, *Perestroika*, Gorbachev himself admitted to being unsure about his 'end goals' (Gorbachev, 1987: 35). Yet there remains little doubt that Gorbachev came to power a reformer. He had made this plain in a number of key-note speeches leading up to his appointment as General Secretary (see Gorbachev, 1995a: 271). A speech to an ideological conference in December 1984 was of particular importance in this regard; for in that speech, he outlined in some detail many of the ideas which later became known as perestroika (Gorbachev, 1984).

However, it was also clear that Gorbachev wanted reform to revive communism, not to bury it. Thus, in his acceptance speech to the politburo after his appointment as General Secretary, he said:

> 'We do not need to change policy. It is correct and it is true. It is genuine Leninist politics. We need, however, to speed up, to move forward, to disclose shortcomings and overcome them and realize our shining future' (Remnick, 1993: 520).[2]

Gorbachev's surprisingly conservative statement could be dismissed as a new leader pandering to his audience. Certainly, his speech to the Central Committee shortly afterwards put more emphasis on the need for change. Nevertheless, two years later in *Perestroika*, his manifesto for reform, he was still writing: 'Any hopes that we will begin to build a different non-socialist society and go over to the capitalist camp are unrealistic and futile' (Gorbachev, 1987: 37). And as late as March 1991, Gorbachev declared: 'I am not ashamed to say that I am a communist and adhere to the communist idea, and with this I will leave for the Other World' (*International Herald Tribune*, 26 December 1991).

---

2   David Remnick, an American journalist, who wrote the bestseller, *Lenin's Tomb*, was the first to gain access to the minutes of the emergency politburo meeting on 11 March 1985. The full transcript is now available in *Istochnik*, 0/1993: 68-75.

By this time, however, Gorbachev's view of communism had changed. From 1987, he began to challenge some of the core beliefs of Marxism-Leninism. Thus, he implicitly rejected the concept of the vanguard party. In *Perestroika*, he admitted that the party did not always know best (Gorbachev, 1987: 152). He recognised the existence of diversity in the Soviet Union, but welcomed rather than feared it. He referred favourably to the term pluralism - or socialist pluralism, as he called it at first: 'A conflict of opinion generates thought,' he wrote at the time (Gorbachev, 1987: 77). Brezhnev had said, trust the cadres, Gorbachev was saying, trust the people (*Pravda*, 11 December 1994). This was a truly revolutionary call in a one-party system.

Gorbachev also favoured limits to the power of the Soviet state (Gorbachev, 1987: 105). He advocated a law-governed state - a state in which all Soviet citizens were equal before the law (*Soviet News*, 30 November 1988). The law, Gorbachev said, should be based on clear rules and not on subjective criteria, such as the furtherance of the revolution. The state should also be neutral. It should not favour one class over another. Its power should be constrained in law by a system of 'socialist checks and balances'. The Soviet state was later divided, like in the US, into three branches: the executive, the legislature, and the judiciary.

Political reform went through three phases. In the first phase, 1985-87, Gorbachev's main policy innovation was glasnost. Glasnost is usually translated as openness, but it had broader implications, including individual freedom and human rights. During this period, the media was freer and the arts livelier than at any time since the Khrushchev thaw. The *gulags* were opened up too and political prisoners began to come home. Gorbachev also prepared the ground for the second phase of his reforms, 1988-90, when perestroika was radicalised. At the June CPSU Conference of 1988, Gorbachev unveiled his plans to democratise the structures of state. These dramatic reforms included competitive elections in March 1989, the creation of a new and fully functioning parliament, and the introduction of a presidential system in March 1990. During this period, the party also formally abandoned its vanguard role in Soviet society. In the third phase, 1990-91, Gorbachev discovered his innovations had led to a loss of power and authority at the centre. This period was spent attempting to regain control, first through abandoning reform in the winter of 1990-91, and then through a renewed alliance with Yeltsin and the radicals. Both efforts failed. Effective power had already passed to the republics and regions.

Perestroika had led neither to a viable democratic socialism or a functioning multi-party democracy. Why was this? Why did perestroika end in the collapse of communism? There are three general explanations. The first argues that the Marxist-Leninist system was essentially unreformable (Malia, 1990; Kirkpatrick, 1989; and Remnick, 1993). Gorbachev sought some kind of middle way between neo-Stalinism and liberal democracy, but this, it was said, was both theoretically and practically impossible. A democratic one-party system was a contradiction in terms. In democratic conditions, how could other parties be prevented from forming? How could the guaranteed monopoly right to rule be justified? David Remnick argued: 'Once the regime eased up enough to permit a full-scale examination of the Soviet past, radical change was inevitable. Once the system showed itself for what it was and had been, it was doomed' (Remnick, 1993: xi).

Both of the remaining two explanations reject the idea that reform in a Soviet-type system was impossible. After all, the Soviet Union reformed itself after Stalin's death and different forms of communism existed around the world. In China, for example, Deng Xiaoping from 1978 introduced market reforms within a Marxist-Leninist political framework which soon led to some of the highest growth rates in the world. In Yugoslavia too, Tito introduced far-reaching economic and political reforms after the split with Moscow in 1948 which allowed far greater personal freedom than in most other communist states. There was, therefore, no apparent *a priori* reason for the failure of reform in the Soviet Union. It all really depended on the chosen definition of reform.

The two remaining explanations, therefore, place more emphasis on Gorbachev's personal role. Critics blamed his naivety, malice, incompetence, or some kind of combination of all three, for the chaos which engulfed the country from the late 1980s (see, for example, Yeltsin, 1990 and 1994; Kagarlitsky, 1992; Ligachev, 1993; and Boldin, 1994). Supporters, on the other hand, cast Gorbachev as the hero not the villain of the piece (see Brown, 1996: 315-318). This third view argued that Gorbachev was one of only a handful of party leaders in the early 1980s who recognised the urgent need for reform. He was prepared to take personal and political risks to introduce changes which were to the long-term benefit of the country. Gorbachev made mistakes and errors of judgement but, it was argued, his political achievements - most notably, the abandonment of terror and the end of the cold war - far outweighed them. Moreover, Gorbachev's failures were less a result of his own failings and owed rather more to bureaucratic obstructionism and the sheer enormity of the task he faced in 1985.

All these theories have much to offer. It did appear that Gorbachev underestimated the systemic barriers to change when he first came to power. Interestingly, however, when the difficulties became obvious to all, Gorbachev did not retreat, as might have been expected, rather he accelerated the process of reform. *'Protsess poshel'*, was his slogan. 'The process has started', and the implication seemed to be that it could not be stopped. Apart from a six-month period in the winter of 1990-91, Gorbachev did indeed maintain the momentum for reform. His policies promoted democratisation but many of his manoeuvres were also designed to maintain his position in power. Moreover, the success (and failure) of his reforms varied greatly across different issue areas. The outcome of reform was also often unanticipated or even the opposite of what had been intended. This will be shown below and in the subsequent chapters.

Yet, by most criteria of the term, Gorbachev was a 'great man' (Brown, 1996: 316). He was one of a handful of figures who could claim to have changed history. Whether by accident or by design, the world looked different after he left office. The past had become a different country. This was Gorbachev's greatest legacy.

## Gorbachev's political reforms

Traditionally, the General Secretary built up his power and authority through the manipulation of personnel policy and the construction of a personality cult. This process usually took some time. Gorbachev, however, was able to quickly impose his authority on the party. His leading conservative rivals, Grigory Romanov and Viktor Grishin, were both rapidly removed from the politburo. Romanov in July 1985 and Grishin the following February. Gorbachev promoted reformers and proven administrators to replace the old hands. In April 1985, Yegor Ligachev became a senior secretary and Gorbachev's effective deputy. Eduard Shevardnadze replaced the long-serving Andrei Gromyko as Foreign Minister in July. Nikolai Ryzhkov became Prime Minister in September and Boris Yeltsin became Moscow party chief the following December. A number of radical thinkers were also appointed in this period as political advisers, including Alexander Yakovlev, Georgy Shakhnazarov and Anatoly Chernayev.

Radical changes affected every level of the party. At the 27th CPSU Congress in February 1986, twelve out of twenty-seven politburo members and forty percent of Central Committee members were newly elected. By the end of the summer, fifty percent of republic and regional first secretaries had also been replaced. These were sweeping changes which contrasted sharply with Brezhnev's policy of 'stability of cadres'. The changes were a necessary precursor to reform. However, Gorbachev remained disappointed by the continued conservatism of party and state. It was not enough to change personnel, he had to change political structures too.

*Glasnost*

Gorbachev formally unveiled his policy of perestroika at the 27th CPSU Congress in 1986 (Gorbachev, 1986). Its most radical innovation in political terms was the policy of glasnost. Glasnost had both moral and practical implications. At a general level, glasnost was intended to open up the system and end the stultifying conformity of the Brezhnev years. A greater openness would allow the public to voice their opinions and encourage more informed and responsible decision-making (Gorbachev, 1987: 32-33). Gorbachev also wanted the media to more closely reflect the views and concerns of the public (Gorbachev, 1987: 76). The media could, therefore, become an effective intermediary between the governors and the governed. However, Gorbachev did not necessarily view the media as independent of the state. In a speech to the media in October 1988, he said:

> 'Publish everything. There should be pluralism of opinions. But its orientation should be towards protecting and strengthening the line for perestroika and the cause of socialism' (*Pravda*, 25 September 1988).

Glasnost was a theme Gorbachev frequently returned to in his early months in office, but it was only after the tragedy at Chernobyl that glasnost was transformed from aspiration into reality.

The accident occurred in the early morning of Saturday 26 April 1986 at the Chernobyl nuclear plant near Kiev in the Ukraine. One of the four reactors exploded in what was meant to be a controlled experiment. Gorbachev and the politburo were informed five hours later when the firemen were unable to put out the fire (Medvedev, 1986: 259-60). Three days after the disaster, the whole of the neighbouring town, Pripyat, was evacuated. It was the worst nuclear accident in history. Several died in the attempt to control the explosion, thousands have since died from the subsequent radiation fall-out. Yet the accident went unreported in the Soviet media until Swedish authorities detected abnormally high levels of radiation coming from the Soviet Union. Finally, in a small news item on Moscow TV on the evening of 28 April, it was reported that a reactor at Chernobyl had been damaged and aid was being given to those that had been injured (White, 1993: 98).

Chernobyl represented a crisis for Gorbachev and his reform policy. The official delay in announcing the disaster endangered the lives of people who lived in the region. The inadequate coverage after the initial announcement added to a general feeling of panic in the country. The people did not trust their leaders. They certainly did not trust their media. Many tuned into foreign radio stations to try to find out what was really happening. Yet, it was almost three weeks after the accident, on 14 May, before Gorbachev went on TV to give a more detailed statement. It was not considered to be one of his most assured performances. He generally tried to downplay the dangers of the accident and criticised the inaccurate reporting of the Western media. More positively, however, he argued that Chernobyl had shown the urgent need to press ahead with glasnost (*Pravda*, 15 May 1986).

Shevardnadze later said, Chernobyl was the first test of glasnost, and it failed (Shevardnadze, 1991: 175). Yet the accident provided an important stimulus for reform. Gorbachev knew that censorship in the information-saturated modern world had become more difficult. Chernobyl showed it could also be dangerous. In the circumstances, it became far more problematic for hardliners to resist the reformers' call for greater openness. Gorbachev later acknowledged that Chernobyl had been 'a turning point' in terms of the development of glasnost in the USSR (Brown, 1996: 163).

Political prisoners were being released before Chernobyl, but the process speeded up thereafter. The most well-known dissident still active in the Soviet Union was Andrei Sakharov. He had been exiled to Gorky in 1980 after his criticism of the Soviet invasion of Afghanistan. Gorbachev rang him up personally in December 1986 and told him his exile was over. He was invited back to Moscow to play a role in the unfolding drama of perestroika. In February the following year, a formal amnesty was announced for all political prisoners jailed under Brezhnev, and by 1989 the annual *Amnesty Report* announced that all political prisoners had been released. In July of the same year, the criminal code was amended to disallow imprisonment for political crime.

Before that however, in the spring of 1988, glasnost confronted a second major crisis. It came in the unlikely form of a letter to the conservative newspaper, *Sovetskaya Rossiya*, from Nina Andreyeva, a little known chemistry lecturer from Leningrad. In the letter she attacked glasnost and complained about the media's persistently negative criticism of Soviet history. In particular, she sought to defend the traditional view of Stalinism as a harsh but necessary period when the Soviet Union built up its industrial and military might, enabling it to defeat Hitler and become a respected superpower in the post-war era (*Sovetskaya Rossiya*, 13 March 1988).

Although her argument was little different to the official view presented by Gorbachev only a few months earlier at the seventieth anniversary of the Bolshevik Revolution (*Pravda*, 7 November 1987), the letter was viewed by reformers as a direct challenge to perestroika. This was largely because the letter was so strongly promoted by Yegor Ligachev, who had emerged as the leading conservative in the politburo. Ligachev has since denied ordering the editor of *Sovetskaya Rossiya* to publish the letter, but he has acknowledged praising it at a meeting of newspaper editors which he chaired whilst Gorbachev was out of the country (Ligachev, 1993: 301).

When Gorbachev returned to Moscow, Nina Andreyeva's letter became the focus of a fierce debate in the politburo. Significantly, the debate was held behind closed doors and went unreported in the Soviet media. Finally, however, after two full days of discussion, *Pravda* published an anonymous editorial (in fact, written by Alexander Yakovlev) repudiating the contents of the Andreyeva letter (see Boldin, 1994: 143). The editorial said there was no alternative to perestroika and any delay in its implementation would be damaging to the Soviet Union and international communism (*Pravda*, 5 April 1988).

The media had feared at the time that Andreyeva's letter signified the end of reform, and for three weeks there had been a self-imposed silence (see *Moscow News*, no. 17, 1988). However, after the *Pravda* editorial, the process of glasnost accelerated. Cultural life became more diverse. Previously unpublished books were made available, including Solzhenitsyn's *Gulag Archipelago* and George Orwell's *1984*, both of which were issued in 1989. The press became more critical and state control over the media was formally abandoned in July 1990.

If Chernobyl really started the process of glasnost, then the Andreyeva letter changed its nature. After April 1988, glasnost ceased to be a process managed and controlled by the party and became a more independent and spontaneous movement. A civil society was slowly emerging.

*Democratisation and the decline of the party*

The process of democratisation really began at the 19th CPSU Conference in June 1988. Gorbachev introduced three central ideas: competitive elections; a functioning parliament; and the separation of powers. These were discussed over the following weeks and formally approved in November and December (see *Vedomosti verkhovnogo soveta SSSR*, Moscow, 7 December 1988: 831-857). The British professor, Stephen White, summed up Gorbachev's ideas on democratisation as follows:

'The animating principle throughout was the control and limitation of executive power in the interests of greater public involvement in all spheres of Soviet life...' (White, 1993: 30).

At first, Gorbachev had wanted to democratise the party but he was unable to overcome fierce opposition in the party apparatus. He, therefore, switched his attentions to the state. Democratisation of the state met with fewer objections. Lenin had taken power in 1917, not in the name of the Bolshevik Party but in the name of the Soviets (the councils of workers, peasants and soldiers). His slogan had been: 'All power to the Soviets', Gorbachev was now using Leninist rhetoric to call for 'More power to the Soviets' (see Urban, 1990). Such a proposal was more difficult for ideologues to reject. Interestingly, a number of conservative figures, including Yegor Ligachev, actively supported the idea of transferring more executive power to state bodies. It was the rushed manner in which it was attempted that provoked criticism (see Ligachev, 1993: 274-5).

The most eye-catching of Gorbachev's reforms was the creation of a new parliament - the tricameral Congress of People's Deputies (CPD). This was a large body with 2,250 deputies with two of the three chambers elected directly by the people. The main duty of the Congress was to elect a smaller body, the 542-strong Supreme Soviet, which sat for far longer and had much greater powers than its predecessor. According to the amended constitution, the Supreme Soviet could both initiate and review legislation as well as monitor government appointments. At the judicial level, a Commission of Constitutional Review (a kind of weaker US Supreme Court) was also created to oversee the workings of the Congress and other state bodies.

Although the reforms seemed far-reaching, many at the time believed little would change in practice. The main reason for this scepticism was the executive power of the CPSU, whose structure and organisation remained untouched by the reforms. The party retained its guaranteed monopoly right to rule and appeared to be in a good position to dominate both the electoral process and the new legislative body. This was so for four main reasons. First, the proposed election to the CPD did not allow multi-party contests, only multi-*candidate* ones. Non-party candidates could stand against party members, but only as independents, not as part of an organised opposition party. This clearly gave the party a major advantage in terms of finance and campaigning. Second, a quarter of all constituencies in the first elections to the CPD in March 1989 still only had one candidate. Third, the third chamber of the CPD was made up of seats reserved for the CPSU and other Soviet organisations, almost guaranteeing representation in the Congress for top establishment figures. Finally, the more powerful Supreme Soviet was elected indirectly by the Congress of People's Deputies. This offered the party yet another opportunity to filter out politically undesirable deputies.

For once, however, the sceptics were proved wrong. The elections which took place on 26 March 1989 were a turning-point in Soviet history. 87 percent of the deputies elected to the Congress of People's Deputies were Communist Party members. Yet, the election was not seen as a victory for the party. About twenty percent of the officially sponsored candidates were defeated, and some, like politburo member Yuri Solovyev, stood in single candidate constituencies but failed to get the required absolute majority. Radical non-conformists, on the other hand, performed strongly, especially in urban constituencies. Most notably, Boris Yeltsin, condemned to the political wilderness after being sacked from the politburo in February 1988, swept to victory as a radical in the Gagarin constituency in Moscow with an amazing 89 percent of the vote, and this despite a virulent campaign against him in much of the party press.

Yegor Ligachev accepted that the party had been discredited by the vote but blamed a lack of leadership at the top. The CPSU issued a manifesto but, he complained, it failed to campaign in any organised way during the election. He wrote:

> '... the Central Committee offered no political orientation, and the local Party offices were helpless. For the first time, there were no clear directives from the centre on how to behave. And this came during an election campaign when the question of power was being decided' (Ligachev, 1993: 92).

The election certainly had a major impact on the party. Party discipline and party unity broke down as party members campaigned against each other for votes. Moreover, the eventual victors owed nothing to the CPSU or the political leadership for their electoral success. Deputies felt loyalty only to the constituency which had elected them. To a large extent, this was what Gorbachev had intended. Indeed, he further encouraged the centrifugal tendencies in the party when he decreed that party members in the CPD no longer had to vote as a single bloc. This ended the Brezhnev tradition of unanimous voting, but the leadership also began to lose its authority over the membership, which in turn eroded the party's ability to impose its will on the country.

Institutional reform of the party had begun slowly when the Central Committee secretariat was broken up in September 1988 into six commissions. Traditionally, the secretariat had been second in influence only to the politburo. It was the administrative arm of the party and the political base from which all General Secretaries had emerged since Stalin. Yet after its abolition as a unified body, conservatives complained that it had an immediate and dramatic effect on executive discipline and control over the party rank and file. Ligachev wrote: 'The center seemed to vanish, and vertical ties as well' (Ligachev, 1993: 110).

Once again, Gorbachev acted to speed up, not slow down this process. In December 1989, political platforms (in practice party factions) were permitted to organise in the CPSU as the party divided along political and national lines. Then, in February 1990, the CPSU abolished article six and gave up its guaranteed monopoly right to rule. At the same time, it also agreed to set up a state presidential system, based on the American or French experience, the following month. This latter change was probably the most dramatic of all. It formalised the shift of executive power from the party to the state. The President took on the powers of the General Secretary. The CPSU continued to exist but as a political party which had to compete for power with others at the ballot box. Nowhere was the emasculation of the party more obvious than in the new role of the politburo. The politburo, for so long the most powerful body in the USSR, no longer discussed matters of state, but concerned itself solely with party affairs. It was the equivalent of reducing the British Cabinet to the status of Tory Central Office.

Effectively, the Marxist-Leninist system was abolished in March 1990. However, this political revolution was scarcely forced upon the leadership. On the contrary, Gorbachev chose to dismantle the system. It was true that the one-party system had come under considerable pressure by early 1990. An estimated 60,000 independent groups and 500 political parties had been formed by this time (Sakwa, 1990: 203), and ethnic problems were creating difficulties outside Russia too (see chapter 3). However, it is also true that Gorbachev's inner circle had been discussing these radical reforms long before there was any sign of political crisis. In 1985, Yakovlev wrote to Gorbachev recommending the legalisation of party factions as a prelude to the introduction of a multi-party system. The idea was not dismissed out of hand by Gorbachev because it was anti-Leninist, as one might have supposed, but simply because it was premature

(Remnick, 1993: 298-9). In 1987, the introduction of a presidential system was being seriously discussed and in 1988, the abolition of article 6 (White, 1993: 65; Brown, 1996: 194). It is also worth bearing in mind that Gorbachev approved the idea of a multi-party system for Hungary in a meeting with its party leader, Karoly Grosz, as early as July 1988 (see chapter 5).

Gorbachev presented the changes as part of the overall process of democratisation. That, of course, was true - at least in part. However, Gorbachev's attitude towards the presidency also revealed other motives. According to the newly amended constitution, the President had to be elected directly by the people, but Gorbachev was eager to avoid such a process. So, he manipulated the rules to get himself elected unopposed by the Congress of People's Deputies. He received 59 percent of the eligible vote, but his unwillingness to face the people, or indeed any competitive election, undermined his reputation at home as a democrat (see Poptsov, 1995: 32).

Yeltsin, in contrast, had frequently risked his career for perestroika. He had been sacked from the politburo in 1988 for speaking his mind and put himself up regularly for election by the people. In July 1990, he also walked out of the party, whilst Gorbachev hung on to his position as General Secretary. Increasingly, Yeltsin was viewed by the Soviet people as the reformer and Gorbachev as the conservative. It was also from spring 1990 that Gorbachev's popularity began to slump. Thus, in May 1990, for the first time, he was overtaken in the opinion polls by Boris Yeltsin (Brown, 1996: 6). Gorbachev was never to recover his position.

What then were the real reasons for Gorbachev introducing the presidential system? First, it was a centralising measure to try to counter the growing power of the republics and regions; and second, it was an attempt to secure Gorbachev's position in power. Gorbachev was greatly concerned about historical precedents. For he was conscious that the last reformist leader, Nikita Khrushchev, had been overthrown by a simple majority in the politburo. He was determined to prevent that happening again (Ligachev, 1993: 123-128; Brown, 1996: 182). Therefore, he wanted to broaden his power base and weaken the power of the party which he saw as the major threat to his position. Thus, he amended the constitution so that a serving President could only be removed during a term of office if he violated the constitution and a two-thirds majority of the CPD approved impeachment.

As Gorbachev took yet more power during the course of the year, many accused him of wanting to become a new Tsar. A Moscow journalist wrote: 'From now on Gorbachev is to be President, the parliament, the government and the ruling party simultaneously' (*Moscow News*, 28 September-2 October 1990). It was certainly true that by the autumn of 1990 Gorbachev had accumulated a formidable array of powers. Yet, his powers were more formal than real. In practice, Gorbachev found his authority eroding. He could issue decrees, but increasingly he was unable to implement them. Power continued to leak from the centre.

## The lurch to the right

The 28th CPSU Congress in July 1990 was the high point of Gorbachev's reformist zeal. The CPSU not only approved the abolition of article 6 from the constitution and the introduction of a presidential system, it also voted to remove Yegor Ligachev, the leading conservative, from the party leadership. It seemed the road to reform had been cleared of all obstacles. But this impression was misleading. Opposition forces licked their wounds and began to reassemble their forces in the autumn. The group, *Soyuz* (Union), made up largely of military officers, played a prominent part in this counter-offensive.[3] As the economy declined and ethnic tension rose, the pressure mounted on Gorbachev to abandon perestroika (Gorbachev, 1995a: 583-7). This culminated in a meeting with military officers on 13 November when Gorbachev was told to reverse the direction of his reforms or risk the consequences (Miller 1993: 166).

For some time, Gorbachev had tried to present himself as a centrist - a man who recognised the need for reform but had the clout to keep the radical extremists at bay. As positions polarised in the country, however, this became a more difficult role to play. Gorbachev's natural constituency was the reformist wing of the party, but in the winter of 1990-91 he shifted to the right. Gorbachev has since portrayed this move as a temporary tactic 'to allow the democratic process to gain sufficient stability to ease out the old ways and to strengthen people's attachment to the new values' (Gorbachev, 1991: 13). There is little evidence to back up his account (see Poptsov, 1995: 39). It seems far more likely that Gorbachev shifted to the right to strengthen his position in power. He thought the Soviet people craved strong leadership, and he hoped by adopting a tougher stance, he would be able to undercut Yeltsin's growing support. 'Society had

---

[3] For a brief period, *Soyuz* appeared to be a very powerful opposition group, but it split over its reaction to the August coup and subsequently disappeared from the political scene.

moved to the right,' Gorbachev said at the time, 'government policy had to follow suit' (Arbatov, 1992: 333).

Gorbachev began to squeeze out leading reformers from his administration. They included Interior Minister, Vadim Bakatin and economic advisers, Stanislav Shatalin and Nikolai Petrakov. But most dramatic of all was the resignation on 20 December 1990 of Gorbachev's long-time friend and colleague, Foreign Minister Eduard Shevardnadze, who left office making dire warnings of impending dictatorship. As the reformers departed, Gorbachev brought in many known hardliners, such as Valentin Pavlov who became Prime Minister and Boris Pugo who took over as Interior Minister. Both later emerged as leading conspirators in the August coup.

Gorbachev also backed moves by hardliners in early spring 1991 to remove Yeltsin as chairman of the Russian Congress (see Arbatov, 1992: 335). When reformers in March announced public demonstrations in support of Yeltsin, 50,000 troops were deployed on the streets of Moscow. Gorbachev authorised law enforcement bodies to 'use all necessary measures to ensure appropriate public order in the capital' (Remnick, 1993: 421). The Soviet capital was tense. Violence on the scale of Tiananmen Square in Beijing looked possible. But when it became clear that the demonstration would go ahead anyway, Gorbachev, to his credit, backed off. The demonstration went ahead and Yeltsin retained his position as chairman.

To avoid such threats in future, Yeltsin decided to emulate Gorbachev at the union level and create a presidential system in the Russian republic. The constitutional change was approved by referendum and an election was held on 12 June. Despite a vigorous campaign against Yeltsin in much of the media, Yeltsin won with 57 percent of the vote from a field of six candidates. It was the third time in three years that Yeltsin had won elections - in 1989 for the CPD, in 1990 for the Russian Congress, and now in 1991 for the Russian presidency. Gorbachev finally had to accept that his attempts to defeat his great rival had failed.

### The August Coup

Gorbachev ended his six-month flirtation with conservatism in the spring of 1991. But as Gorbachev changed course once again, he found himself more isolated than ever. The reformers no longer trusted him and the conservatives were outraged by his latest betrayal. In April, the conservatives forced the Central Committee to discuss Gorbachev's future, and in June Pavlov attempted to get the President's powers transferred to him as Prime Minister. Both attempts failed to shift Gorbachev. This should have been a warning to the hardliners that they lacked support in the party, but the campaign against Gorbachev continued.

In July 1991, the hardline newspaper, *Sovetskaya Rossiya*, published an article, 'A Word to the People', written by twelve conservatives, including Gromov, Deputy Minister of the Interior, and Varennikov, Chief of Ground Forces, saying the reformers had led the country to ruin. It called on 'healthy forces' to save the country from 'humiliation' and 'fratricidal war'. The letter called for emergency measures and declared that the military was prepared to act if the President did nothing (*Sovetskaya Rossiya*, 23 July 1991). This was effectively a call for a coup d'etat. Yet, Gorbachev took no action. He still believed his position was secure (see Gorbachev, 1991).

This proved to be a fatal mistake. Whilst Gorbachev was away on holiday in the Crimea, a small group of hardliners finally decided to act. On Sunday 18 August 1991, Gorbachev and his family were placed under house arrest at the presidential dacha on Foros. All communications with the outside world were severed. A Committee of State Emergency was set up which publicly announced on 19 August that Gorbachev had fallen ill and was unable to fulfil his state duties as President. In accordance with the constitution, Vice President Gennady Yanayev took over during the President's incapacitation. A statement issued by the conspirators declared a state of emergency. The measure had been taken, it went on, because perestroika had 'come to a dead end' and the country had become 'ungovernable' (*Pravda*, 19 August 1991).

Troops secured the city of Moscow and the Emergency Committee issued a series of decrees. Independent newspapers, radio and TV stations were closed down. All opposition activity was banned. Tanks were deployed on the streets of Moscow and a list was drawn up of seventy leading radicals to arrest (Yeltsin, 1994: 67-73). These intimidatory tactics failed to work, however. The coup collapsed after only three days and the hope of holding the Soviet Union together collapsed with it. Gorbachev returned from exile to what he himself called a 'different country' (Gorbachev, 1991: 38). Despite initially expressing continued faith in the ability of the CPSU to reform (*Pravda*, 23 August 1991), Gorbachev resigned as General Secretary on 24 August and closed down the Central Committee, the secretariat and politburo. The coup had not propped up the system, as intended, but hastened its end. Why was the coup such a failure?

First, the coup was badly planned. The conspirators could find no convincing figure to act as leader and the members of the Emergency Committee who presented themselves at the press conference on 20 August were an undistinguished group of little known hardliners. The figure-head of the Emergency Committee, Gennady Yanayev, was a particularly pathetic figure who was reportedly drunk throughout the crisis. He was unable even to convincingly identify the aims of the coup. Did he want an end to perestroika, or a return to perestroika without Gorbachev? The message was confused.[4]

Second, Gorbachev refused to resign or support the emergency measures as many of the conspirators had hoped (Gorbachev, 1991: 27-28). Gorbachev's refusal was vital in undermining the claim of the Emergency Committee to be acting within the law. The claim that Gorbachev was ill was transparently false since the plotters were unable to provide any substantiating evidence.

Third, Yeltsin provided a focus for opposition to the coup. Yeltsin's brave stance against the coup led to splits amongst the conspirators as well as in the political and military establishment more generally. Having been elected in June 1991 as Russian President, Yeltsin had far more authority on the territory of Russia in most people's eyes than any self-appointed Emergency Committee. Some regiments defected to the side of the White House. Others, like the elite Alpha group ignored orders from their superiors and refused to use force against their compatriots (*Izvestiya*, 4 September 1992).

Finally, popular opposition to the coup limited the options for the Emergency Committee. The conspirators had misjudged the situation. They had thought it necessary only to proclaim power and place tanks on the streets of Moscow to win the obedience of both people and party. The Soviet Union, however, had changed. The people were no longer so afraid. The political elite was split and power in the Soviet Union had been devolved more to the regions and republics. Organising a coup was far more complex than it had been back in 1964 when Nikita Khrushchev was overthrown (Grachev, 1995: 100). Since the conspirators, to their credit, were unwilling to spill blood on the scale of Tiananmen Square, they had little option but to back down.

However, as one of Gorbachev's own advisers has written, it would be misleading to suggest that Russia rose up against the coup in the name of democ-

---

[4]  Such confusion was evident in a book written by a central figure in the coup, Prime Minister Valentin Pavlov (1993). He tried to argue that the coup never really happened. He denied that Gorbachev had been under house arrest and that his communications with the outside world had been severed. He implicated Gorbachev in the plot whilst at the same time trying to dismiss the whole affair as a catalogue of misunderstandings. There is little evidence to support Pavlov's version of events (see Stapankov and Lisov, 1992).

racy (Grachev, 1995: 34). In fact, protest was largely confined to the large cities of Moscow and Leningrad. Yeltsin's call for a general strike went largely unheeded except in a few mining areas. Polls taken at the time indicated 80 percent of military officers and 40 percent of people in the provinces actually supported the coup (Shevtsova, 1992: 7). Even in Moscow, opposition was limited. When Yeltsin made his famous speech on top of the tank on that first Monday morning, there was a crowd of only about a hundred outside the White House (Steele, 1994: 73). On Monday evening, it had grown to several thousand, but it was only when the coup showed signs of collapsing that the numbers swelled to 50,000 or more.

In truth, the Soviet people were deeply divided over the events of August 1991. The coup did not fail because of popular opposition. It failed because the plotters acted too late. The Marxist-Leninist system they wished to save no longer existed. Gorbachev had dismantled it back in March 1990. However, as Gorbachev acknowledged in his resignation speech, it was easier to dismantle the old system than construct a new one (*The Independent*, 26 December 1996). Thus, when Gorbachev left office in December 1991, his revolution was incomplete. He had democratised the system but he had not created a democracy. Gorbachev introduced competitive elections, he founded more accountable and responsible political institutions; but he could not create a democratic political culture. This takes time. Some Russians believe it is an impossible task - they argue, their country is too big for democracy, their culture too collectivist. But national cultures do change. They change with the generations and they change with social circumstances. To gain legitimacy in Russia, democracy has got to start producing the goods. It must provide efficient government as well as election campaigns, stability as well as freedom, and above all, raised living standards for the average Russian citizen. It is still a long road. The Gorbachev revolution continues.

# Chapter Two

# THE COLLAPSE OF THE SOVIET ECONOMY

The Soviet economy always looms large whenever the collapse of communism is discussed and there can be little doubt that Gorbachev introduced perestroika because of poor economic performance over a prolonged period (see Gorbachev, 1987: part one). Economic problems also affected Gorbachev's foreign policy - much of his new thinking was aimed at reducing the burden of defence spending and facilitating the integration of the USSR into the world economy.

Gorbachev's reforms started cautiously. In the period 1985-87, economic reform was known as *uskorenie* (acceleration). As the name suggests, it envisaged improved growth and efficiency but it did not imply any change to the basic structure of the Soviet command economy. In 1987, however, Gorbachev began to contemplate more radical reform. The policy included moves towards non-state owned property; a relaxation on trade restrictions and foreign investment; and most important of all, a greatly reduced role for central planning and the introduction of some market indicators into the Soviet economy. A third phase began about 1990 as Gorbachev's economic reforms were generally acknowledged to have failed and a furious debate over future policy was taken up by officials and economists alike (see Aslund, 1989; and Goldman, 1991). The debate was only resolved in January 1992 (after the collapse of the USSR) when Yeltsin announced a policy of 'shock therapy' which promised the complete abandonment of the command economy and a rapid shift to private property and the market.

What were the causes of the Soviet economic crisis of the late 1980s? Three views predominate. The first argues that there were systemic problems in the Soviet economy which reform could not overcome (see, for example, Kennan, 1947; Malia, 1990; and MccGwire, 1991). Although this is undoubtedly true, this view, at least in its starkest form, has difficulties in explaining the timing of the economic collapse. Why did it occur in the late 1980s, more than fifty years after Stalin had brutally imposed the command economy on his country? The second explanation answers this by arguing that the Soviet economy was reasonably effective in its early years, but was unable to cope with the changing economic and political circumstances of the late twentieth century. In other words, the command economy became a victim of the modernisation process (Deudney and Ikenberry, 1991). The third view places more stress on the issue of leadership, arguing that poor economic management, which pre-dated Gorbachev but climaxed in his period of office, led to stagnation and then collapse (Ellman, 1992).

## Systemic problems

The Stalinist economic system was designed to be the antithesis of capitalism. Private property and the market were abolished in favour of state control over virtually the entire Soviet economy. Instead of the invisible hand of the market distributing goods according to the criteria of supply and demand, the Soviet state allocated goods according to political, not economic, priorities. In theory at least, goods were distributed according to need rather than wealth. Liberal economic theory argued that such intervention simply distorted the workings of the economy and produced sub-optimal and irrational results (see, for example, Hayek, 1944). The Soviets, on the other hand, argued that the invisible hand of the market did not maximise economic advantage for the maximum number of people. Instead, the system operated at increasingly lower levels of competitive equilibrium (despite periods of growth) which led to mass unemployment and a collapse in demand. Capitalism did not benefit all equally, but operated to maximise profit for the ruling class. For Moscow, distortion of the free market was vital to ensure social justice and to maximise state investment.

In the inter-war years, such arguments won support as Western countries were unable to recover from deep recession. The USSR, in contrast, industrialised rapidly in the 1930s and after war became an economic power - in gross terms, at least - second only to the United States. What was most impressive was that record levels of growth were achieved without any significant unemployment or inflation. The Soviet Union had managed to break the cycle of boom and bust. In economic terms, the Stalinist experiment looked a success. In human terms, of course, the costs were extreme, including labour camps and mass terror.

The system did not collapse after Stalin's death, however, as many had predicted. Instead, the economy continued to function without the use of mass terror, albeit at lower rates of growth. Stalinist brutality was replaced by a form of paternalist authoritarianism. Consumerism remained severely restricted in comparison to the West, but welfare policies were broadened and extended. Education and health were free, as in Britain and some other Western countries, but the Soviet state also provided housing, energy resources, water, public transport and food at nominal prices. The quality of welfare, however, was variable across the country. Education was generally good; housing, on the other hand, was often of very poor standard with many families living in communal flats. Nevertheless, the welfare system did provide considerable personal security for all Soviet citizens. The most important aspect of this was a guaranteed job for life.

The achievements of the Soviet Union were real enough, but inherent economic problems existed in the system. The most prominent was the concept of the plan. The Western capitalist system also generates plans at both the macro and micro level; in the USSR, however, the plan was not a general strategic plan but the basis of all economic activity. As a result, the plan had to be detailed down to the number of screws required for a furniture factory in Novosibirsk. The amount of information required to devise a rational and balanced plan was so great that the task was always likely to be beyond even the most diligent of bureaucrats. This was certainly the view of Gorbachev. After he came to power, he publicly stated that to run an economy the size of the Soviet Union from Moscow was 'absurd' (*Pravda*, 9 April 1986).

Moreover, in the absence of the market, it was also difficult to devise suitable criteria to judge the performance of an enterprise. Throughout the period, the main criterion chosen was output. Output was easily measured for most if not all industries and the target could be ratcheted up each year to ensure overall growth in the Soviet economy. Thus, workers and management were paid when the output quota was fulfilled, and bonuses given when it was over-fulfilled. However, the by-product of such simple, single targeting was wholly predictable.

First, the enterprise was only interested in production. It had no interest in selling its products. There was no incentive at all for the enterprise to seek out new markets, whether at home or abroad. Moreover, consumer demand was irrelevant in terms of the perceived success of the enterprise. As a result, enterprises were churning out poor quality goods which in some cases failed even to serve the basic purpose for which they were made. In a shortage economy without competition, there was nothing the consumer could do.

Second, cost was irrelevant to the individual enterprise. All capital, including money for wages, came directly from the state. As a result, there was an effective conspiracy between the workers and management against the central planners. The enterprise sought to keep output targets as low as possible so that the fulfilment of the plan was as easy as possible. At the same time, it sought to exaggerate the cost of production, by maximising the amount of inputs, including labour, required to achieve these minimal output targets. As there was a general problem getting the necessary inputs of the right quality on time, such over-estimates were not wholly irrational. Nevertheless, the result was that labour and resources were idle for long periods during the monthly economic cycle.

This, in turn, meant that productivity remained low. This was a characteristic of all Soviet production. Productivity was far below that in the West. In 1980, a US farm worker produced enough to feed 65 people per year; the Soviet equivalent, only enough for six people (Kennedy, 1987: 556). The disincentive to cut costs meant that the USSR was left behind in the technological revolution of the 1970s. The installation of new machinery only created problems for the management. It disrupted production and endangered monthly output quotas. It also required the retraining of the labour force. Forces favouring inertia proved irresistible. The Soviet Union was still making 1950s cars in the 1980s.

There was also an incentive to conceal accurate statistics, notably to claim target fulfilment even when this had not been achieved. Who would ever know? The director did not take responsibility for the profitability of the enterprise. Everyone distorted the figures, from the highest to the lowest in the land. Even Gorbachev, in the days before he became General Secretary, was denied access to the budget by his party boss, Yuri Andropov (*Pravda*, 10 December 1990). A Panglossian complacency benefited workers and the entire administrative class. It was a producers' market. Only the consumer lost out.

Finally, shortages became endemic to the Soviet economy. In the absence of market indicators, prices did not reflect value. Prices were fixed at the centre based on political rather than economic criteria. As a result, money lost the power it has in capitalist economies. In the West, goods are rationed according to price.  Consumers decide whether to buy a desired article on the basis of affordability.  In the Soviet Union, this was rarely an issue.  Russians out shopping talked not about cost but availability.  The most useful Russian word in this context was *dostat'*, which roughly means, 'to get hold of'.  Where can I get hold of car tyres?  Where did you get hold of those clothes?  Goods in the USSR were rationed according to availability.  Therefore, shortage was not an accidental by-product of the command economy but a vital and central feature of the system.

The shortage economy also induced hoarding among consumers.  As cost was not usually prohibitive (except for certain luxury goods), it made sense for consumers to buy more goods than needed to hedge against future shortages.  Balconies and cellars in Soviet apartment blocks were nearly all stashed up with all sorts of goods to help the residents get through difficult times ahead.  However, actions that were wholly rational from the individual consumer's point of view, only made future shortages more likely.

It could be argued that rationing on the basis of availability rather than affordability is potentially a fairer system.  In reality, the system gave power to those with access to goods and privileged access to those with power.  The party high-fliers had access to goods, services and welfare which were simply unavailable on the street no matter how long the queue (Arbatov, 1992: 83-87).  This system of perks won loyalty to the system amongst the privileged, but it also created resentment amongst the masses.  Yet virtually everyone in the Soviet Union had a commodity or service, whether as a hairdresser, headteacher or shopkeeper, which could be traded in a shortage economy outside the official channels of distribution.  Little wonder that corruption and the black market grew exponentially through the Brezhnev period.

It was difficult to see how such inherent contradictions could be resolved within a centrally administered plan.  The state attempted it, however, by creating an economy based on clear priorities.  Top priority sectors received most state investment, which in turn attracted well-motivated and well-educated personnel because of the higher wages, better working conditions and welfare facilities.  This can partly explain the relatively strong performance of some sectors, such as heavy industry, the arms industry, chemicals, electricity, oil and transport.  It can also help explain the appalling performance of low priority sectors - most notably, the almost non-existent service industry.  However, priority planning can, at best, only be a partial explanation for the great diversity in performance between different sectors of the Soviet economy.  Agriculture, for example, remained a problem despite it becoming a priority during Brezhnev's term of office. The fact is, some sectors were simply better suited than others to the structures of the command economy.

The defence industry, for example, was uniquely well-suited to the command structures of the Soviet economy. The defence industry has only one consumer to satisfy - the military - whose orders are placed many years before the final delivery. The relatively few military goods produced each year means that they can be individually inspected for quality. The one complicating factor is that military equipment is a complex and sophisticated manufactured product. However, massive efforts, in terms of money and manpower, meant that the Soviet Union kept up with the United States in most areas of defence - but at the expense of the civilian economy. At least 15 percent of GNP was devoted to defence and the Soviet economist, Abel Aganbegyan, estimated that as much as a third the entire Soviet workforce was engaged in military-related work (Walker, 1987: 38).

The consumer goods industry is a very different kettle of fish. The consumer goods industry has to respond to the demands of literally millions of individual consumers with varied and rapidly changing needs and desires. Design and quality is a vital part of the product. Therefore, the consumer goods industry has to be flexible, responsive to issues of supply and demand, and with effective distribution and innumerable sales outlets. Such requirements were the very antithesis of the Soviet command economy. As a result, most consumer goods were in short supply and of poor quality.

Agriculture faced many of the same problems as the consumer goods industry, particularly in terms of distribution. However, food was a fairly basic product which is relatively easy to produce. Technology has a role to play in agricultural production but it is far less important than in most other sectors of the economy. An apple is an apple, and it has remained roughly the same in quality and design throughout time. Yet agriculture remained the Achilles heel of the Soviet economy. In Stalin's time, this could be explained by low investment, but priorities changed and in the 1970s agriculture consumed between a quarter and a third of all state investment. Diets in the Soviet Union improved over the period, but this fact could scarcely explain the failure of the state to meet the rising demand of consumers.

In fact, it was a systemic rather than a policy problem. The attempt to industrialise' work processes in agriculture failed dismally. Agriculture cannot respond easily to central plans. Output is dependent on climate, soil and the seasons, so many food products cannot be produced monthly on order like in industry. Food also requires good storage and rapid distribution, both of which were chronically bad in the USSR, largely because such activities were difficult to measure in terms of raw output figures. It was estimated that between 30 and 50 percent of food failed to reach retail outlets (Goldman, 1991: 50). Finally, the long period between sewing and reaping or birth and slaughter requires a major personal commitment on the part of agricultural workers. Such a commitment was lacking in almost all spheres of economic life in the Soviet Union.

Therefore, many have argued that private ownership is even more important in agriculture than industry. Even Stalin was forced to accept some private ownership in agriculture when he permitted private family plots. Without these plots, famine would have been an ever present phenomenon in the USSR. Under three percent of agriculture under Brezhnev was private, yet it provided a quarter of the food on sale. Claims can be made for state-owned industry in the Soviet Union, but collectivised agriculture was an abysmal failure wherever in the socialist world it was tried.

In passing, it is worth noting, of course, that the market in the West has also found difficulties in providing food without significant state intervention. The European Union, for example, has the Common Agricultural Policy (CAP) with guaranteed prices, butter mountains, wine lakes and even subsidy to farmers for allowing fields to lie fallow. The cost of CAP to a British family of four is an estimated £20 per week. The continued existence of CAP is evidence of the failure of the market in Western Europe, but the unique achievement of the Soviet system of agriculture is that its state subsidies produced shortages rather than surpluses.

Given all these systemic faults, it is a wonder the economy did not collapse long before the 1990s. Alexei Kiva, the Soviet commentator, wrote that the Soviet system was exhausted by the mid-1960s, but it was kept going by the plunder of its rich natural resources - oil, gas, timber, gold and diamonds (Kiva, 1992: 17). This was partly true, but it was still the case that the Soviet economy created its own laws which kept it functioning in its own way. Living standards rose dramatically after the war, with people better fed, better clothed and able in greater numbers to enjoy luxury goods, such as cars and televisions. Four pillars were essential to the functioning of the Soviet economy. First, Marxist-Leninist ideology to legitimise the command economy; second, repression of some form to discipline the workforce in the absence of monetary incentives; third, the active participation of the party to circumvent the irrationalities of the plan; and fourth, the central bureaucracy to implement policy. It is notable that Gorbachev attacked all four pillars during his time in office.

## Economic slowdown

Although there is disagreement over the actual rates of growth in the Soviet period, few doubt that growth slowed from the late 1950s, (see table 2:1). To some extent, this was only to be expected. The very high growth rates of the Stalinist period could never have been sustained over the long term. Further-more, the average rate of growth over the post-war period compared favourably with most in the West. The main concern, however, was that a new equilibrium around a relatively stable average rate of growth was not found. Instead, the decline continued inexorably and even quickened in the last few years of the Brezhnev administration. Why did this happen?

Table 2:1
**Different Estimates of Average Annual Rates of National Income  Growth**
(in percentages)

|  | **Official** | **CIA** | **Khanin** |
|---|---|---|---|
| 1965-70 | 7.7 | 4.9 | 4.1 |
| 1970-75 | 5.7 | 3.0 | 3.2 |
| 1975-80 | 4.2 | 1.9 | 1.0 |
| 1980-85 | 3.5 | 1.8 | 0.6 |

*Source:* Mark Harrison, 'Soviet Economic Growth Since 1928: The Alternative Statistics of G. I. Khanin', *Europe-Asia Studies*, vol. 45, no. 1, 1993: 146.

Probably the most important reason for the economic slowdown was the need to shift from extensive to intensive growth. Stalin's policies produced growth through the manipulation of under-utilised resources, including labour resources. Everything was determined by the need to industrialise. Cost and waste, in-cluding human cost and waste, were irrelevant. The *gulags* were set up largely to provide slave labour to carry out crucial tasks in the industrialisation process, such as mining, building roads, and even constructing the famous Moscow *Metro*. Slave labour is undoubtedly cheap, but it is inefficient and the quality of output low. Such a labour system can only be employed for basic, simple jobs where skilled and creative work is minimal. After the foundations of the new industrialised Soviet Union had been laid, the state required an increasing number of educated and well-motivated employees.

The post-Stalinist Soviet Union also required greater productivity as it became increasingly apparent to the political leadership that the resources of the country were not infinite. There was little potential for growth in the workforce as the birth rate slowed in the Brezhnev period, and whilst natural resources were abundant in the Soviet Union they tended to be located away from the main population centres. For example, 90 percent of energy resources were located east of the Urals (Nove, 1992: 390). The increasing difficulty in exploiting such natural resources led to a greater awareness of cost.

Productivity in the post-Stalinist era improved, but not as much as the leadership wanted. Apart from the systemic problems already mentioned, two reasons predominated. First, the Soviet Union found itself left behind in the post-industrial technological revolution of the 1970s. As this revolution was concerned with the distribution of information, it was never one that Brezhnev was likely to embrace. A formidable bureaucracy had been built up over the years to restrict access to information. Even something as basic as photocopying was severely restricted. The Soviet leadership was genuinely worried by the political implications of the revolution in home computers and telecommunications. Leonard Geron, revealed how backward the USSR was in the late 1980s when he found that it was '... not possible to have more than sixty-eight simultaneous phone calls between the Soviet Union and Britain, including faxes, or more than thirty-two with the United States' (Geron, 1990: 67).

Second, there was no incentive to cut costs because of external competition. The Soviet Union was missing out on the rapid growth in trade which was revolutionising the world economy. World trade increased five-fold between 1948 and 1971 (Kennedy, 1987: 535) whilst the inefficient, autarkic Soviet economy continued to shelter behind a wall of bureaucracy. In the 1970s, Brezhnev encouraged more trade, but he wanted imports to fill gaps in Soviet production not to compete with domestic products. Soviet exports were generally in natural resources and raw materials. The only manufactured goods exported in significant quantity were arms and other military-related equipment. Soviet trade to the West increased from 4.7 billion rubles in 1970 to 31.6 billion in 1980, but this increase was largely due to a ten-fold increase in the price of gold and petrol (Hough, 1988: 55). Although Soviet trade in gross terms rose, its world share actually fell in the period of detente from 1.8 percent in 1970 to 1.6 percent in

1982 (Geron, 1990: 28). This was a clear sign that Soviet manufactured goods were increasingly uncompetitive on the world market. In comparison, the US share rose from 12.9 percent in 1970 to 14.5 percent in 1985 (Walker, 1993: 332).

Third, Brezhnev's policies compounded his problems by allowing military spending to rise as a percentage of the GNP at a time when growth was slowing. This led to acute shortages for many basic products in the civilian sector (Nove, 1992: 389). Even if official statistics denied it, from the late 1970s virtually everyone on the street would privately agree that all sorts of goods, from specific varieties of cheese to materials for curtains and clothes, were no longer available in the state shops. At the same time, discipline slipped during the Brezhnev period. Ideological zeal faded from view among both the elite and the mass of the population. Brezhnev turned a blind eye to the rise in corruption and the people lost any remaining respect for the party leadership. The Soviet people in the 1970s seemed lethargic and alienated. 'I pretend to work and you pretend to pay me' became the motto of the times.

It was obvious, therefore, that in the Brezhnev era the Soviet economy was operating at a sub-optimal level. However, the Soviet people were not pressing for change (Nove, 1992: 397). For as the Western economist, Michael Ellman, has convincingly argued, all the evidence suggests that the Soviet economy in 1985, when Gorbachev came to power, was not facing a systemic crisis. Ellman wrote, 'Both by world standards and by the standards of the Soviet past, the situation was not so bad in the early 1980s'. The problems in the USSR, he said, could not compare to the crisis in Poland in the early 1980s, nor to the recession of the inter-war years (Ellman, 1992: 17). In the Soviet Union, inflation and unemployment remained low, there had been no dramatic fall in living standards and Moscow's international credit rating was high. Why then did Gorbachev decide to embark on a programme of reform?

The most important factor was the growing gap in living standards between the USSR and the West. Over the period, 1965-85 the USSR's share of world GNP had fallen from 15.3 percent to 13.8 percent (Davis, 1990: 88). The Soviet Union had missed out on the information-technology revolution of the 1970s, and the trade boom of the 1980s, and this had adversely affected its competitiveness internationally. Japan had overtaken the Soviet Union in gross GNP terms in the 1980s to become the world's second largest economy, and the Newly Industrialising Countries (NICs) of the Far East were overtaking Moscow in per capita terms (*Moscow News*, 8 May 1988). Trade barriers could protect domestic industries, but they could not protect the Soviet economy from comparative international decline which ultimately threatened the status of the USSR as a superpower. This was Gorbachev's central dilemma.

Reform could have taken many forms. Increased discipline, more stream-lined planning, or the gradual introduction of the market and foreign invest-ment. Gorbachev chose a more radical course from 1988 and Ellman blames his administration for the ultimate demise of the communist system. The end of the command economy, he wrote, 'was by no means doomed to extinction in the late 1980s. Its eventual ruin was the result of a conscious choice on the part of the political leadership' (Ellman, 1992: 16). Whilst other economists differ on the relative strength of the Soviet economy in the 1980s, there was general agree-ment, even amongst Gorbachev's advisers, that the reforms precipitated eco-nomic collapse (Boldin, 1994: 77; and Petrakov, in Pryce-Jones, 1995: 102; see also Aslund, 1989 and Goldman, 1991).

**The Gorbachev period**

Soon after Gorbachev came into office, he described the Brezhnev period as one of stagnation and inertia. He said the economy was in a state of pre-crisis and needed radical reform. At the 27th CPSU Congress in 1986, he set out his fifteen year manifesto and announced that growth would double and productiv-ity would rise two and a half times by the year 2000. This would be achieved through a policy of *uskorenie* (acceleration), which involved an increase in state investment allied to greater discipline at the workplace. The tightening of disci-pline took a number of forms. It included a stricter application of rules govern-ing the quality of goods produced at the enterprise, whilst at the other extreme, a rigorous anti-alcohol campaign which did appear to have some success in both lowering mortality rates for young males and improving productivity at work.

*Uskorenie* also had some success in improving growth rates. Estimates of growth over the period 1985-87 varied from two to three percent per year (see Harrison, 1993: 146). Gorbachev soon expressed disappointment, however, since the growth rates were too low to achieve his long-term goals of closing the gap on the West. Moreover, the high rates of investment in machine-building and other areas of the Soviet economy also meant that disposal income per capita actually dropped during this period. This contributed to a general feeling of disillusionment with perestroika amongst the people of the Soviet Union.

The problem for Gorbachev was that his policy led to a severe drain on the state budget. He announced a raft of worthwhile policies but they all involved a major increase in state spending. For example, pensions were raised for the first time since the late 1950s and an ambitious programme of house-building was unveiled. But there were no corresponding cuts in spending elsewhere. Defence spending, for example, continued to rise until 1989. At the same time, state revenue was reduced as a result of Gorbachev's anti-alcohol campaign and the dramatic drop in international oil prices from $53 per barrel in 1983 to $10-12 per barrel in 1986. It was estimated that Moscow lost $20 billion per year on oil revenues as a result (Galeotti, 1995: 22). Since Gorbachev himself had stated that growth since the late 1960s had been wholly dependent on revenue from oil and alcohol, the subsequent budget crisis was totally predictable (see *Marxism Today*, June 1988).

However, Gorbachev appeared to attribute the crisis to the economic system itself and called for more radical, more fundamental change (Pryce-Jones, 1995: 5). Some of his reforms were sensible and in more favourable circumstances may have been more successful. These included policies to encourage foreign investment into the USSR, including legislation in January 1987 to allow joint ventures on Soviet soil. Although the process was relatively slow and had little impact on the Soviet economy as a whole, Western goods became more readily available, especially in Moscow and other metropolitan centres. At the same time, small, but important, steps were taken to ease trade restrictions and encourage the reintegration of the USSR into the world economy.

In July 1987, the state monopoly over ownership was broken when private farms and co-operatives were legalised. The main effect was in agriculture and the service industry where co-operative shops and restaurants began to trade. The public, however, was often very critical of the co-operatives which were accused, often rightly, of speculation. Again, patience on the part of the leadership might have produced results. Instead, the hardliners insisted on draconian tax laws to cap profits. But higher taxes did little to bolster state reserves and only led to distrust on the part of the new entrepreneurs.

The centre-piece of Gorbachev's new radical reform programme, however, was the Law on State Enterprises which was passed in 1987 and came into operation the following January (*Pravda*, 1 July 1987). It was a complex piece of legislation but essentially it devolved power to the individual enterprise which, under Gorbachev's new scheme, was obliged to make a profit. The reform was known as *khozraschet* (cost-accounting). In theory, the enterprise director would make all the important decisions over investment, personnel issues and the production of goods. It was hoped that a climate of competition amongst enterprises would make them more responsive to consumer demands in terms of price and quality. An enterprise's performance would be judged ultimately by the market criteria of profit and loss. The economy would remain socialist, however, since severe restrictions would remain in place over the hiring of personnel, whilst the so-called commanding heights of the economy - essentially strategic industries, such as banking and other financial institutions - would remain in state hands.

There were, however, at least three major problems with *khozraschet*. First, it was too ambitious with as many as 60 percent of firms going over to a system of cost-accounting on 1 January 1988. It has to be remembered that this was a wholly new and untried system and there was little sign that the possible problems of the system had been seriously discussed. *Khozraschet* was a high risk experiment foisted on a public largely ignorant of its implications. Second, the Soviet economy contained many huge enterprises with effective monopoly control over products. In the absence of competition, the easiest way to maximise profits was simply to raise prices wherever possible. Moreover, the state could not afford to allow such important enterprises to go bankrupt because of the social effects of mass unemployment. Third, the experiment was half-baked. Due in part to understandable bureaucratic opposition, the original reform proposal was watered down allowing the state to maintain its dominant position in the economy. The centre continued to send down plans and output targets, severely limiting the ability of enterprises to act independently. Investment still largely came from the state, and the state continued to subsidise unprofitable enterprises. Most wholesale prices remained fixed by the authorities and without free prices, concepts such as profit and loss were rendered meaningless.

The adoption of *khozraschet* resulted in a drop in deliveries to the state and a fall in production of 35 percent between 1988 and 1991 (Pryce-Jones, 1995: 101). This was due to a mixture of confusion and dislocation caused by the new system. Anders Aslund, who later acted as a Western adviser to the Yeltsin government, argued that *khozraschet* accorded the enterprises 'substantial rights but little responsibility' (Aslund, 1995: 29). The relaxation of central controls also meant that more goods found their way on to the black market or into the hands of legitimate private traders who were prepared to pay far more than the official state prices. The state system of distribution began to break down fuelling inflation in the non-state sector. Inflation hit double figures in 1988, rising rapidly to 2-5 percent per week in 1991 whilst wages rose 70 percent over the same period (Ellman, 1992: 2; Aslund, 1995: 48).

Links between the enterprise and the centre broke down. This led to a crisis in the whole distribution system throughout the country. Shortages, typical of the Soviet system, became acute. Rationing of goods became commonplace, with meat rationed in half the regions of the Russian Republic by late 1988 (Galeotti, 1995: 96). The ensuing economic chaos led to absurd levels of parochialism as regions and even some cities declared sovereignty. It was a desperate attempt to prevent the uncontrolled flight of basic goods out of certain areas. At one point, Moscow citizens had to show identity cards to buy certain products in their own neighbourhood shops. Such parochialism indicated that the centre had lost effective control of the economy.

The decline in production and the inability to collect taxes from the republics and regions led to a soaring budget deficit. It rose from three percent of GNP in 1987 to ten percent in 1989, and to at least 20 percent by the end of 1991 (Aslund, 1995: 52). The trade deficit grew from $18.3 billion in 1985 to $56.5 billion in 1991 (Aslund, 1995: 49). At the same time, oil production slumped from 12.5 million barrels per day in 1987 to 9 million in 1992 (Utagawa, 1992: 53). In the period, 1986-90, trade declined by 7.4 percent - imports rose by 1.9 percent but exports dropped 16.2 percent (*Soviet Weekly*, 30 May 1991).

The failure of *khozraschet* stimulated further debate over the way forward for the Soviet economy (see *Soviet Weekly*, 11 October 1990). In December 1989, Gorbachev appointed his first full-time economics adviser, Nikolai Petrakov, who was a well-known proponent of the market. Petrakov believed his appointment indicated Gorbachev's desire to move quickly towards the market (Brown, 1996: 149). Gorbachev persuaded Yeltsin to help create a working group, led by Stanislav Shatalin and Grigory Yavlinsky, to devise a plan of transition. The group worked intensively over the summer of 1990 and finally came up with a plan which advocated a transition to the market in only 400 days. Later, the proposal became known as the 500-day programme, not because of growing caution or because of any reassessment of practicability, but simply because it was thought to sound better (*Izvestiya*, 30 August 1994).[1]

Gorbachev, at the 28th CPSU Congress in July 1990 appeared ready to accept the Shatalin-Yavlinsky programme, but in the autumn drew back as conservative forces strengthened and fears grew over the implications of such a sudden lurch to the market (see chapter 1). In December, a more gradual, step-by-step

---

[1] The 238-page document was published as *Perekhod k rynky:Chast' odin': kontseptsiya ii programma* (1990), Arkhangelskoe, Moscow.

approach, sponsored by Prime Minister Ryzhkov was formally approved by the Supreme Soviet. But it was all too late. The economy continued to contract through 1991 at an alarming rate. By now, few doubted that the command economy in the USSR was doomed. It was less a case of whether to introduce the market, but how best it should be done (see Aslund, 1995: 39-40).

Why did the Soviet economy collapse so precipitously in 1990-91? Michael Ellman, a Western economist, argued that Gorbachev failed to understand the laws of the command economy and systematically removed the main pillars holding the economy together: Marxism-Leninism, the CPSU, repression, and the central bureaucracy. Gorbachev believed he had to weaken the party and state to get his reforms accepted. Unfortunately, as shown in the previous chapter, this meant he no longer had the means to implement them. Alec Nove argued that Gorbachev needed a strong government for reforms to have a chance (Nove, 1992: 418). The growing nationalism, regionalism and workers' unrest only made his task more difficult (see chapter 3).

It also seems Gorbachev failed to fully comprehend the nature of the Soviet economy. For the Soviet Union was never a consumer society. Instead, the economy was created to serve the interests of national power and prestige. It required strong leadership and individual austerity to provide investment in prestige areas, such as the military, culture and sport. In return, the system offered a form of paternalism which included a secure job and extensive welfare. The Soviet Union was not alone in adopting what might be called a 'collectivist ethic' in its economic programme. Japan, in a very different society, by all accounts, adopted a posture that contained at least some similarities (see van Wolferen in *International Herald Tribune*, 27 June 1994). The collectivist ethic, in common with other philosophies around the world, at its heart represented a rejection of the Western ethic of conspicuous consumption.

However, Gorbachev was a committed Westerniser. He wanted to create a consumer society based on the individual rather than the collective. His reforms required a change of culture as well as economics. It was an enormous task. Few in the Soviet Union appeared to realise just how big. They believed that the basic organism was so strong that it could adapt and survive virtually any reform programme. Gorbachev argued that reforms in the past had failed because they had been too timid (Gorbachev, 1987: 84). But Gorbachev's economic reform failed because his aims were too ambitious and his policies were not ambitious enough to achieve them.

Gorbachev supporters argued long and hard that perestroika was hijacked by saboteurs (see, for example, Brown, 1996: 131-3). It was true that opposition to his reforms existed and this reduced the chances of success, but sabotage was not a critical factor in their demise. Indeed, the failure of the reforms can be fully understood without any recourse to sabotage at all. As Ellman wrote, 'The economy was not wrecked by saboteurs. The immediate causes of the partial collapse were the actions of the leadership itself, its destabilising institutional changes and economic policies' (Ellman, 1992: 27). The Soviet economy needed reforming in 1985 but Gorbachev exacerbated rather than solved the problems he inherited.

# Chapter Three

# THE NATIONALITIES PROBLEM AND THE END OF THE SOVIET UNION

The USSR was a massive multi-ethnic state. It covered a sixth the surface of the globe and stretched over eleven time zones. According to the 1989 census, the Soviet population was 290 million made up of 128 different nationalities. Simply by dint of its geography, the Soviet Union was both Asian and European, and this was reflected in a great diversity of cultures. One commentator, Victor Zaslavsky, remarked that the USSR was as unlikely an alliance as one between Norway and Pakistan (Bremmer and Taras, 1993: xxii). This analogy may have been an exaggeration, but it nevertheless highlighted a basic problem for Soviet leaders. What possible mutual interests could entice all these different nations to join together in a single state?

To cope with this problem, the Soviet Union was created as a federation, divided along national lines into fifteen Union Republics and other sub-groupings. All these national administrative regions were given rights in Soviet law. The Union Republics even had the right to secede according to article 72 of the 1977 Constitution. In practice, these rights were more formal than real, but the continued existence of the federation was evidence of the strength of nationalism throughout the Soviet period. It was notable that no leader, not even Stalin, dared to abolish the federation in favour of a unitary state.

Despite the obvious potential for nationalist conflict, Moscow argued from Stalin's time that nationalism had ceased to be a problem in the Soviet Union. This accorded with the Marxist view that nationalism was a bourgeois ideology which would fade under socialism. Nationalists, according to Marxists, put forward the bogus idea of a common national interest to unite the country and legitimise the existing power structures in society. No harmony of interests was possible, however, whilst the exploitative nature of capitalism continued to exist. The unity of interest promised by nationalism was only possible under communism.

Moscow argued that there was increasing evidence to support the Marxist analysis in the case of the Soviet Union. Statistics were presented to show that the nations of the USSR were drawing together and differences disappearing. As part of the process of modernisation, Soviet society was becoming more urban, more educated, and more mobile. Party membership was more evenly spread across the nations whilst the job market appeared more open than ever before (White, 1993: 150-51). In the 1970s, Brezhnev went so far as to declare that the nationality problem in the Soviet Union had been solved (Brezhnev, 1974: 30).

This appeared premature even at the time, but some Western commentators argued that Soviet nationality policy had indeed been something of a success. Although reports of ethnic tension were common, there were few known cases in the post-Stalin period of national unrest. Surveys indicated that nationalism was not a major issue among the Soviet people, and the young in particular indicated general satisfaction with the direction of nationalist policy (White, 1993: 151). Furthermore, there was a general assumption that the state had both the repressive powers and the political will to prevent national unrest from reaching a scale which could pose a threat to the state (McAuley, 1984: 204).

This analysis, however, proved badly mistaken. It underestimated both the resilience of nationalism and the willingness of the party leadership to contemplate change. The brutal repression of nationalism throughout the Soviet period succeeded in preventing the organisation and articulation of national views, but it was unable to obliterate national difference. Therefore, the nation remained an important form of identity for the majority of Soviet people. When Gorbachev introduced democracy on a scale never expected nor experienced before in the Soviet Union, it gave the nations the right to organise and disseminate an alternative worldview to that of Marxism-Leninism.

Any reformist leader in the Soviet Union would have encountered grave difficulties in dealing with the nationality problem. The repressive policies towards the nationalities had stored up trouble for the future. Demands for devolution in a highly centralist state were inevitable and calls for secession, at least among some republics, were always possible. It will be argued below, however, that the dissolution of the Soviet Union was not inevitable. In a referendum held in the spring of 1991, the majority voted to stay in the USSR. Even after the centre had fragmented following the abortive August coup, most leaders sought to salvage some kind of Union Treaty. After the formation of the Commonwealth of Independent States (CIS), few wished to return to the Soviet Union, but its dissolution met with little enthusiasm. Independence solved few problems; it created others; and it could not even solve the nationality problem itself. Nationalism remains a major threat to economic recovery and political stability throughout the former Soviet Union

## The Rise of Nationalism

When Gorbachev came to power, he was aware of the economic and social problems which beset his country, but despite Ukrainian blood on his mother's side, he appeared largely ignorant of the national question (see Brown, 1996: 256-7). This may have been because he had never held a political office outside the Russian federation. His early speeches on the issue were conservative and contrasted markedly with his reformist attitudes on most other domestic issues. As late as 1987, he was still repeating the Brezhnev line that the nationality question had been settled (*Soviet News*, 27 September 1987).

The few demonstrations of national discontent in the first years of the Gorbachev administration could be dismissed as isolated, unrepresentative cases. But as the nationalist movement spread and radicalised from 1988, this position became untenable. Gorbachev came to acknowledge that nationalism was a problem, but argued that nationalist demands could be satisfied within the framework of perestroika. Glasnost allowed the articulation and dissemination of nationalist views, whilst the practical effect of democratisation and economic reform was the devolution of power from the centre. Gorbachev also welcomed the articulation of nationalist views as a sign of perestroika in action. He even encouraged the formation of the nationalist popular fronts which began to emerge from 1988 (Pryce-Jones, 1995: 172).

Initially, the popular fronts gained Gorbachev's support by adopting the terminology of perestroika. However, it soon became clear that they had a different and more radical agenda. Devolution was not enough, the nationalists wanted sovereignty. Sovereignty for the majority of nationalists did not mean independence, but simply that republican law should take priority over union law. Nevertheless, in the context of the USSR, this remained a revolutionary demand which challenged the future existence of the union. Estonia was the first republic to declare sovereignty in November 1988, but by October 1990 all the Union Republics had followed suit. Nationalism received a further boost during the March 1989 elections when some members of the popular fronts won seats in the Congress of People's Deputies.

The party was deeply worried by the turn of events, but it was paralysed by splits and dithered over the future course of action. Party meetings devoted to the topic were announced but then postponed. Thus, it was only in September 1989, as Eastern Europe was unravelling, that the Central Committee finally met in full session to discuss the nationality crisis. In the revolutionary atmosphere of that autumn, the Central Committee decisions looked conservative and cautious. On the positive side, the principle of equality of nations was re-emphasised and policies promoting the devolution of power and greater cultural rights were promised. Such goodwill gestures towards the nationalists were undermined, however, by other countervailing decisions. The most important of these was the reiteration that the party would retain its key centralising role in Soviet society (*Pravda*, 24 September 1989).

After the popular fronts in Georgia and the Baltics won the republican elections which were held in 1990, Gorbachev had to shift position again. He acknowledged that perestroika alone was insufficient to satisfy nationalist ambition and began to search around for legal and constitutional reforms which would maintain the union whilst allowing considerable autonomy to the republics. The problem was that Gorbachev often seemed to offer more than he could deliver. Thus, on a visit to the Baltic Republics in January 1990, Gorbachev told his hosts that he was working on a law which would grant them independence. However, when the law was published the following April, it was something of a let-down (see *Pravda*, 7 April 1990).

Nationalists argued that the law made secession too difficult. The law insisted on the holding of a referendum and a two-thirds majority for secession to go ahead. This was a high hurdle to jump since the titular nationality often constituted less than a two-thirds majority in their Union Republics (see table 3:1). Even if the required majority was achieved, sub-republican regions held the right to maintain links with the centre. A number of sub-republican regions utilised this right to effectively secede from their Union Republic. The most notable cases were Trans-Dniester in Moldavia, and South Ossetia and Abkhazia in Georgia. This proviso made independence less viable for many republics and contributed to the subsequent conflicts in those areas.

Table 3:1
**Nationalities in the Soviet Union**

| Republic | Pop. in millions | % Titular pop. | % Russian pop. | Dominant Religion |
|---|---|---|---|---|
| **Slav** | | | | |
| Russian | 147.0 | 83 | - | Russian Orthodox |
| Ukraine | 52.0 | 73 | 21 | Russian Orthodox |
| Belorussia* | 10.2 | 80 | 13 | Russian Orthodox |
| **Non-Slav European States** | | | | |
| Moldavia* | 4.3 | 64 | 12 | Romanian Orthodox |
| Lithuania | 3.6 | 80 | 9 | Catholic |
| Latvia | 2.8 | 53 | 33 | Protestant |
| Estonia | 1.6 | 65 | 30 | Protestant |
| **Caucasus** | | | | |
| Azerbaijan | 7.0 | 78 | 5 | Shi'a Muslim |
| Georgia | 5.4 | 65 | 6 | Georgian Orthodox |
| Armenia | 3.5 | 90 | 1 | Armenian Orthodox |
| **Central Asia** | | | | |
| Uzbekistan | 20.0 | 69 | 8 | Sunni Muslim |
| Kazakhstan | 16.5 | 36 | 30 | Sunni Muslim |
| Tajikistan | 5.0 | 59 | 7 | Sunni Muslim |
| Kirgizia* | 4.2 | 48 | 21 | Sunni Muslim |
| Turkmenistan | 3.5 | 69 | 9 | Sunni Muslim |

* Belorussia was later known as Belorus; Moldavia as Moldova; and Kirgizia as Kyrgyzstan.

*Source:* Adaption of *Vestnik Statistiki*, no. 10, 1990: 69-76.

Gorbachev's attempts to cobble together a new union treaty to replace the 1922 version was equally controversial. After much delay, a first draft was published in November 1990 which continued to envisage a dominant role for the centre. Amendments were subsequently accepted, however, which devolved more power to the republics. Finally, Gorbachev tried to settle the matter through a referendum on a new Union Treaty which was held on 17 March 1991.

Gorbachev set the question: 'Do you consider it necessary to preserve the Union of Soviet Socialist Republics as a renewed federation of equal, sovereign republics in which human rights and freedoms of all nationalities will be fully guaranteed?' The exact nature of this 'renewed federation' was ambiguous, but the general question was clear.  Do you support the continued existence of the union?  Six of the fifteen union republics - the Baltic Republics, Georgia, Armenia and Moldavia - refused to participate in the poll.[1]  For some, this meant that the referendum was rendered redundant.  However, the results do reveal a number of important points (see table 3:2).

Table 3:2
**Results of the March 1991 Referendum**
(in percentages)

| Republic | Turnout | Yes | No | Absolute majority |
|---|---|---|---|---|
| Azerbaijan | 75.1 | 93.3 | 5.8 | 69.7 |
| Belorussia | 83.3 | 82.7 | 16.1 | 68.9 |
| Kazakhstan | 88.2 | 94.1 | 5.0 | 83.6 |
| Kirgizia | 92.9 | 94.6 | 4.0 | 87.7 |
| Russia | 75.4 | 71.3 | 26.4 | 52.8 |
| Tajikistan | 94.4 | 96.2 | 3.1 | 90.2 |
| Turkmenistan | 97.7 | 97.9 | 1.7 | 95.7 |
| Ukraine | 83.5 | 70.2 | 28.0 | 58.1 |
| Uzbekistan | 95.4 | 93.7 | 5.2 | 89.0 |
| Total | 80.0 | 76.4 | 21.7 | 56.0 |

*Source:* Adapted from *Izvestiya*, 28  March 1991; and Commission on Security and Co-operation in Europe (1991), *Referendum in the Soviet Union*, US Government Printing Office, Washington DC.

---

[1]  These six republics remained throughout the Soviet period the least willing to contemplate accommodation with Moscow.  They were unwilling to sign the Union Treaty in August 1991 and wanted nothing to do with Gorbachev's efforts to cobble together an alternative after the August coup failed.

The most important point to note is that in the spring of 1991 - only nine months before its final demise - there was no overwhelming majority in favour of the dissolution of the Soviet Union. On the contrary, the results show that a large majority favoured the continuation of the union. 56 percent of the total Soviet electorate (including non-participant republics), 61 percent of the electorate in all participating republics, and 76 percent of actual voters supported the union.

The result, however, was not quite as satisfactory for Gorbachev as it may at first appear. For it also showed the polarity of opinion across the country. Whilst the Central Asian and slavic republics were voting overwhelmingly in favour of the union, alternative polls in the Baltics and Caucasus provided equally convincing majorities in favour of independence. There were also divisions in opinion between town and country. This was most apparent in the slavic republics where the bigger cities were less likely to support the union. Both Moscow and Leningrad in Russia voted narrowly in favour of Gorbachev's proposal. In Kiev, the capital of the Ukraine, just 44 percent voted for the union, whilst in the western city of Lvov (only integrated into the USSR in 1940) the percentage was down to 25 percent. For all its intrinsic interest, it could be argued that in policy terms the poll solved nothing.[2]

The alternative referenda in the Baltic Republics and Georgia represented a direct threat to the union. However, republics and regions were also undermining the centre in other less direct, but no less decisive, ways. The most important instance of this was the issue of tax. In what has been called the biggest tax strike of all time, the republics refused to co-operate and send locally collected taxes to Moscow. Yeltsin, from mid-1990, held back approximately two-thirds of tax payments due to the centre (Pryce-Jones, 1995: 368). Inevitably, this led to a major budget crisis which paralysed the Soviet government.

Yeltsin also manipulated the crisis to his own advantage. In June 1990, he declared sovereignty for Russia - the biggest and richest republic - effectively creating dual power in Moscow. In the March 1991 referendum, the Russians, whilst voting in favour of the union, also voted for a directly-elected executive President, a post that Yeltsin filled in the subsequent election in June. Yeltsin was usurping Gorbachev's authority - a point Yeltsin was willing to drive home at every opportunity. When the miners went on strike in early 1991, it provided

---

2  This was even the view of Gorbachev's adviser, Shakhnazarov, see *Soviet Weekly*, 30 May 1991. Most western commentators agreed (see, for example, Lapidus, 1992: 63).

Yeltsin with a good opportunity. The strike was threatening to bankrupt the economy, but Gorbachev had neither the funds nor the authority to get the miners back to work. Gorbachev had to turn to Yeltsin to broker a deal.

In return, Gorbachev ended his six-month flirtation with the hardliners and negotiated the Novo-Ogarevo agreement with Yeltsin in April 1991. The agreement offered amendments to the Union Treaty which the people had voted on only a month earlier. A final version was agreed in June which granted the republics consultation rights over defence, foreign policy, energy, communications, transport and the union budget. On all other issues, however, the law of the republics took precedence. Most important of all, the republics were the sole collectors of taxation, leaving the centre without any direct means of obtaining revenue. It left the centre vulnerable and dependent on the goodwill of the republics. The usual six republics refused to participate, but the date of 20 August was set for the rest to sign the new Union Treaty (see *Pravda*, 15 August 1991).

Gorbachev's opponents, with some reason, feared the proposed confederation of sovereign states was unviable and would simply quicken the process of disintegration (see *Sovetskaya Rossiya*, 23 July 1991). The August coup represented a desperate attempt by a handful of Gorbachev's colleagues to preserve the union. On 19 August 1991, the day before the treaty was due to be signed, Gorbachev was ousted and a state of emergency was announced. The coup leaders in their initial statement said that extremist forces had embarked on a mission of 'liquidating the Soviet Union' (*Pravda*, 19 August 1991). Lukyanov, head of the Supreme Soviet and a man who had known Gorbachev since his student days, argued that the treaty contained certain omissions, including the absence of any concept of all-union property and the lack of any independently financed union budget.

Support for Gorbachev was lukewarm in most parts of the Soviet Union, but the coup collapsed largely because of splits in the party and military (see chapter 1). The failure of the putschists represented a victory for Yeltsin in his long-standing power struggle against both Gorbachev and the hardliners. As the centre shattered, the Baltic Republics declared independence. This time independence was recognised by Moscow and the international community. Other republics followed the Baltic lead and declared independence over the next few months.

Yet, Gorbachev, with the support of the majority of national leaders, tried to resurrect the Union Treaty after August. In the circumstances, it had to be a far looser arrangement than the one originally envisaged in August, but agreement was finally reached on 14 November with nine republics for a Union of Sovereign States. The agreement allowed for a directly elected president and a bicameral legislature, but the centre would have powers only in those areas specifically designated to it by the republics (White, 1993: 181).

The whole plan was effectively scuppered, however, when 90 percent of the Ukraine electorate voted for independence on 1 December. Since Russia had little desire to be left stranded in a union with just the five Central Asia republics, Yeltsin organised a meeting of the three slavic republics at Belovezhskaya *pushcha* near Minsk in Belorussia. On 8 December, a joint communique announced the dissolution of the Soviet Union and its replacement by the Commonwealth of Independent States. On 21 December, CIS membership was extended to non-slavic republics, and all the Soviet successor states joined, except the Baltic Republics and, initially, Georgia.

Gorbachev had not been informed of the plans to abolish the Soviet Union. His supporters described the Minsk agreement as a second coup and many of Yeltsin's own supporters, including Rutskoi and Khasbulatov, were unhappy about the President's unilateral initiative (Diuk and Karatnycky, 1993: 245; Khasbulatov, 1993: 222). There was, however, little Gorbachev could do, and he resigned on Christmas Day. The Soviet Union ceased to exist on 1 January 1992.

The dissolution of the Soviet Union solved some nationalist problems, but it exacerbated others. This was because the nature and intensity of nationalism varied enormously across the country. In some cases, notably in the Baltic Republics, the demand was vertical and directed against the centre. In those cases, anti-Russianism played a large part in the mobilisation of the people. Vertical demands could be largely satisfied through the granting of independence and the withdrawal of a Russian presence. In other cases, notably in the Caucasus, the demands were also horizontal or inter-regional. Horizontal nationalist claims could well involve calls for independence, but anti-Russianism played a lesser role. Instead, the main challenge to the nation was perceived to come from other nations inside or outside its borders. In these cases, the centre could act in a more positive role as a mediator on issues such as minority rights or territorial disputes. The collapse of the centre, in these circumstances, led to greater conflict. Finally, a form of nationalism emerged, notably in Yeltsin's Russia, which the *Guardian* journalist, Jonathan Steele, has called 'instrumental nationalism' (Steele, 1994: 328; see also Grachev, 1995: 136-7). In this case, nationalism was a means rather than an end. Leaders employed nationalist terminology, not in the name of self-determination, but to undermine opponents and to legitimise alternative policies.

Inevitably, these definitions offer only a rough guide. It was quite possible for all three types of nationalism to co-exist in one republic. However, the rest of the chapter will attempt to show the relevance of this categorisation by looking at the different sources of nationalism in various regions of the Soviet Union.

## The Baltic Republics

Two issues most galvanised nationalist opinion in the Baltic Republics. The first was the forcible reintegration of the region into the Soviet Union in 1940; the second was Russian immigration. The Baltic peoples protested that their membership of the Soviet Union, based on the Molotov-Ribbentrop pact of 1939, was illegal. Although Moscow had always claimed that the Baltic Republics voluntarily integrated into the USSR, this was proved to be false when the secret protocols to the Molotov-Ribbentrop pact were published in the Baltic Republics for the first time in 1988. This admission radicalised opinion, and on 23 August 1989 - the fiftieth anniversary of the pact - two million people held hands to form a human chain across the three republics in protest over their forced integration into the USSR.

Membership of the USSR was perceived, especially by two Baltic Republics, Estonia and Latvia, to be a threat to their national cultures. For the numbers of native Estonians and Latvians in their respective republics had fallen precipitately over the Soviet period. In Estonia, the proportion of native Estonians fell from 90 percent in 1940 to 65 percent in 1989; and in Latvia the titular population fell from 77 percent to 53 percent over the same period. In both cases the Russian minority numbered over 30 percent and made up a majority in some of the bigger towns and cities. This demographic shift was blamed on the forced exile of three quarters of a million Balts in Stalin's time and the encouragement of Russian immigration to the region thereafter. Only in Lithuania could the native population feel more secure. 80 percent of the republic was Lithuanian, but ethnic tensions remained with the smaller Russian and Polish minorities.

Baltic nationalism was anti-Russian and anti-Moscow. The Baltic culture was Westernised and tended to look on the more Asiatic culture of the Russians as inferior. The Baltic people had thrown off feudalism almost a century before the Russians and had a far longer experience of representative government. The inter-war years proved that the three republics could exist and prosper as independent, sovereign states. Since then, it was generally felt that membership of the Soviet Union had restricted political and economic development in the region.

Therefore, the Baltic Republics were at the forefront of the popular front movement. It soon abandoned the agenda of perestroika as the population recognised that more radical goals were attainable. The communist parties in the region began to split as many members joined the popular fronts. Through the course of 1989, the communist parties of the Baltic Republics often threatened to disassociate from the CPSU, before the Lithuanian party finally took that historic step in December. The move failed to convince the population that the party had changed, however, and in February 1990, the Lithuanian popular front, Sajudis, won a majority of seats to the republic's parliament, and its leader, Vytautas Landsbergis, declared independence on 11 March. More cautiously worded declarations of independence were also issued in the following weeks from both Estonia and Latvia.

Gorbachev feared that compromise in the Baltics could lead to the total disintegration of the USSR and ultimately civil war (Pryce-Jones, 1995: 159). He therefore attempted to isolate Vilnius and imposed a three-month economic blockade on Lithuania to get the declaration reversed. An uneasy truce followed until January 1991 when a bogus National Salvation Committee, backed by the Soviet military, made a bid for power in both Lithuania and Latvia. During an attack on the main television tower in Lithuania, fourteen people were killed and a makeshift barricade was erected to protect the parliament building in Vilnius. In similar military action in Latvia, five people died. However, the coup in the Baltics failed and the action was aborted.

The reasons for the failure of the coup are not entirely clear, but a number of possibilities suggest themselves. First, the nationalist governments were popularly elected and enjoyed massive support, even from many Russians living in the region. Therefore, a clampdown risked considerable bloodshed, and any non-nationalist government subservient to Moscow would have been seen as a quisling. Second, the party leadership in the republics as well as at the centre was split and divided over the future course of action. The situation in Moscow had changed dramatically since Yeltsin's election as chairman of the Russian parliament in May 1990. During the crisis, Yeltsin flew to Tallinn and signed a mutual support pact with the Baltic Republics and made a personal appeal to the Soviet military in the region not to use force against the people. Finally, the region had strong lobbies in the West. They backed the view of the nationalists and argued that the Baltic Republics were a special case - in international law, the Baltic Republics were not formally a part of the Soviet Union and, therefore, should be given their independence. Since they were so small, it was claimed that secession would not automatically lead to the disintegration of the Soviet Union as a whole.

Gorbachev argued he knew nothing of the January coup attempt in Lithuania and Latvia (Gorbachev, 1995b: 507). Others have backed up this claim (see Shevardnadze, 1991: 177; and Brown, 1996: 280-84). It is probably true that Gorbachev never gave the order to use force, but he undoubtedly helped to create the atmosphere of crisis after his shift to the right in the winter of 1990. The National Salvation Committee called for direct presidential rule, something Moscow itself had talked about earlier. Furthermore, Gorbachev also approved the deployment of airborne troops to the region and publicly defended the need for a crackdown at the time (Beschloss and Talbott, 1993: 309). On the other hand, Gorbachev deserves credit for drawing back from the brink and calling off further violence. In this respect, the West's position was not inconsequential, since Gorbachev had hitched his reform package by this time to the wagon of Western aid and he was reluctant to risk alienating his new allies.

Whatever Gorbachev's role, the January events were a crystallising moment for the future of the Soviet Union. Both the hardliners and reformers lost faith in Gorbachev. The hardliners accused Gorbachev of indecisiveness, whilst the reformers accused him of authoritarian instincts. For their part, the people of the Baltics became convinced that only full independence could prevent further atrocities and allow the development of democracy and market reforms. The referenda held in February and March 1991 showed 90 percent in Lithuania favoured independence; in Latvia and Estonia the majorities were only slightly less convincing - 74 and 78 percent respectively. Soviet rule in the Baltic Republics was doomed.

## *The Caucasus*

The situation in the Caucasus was rather different to the Baltic Republics. The Caucasus had been a part of the Russian empire for much longer and the people tended to be less anti-Russian. National identity had been forged not only in contradistinction to Russia, but also to their regional neighbours. The Caucasus was an ethnically mixed and traditionally volatile region. As a result, Moscow was seen as a potential mediator in inter-regional crises. This was the case in Armenia, in particular, where Moscow was perceived to be a powerful defender against Yerevan's traditional enemy, the Turks. The Armenians were aware of the close cultural links between the Azeris and Turks, making relations between the two Soviet republics uneasy.

The tension was contained, however, until the issue of Nagorno-Karabakh exploded on to the international scene in 1988. Nagorno-Karabakh was an autonomous republic located on Azeri territory but only six kilometres from the Armenian border. The majority of the 160,000 population was Armenian, but to appease Baku, the region was placed under Azeri jurisdiction in 1923. On 20 February 1988, the people of Nagorno-Karabakh voted to secede from Azerbaijan and rejoin Armenia. This vote provoked demonstrations in both Union Republics which soon escalated into racial attacks and ethnic cleansing, which pre-dated the wars in Yugoslavia.

Moscow was opposed to the redrawing of borders for fear this would open up a Pandora's Box. It was reckoned there were over thirty other territorial claims within the USSR alone. Gorbachev's decision made sense, but the implication for Yerevan was that Moscow was siding with Baku. The violence increased as Azerbaijan imposed a crippling economic blockade on Armenia. Moscow decided to impose direct rule on Nagorno-Karabakh in January 1989, but after failing to negotiate a compromise between the two sides, it was lifted some six months later.

The abandonment of direct rule led to a worsening of the situation over the winter. As Baku's position deteriorated, the Azeri Popular Front made a dramatic bid for power in January 1990. In contrast to Lithuania a year later, the Soviet military moved massively into Baku and was successful in defeating the coup. 30,000 Soviet troops were deployed on the streets of the Azeri capital and they broke through barricades to restore the communist government in the republic. According to official statistics, 120 people died. Gorbachev defended the military action as necessary to maintain the constitutional government, and he was backed by the US. Moscow and Washington appeared united in their fear of Islam. The action, however, had no appreciable effect on the situation in Nagorno-Karabakh (see chapter 10).

In sum, Moscow's relationship with both republics was very different to that with the Baltic Republics. Both Armenia and Azerbaijan wanted Moscow to intervene in the conflict and act as mediator. The crisis escalated, not because of interference by the centre but because of its growing weakness. As a result, both sides became disillusioned with Moscow when it proved incapable of finding a solution acceptable to either side. Increasingly, views inside the two republics polarised and they adopted policies more independent of Moscow.

Georgia, the third republic in the Caucasus, was orthodox Christian like Armenia and, at least in Soviet terms, relatively wealthy. The Georgians boasted an ancient history and enjoyed a reputation for flamboyance and relative independence within the Soviet system. On the debit side, this Georgian free spirit led to extensive mafia operations in the republic; on the credit side, it led to a livelier cultural life with, for example, more challenging films, such as Abuladze's *Repentance*, being made there during Shevardnadze's time as Georgian First Secretary.

Nationalism was strong in Georgia and a mass movement for greater autonomy began to build up after Gorbachev took power. The generally accepted turning-point came in April 1989 when a peaceful demonstration in Tbilisi was brutally suppressed by the authorities leaving at least nineteen dead (*Soviet Weekly*, 15 April 1989). The demonstration was not directed at Moscow but at the region inside Georgia, Abkhazia, which was campaigning for independence. The role of the centre has remained a matter of great debate. Both Gorbachev and Ligachev have denied giving the order to use force to suppress the demonstration (Ligachev, 1993: chapter 4 and *Moscow News,* 7-13 August 1996). Their position appeared largely vindicated when an independent commission put most of the personal responsibility for the violence on the local party leadership and the military (Brown, 1996: 266).[3]

After the tragedy, the people turned for succour to the long-time dissident, Zviad Gamsakhurdia. His Round Table/Free Georgia coalition won the republic election in October 1990 and in the subsequent referendum on 30 March, 98 percent of Georgians voted for independence, which was duly declared early in April. The following month, Gamsakhurdia was elected President of Georgia with an overwhelming majority of 86 percent. In office, however, he pursued an ultra-nationalist policy and denied full civil rights to non-Georgians. As only 65 percent of the republic was made up of ethnic Georgians, this was always likely to cause problems. In response, the autonomous republics of South Ossetia and Abkhazia, whose status was challenged by Gamsakhurdia, declared their intention to secede and the country descended into civil war (see chapter 10).

*Central Asia*

Central Asia was the poorest part of the Soviet Union. Predominantly Muslim, it remained a largely rural area with low levels of educational achievement. The region had suffered from Soviet repression, but the traditional way of life remained surprisingly intact. This meant that nationalism was never strong. Instead, primary allegiance was to the family, region or tribe, whilst the national

---

[3] Two of the leading figures in Yeltsin's new administration after the June 1996 election were implicated in the military action. They were Alexander Lebed, Yeltsin's chief of the Security Council, and Igor Rodionov, Minister of Defence.

intelligentsia and middle class (so vital for successful nationalist movements) was relatively weak. The political elite was also reluctant to manipulate nationalism for their own ends. The ethnic mix and the arbitrary nature of the borders between the five republics meant a rise in nationalism could very easily spill over into violence. Instead, the political elite tended to turn to Islam, which sought unity rather than national division.

This is not to say that nationalism did not exist in Central Asia. It very clearly did. Complaints were raised, for example, over the supposed colonial status of the region. Russians were perceived in some way as colonial masters, generally taking the higher skilled jobs and enjoying higher living standards in these republics than the titular nationality. The economy too was typical of colonial dependencies, being based on raw materials and the export of a single product.

In fact, the first instance of nationalist violence in the Gorbachev period took place in Kazakhstan. As part of Gorbachev's more general crackdown on corruption, Dinmukhamed Kunayev, a native Kazakh, was sacked as party boss in 1986 and replaced by Gennady Kolbin, a native Russian. This was seen as a slur on the Kazakh nation and an abandonment of an unwritten rule under Brezhnev that all first secretaries should be local. Two people died in the subsequent demonstrations. The intensity of national feeling could be exaggerated, however, since rumours suggested the rebellion was orchestrated by Kunayev's associates. Whatever the truth of the situation, Gorbachev learnt his lesson. Kolbin's successor in 1989 was Nursultan Nazarbayev, a native Kazakh.

Brutal inter-ethnic conflict has broken out elsewhere in Central Asia too. For example, in the Ferghana Valley in July 1989 between the Meskhetians and Uzbeks; and in Tajikistan between various tribes in September 1992 (see chapter 10). The threat of further violence also remains a constant danger in the future. This nationalism, however, rarely articulated itself in terms of secession from the Soviet Union. The vast majority voted in the March 1991 referendum to stay as members of the USSR. Party control over the media may have played a role in the remarkably high percentages voting yes, but no one doubts that the result reflected the general mood of the people. The Soviet Union provided economic subsidy and political stability. The people of Central Asia did not campaign for independence, rather it was thrust upon them.

*The slav republics*

In the slav republics, nationalism was stronger than in Central Asia, but it was highly divisive. Was the real basis of common identity religious, racial or national? The histories of Russia, Belorussia and the Ukraine had been inextricably intertwined for centuries. Many Russians, in particular, were unwilling to accept that either Belorussia or the Ukraine constituted true, independent nations (see, for example, Solzhenitsyn's views in *Literaturnaya gazeta*, 18 September 1990).

Nationalism in Belorussia was always of limited importance, but the situation in the Ukraine was very different. The people of the Ukraine were proud of their distinctive history and especially their record of nationalist resistance to the Bolshevik regime. Territorially, the Ukraine was three times the size of France with a population only slightly smaller at 52 million. It boasted some of the richest agricultural land and the most advanced industry in all of the Soviet Union. After Russia, the Ukraine was politically and economically the most important republic in the Soviet Union.

No one seriously doubts Ukraine's claim to be a distinct nation. However, its distinctiveness has been somewhat blurred over the years due to its close ties to Russia. In practice, the Ukraine could be divided into three distinctive regions. In the east, the republic was populated predominantly by Russians. In the centre, ethnic Ukrainians predominated, but through inter-marriage, ethnic mixing and long-term socialisation by the Tsars and the Soviets, they were relatively well Russified. Finally, in the west, the Ukrainians had been a part of Poland until absorption into the Soviet Union in 1940. In this western, Catholic part of the Ukraine, integration was less complete and anti-Russian and anti-communist nationalism strongest. These differences made any coherent nationalist movement difficult to assemble.

However, nationalism did begin to emerge after the Chernobyl disaster of April 1986. The environment, as in many other republics, was a stimulus to greater national awareness. The desire for an end to state-supported Russification was another. For the patronising attitude of many Russians towards Ukrainian language and culture was a matter of deepening resentment among native Ukrainians. A popular front called *Rukh* (the Movement) was formed in late 1988 to articulate these concerns. It grew rapidly in importance after the fall in September 1989 of the hardline, Brezhnevite First Secretary, Shcherbitsky. Although Ukraine voted solidly in March 1991 to stay in the union, the dramatic reversal of that vote in the second referendum in December was crucial in bringing down the USSR.

Why did this shift in opinion occur? There are two possible reasons. First, economic and political conditions deteriorated sharply after the first referendum and this led to increasing public disillusionment. Second, the leadership, recognising this shift in public opinion, attempted to evade responsibility by cynically adopting the language of nationalism. Thus, the government began to emphasise the distinctiveness of Ukrainian culture. It purposefully portrayed the Ukraine as a wholly European nation to differentiate it from Russia. It suggested that the Ukraine could become an economic power in Europe if only it were released from the incubus of the USSR. Yet, independence proved to be no panacea. The Ukrainian economy proved less robust than many had supposed. It remained, in fact, highly dependent on Russia - especially for energy - and this dependence contributed to its rapid economic decline after the collapse of the Soviet Union.

In both the Tsarist empire and the USSR, Russia was the dominant nation. In some sense, this was natural given its size and economic power. However, it became a cause of deep resentment in non-Russian areas. Soviet authorities like their Tsarist predecessors promoted Russian culture as superior to all others and the Russian language became the *lingua franca* inside the Soviet Union. A common perception also took hold that Russians were preferred for the top jobs in the country. This may have been exaggerated, but key positions in the party and military were certainly reserved for Russian nationals. This may have been more justifiable in 1922 when 72 percent of the Soviet population was ethnic Russian, but by 1985 barely half the population was Russian and, moreover, the non-Russian groups were, with only a few exceptions, just as well educated.

The Russian people, however, tended to see the nationalist question in a rather different light. A common view was that the Russian national interest had been sacrificed for the good of the union. Some Russian nationalists - most notably, Vladimir Zhirinovsky - were known as the 'empire builders' and they accepted these sacrifices in the name of a Greater Russia. Empire builders argued that no Russian national identity had existed separate from empire, and therefore, its power and self-image rested on maintaining an empire of Tsarist, Soviet or post-Soviet variety.

Other nationalists, like Alexander Solzhenitsyn, rejected the empire builders' analysis (see *Literaturnaya gazeta*, 18 September 1990). They argued that Russia had suffered as much as any nation under communism, and it needed to recover its true spiritual essence alone and without the encumbrance of empire. They were known as 'nation savers'. Russia, they said, was potentially the richest nation in the USSR, yet due to subventions to other areas of the union, it remained one of the poorest republics. Russian nationalism had been actively discouraged by Soviet leaders with Russia denied many national institutions taken for granted in other republics, such as a Russian TV channel and even its own Communist Party.

Yeltsin, on the other hand, was more of an 'instrumental nationalist'. He was no Russian nationalist himself, but he recognised a growing mood in the country which felt that Russia had become the milk cow of the USSR. Yeltsin skilfully manipulated this mood to his own advantage. A number of Yeltsin's key advisers, such as Kozyrev, Gaidar and Burbulis, believed that democracy was impossible as long as the Soviet Union continued to exist. Empires, it was argued, could only be held together by force. Moreover, the forces of reaction were increasingly thought to reside in the union institutions of party and state. Yeltsin, therefore, used his popular support to undermine Gorbachev, the centre and ultimately the Marxist-Leninist system itself (Grachev, 1995: 66).

Yeltsin presented himself as the people's defender against central maladministration and repression. He supported the Baltic Republics in their drive for independence and in August 1990 challenged the regions inside the Russian Federation to 'take as much sovereignty as they could digest' (*Pravda*, 9 August 1990). However, the policy soon changed after Yeltsin ousted Gorbachev and he himself sat in the Kremlin. Then he was prepared to use uncompromising force, on a scale far greater than that of Gorbachev, if he felt it necessary to further Russian national interests. In Chechnya, for example, the death toll of 30,000 since December 1994 far exceeded 'the total number killed by the Soviet army and Ministry of Interior troops in all Soviet republics during the entire Gorbachev era' (Brown, 1996: 282-3).

In fact, support in Russia for the end of the Soviet Union was always equivocal. Whilst popular fronts were being set up throughout the USSR, no popular front of any significance was set up in Russia. Nationalism in Russia remained relatively weak. In large part, this was due to the divergent views on the nature of Russian nationalism and the continued commitment amongst many to some kind of Russian empire. The Soviet Union was brought down, not by the Russian people, but by other minority nations. In the circumstances, it was important that the new political structures should, as soon as possible, receive formal approval from the Russian people. But, in contrast to other republics, no referendum or presidential election was ever held in Russia to ratify the dissolution of the Soviet Union or the creation of the CIS. In September 1994, a poll found that seventy percent of Russians regretted the breakup of the Soviet Union, although only a minority thought it could be reconstituted (Brown, 1996: 378).

The Russian people had been brought up to feel pride in their belonging to a huge country and a superpower. It was difficult to come to terms with the change in status. The collapse of the Soviet Union was simply the most dramatic example of Russia becoming just another country. A country, moreover, bereft of pride as it pleaded for Western aid and technical assistance. The loss of the Russian empire was always going to be more difficult to deal with for Russians than other nations in the Soviet Union. The election results of December 1993 and 1995 showed that thoughts of empire still lingered on.


## Conclusions

Gorbachev admitted publicly that his nationality policy was his greatest failure. It ended in the collapse of the Soviet Union and the escalation of nationalist violence. Gorbachev fought to the end to try to preserve some kind of union and this put terrible strains on his policy of perestroika. In the winter of 1990-91, he even seemed prepared to sacrifice his reforms to keep the Soviet Union together. And he was justly criticised for that. However, he was surely right to fear the possible consequences of nationalism. The problems of dismantling the political, economic and military structures which bound the USSR together were enormous. Concrete gains, on the other hand, have been few. Independence tended to produce populism rather than democracy; conflict rather than unity; and economic decline rather than prosperity. The Soviet successor states could not even claim to have escaped economic and political dependency on Moscow. Only the Baltic Republics have been able to fully escape the Russian embrace. Independence, it seemed, was easier to declare than achieve.

The leading commentator on the nationality problem in the former Soviet Union is the French conservative academic and politician, Helene Carrere d'Encausse. She has acknowledged the problems for the nations of the former Soviet Union in adapting to independence, but still views nationalism positively as a necessary step towards democracy. Nationalism, she wrote, is a 'distinctive feature of civilized humanity. It represents some progress over primitive society, not a regression toward it' (Carrere d'Encausse, 1991: 236). Undoubtedly, nationalism's central demand for national self-determination retains a basic democratic core. The right of a people to decide their own government remains a fundamental right which no liberal would wish to dispute. In the case of the USSR, nationalism revealed its emancipatory nature as it contributed to the collapse of the Soviet one-party system. Nationalism also has the potential to unite a population and prevent disorder through the public's identification with the state.

The liberal vision of nationalism emphasises the civil rights of all citizens living under the jurisdiction of the nation-state. This, however, has tended to be the practice of only the most confident and secure nation-states. Elsewhere, leaders have tended to define nationalism in a more limited way - in terms of ethnicity (see Smith, 1991). More insecure nations fear their culture could be submerged or suppressed. They seek to defend it against external challenge and internal subversion. They also seek to define their own nation-hood in more absolutist terms. Such nationalism tends to exclude rather than include. It seeks scapegoats for failure and usually finds them in internal minorities or external threats.

These are the dilemmas facing the political leaders in the Soviet successor states. As the new independent states scramble to find new group identities in the post-Soviet world, it is difficult not to embrace ethnicity as a unifying concept and a legitimising force. Yet, responsible leaders recognise that it is only if a more liberal version of citizenship takes hold in the former USSR, with full rights accorded to all inhabitants, that there can be any hope of long-term peace and stability in the region.

# Chapter Four

# DEFENCE POLICY AND ARMS CONTROL

Russian leaders have traditionally emphasised the importance of a strong state and a strong military. The general perception in Russia is that military weakness is punished by invasion and occupation, whilst military strength is rewarded with empire and great power status. The Bolshevik Revolution only served to reinforce such perceptions. In 1917, the Soviet Union stood alone as the first communist state. Marxist-Leninist ideology pledged Moscow to international revolution, but the country was militarily weak and encircled by hostile powers. Twice in its history, the USSR was invaded from the West - in 1918 at the time of the civil war, and in 1941 when the Nazis almost captured Moscow.

The impact of World War II on the Soviet Union was devastating. The Soviet army bore the brunt of the fighting against the Nazis. Over twenty million lives were lost and much of the west of the country was laid waste. Yet as the Grand Alliance broke up after the defeat of the Germans, Moscow once again faced a threat from the West. This time it was led by a resurgent and self-confident America. Moscow was never able to match America's economic power, but it emerged from the rubble of World War II an undisputed military superpower.

In the immediate post-war period, Soviet status rested solely on its formidable land army which had proved itself so recently in battle against the Nazis. It was only in the late 1960s, however, that Moscow became a genuine global power when it began to build up its navy and air force. True superpower status, however, came to be judged in terms of nuclear capability. Washington led in this latest technology too. America was the first to develop atomic weapons and to date remains the only country ever to have used them when bombs were dropped on Hiroshima and Nagasaki in August 1945. Although the use of atomic weapons against Japan was justified by President Truman as a means of bringing the Asia-Pacific war to a speedy conclusion, few doubted that it was also meant to show to the world (and most particularly to Moscow) America's overwhelming power in the post-war world (see Alperovitz, 1995).

The US held the monopoly of nuclear weapons until the Soviets tested their own device in 1949. However, the US mainland remained invulnerable to a nuclear strike until the mid-1950s when Moscow began to develop its long-range bombers and rocket technology. Thereafter, the nuclear relationship between the superpowers began to shift. For the first time, the American people shared the experience of living in a country under the constant threat of a nuclear strike. After 1961, the USSR began a massive military buildup which culminated in Moscow achieving rough strategic parity with the US by the time of the SALT I agreement in 1972. The US remained ahead in number of warheads and in most areas of technology, but the Soviet Union more than compensated for this through the development of more powerful missiles.

### Table 4:1
### Total Number of Nuclear Strategic Warheads for
### the Soviet Union and the USA

|      | USA    | USSR   |
|------|--------|--------|
| 1964 | 4,180  | 771    |
| 1968 | 4,839  | 1,605  |
| 1972 | 7,601  | 2,573  |
| 1976 | 10,436 | 3,477  |
| 1980 | 10,608 | 7,480  |
| 1984 | 11,500 | 9,626  |
| 1988 | 13,000 | 10,834 |
| 1990 | 11,966 | 10,880 |

*Source: SIPRI Yearbook 1991*, Brassey's for IISS, London: 21.

There were growing doubts in the West, however, that Moscow was satisfied with strategic parity. As the Soviet buildup in nuclear weapons continued inexorably through the 1970s, a growing number of analysts feared that Moscow had aggressive intentions towards the West. Richard Pipes, the conservative writer who later became adviser to President Reagan, argued that Moscow had been developing a war-fighting strategy since 1961 (see Pipes, 1977). As the term implies, this would mean that Moscow had adopted a strategy to fight and win a nuclear war. For such a strategy to have any credibility, it required two things as a basic minimum - a first-strike capability, and defences which could both protect command and control headquarters and minimise physical destruction to the country.

There were some grounds for giving credence to the views of the conservative right. First, although Moscow always denied it was planning to fight a nuclear war, it never formally accepted the concept of Mutual Assured Destruction (MAD). Second, in the late 1970s, there were signs that Moscow was upgrading its nuclear defences as the civil defence programme gained more funding and the BMD facility around Moscow was modernised. But most worrying of all, there was also some evidence that Moscow was trying to develop a first-strike capability. Moscow clearly never achieved the kind of numerical superiority required for a successful war-fighting strategy, but the US became concerned over Soviet ICBM systems. ICBMs have always been considered by strategists to be quintessentially first-strike weapons because of their speed, accuracy and throw-weight. Roughly 60 percent of the Soviet strategic triad was placed on ICBMs compared to 20 percent in the case of the US, and in the first four years of SALT (a period of supposed arms control), Moscow introduced no less than three new ICBM systems - the SS9, the SS19, and the giant, multi-warheaded SS18.

The conservative right argued that the Soviet nuclear deployment policy had opened up a so-called 'window of vulnerability' which would give Moscow a significant advantage in any future crisis with the US. In this scenario, it was argued that Moscow had gained the capability to take out as many as 95 percent of the American ICBMs in a massive, surprise first strike. This, it was argued, would leave Washington with only two options - to use their less accurate and more vulnerable forces to attack Soviet cities and economic centres in the knowledge that Moscow still retained sufficient force to strike back again with its remaining nuclear forces; or seek a negotiated settlement. Naturally, this stark choice, which became known as the suicide or surrender option, was deemed unacceptable and helped legitimise Ronald Reagan's decision to dramatically increase American military spending in the early 1980s.

The American right had justification in describing the Soviet military buildup as disturbing. It was an exaggeration, however, to argue that Moscow had gained a first-strike capability. Indeed, the Scowcroft commission, set up by President Reagan to look into the matter, reported in 1983 that no 'window of vulnerability' existed (ACA, 1989: 60). For such vulnerability to exist, the report said, it would have required both optimal performance and complete surprise on the part of the Soviets so that all the American missiles were hit whilst still in their silos. The Soviet leadership would also have had to discount the effect of a retaliatory strike by the Americans, which might have been unable to take out all the remaining Soviet ICBMs, but would still have represented a devastating attack on USSR territory. In effect, Scowcroft said, MAD still existed.

Liberal critics further argued that Moscow's intentions were not aggressive. Whilst the conservatives viewed Soviet deployment strategy with growing unease in the late 1970s, liberals detected signs of moderation (see Holloway, 1983; and Jacobsen, 1990). Evidence for this was Brezhnev's speech at Tula in 1977, when he rejected the idea of superiority and, publicly for the first time, declared strategic parity to be official Soviet policy (*Pravda*, 19 January 1977). This commitment was accompanied by a slow-down in the *growth* of military spending from 4 percent per year in the period 1966-76 to 2 percent 1976-85.[1] Then at the 26th CPSU Congress in 1981, Brezhnev appeared to wholly repudiate any thought of a war-fighting strategy when he declared that victory in nuclear war between the superpowers had become a meaningless concept (*Pravda*, 24 February 1981). Why then did Moscow never formally accept MAD as a concept?

A number of Western analysts explained this apparent contradiction by arguing that Moscow simply had a different concept of nuclear deterrence to the West (Garthoff, 1990; MccGwire, 1991). In this interpretation, Moscow accepted the notion of nuclear deterrence but believed MAD to be insufficient to ensure peace. For Moscow, MAD was flawed as a concept since it was based on the idea of deterring a rational leader who would see that the costs of war outweighed any possible benefit. The Soviet leadership, however, always took seriously the possibility of unauthorised, accidental or irrational launch (see, for

---

[1] *Soviet Imperatives for the 1990s*, Hearing Before the Subcommittee on European Affairs of the Committee on Foreign Relations US Senate, 99th Congress, 1st Session, 12 September 1985, Part 1, US Government Printing Office, Washington, 1986: 26.

example, Gorbachev, 1987: 141). If nuclear war were to break out, Moscow wanted a strategy to bring it to a speedy conclusion with the minimum of destruction to the country. MAD, in contrast, demanded the total destruction of the planet in an orgy of wild and wanton violence. Moscow, it was argued, was simply looking for a more credible deterrent than MAD; it was not planning to fight and win a nuclear war.

The problem with Moscow's concept of nuclear deterrence, however, was that it *looked* offensive. Few in the West believed that Moscow wanted war, but the Kremlin acted as though it was planning for just such an eventuality. The Soviet concept required of potential enemies the subtlety to differentiate between intentions and capability. This was not a familiar characteristic of military officers in any country whose perceived duty was to plan for worst-case scenarios. To add to the confusion, Soviet defence policy was suffused with ambiguities. These were rarely teased out or clarified by Soviet experts due to the secrecy that shrouded every aspect of defence policy in the Soviet Union. Thus, Brezhnev declared parity official policy at Tula, but he failed to say that the concept of parity had changed. After the Sino-American rapprochement of the detente period, Moscow wanted parity not just with the United States but with all potential enemies in any putative alliance against the USSR (*Moscow News*, 2 October 1988). Inevitably, such a broad definition of parity led to a further increase in Soviet defence spending. This failed, however, to increase Moscow's feeling of security. On the contrary, it only led to greater insecurity as the Soviet military buildup fed suspicion amongst Moscow's rivals and contributed to the spiralling arms race in the 1980s. This was a classic example of the so-called 'security dilemma' which Gorbachev was so keen to resolve.

## Gorbachev's new thinking

New thinking on defence really began in July 1985 when Gorbachev spoke to the entire Soviet military command in Minsk and outlined his hopes for the future (Oberdorfer, 1992: 113-4). He hoped to end the threat of nuclear war and superpower conflict, and put forward a number of policy initiatives to try to achieve these ends.

First, he re-emphasised the view that nuclear war was unwinnable. This statement was formalised at the Geneva summit of 1985 when both Reagan and Gorbachev declared that 'nuclear war cannot be won and should never be fought' (ACA, 1989: 6). Extending this idea logically, Gorbachev argued that nuclear weapons were unusable and therefore should be abolished. In January 1986, he put forward an ambitious step-by-step proposal to achieve this goal by the year 2,000.

Second, he sought to end the arms race. Gorbachev argued that the arms race itself had become a major threat to peace with technology a major destabilising factor (Gorbachev, 1987: 218). It was an argument too easily dismissed by the Western defence establishment. It only took thirty minutes for an ICBM to hit its target, and by the early 1980s, 80 percent of all ICBMs were on a state of alert, and were ready to launch on warning. Gorbachev, therefore, was eager to break through traditional cold war thinking on arms control. Important in this respect was his abandonment of the concept of parity. Parity implied a need on both sides, irrespective of defensive needs, to match the other's every missile system. In rejecting such thinking, Gorbachev was able to contemplate innovations such as unilateral concessions and asymmetrical cuts. Such innovations were also designed to reduce mutual fear and suspicion.

Gorbachev downplayed the role of force in international relations and argued in favour of a world without war (Gorbachev, 1987: 141; and *Pravda*, 8 December 1988). Instead, he favoured the resolution of inter-state tensions through diplomacy and negotiation. Political security, he said, should always take priority over military security (Gorbachev, 1987: 141). Governments should try to deal with the underlying causes of tension rather than just its symptoms. In other words, crisis prevention was always preferable to crisis management. At the same time, Gorbachev sought to allay fears about Soviet military strategy by abandoning Moscow's offensive military posture. Gorbachev promoted the concept of mutual security - no country, he said, could be more secure at the expense of another (Gorbachev, 1987: 142). Therefore, military deployment should always emphasise deterrence, or defensive defence, at both the conventional and nuclear level. Such thinking strongly implied the need for deep cuts in arms and troop levels.

Gorbachev faced opposition to his ideas both at home and abroad. Mrs Thatcher was only one of the most prominent Western leaders who was dismissive of his ideas on nuclear disarmament. At home, his ideas often met with similar scepticism. His benevolent view of the West was particularly controversial. Conservatives, such as Yegor Ligachev and Boris Gromov, still portrayed the West as a military threat to the USSR (see *Pravda*, 6 August 1988; MccGwire, 1991: 370). In the light of which, it was scarcely surprising that unilateral concessions by Gorbachev were strongly resisted by the military and the spirit, if not the word, of certain agreements were sometimes wilfully undermined.

Nevertheless, Gorbachev achieved a lot in a short period of time. The Defence Council formally approved new thinking in 1986 and the Warsaw Pact formally adopted the concept of defensive defence as policy in May 1987. How did Gorbachev manage it?

First, Gorbachev used his power to purge the military officer class and bring in others more sympathetic to his ideas. Second, he gained public support for his policies through appeals to the Soviet people over the heads of the military and party *apparatchiki*. Third, civilian scrutiny of defensive matters was greatly increased as non-military personnel were appointed to key defence bodies, such as the Defence Council. An arms control department was also set up in the Foreign Ministry for the first time. Fourth, Gorbachev was able to convince his military high command that his arms control initiatives were in the best interests of the Soviet Union. It was only when the Soviet Union began to unravel, that his defence policies were viewed in a rather different light. This will be shown below.

## Arms Control

By the time of Brezhnev's death, there were few supporters of arms control in the West. Critics on the left pointed out that the nuclear arms race had continued for all the efforts of SALT. Critics on the right blamed the Soviet Union which, they charged, had consistently cheated on all its major arms agreements (see Gray, 1984). In the Soviet Union, the consensus in favour of arms control had proved stronger. However, Yuri Andropov called for a review of policy in 1982 in the light of Reagan's military buildup. The new General Secretary adopted a tough negotiating stance and backed the Western peace movements which were opposed to the deployment of Cruise (GLCMs) and Pershing-2 missiles in Western Europe. When deployment went ahead on schedule in the winter of 1983, the Soviets walked out of the Strategic Arms Reduction Talks (START), the successor to SALT. Arms control appeared dead and the second cold war had reached its lowest point.

Yet even in the darkest days of the second cold war, there was never a complete reversal to the 1950s. Despite Reagan's antagonism, there remained a significant domestic and international constituency in favour of arms control. The main problem for Reagan was finding any alternative. For despite all the problems with arms control, a complete stand-off looked even less attractive and only added to the feeling of tension and distrust on both sides. Therefore,

Reagan shifted position and by the time of his second term he was far more positive towards the concept of arms control. Fortunately, this coincided with Gorbachev's appointment in Moscow as General Secretary. Thus, new talks were set up for March 1985. Parallel discussions were held under the rubric of Nuclear and Space Talks on three areas of contention: INF, strategic forces and SDI. Talks on conventional forces continued, but they only began to make progress after the MBFR framework was abandoned and the more flexible CFE structure put in its place in March 1989. These four areas will be explored below.

*The INF Treaty*

In 1979, NATO decided to deploy Cruise and Pershing-2 missiles in Western Europe. It is commonly thought the decision was taken to counter the 1977 Soviet deployment of medium-range SS20s. In fact, the decision had broader implications. European leaders had become worried that the Soviet Union were planning to fight a nuclear war limited to the European continent. The SS20s were viewed as an important part of such a strategy. For they could strike all of Western Europe without posing any direct threat to the United States. The West would be left only with its strategic nuclear weapons. Would the US use them? The temptation for Washington to stay out of the conflict and avoid the risk of a retaliatory strike would be enormous. This was the main problem INF deployment was meant to resolve. Cruise and Pershing not only offered greater flexibility in the event of a Soviet attack, they also tied the US more firmly to Europe since an American finger would be on the INF button (Kissinger, 1994: 776-7).

The Soviet leadership, for its part, viewed the NATO decision as provocative. Moscow did not accept that the SS20s posed a new threat to European security. Moscow claimed the SS20s, armed with three highly accurate warheads, were simply a modernised version of the SS4s and SS5s, which had become vulnerable to Polaris A-3 weapons deployed on US submarines (Galeotti, 1995: 59). The SS20s were more survivable since they were mobile and equipped with a rapid reaction time. For that reason, deployment was seen as justified. The Soviet Foreign Minister, Andrei Gromyko, argued that the SS20s had not materially affected the military balance in Europe (Gromyko, 1989: 300).

According to Moscow, the same could not be said for Cruise and Pershing-2. The latter, in particular, was perceived to be a first-strike weapon which could hit targets in the Soviet Union with great accuracy in only four to six minutes.

Moscow entertained some genuine concerns over Pershing, but the 108 warheads NATO planned was a number below that required of a first-strike force. As for Cruise, the missiles were too slow ever to be seriously counted as having first-strike potential. However, in the spirit of the cold war, Moscow made every effort to prevent the deployment of Cruise and Pershing. Andropov was particularly energetic in this regard, with a whole series of propaganda assaults on the West, including war scares which created as much panic in the Soviet Union as on its intended foreign audience (see Talbott, 1984).

There was, however, genuine public disquiet in the West over this new twist to the arms race. In Europe, peace movements campaigned against INF deployment; in the US, they called for a freeze in the deployment of new nuclear systems. Reagan responded in 1981 by proposing the zero option. The West would not deploy Cruise and Pershing if Moscow withdrew its SS20s. This was a clever proposal that allowed Reagan to present himself as more radical than the protestors. The President was seeking to cut back on arms whilst the peace movement was proposing either a general freeze or one-sided concessions. However, Moscow dismissed the zero option as 'absurd' (*Pravda*, 27 May 1985). Nobody in Washington was surprised. Reagan's proposal would amount to the USSR giving up something for nothing - the SS20s were already in place, Cruise and Pershing were not. This was not the way the cold war system worked.

The result was a stalemate until Gorbachev appeared on the scene. The new Soviet leader made a number of important concessions which made it possible to sign the INF treaty on 8 December 1987. First, in February 1987, he de-linked Star Wars from an agreement on INF. This was significant since the original rationale for the framework of the Nuclear and Space Talks from the Soviet point of view had been to emphasise the interdependence of all agreements. Gromyko had been insistent that no progress could be made on START or INF without American concessions on Star Wars. Gorbachev held to this line through 1985 and 1986, but it was later abandoned as a negotiating strategy. This made good sense since Star Wars was a defence against strategic nuclear forces, not against low-flying short and intermediate range missiles. Second, in April 1987, Gorbachev not only accepted Reagan's initial zero-option, he went further and accepted what became known as the double-zero option in which shorter range intermediate nuclear missiles (SRINF), as well as the original longer range INF (IRINF), were eliminated. Thus, the final INF agreement included all land-based nuclear weapons with a range of 500 to 5,500km. Finally, he accepted that French and British forces would not be included in the deal.

Although the treaty only involved four percent of the total nuclear arsenals of the two superpowers, the agreement was not unimportant. It was the first time a whole class of nuclear weapons had been abolished by a superpower treaty. It was also seen to be a breakthrough in relations because of a number of innovations on the Soviet side. First, Moscow agreed to asymmetrical cuts. Moscow got rid of 1,836 missiles compared to 859 on the American side. More significantly, for the first time the Soviet Union accepted the idea of on-site verification. The INF agreement allowed foreign experts to inspect military bases to monitor the compliance of the treaty. In the past, the two superpowers had to rely on satellites. On-site verification meant that it would be far more difficult for either side to cheat - a charge Reagan had levelled at the Soviets as an excuse for not wanting arms control.

Because of these concessions, the INF Treaty was controversial inside the Soviet Union. It has been rumoured that Sokolov, the Defence Minister at the time, was removed in May 1987 as a result of his opposition to the treaty. There were particular doubts expressed over on-site verification (which a few years earlier would have been called spying) and the non-inclusion of British and French missiles. There was some opposition to asymmetrical cuts, but overall that proved less of a problem since many of the Soviet weapons involved were old and would have to have been scrapped anyway (Arbatov, A., 1989b: 121).

The West has since portrayed the treaty as vindication of its hardline policies - and vindication, in particular, of the NATO decision to deploy Cruise and Pershing in the face of mass protests in Western Europe.[2] Certainly, if the West had decided against deployment, there would have been little incentive for Moscow to have withdrawn its intermediate-range nuclear forces. Nevertheless, the treaty should not be seen simply in terms of a victory for Western diplomacy (see Risse-Kappen, 1991). Although everyone in the West was happy at the disappearance of the SS20, many Western strategists were worried by certain aspects of the INF treaty (see Davis, 1988).

Mrs Thatcher was certainly dubious of its merits and called a meeting for November 1988 to reaffirm Nato's commitment to nuclear deterrence and the modernisation of short-range nuclear missiles (Thatcher, 1993: 771). There were particular concerns that the double-zero decision undermined NATO's flexible response and weakened the nuclear link between Europe and Washington. Soviet long-range nuclear weapons, SS24s and SS25s, could still hit all the INF

---

[2]   See, for example, the views of Paul Warnke, who had been a consultant to the State Department in 1979 (Partos, 1993: 234-5).

targets in Western Europe whilst the West had negotiated away the land-based missiles which could hit Soviet territory. As the Warsaw Pact still retained its conventional superiority, the Soviet bloc was, arguably, better placed strategically after the INF Treaty than before it.[3] Jeanne Kirkpatrick, the former US Ambassador to the UN, summarised these fears when she said that the INF Treaty undermined a 'basic component' of the NATO deterrence system. 'On balance,' she said, 'the treaty leaves Europe somewhat more vulnerable and the Soviet Union somewhat less vulnerable, and the alliance somewhat weaker' (Kozlova, 1989: 126).

The Soviet military, meanwhile, could be comforted with the thought that there was no longer the threat of Pershing-2 in Europe. The new Defence Minister, Dmitri Yazov argued that the treaty had made limited nuclear war in Europe impossible (*Izvestiya*, 10 February 1988). Gorbachev had shown not only flexibility but also great skill in negotiating a treaty that both improved Soviet security whilst simultaneously easing East-West tensions.

## The CFE Treaty

The West became worried that Europe had been de-nuclearised by the terms of the INF treaty, and Mrs Thatcher among others demanded that conventional force reductions would be required before any further talks on nuclear matters would be considered. Gorbachev had become sensitised to the Western point of view and recognised that the number and deployment of troops and equipment could be perceived as threatening. He wanted to show his genuine commitment to arms control. This he did in a key-note speech to the General Assembly of the UN on 7 December 1988. He impressed on his audience that the Soviet Union had no aggressive intentions and to emphasise this he announced unilateral cuts in troop levels of 500,000 by the year 1990. 50,000 troops were to be removed from Eastern Europe and the rest from the Asian part of the USSR. Moscow's Warsaw Pact allies followed suit, and announced further cuts in troop forces of around 56,000. Gorbachev also insisted that Soviet deployment would no longer be offensive. To this end he announced a 20 percent cut in the number of tanks and artillery and reductions in bridge-building equipment (*Pravda*, 8 December 1988).

---

[3]  For this view from the perspective of an American conservative, see Glynn, 1992: 353; and from the Soviet perspective, see Trofimenko and Podlesnyi, 1988: 76.

The cuts were generally welcomed in the West although many remembered that Khrushchev had proposed a cut of one and a half million troops in 1960 without fundamentally changing the superpower relationship. Others thought the timing of the speech indicated that it was a propaganda gambit aimed at putting more pressure on Western governments to stop the modernisation of NATO's Lance missile. All viewed Gorbachev's unilateral offer as only a first step. For even after the cuts, the Soviet Union would still be able to call on about 3.5 million troops backed by a formidable number of tanks and artillery which far outnumbered NATO.

The unilateral cuts, however, were resisted by some in the Soviet military. The Chief of the General Staff, Sergei Akhromeyev, resigned on the eve of Gorbachev's speech to the UN, although he later insisted that he always favoured the cuts and he remained as Gorbachev's adviser on arms control. Overall, the UN speech was successful in showing Soviet goodwill and provided extra impetus for the multilateral talks on conventional forces in Europe.

After the years of log-jam over agreeing conventional force reductions during the MBFR talks which lasted from 1973 to 1988, there was far more flexibility in the CFE negotiations which began in March 1989. There were disputes over the number of troops and the quantity of military equipment each side held - the WTO claimed rough military parity in Europe whilst NATO argued that the socialist bloc had clear superiority. Akhromeyev argued that the NATO estimates ignored naval forces and the ability of the US to deploy six tank and motorised divisions in ten days (*Soviet News*, 15 March 1989).

Nevertheless, the CFE Treaty was signed by twenty-two NATO and Warsaw Pact states in Paris in November 1990. Once again, it was the Soviet side that agreed to asymmetrical cuts (see table 4:2). The Warsaw Pact agreed to cuts of approximately 50 percent and NATO to cuts of ten percent. There was still, however, parity in tanks and heavy artillery between the two military blocs, and a separate agreement reduced each superpower to 195,000 troops in Central Europe. The aim of the agreement was to remove the fear of surprise attack and re-emphasise Gorbachev's ideas on defensive defence.

However, the significance of the treaty was entirely overtaken by the events in Eastern Europe in 1989. By the time the treaty was finally signed, Germany was reunified whilst the CMEA and Warsaw Pact were in the last stages of disintegration. The revolutions in Eastern Europe had shocked the world, not least the Soviet military, which was particularly taken aback by the speed of events. As the superpower status of the USSR appeared to unravel, the military became more concerned about the implications of the CFE Treaty.

The treaty had been based on the assumption that the two military organisations, NATO and the Warsaw Pact would continue to exist. Ceilings of two
thirds of the alliance totals for individual countries had been made on that basis.
As the Warsaw Pact disintegrated, the USSR (and later Russia), as an individual
state, was put in an inferior numerical position vis-a-vis NATO which continued to exist as an alliance (see table 4:2). Moscow, in accepting parity, had also
ignored naval and airforce advantages on the NATO side, as well as its technological superiority in many areas (Beschloss and Talbott, 1993: 363).

Table 4:2
**Conventional Forces in Europe: From the Atlantic to the Urals**

|  | 1988 | | 1994 | 1988* | | 1994* |
| --- | --- | --- | --- | --- | --- | --- |
|  | **NATO** | **WTO** | **max limit** | **USA** | **USSR** | **max limit** |
| Tanks | 22,000 | 60,000 | 20,000 | 5,700 | 46,000 | 13,000 |
| Armoured Vehicles | 27,000 | 63,000 | 30,000 | 5,500 | 45,000 | 20.000 |
| Artillery Pieces | 21,000 | 61,000 | 20,000 | 2,650 | 47,000 | 13,700 |
| Combat Aircraft | 6,300 | 14,000 | 6,800 | 800 | 11,000 | 5,150 |
| Helicopters | 2,000 | 3,000 | 2,000 | 700 | 2,800 | 1,500 |

*No single state was allowed more than two thirds of the alliance totals.

*Source: International Herald Tribune*, 20 November 1990.

As a result, the hardliners in Moscow began a concerted campaign against
many aspects of new thinking, opening up a public split between the Defence
and Foreign Ministry. The military had become increasingly unhappy at the

way Shevardnadze had put forward initiatives on arms control without consulting the Soviet defence community (Beschloss and Talbott, 1993: 118). In retribution, the military made use of loopholes in the treaty to subvert its spirit. Thus, before the treaty came into force, equipment was shifted out of Europe, east of the Urals, to take it outside the terms of the treaty. At the same time, troops were redesignated as naval guards, who (at Western insistence) had not been covered by the original agreement.

After the collapse of the Soviet Union in December 1991, the numbers in the CFE treaty had to be readjusted again. An agreement was reached among the Soviet successor states in July 1992. Russia was to have almost one and a half million troops - more than Germany, France and the United Kingdom put together. However, Moscow was still dissatisfied. Most importantly, Moscow felt constrained by the terms of the treaty from a major re-deployment of troops and equipment to the south in line with its security preoccupations in the Caucasus (see, for example, *Krasnaya zvezda*, 21 October 1993). As a result, special arrangements had to be made to avoid Russian non-compliance when the treaty came into operation in November 1995 (see chapter 11).

## START I and II

The INF and CFE treaties were important and played their part in ending the cold war in Europe. For the United States, however, the strategic balance was always the most important. In March 1985, START talks resumed and agreement was quickly reached to cut their strategic nuclear arsenals by 50 percent. This was formally adopted as the negotiating position of the two superpowers at the Geneva summit in 1985. The actual course of the negotiations, however, proved slow. The Americans argued that START should primarily target first-strike weapons, in other words the Soviet heavy, MIRVed ICBMs. Moscow, on the other hand, called for percentage cuts across the board. Negotiations also became bogged down over the Strategic Defence Initiative (SDI) with Moscow insisting up to 1988 that any progress on strategic nuclear weapons had to be linked to this issue.

Despite a big investment in START from both Gorbachev and Reagan, there was no treaty ready until after the cold war had formally come to an end. Reagan had long since left office, so it was George Bush who finally went to Moscow in July 1991 to sign START I. The terms of the treaty disappointed many who had become used to dramatic cuts and the rhetoric of US-Soviet co-operation. The actual cuts were only 30 percent over a seven year period despite the official claim of 50 percent. The discrepancy was due to arcane methods of counting which deliberately under-estimated the number of warheads carried by bombers and other missile launchers.

Georgy Arbatov, head of the US and Canada Institute, was dismissive of the treaty which he described as being steeped in cold war thinking (*Soviet Weekly*, 8 August, 1991). In fact, the cuts only brought the strategic nuclear weapons down to the levels of the 1970s, and although the Soviet Union agreed to destroy half of its SS18s, most of the missiles which were to be destroyed were old and due for decommissioning anyway. START I also paid little attention to the question of improved technologies and the modernisation of weaponry. The quality of weapons had long ago become more relevant than the simple numbers game. In sum, START appeared bedeviled by the familiar problems of 1970s arms control.

Table 4:3
**After  START: Projections of US and Russian
Strategic Nuclear Warheads**

|  | START  I | | START II ( by year 2003 ) | |
|---|---|---|---|---|
|  | **USA** | **Russia** | **USA** | **Russia** |
| ICBMs | 1,400 | 3,153 | 500 | 531 |
| SLBMs | 3,456 | 1,744 | 1,728 | 1,744 |
| Bombers | 3,700 | 1,552 | 1,272 | 752 |
| Total | 8,556 | 6,449 | 3,500 | 3,027 |

*Note:* The numbers are estimates. They are within treaty limits but, because of national force restructuring choices, do not necessarily match them.

*Source: The Arms Control Association*, Fact Sheet, 19 June 1992.

The arms control process only really changed its nature after the collapse of the Soviet Union and the emergence of Yeltsin as leader of the new Russian state in 1992. Commentators then began to refer, not to the arms race, but the disarmament race. After a series of unilateral moves, a follow-up START II treaty was signed in January 1993. START II decreed cuts in the nuclear arsenals of both powers of 50 percent again on top of START I (see table 4:3). The agreement stated that either side would have a maximum of 3,000 to 3,500 strategic nuclear weapons by the year 2,003. (Or the year 2,000 if the United States gave material assistance to the Russians in the disarmament process.) Cuts would begin after ratification by all parties of START I. The dramatic cuts received most attention) but even more important was the agreement to dismantle first-strike potential on both sides. Therefore, cuts fell disproportionately on ICBMs, and in contrast to START I, the two sides also agreed to dismantle their most modern weapons systems. The US gave up its Minuteman and MX, the Soviet Union its 154 SS18 missiles. Another important decision was the banning of all MIRVs on ICBMs. MIRVs were perceived to encourage a first strike against them since one incoming missile could knock out up to ten warheads.

The air force and submarines were less affected since their missiles were not considered to have first-strike capability. Aircraft were too vulnerable and too slow to pose a credible threat of a surprise first strike. SLBMs, on the other hand, were the archetypal second-strike missiles. They were too inaccurate to be used in a counterforce attack, but were invulnerable to a first strike. Nevertheless, as a sign of goodwill, the US agreed to give up half of its nuclear warheads on its most sophisticated submarines.

This US concession failed to satisfy the Soviet military, however, since it still left the US with the core of its naval and airforce in place. The SS18, on the other hand, was the centre-piece of Russia's strategic force and its abolition required a radical revision of nuclear strategy. In these circumstances, rough parity in strategic nuclear weapons was scarcely sufficient for Russian military strategists, especially when America retained its traditional advantage in the quality of equipment (see chapter 11).

## SDI

In March 1983, President Reagan made a dramatic speech which came to dominate the defence debate in most of the world's capitals. After the minimum of consultation with his defence experts, Ronald Reagan argued in favour of research into space-based defence. Both Moscow and Washington had long been researching various aspects of ballistic missile defence but Reagan's Star Wars speech had the effect of both politicising the debate and sending it to the top of the defence policy agenda.

Star Wars was supported in the West for different reasons. Reagan was one of the few who actually believed in the idea of a comprehensive defence shield to protect against a massive Soviet nuclear attack. He was genuinely appalled that the United States had no protection whatsoever against any nuclear strike. The concept of Mutual Assured Destruction clearly troubled him. 'Wouldn't it be better,' he asked 'to save lives rather than avenge them?' (ACA, 1989: 74). He offered to share SDI technology with the Soviet Union to replace MAD with MAS (Mutual Assured Security). His declared aim was to make nuclear weapons 'impotent and obsolete' (ACA, 1989: 74). Reagan had found a populist topic. With his personable smile, he was able to sell the idea to a large proportion of the American people. Government advertisements on TV at the time showed cartoon children playing under a massive Star Wars rainbow as incoming Soviet weapons bounced off the impermeable shield.

The idea of ballistic missile defences had been abandoned in the 1970s on the grounds that they were impractical. No defence could be one hundred percent perfect and even if only a few warheads got through, it would wreak unacceptable damage. Strategists, therefore, welcomed the ABM Treaty of 1972 on two grounds. First, it halted what could have been a very costly, and wasteful, arms race in defensive missiles. Second, the treaty implied that both sides accepted the logic of MAD. As the Soviets had developed ever more powerful warheads and almost quadrupled the number of strategic weapons through the 1970s, the arguments against a ballistic defence system seemed all the greater when Reagan came into office in 1981.

However, Reagan was told by scientists, such as Edward Teller father of the H-bomb, that technological breakthroughs had made realisable the prospect of a defensive shield in space. So the SDI Organisation (SDIO) was set up to enquire into the feasibility of the project. Paul Nitze, the experienced arms control hand, stated in 1985 that for SDI to go ahead it had to be 'survivable and cost-effective at the margin' (ACA, 1989: 77). In other words, Nitze was demanding that it had to be cheaper for Washington to deploy Star Wars than for Moscow to deploy counter-measures. This was always going to be a tall order given the array of relatively cheap counter-measures Moscow could devise. The most obvious was to launch more missiles which would swamp the Star Wars defences. Other possibilities included decoy warheads, the installation of equipment which could jam the SDI technology, or an increase in anti-satellite weaponry to shoot down American space-based technology.

Nevertheless, some strategists who rejected Reagan's ideas of a comprehensive space shield idea still supported continued Star Wars research. Some believed that SDI could provide enhanced defence for America's vulnerable ICBMs and hence improve deterrence (*Washington Post*, 28 June 1987). Others saw it as having political advantages. On the one hand, Reagan's concept of MAS appealed to large swathes of public opinion and allowed the Reagan administration to capture the moral high ground. After all, the President was thinking about protecting America, whilst traditionalists talked about defence in terms of Mutual Assured Destruction. Others amongst Reagan's advisers, including figures such as Robert McFarlane and Richard Perle, perceived Star Wars more in pragmatic terms, simply as a useful bargaining chip in negotiations with the Soviet Union (Glynn, 1992: 348). However, the majority of arms experts in the West was opposed to Reagan's Star Wars initiative. SDI represented a significant shift from the doctrine of MAD. Any effective defence would give Washington a first-strike capability since the US would remain invulnerable to any retaliatory strike behind its Star Wars shield. Even if SDI failed to work, it was likely to destabilise the international system by leading to an arms race in defence weapons in apparent contravention of the 1972 ABM Treaty.[4]

The initial response to Star Wars in Moscow was verging on the apoplectic. Andropov declared that SDI represented 'a bid to disarm the Soviet Union in the face of the US nuclear threat' (*Pravda*, 26 March 1983). Moscow did not believe the Reagan offer to share the Star Wars technology since the weapons could easily be adapted for offensive purposes. The Soviet scientific establishment was split for the first few years over the practicability of the SDI project. Andropov's advisers appeared to believe SDI was credible and affordable at least as a partial, if not a complete, defence against a second strike (see Meyer, 1985: 275; and *Krasnaya zvezda*, 26 September 1984). In the less paranoid world of the Gorbachev Kremlin, more Soviet scientists sounded sceptical (see Velikhov, 1986). Gorbachev's own scientific adviser, Roald Sagdeyev was more outspokenly dismissive, describing SDI as 'science fiction' (Partos, 1993: 227). Nevertheless, Moscow had considerable respect for American technology, and obviously felt that they could not take the risk of ignoring the challenge of SDI (MccGwire, 1991: 75).

How was the Soviet Union to respond to the Reagan initiative? There appeared

---

4  Washington always denied that SDI was a violation of the ABM Treaty. Although the treaty explicitly banned the deployment of ballistic defences in space, exotic technologies were not mentioned. This permissive view of the ABM Treaty became known as the Sofaer Doctrine.

to be three alternatives. Kill Star Wars; match the American project; or adopt counter-measures to render Star Wars inoperable. The logic of the cold war suggested that if the US were successful in deploying Star Wars, then the Soviet Union would have to emulate the American project (Regan, 1988: 297).

It has been argued, however, that the Soviet Union could never have matched the American project, and the Kremlin was well aware of this. This may have been so, but it was a risky strategy for the Americans to adopt. The Soviet Union was judged to be behind in the most important technologies concerned with SDI, such as micro-electronics and computers, but the USSR had other advantages. It had greater operational experience of BMDs, having modernised its defence system around Moscow in the late 1970s, and it also had a greater capability for putting payloads in space. The Soviet Union was also ahead in some of the most advanced technologies with particular relevance for SDI, most notably particle beams (Glynn, 1992: 342). Moscow had caught up before in military technology and, if SDI was practicable, there was little reason, from the scientific standpoint, to suppose they could not do likewise in the case of Star Wars. However, the Soviet Union had no desire to embark on a qualitatively new arms race in defensive weapons in space which would be a terrible burden on an already over-stretched economy. Some estimates of the possible cost of Star Wars were as high as $1 trillion (Meyer, 1985: 276). Therefore, on the grounds of military doctrine, economic cost and technological difficulties, the Soviet Union wanted SDI stopped.

First of all, Andropov attempted to kill Star Wars through threats. The cold war was intensified and the arms race heated up. The Soviet standoff singularly failed to budge Reagan on his pet toy and tangibly increased East-West tension. After Andropov's death, a new strategy was attempted under Gorbachev's direction. Now Gorbachev attempted to kill off Star Wars through inducements rather than threats. Moscow returned to the negotiating table after a break of about fifteen months in the spring of 1985 and Gorbachev began to offer dramatic arms cuts if Reagan agreed to abandon SDI. This was Gorbachev's negotiating position at both the Geneva and Reykjavik summits although he had no greater success in reducing Reagan's commitment to Star Wars.

Initially, Gorbachev's demand on SDI was fundamentalist, not even allowing any research on space-based technologies. This was not a credible position, especially since the Soviets were conducting research themselves, as Gorbachev admitted in 1987 (ACA, 1989: 85). Gradually, over time, Gorbachev's position on SDI softened and he sought to delay deployment rather than stop it altogether. In March 1986, Gorbachev said he was no longer seeking a total ban, instead his attention transferred to strengthening the terms of the ABM Treaty by allowing no escape for a minimum of ten years. By early 1987, Gorbachev's position changed again as he began to come to terms with the idea of an active Star Wars. In February, the INF talks were de-linked from SDI, and then in April Gorbachev told George Shultz, Reagan's Secretary of State, that Moscow was prepared to tolerate any BMD activity as long as it was not in space (*Pravda*, 15 April 1987). By December, Moscow was willing, in effect, to accept any research, development and testing. It appeared the Star Wars issue had come full circle. Why had the Soviets effectively accepted the right of the Americans to develop SDI?

First, the Soviet Union thought deployment of SDI was becoming increasingly unlikely. Both the US and the Soviet Union had come to realise by 1987 that major technical difficulties existed. The goals of the American project were constantly being downgraded whilst costs continued to soar (Arbatov, A., 1989b: 62-67). Two strong supporters of SDI in the US left office in this period - Secretary of Defence Weinberger in November 1987, and the head of the SDIO Abrahamson in 1988. Furthermore, Reagan's reputation had taken a fall since Irangate, and Congress was less willing to fund Star Wars at a time when the budget deficit was growing. In December 1987, Congress cut the SDI bill by a third and banned testing in space. Second, the scientific and defence community in Moscow had revised its view and decided that the Soviet Union could tolerate even an active Star Wars system (Puschel, 1989: 43; Sagdeyev, 1994). As the cold war mentality faded, Moscow no longer felt the need to match every new American innovation. If SDI ever came to fruition, it was believed that counter-measures would be relatively cheap and effective. An official report of 1985 argued that 'counter-measures could be set up more quickly than SDI and would cost only one or two percent as much' (Shenfield, 1985; see also Velikhov, 1986).

After Reagan left the scene, Star Wars slipped down the American foreign policy agenda until Bill Clinton in 1993 pronounced it dead.[5] Clinton said research into ground-based defences would continue but deployment in space would not go ahead (*International Herald Tribune*, 15 May 1993). The estimated cost of even the more limited Star Wars programme (known as GPALS) devised by President Bush, was as high as $43 billion. The SDI project up to

---

5 However, the new republican Congress that came to power in January 1995 has expressed an interest in reviving Star Wars in some form.

1993 had already cost $32 billion with very little in the way of results to show for it. The most dramatic technological breakthroughs claimed by the SDIO were later proved to be fraudulent.

For some, SDI represented a grotesque waste of money on a project that was little more than a personal pipe-dream of President Reagan. Others, like Bush's Secretary of State, James Baker, have given Star Wars pride of place in explaining the end of the cold war and the change in Soviet foreign policy from the mid-1980s. What is the evidence?

Many Soviet officials and military experts have accepted that the Star Wars initiative led to a radical reassessment of Soviet defence policy (see MccGwire, 1991: 115). This would scarcely be surprising, given the radical shift in American military strategy that such a deployment would imply. Some evidence exists to suggest that SDI was one reason for the Soviets agreeing to reconvene the arms talks in 1985. It is possible too that Gorbachev may have de-linked INF after he heard that Reagan in 1987 had called for an intensified effort to make strategic defences a key component of American nuclear strategy (ACA, 1989: 37). On the other hand, it was only after Soviet experts had re-evaluated the feasibility of SDI from 1987 that any of the arms agreements went ahead (Beschloss and Talbott, 1993: 118). This brings us to the fundamental question - how far did Reagan's military buildup force Moscow to make concessions?

### Reagan's role in securing arms control

Reagan came to office with the aim of altering the military balance to allow the US once more to negotiate from a position of strength. In his phrase, America had to build up to build down. By 1984, with the modernisation of the strategic triad, it was claimed that he had achieved his aim. Therefore, it was legitimate once again to actively pursue arms control with the Soviet Union (Oberdorfer, 1992: 129).

It is doubtful, however, as Soviet commentators noted at the time, that there had been any dramatic shift in the strategic balance over the period 1981-84 (Trofimenko and Podlesnyi, 1988: 75). On the whole, Moscow kept pace with Washington in the arms race in the 1980s. The Soviet Union continued to increase its defence spending throughout the Reagan presidency and developed a number of new weapons systems, including two new mobile ICBMs - the SS24 and SS25. When Reagan became President, the Soviet Union had just under 8,000 strategic warheads; when he left office in January 1989, there were almost 11,000 warheads aimed at the United States. The United States had improved its second-strike capability with the introduction of the Midgetman and the MX, but at great cost and with only minimal gains. One thing can be said unequivocally. The arms race gathered pace through the 1980s at great cost to the economies of both the US and USSR. It was the opposite of a race in Alice in Wonderland - everybody raced and everybody lost.

However, the economic cost of the arms race was another important part of Reagan's overall strategy. Reagan's stated aim was to arm the Soviets to death: 'The Soviet Union,' he said in 1978, 'cannot possibly match us in an arms race' (ACA, 1989: 33). Furthermore, he deliberately tried to stimulate the arms race in areas of high technology where the Soviets were less able to compete (Garthoff, 1994: 508). SDI was simply the most obvious example of this. As a result, the arms race received another twist in the 1980s. Moscow faced the prospect of a major increase in defence spending just to maintain levels of parity. Reagan, it is said, left the Soviet Union with just two options - continue to tough it out and risk bankruptcy or surrender on American terms.

Unquestionably, the Soviet Union had been spending too much on defence over a prolonged period of time and this had held back overall economic development. By 1985, the Soviet Union spent (depending on which estimate you choose) between 15 and 30 percent of GNP on defence. Moreover, annual growth in defence spending continued to rise after Gorbachev came to power - from two percent to three percent in the period 1985-88. However, this increase scarcely seemed sufficient to explain the seismic shift in Soviet policy under Gorbachev (see Garthoff, 1994: 506; and Chernoff, 1991: 125). The technological challenge was more worrying for the Soviet Union, but no evidence has come to light of extra investment being put aside in this period for research and development into SDI or other high technology weaponry (Garthoff, 1994: 517).

Thus, critics of Reagan suggest he had little impact on Gorbachev's new thinking. Indeed, many have argued that his policies of brinkmanship were provocative and unsuited to the nuclear age. The security expert, Michael MccGwire, has gone much further and argued that Reagan's policies did not precipitate change, they actually delayed it. MccGwire argued that a radical review of defence strategy was already under way in the Soviet Union before Reagan came to power, and the US military buildup in the early 1980s had the effect of putting the process back several years (MccGwire, 1991: 386). This may be an exaggeration, but MccGwire is right in placing the emphasis for change on Gorbachev. For four years, Reagan pursued his hardline policy but achieved nothing. It was only when Gorbachev came to power that agreements were finally reached (Trofimenko and Podlesnyi, 1988).

Gorbachev was desperate to end the arms race, not only to cut back defence spending, but also for its own sake. For the arms race had long since lost any rational purpose (see Arbatov, A., 1989a). Even those theorists who believed in the concept of nuclear deterrence were ready to accept that the two superpowers had reached absurd levels of overkill. Dramatic reductions, therefore, could be undertaken without undermining nuclear deterrence. Gorbachev, of course, wanted complete nuclear disarmament, but his more conservative colleagues accepted arms cuts, not because of perceived Soviet weakness, but because of its perceived military strength. The Soviet Union, for the first time in its history, no longer feared invasion and occupation. Its security was safe. And it was this, rather than any American pressure, which encouraged the Soviet military to accept Gorbachev's new thinking.

# Chapter Five

# THE REVOLUTIONS IN EASTERN EUROPE

Eastern Europe in the cold war period was clearly a top foreign policy issue for Moscow. Stalin wanted a buffer zone after the war and he believed the only way to ensure Soviet security was through the imposition of Soviet-type systems throughout the region. Communist leaders were only trusted if they were chosen and wholly accountable to Stalin. When Tito sought to defy Moscow in 1948, he was expelled from the Cominform and Stalin decided to tighten his grip over the rest of the region. Stalin's successors attempted to change Moscow's relationship with Eastern Europe. Instead of Stalin's iron grip, they tried to encourage greater legitimacy for the communist regimes in the region. In most cases, this proved impossible. The brutality of the Stalinist period alienated even those, like the Czechs, who had been more open to Moscow and Marxism-Leninism at the end of the war.

At the 20th CPSU Congress in 1956, Nikita Khrushchev raised hopes in Eastern Europe when he spoke of different roads to socialism. But when Soviet dominance was challenged in Hungary shortly afterwards, Soviet troops invaded and crushed the popular uprising. Remaining hopes that the system could be reformed were finally extinguished in 1968 when the Prague Spring in Czechoslovakia was suppressed by force. The leader of the reform movement, Alexander Dubcek, was a communist who went out of his way to insist on his loyalty to Moscow. He was not seeking to overthrow communism nor leave the Warsaw Pact. His stated aim was simply to create socialism with a human face. But even that was too much for Brezhnev. Warsaw Pact troops invaded Czechoslovakia on 20-21 August and in so doing convinced many intellectuals that change could only come through the overthrow of the communist system. The Soviet daily, *Pravda*, later justified the invasion in the context of the limited sovereignty of East European states; in the West, it became known as the Brezhnev Doctrine. In effect, the doctrine claimed the right for the Soviet Union to intervene in the internal affairs of allied states to preserve and protect the Marxist-Leninist system throughout the region (*Pravda*, 26 September 1968).

This was the last time Warsaw Pact troops invaded another Soviet bloc state. In Poland, the Jaruzelski government was able to contain the rise of Solidarity internally through the imposition of martial law in December 1981. It is not entirely clear from the evidence available how close Moscow was to military intervention in this case. What is clear, however, is that Moscow openly threatened intervention, conducting major military manoeuvres during the crisis along the Polish border.[1]

Therefore, in 1985 when Gorbachev came to power, the Brezhnev Doctrine appeared firmly in place. Few in the West expected any radical change in policy towards Eastern Europe and no one expected that the Soviet Union would voluntarily withdraw from the region. Thus, the American academic, Karen Dawisha, argued in 1988 that 'the Soviet Union will not peacefully relinquish fundamental control over Eastern Europe in the military and security field' (Dawisha, 1988: 197); and a year later Zbigniew Brzezinski, the former National Security Adviser to President Carter, was writing of Poland that 'a dramatic collapse of the regime ... would almost certainly produce a Soviet intervention' (Brzezinski, 1989: 128). Yet from 1989, the communist regimes in all East European countries were dismantled without the Soviet Union firing a shot. In 1991, the Soviet-dominated alliance organisations, the Warsaw Pact and the Council of Mutual Economic Assistance (CMEA), were both abolished and Soviet troop withdrawal from Eastern Europe was completed by the summer of 1994. How did this happen? Why did Moscow allow it to happen?

There are two basic views. The first argues that Gorbachev had little alterna-

---

[1]  Much archival evidence suggests that Moscow had no immediate plans to intervene in Poland before the imposition of martial law in December 1981 (see Pryce-Jones, 1995: 214-215). However, two Soviet army officers have stated that the Soviet army was on the point of invasion before General Jaruzelski chose to act (*Moscow News*, no. 15, 1992 and no. 27, 1992).

tive but withdrawal (Gati, 1990; Pravda, 1992; and Dashichev, 1994). Communism in Eastern Europe was bankrupt as an ideology and the majority of East European leaders recognised this fact. Gorbachev may have initiated reform in the region, but he neither anticipated nor desired its revolutionary outcome. Gorbachev was working for a socialist, pro-Soviet alliance in Eastern Europe based on consent rather than coercion. When this proved an impossible option, the region was engulfed by revolution. The British scholar, Alex Pravda, described Soviet policy towards Eastern Europe in 1989 as 'reactive permissiveness', and Jonathan Eyal, writing in the same volume, suggested that Soviet policy was 'not to have a policy' (Pravda, 1992: 137; Eyal, 1992: 205).

The second view argues that such an analysis underestimates the radical nature of Gorbachev's thinking. Moscow was not forced out of Eastern Europe, it is argued, but chose to disengage from Eastern Europe as part of Gorbachev's new thinking. The speed of Soviet disengagement was more precipitate than Moscow would have wished but the withdrawal accorded with Gorbachev's overall foreign policy strategy. The West, it is said, was more surprised than Moscow when the Berlin Wall came down in November 1989 (MccGwire 1991; Garthoff, 1994).

What is the evidence? Although much remains unclear, it cannot be disputed that Gorbachev sought to change the nature of relations between Moscow and its East European allies. This was articulated as soon as Gorbachev became General Secretary. Thus, Gorbachev informed his East European colleagues at Chernenko's funeral in March 1985 that the principle of equality and respect for sovereignty would henceforth govern relations between Russia and East European states. Outside interference in their affairs, he said, would no longer be tolerated (Gorbachev, 1995b: 311; Chernayev, 1994: 158). In effect, the Brezhnev Doctrine had been abandoned in the first days of Gorbachev's leadership (Gorbachev, 1995b: 312). This was a dramatic moment in the course of East European history, although it was only in November 1986 that it was formally confirmed by the politburo and the decision privately transmitted to all East European leaders (Garthoff, 1994: 573; Gedmin, 1992: 19). As the dramatic events of 1989 unfolded, Gorbachev came under pressure from hardliners to use force but he stuck by the Soviet Union's earlier commitment to non-intervention (see *Soviet Weekly*, 2 May 1990).

The importance of Soviet permissiveness is hard to exaggerate. Nevertheless, questions remained. To what extent was Gorbachev a passive observer, overwhelmed by events and incapable of action? To what extent did Gorbachev intervene directly to facilitate change? On these questions answers are less definitive. For although participants in the events have been willing to express their views in memoirs and interviews, discrepancies remain in their accounts. However, it is possible to pick our way through contradictory evidence to reach some kind of conclusion on this historic moment in European history.

## The withdrawal

After Gorbachev came to power, the leaders of Eastern Europe were slow to respond to the shift in Moscow's policy. Gorbachev argued that his declaration at Chernenko's funeral was not taken seriously by his allies. The language of equality and sovereignty had been used before, but as Gorbachev later wrote, this time it would be put into practice (Gorbachev, 1995b: 312). However, it was inconceivable to most East European leaders that Moscow would desert its allies in a crisis. Even if Gorbachev were willing to contemplate the loss of Soviet influence in the region, would the hardliners allow it to happen? Reformers and conservatives alike could scarcely believe it.

However, as Gorbachev and fellow politburo members more clearly formulated their new policy in a series of key speeches, the more reform-minded states of Hungary and Poland decided to test the water. Karoly Grosz replaced the long-serving Janos Kadar in May 1988, and went to Moscow the following July to meet Gorbachev. It was a most remarkable meeting during which Gorbachev supported the introduction of competitive, multi-party elections and the total withdrawal of Soviet troops from Hungary (MccGwire, 1991: 321; Gedmin, 1992: 21). After his return home, Grosz prepared his country for democratisation. In February 1989, the leading role of the party was abandoned and a date was set in 1990 for multi-party elections. As events radicalised elsewhere in Eastern Europe, the Hungarian communist party also voted in October 1989 to change its name and formally abandon Marxism-Leninism as a guiding principle of the party. Why did the party take this action?

Hungary was one of the freest and wealthiest states in the communist bloc, but like others in Eastern Europe Budapest was suffering from economic slowdown in the 1980s (see table 5:1). A growing number on the reformist wing of the party believed this was not a temporary problem but a systemic crisis which required a radical, market solution. The elections were meant to legitimise a radical reform package. Since the opposition in the spring of 1989 was weak and little known in the country, the party was confident it would win the elections and head the reform process (Bruszt and Stark, 1992: 43-44). This strategy might have worked if it were not for events elsewhere in the communist bloc. Instead, the revolutionary atmosphere of the time swept the communists from power in the subsequent election of 1990.

Table 5:1
**Average annual growth of GNP in Eastern Europe in %s**

|                | 1961-70 | 1971-80 | 1981-85 | 1986-88 |
|----------------|---------|---------|---------|---------|
| Bulgaria       | 5.8     | 2.8     | 0.8     | 1.9     |
| Czechoslovakia | 2.9     | 2.8     | 1.2     | 1.5     |
| East Germany   | 3.1     | 2.8     | 1.9     | 1.7     |
| Hungary        | 3.4     | 2.6     | 0.7     | 1.5     |
| Poland         | 4.2     | 3.6     | 0.6     | 1.0     |
| Romania        | 5.2     | 5.3     | -0.1    | 0.1     |

*Source: New York Times*, 11 December 1989.

Hungary is an interesting test-case for the various theories outlined in the introduction. For Hungary was the first country to start down the revolutionary road of multi-party democracy. Yet it was revolution by committee and a revolution supported by the party. In the case of Hungary, there was no major economic crisis nor public demonstration of opposition. For these reasons, events in Hungary were neglected by much of the world's media at the time. But it is important to note that the party was not forced from power in Hungary. The party *chose* to introduce a multi-party system, and when it lost the subsequent election in 1990, it retired from government and, in the tradition of democratic politics, became the loyal opposition.

It is true, however, that the party initiated political change in the belief that this would offer the communists the best chance of retaining power in the longer term. In this sense, the Hungarian case could support the theory that the reforms were aimed at preserving rather than dismantling the communist system. On the other hand, this view seems to underestimate the radical nature of the reforms initiated by the party and agreed by Gorbachev in 1988. Even if the party had won the election in 1990, after the political and economic reforms advocated by the party little would have remained of a recognisably Soviet-type system.

In Poland, the economic situation was much worse than in Hungary. A series of major strikes in the spring and summer of 1988 had paralysed the country. The Polish leader, General Jaruzelski, became convinced that he needed Solidarity's co-operation to escape from the political impasse. As a result, he introduced round table talks in February 1989, and events speeded up thereafter. In April, Solidarity was formally unbanned and multi-party elections were scheduled for June.

The election rules were rigged specifically to ensure a communist majority in parliament with 65 percent of the seats in the lower house uncontested and reserved for the communist party (PUWP). The election was not designed to bring the communist era to a close, but to legitimise the continuation of the communist government and its policies. Some Solidarity activists were opposed to the election on these very grounds (Gross, 1992: 62-4). The election, however, did not provide the expected result - in fact, the PUWP was humiliated. The party failed to win a single contested constituency for the lower house and only five communists received the absolute majority required in the single-candidate constituencies reserved for the party. Solidarity, on the other hand, received 80 percent of the vote, and the only contested seat it failed to win went to a non-party billionaire.

The election result created an acute political crisis over the summer. For although the party had lost all legitimacy to rule, Solidarity had no constitutional right to take power. It was at this point Moscow made a series of decisive interventions. In a well-publicised speech on 7 July 1989 to the European Council in Strasbourg, Gorbachev indicated a willingness to tolerate systemic change. He said:

> 'Social and political orders in one or another country changed in the past and may change in the future. But this change is the exclusive affair of that country and is their choice. Any interference in domestic affairs and any attempts to restrict the sovereignty of states, both friends and allies or any others, is impermissible' (Gati, 1990: 169).

After a commitment by the Warsaw Pact to respect sovereignty in July, the Soviet Defence Council also declared the following month that Soviet troops would not be deployed to maintain civil order in Eastern Europe (Zic, 1992: 1231; Oldenburg, 1994: 104).

It was also reported that Gorbachev phoned the Polish Prime Minister, Mieczyslaw Rakowski, on 22 August and told him that the communist party should accept the results of the June election and accept a minority position in a coalition government (Beschloss and Talbott, 1993: 102). This version of events, however, has been denied by Rakowski. In Rakowski's account, Gorbachev simply emphasised his unwillingness to intervene in the internal affairs of Poland (Pryce-Jones, 1995: 210). The latter version is probably closer to the truth, but even this represented a significant shift away from traditional Soviet policy in Eastern Europe. For when Tadeusz Mazowiecki finally formed a Solidarity-led coalition in September, it represented a major turning point in post-war European history. It provided conclusive evidence that systemic change was possible in the Soviet bloc. Nor did Gorbachev attempt to slow down the process of change in other East European countries. On the contrary, he immediately turned his attention to East Germany where he began to actively promote reform.

Emigration had always been the Achilles heel of the East German regime. The Berlin Wall had been erected in 1961 to stem the flood of refugees. Although emigration restrictions had eased since Gorbachev came to power, it proved to be a problem again in 1989. The crisis began in May when Hungary, with great fanfare, cut the barbed wire on its border with Austria. In fact, the event was something of a publicity stunt to improve Hungary's international image. For Hungarians already had freedom of travel. A month earlier in April, as many as 800,000 Hungarians had crossed the border in just one week to do some shopping in Austria (Frankland, 1990: 118). However, when the rip in the iron curtain came to the attention of GDR citizens via West German TV, they began to campaign to be allowed to emigrate through Hungary.

Although Hungary had an agreement with the GDR to return all refugees, it was felt this was no longer in accord with the changing times. Therefore, in September 1989 Budapest decided to allow the East Germans to leave. Many understood that this was a momentous decision. Hungary's Foreign Minister, Gyula Horn, told an American journalist later, 'It was obvious to me that this would be the first step in a landslide-like series of events' (Oberdorfer, 1992: 362).[2] And so it proved. In the four months to December, almost 300,000 East Germans took the opportunity to emigrate through Hungary. When the GDR party leader, Erich Honecker, closed the border to Hungary, his compatriots simply went to Czechoslovakia and camped out in the West German embassy in Prague.

---

[2] Karoly Grosz's successor, Miklos Nemeth, also stated that he recognised the international ramifications of opening the iron curtain (BBC, 1994a).

The desire to emigrate was not unique to the East Germans. Many other East Europeans wanted easier access to the West. The East Germans *were* unique, however, in having a rich neighbour willing to grant emigres full citizenship rights. The welcome for East Germans in the FRG contrasted sharply with the reception for fleeing Albanians in Italy some months later. It was the right of immigration to a foreign country rather than the desire to emigrate that brought down the GDR.

As thousands deserted the GDR, Moscow continued to put pressure on Honecker's government. Back in June 1989, Gorbachev had confided to the West German Chancellor, Helmut Kohl, that Honecker's days were numbered (Gedmin, 1992: 64). In October, as the crisis in the GDR worsened, Gennady Gerasimov, Gorbachev's foreign affairs spokesman, declared the Brezhnev Doctrine had been superseded by the Sinatra Doctrine. 'You know Frank Sinatra's song, My Way,' he said, 'well, Eastern Europe can do it their way'(*The Times*, 26 October 1989).

The same month, Gorbachev went to Berlin for the GDR's fortieth anniversary celebrations. It turned out to be a public relations disaster for Erich Honecker. At a candle-lit procession, Honecker was greatly embarrassed when a chant rose up for Gorbachev. The message was clear. Even the young communists, hand-picked to take part in the procession, rejected Honecker's vision of communism and wanted change. Next day, at a closed meeting of the SED politburo, Gorbachev made it plain that he was dissatisfied with Honecker's leadership (BBC, 1994b) and he finished his address with the famous words: 'He who arrives late in politics is punished by life' (Gorbachev, 1995b: 412).

At last, the SED acted. Honecker was removed on 18 October and replaced by Egon Krenz as General Secretary. Krenz favoured reform, but his reputation was as a hardliner. Back in June, he had even supported the Chinese crackdown in Tiananmen Square (*Neues Deutschland*, 5 June 1989). So the demonstrations continued. 150,000 people took to the streets of Leipzig on 23 October and double that number a week later. In Berlin at least half a million demonstrated against the regime on 4 December whilst thousands more were emigrating via Czechoslovakia.

Krenz recognised that the issue of travel and emigration had to be settled if any resolution of the crisis was to be found. He devised a plan to simplify the procedures for travel which was approved by the SED Central Committee on 9 November. All GDR citizens would still require an exit visa to leave the country but these would be more readily available than previously. Through such a compromise, it was hoped to satisfy public demand for freer movement whilst at the same time allowing the government to maintain some kind of control over the movement of its people.

The plan was to come into effect on 10 November, but it all went badly wrong. On 9 November, politburo member, Gunter Schabowski, towards the end of a press conference carried live on TV, announced the end of all travel restrictions. However, he omitted to state the visa requirement and when pressed further by journalists said he assumed the changes would come into operation with immediate effect. The impact of his words was dramatic. Berliners rushed to the Wall in their thousands and demanded the border guards allow them to cross to the West. Krenz later described the situation as close to civil war (*Moscow News*, 11-17 November 1994). Since the guards were unable to get any advice from superiors, after some hours of confusion, they used their own initiative and allowed the people to cross into West Berlin (McElvoy, 1992: 207-8). The Wall never closed again. Thus, in the final analysis, the cold war ended that night largely as a result of bureaucratic incompetence. A fitting end, some would say, to the communist experiment.

Given the chaotic state of affairs in Berlin at the time, Gorbachev could have been given no forewarning of the fall of the Wall. Nevertheless, he immediately recognised that there was no going back. Gorbachev was not surprised by the event itself, but rather its manner and timing. As far back as 1988, Gorbachev had acknowledged that the issue of the Berlin Wall should be a part of the international political agenda and just before its fall, he had approved Krenz's proposal to permanently open the Wall by the year 2000 (*Moscow News*, 11-17 November 1994).

Moscow appeared less clear, however, over the international implications of the move. Certainly, Moscow was deeply divided about the future of Germany. Shevardnadze said in numerous interviews after the event that he had been ready to consider the reunification of Germany as far back as 1985 and that he had recognised the inevitability of reunification in November 1989 (*Soviet Weekly*, 17 October 1991). Gorbachev also refused to rule it out as a possibility in a meeting with the FRG President in 1987, but argued it was 'premature and harmful' (Gorbachev, 1995b: 152). Nevertheless, when the Wall came down, the official line from Moscow was that the events of 9 November did not effect the GDR's status as an independent, sovereign state (*Moscow News*, 11 November 1994; and Dashichev, 1994: 173). In fact, the Soviet news agency, TASS, declared that the opening of state borders was a means of preserving the GDR and did not presage a 'recarving' of European borders (*Soviet News*, 15 November 1989). The GDR had survived up to 1961 without the Wall in the depth of the cold war - why shouldn't it continue to exist in the new era of East-West rapprochement?

At the time, this view did not seem so fanciful, for the GDR had some surprising supporters. At home, Neues Forum (the main opposition group to emerge during the East German crisis) came out in opposition to both reunification and free market capitalism. On the international scene, President Mitterand and Mrs Thatcher were privately fearful of the destabilising effects of a powerful, reunified Germany in the centre of Europe (Thatcher, 1993: 769). The hope of preserving the GDR as a sovereign state faltered, however, on the rocks of self-determination. The people in the GDR wanted West German living standards combined with West German freedoms.

Although the GDR was not the last European communist state to fall, it was the most important. The balance of power in Europe was based on a divided Germany and the cold war was symbolised by the Berlin Wall. As the Wall came down, other communist states found it impossible to resist the wave of revolution. Nothing, it seemed, could save communism and the communist party. The dominoes continued to fall irrespective of personalities, policies and the state of the economy.

A stable, relatively prosperous country like Czechoslovakia, for example, fell in a matter of days as the party abdicated power on 10 November in what became known as the velvet revolution. In impoverished Romania, on the other hand, Nikolai Ceausescu tried to stay in power by rejecting reform and tightening up on repression. The policy was no more successful than anywhere else in the region. It merely added to the misery of the Romanian population and led to a bloody struggle for power on the streets of Bucharest between the military and the *securitate*. The fighting came to an end when Nikolai Ceausescu and his wife, Elena, were executed on Christmas Day 1989 and their corpses were shown on national TV.

Romania was the last of the Warsaw Pact countries to succumb to revolution. But the mood of revolt soon caught up with the neutral communist states of Yugoslavia and Albania. Free elections were called in Yugoslavia in 1990 which ultimately led to the breakup of the country and the most bloody fighting seen in Europe since the end of World War II (see chapter 12). Albania, due to its isolationist stance and fierce repression throughout the cold war period, was able to withstand revolution the longest. However, news of the Albanian problem in the Yugoslav province of Kosovo radicalised the people in Albania proper. The authorities, as elsewhere in Eastern Europe, were obliged to accept multiparty elections and give up the communist party's guaranteed monopoly right to rule.

Commentators have debated whether the overthrow of communism in Eastern Europe actually constituted a revolution. Timothy Garton-Ash suggested it was a mix of reform and revolution, which he termed 'refolution' (Ash, 1990). The word, revolution, implies a sudden, mass uprising, not just against leaders or policies, but against the political system itself. It is not clear that such a definition always applied to Eastern Europe. In fact, the causes and extent of change varied greatly across the region. In Hungary, mass protest played no role, in East Germany it literally forced the guards to open the Berlin Wall on the night of 9 November 1989. In some countries, such as Romania and Bulgaria, protests were sparked off more by a desire for a change in leader rather than a change of system. In Romania, in particular, the events could be seen in terms of a coup or a bloody power struggle between Ceausescu's friends and enemies. Moreover, the National Salvation Front which emerged as the successor to the communist party was dominated by figures which had served at one time or another with Ceausescu. As communists returned to positions of power in other countries, such as Poland, Hungary and Slovakia, doubts were more frequently expressed over the real nature of change in the region since 1989.

It still seems, however, that revolution is the most suitable word for the climactic events of 1989. For the most important thing to note is the rejection of communism as a system in all East European states. This is found in two vitally important changes common throughout the former communist bloc. First, legitimation to rule no longer rested with Marxist-Leninist ideology but with the people and the ballot box. Second, the command economy was rejected, and a role for market forces and private property was acknowledged in all former communist states. The shift towards democratisation and marketisation varied greatly across the region. Nevertheless, Soviet-style communism had failed as an idea. It was hard to see how it could ever return in any recognisable form. Even most self-proclaimed communists tried to reinvent themselves for public consumption as either nationalists or social democrats.

## The post-revolutionary period

As communism collapsed in Eastern Europe in 1989, Moscow still initially hoped to retain influence in the region because of mutual economic and military interdependence. The results, however, were rather mixed.

The main economic organisation in Eastern Europe, the Council for Mutual

Economic Assistance (CMEA), had few supporters by 1989. It compared badly with its mirror image in the West, the European Community. The CMEA had singularly failed to integrate the communist economies since its inception in 1947 and had scarcely facilitated intra-bloc trade. As it had failed as an institution in the communist era, it was unlikely to have any relevance as the East Europeans abandoned the state planning system. As a result, the CMEA was formally abolished on 28 June 1991, although it had ceased to have any operative function long before that.

A secret International Department document leaked to the West argued, however, that the end of the CMEA did not mean the end of Soviet influence (*Frankfurter Allgemeine Zeitung*, 7 June 1991). On the contrary, it was pointed out that Eastern Europe remained highly dependent on the Soviet Union in economic terms both as a market for consumer goods, which were often uncompetitive on the world market, and as a source of energy and natural resources. The document reckoned that as much as 80 percent of the region's oil and almost 100 percent of its gas came from the Soviet Union. It was hoped, therefore, to use such dependency to defend Soviet interests in the area - a policy which both Gorbachev and Yeltsin followed in Moscow's relations with recalcitrant nationalist leaders in the Soviet republics and successor states.

There was evidence that the USSR was attempting a policy of economic blackmail in the case of Czechoslovakia when Moscow threatened to cut oil supplies after Prague condemned Soviet military action in the Baltic Republics in January 1991. The Czechs responded by threatening unilaterally to leave the Warsaw Pact (Roucek, 1992: 5). It all came to nothing, as the attempted coup in Lithuania and Latvia fizzled out. In any case, the proposed linkage policy collapsed since the state of the Soviet economy gave Moscow little in the way of leverage. In fact, the USSR soon found itself after 1989 facing significant trade deficits with its former East European allies.

The International Department document had been right, however, in sensing the importance of the USSR to the immediate economic prospects of its former allies. The economies of Eastern Europe suffered badly when all trade with the Soviet Union was conducted in hard currency after January 1991. This meant an end to cheap Soviet oil and gas which had been so vital for economic growth in the region. At the same time, the collapse of the Soviet economy meant that trade between the USSR and Eastern Europe was roughly halved in the period 1989-1993 (*Rossiiskie Vesti*, 16 February 1993: 2). As a result, the years immediately after 1989 were very difficult as Eastern Europe began to restructure their economies and were forced to redirect their trade away from the Soviet

Union.

The CMEA was given up without much of a struggle. The dissolution of the Warsaw Pact was a more painful process for Moscow. Soviet leaders were greatly exercised by the emergence of a political vacuum in an area of traditional instability. The fear of renewed encirclement by NATO powers prompted army officers, such as Chief of the General Staff Mikhail Moiseyev, to argue that Soviet troops should remain in Eastern Europe as long as there were US troops on the continent (*New Times*, no. 12/13 1993: 17).

Not all East European states were opposed to a continued Soviet presence in the region. Poland, for example, whilst harbouring vigorous anti-Russian sentiment, also feared the prospect of German revanchism. Polish fears of Germany were largely set aside, however, by the multilateral treaty of unification of September 1990 and the bilateral Polish-German treaty of 14 November when the western frontiers of Poland were fully recognised in international law. In contrast to the Poles, the Hungarians and Czechs believed from the start that the main threat to security and independence came from the USSR. As long as Soviet troops remained on their soil, there was felt to be a danger of the reimposition of Soviet control. In spring 1990, Moscow agreed to start the process of troop withdrawal.

The issue of the GDR was always likely to pose the most difficult problems and this proved to be the case. The central rationale of Soviet post-war policy in Europe had been to prevent the rise of a strong, militarised Germany allied to the West. The division of Germany had been an important part of this strategy. Yet in January 1990, some two months after the fall of the Wall, Hans Modrow, the then East German leader, convinced Gorbachev that the German people would accept nothing less than reunification (*Pravda*, 31 January 1990). Gorbachev decided to accept reunification, in part because Moscow was no longer prepared to subsidise the collapsing East German economy (see Wettig, 1993). Therefore, on 10 February Gorbachev telephoned Kohl to say that the future of Germany was the 'choice' of the German people (Chernayev, 1994: 167).

Moscow accepted reunification but at a politburo meeting in May, Gorbachev still expressed his opposition to the prospect of a reunified Germany in NATO. Ligachev voiced the concern of many conservatives when he declared that NATO was 'approaching the borders' of the Soviet Union (Chernayev, 1994: 167). However, by the summer of 1990, the majority in Moscow had come round to the view, advocated by most Europeans - East and West - that the best way to contain the power of a reunified Germany was through its membership of viable

Western institutions. Thus, Soviet ideas of a neutral Germany or a Germany straddling both NATO and the Warsaw Pact were dropped. By-passing the formal two-plus-four negotiations (involving the two Germanies and the four occupying powers) set up earlier in the year, Gorbachev and Kohl met in Sevastopol in mid-July. In a momentous meeting, Gorbachev agreed to German political union by October, full membership of NATO, and the withdrawal of all Soviet troops from the territory of the former GDR by the end of 1994 (later brought forward to August). The final agreement was signed by the two Germanies and the four occupying powers on 12 September.

In return, Gorbachev won some important concessions. First, he gained commitments on security which were aimed at reassuring Soviet conservatives that a reunified Germany posed no military threat to the USSR or Europe. Thus, it was agreed that the unified German army would have a ceiling of 370,000 troops -100,000 less than the number in the West Germany army at that time. Furthermore, NATO troops would not be deployed in the zone of the former GDR and a unified Germany would remain a non-nuclear signatory of the non-proliferation treaty. NATO also formally committed itself in its July Declaration to reduce and restructure its military forces and to redefine its purpose as no longer anti-Soviet. Second, Kohl agreed to provide DM 15 billion credit, including DM 3 billion to accommodate returning Soviet soldiers. Kohl also promised to act as the Soviet representative in international forums, such as the G7, to lobby for further aid (Oldenburg, 1994: 110).

Despite these concessions, a reunified Germany in NATO was more than many conservatives could stomach. The future Soviet Foreign Minister, Alexander Bessmertnykh, said that hardliners found this 'one of the most hated developments in the history of Soviet foreign policy' (Beschloss and Talbott, 1993: 240). Germany was just one reason for the hardliners in the Soviet Union regrouping over the summer of 1990 (see chapter 1). As they put increasing pressure on Gorbachev, Eastern Europe became worried over the implications for the region of a shift to the right in Moscow.

The Soviet military began to voice concern over the CFE Treaty which had originally been devised on the premise of the continued existence of the two military blocs in Europe. As the Warsaw Pact was in the last stages of disintegration, the treaty appeared to freeze the USSR into a position of permanent inferiority vis-a-vis NATO (see chapter 4). NATO, the Soviet military noted bitterly, showed no signs of disbanding. Meanwhile, the bellicose US reaction to the Gulf crisis seemed to be aimed at re-emphasising America's continued great power status (see chapter 8).

Through much of 1991, the anti-reformist forces in Moscow made threatening noises. There was violence in the Baltic Republics in January which revealed an unstable balance of power in the Kremlin. Fears grew in much of Eastern Europe that the military might seek to restore the Soviet position in the region. Since the continued existence of the Warsaw Pact could be used as a pretext for military intervention, shortly after the attacks on the Baltic Republics, the countries of Czechoslovakia, Hungary and Poland called for the end of the Warsaw Pact by July 1991 (Sheehan, 1992: 35). Gorbachev, concerned about hardliners at home, agreed and simultaneously concluded an agreement with Poland to start troop withdrawal from April of that year.

In many ways, the worst fears of Eastern Europe were realised when the power struggle in Moscow climaxed in the August coup of 1991. There are reasons to believe relations with the West would have worsened had the coup been successful. However, during the coup, international borders remained open and there was no unusual military activity except at Tallinn in Estonia. The emergency committee said little on foreign policy, but what it did say emphasised continuity. Most importantly, the leader of the committee declared that the withdrawal of Soviet troops from Germany would still be completed on schedule. This highlighted two important points. First, there was a reluctant acceptance after the event, even among the hardliners, of the changes in Eastern Europe. Second, it also revealed a desire among all sections of the Soviet elite to maintain reasonable relations with the West.

## Reasons for withdrawal

The Soviet Union had few options in late 1989. Gorbachev himself admitted that the only possible alternative to withdrawal was 'Soviet tanks on the streets and blood on the pavement' (*Vestnik*, August 1990). Yet the Soviet Union was not forced out of Eastern Europe. The evidence shows that Gorbachev began the process of withdrawal back in 1985 when he indicated that the USSR was no longer willing to prop up East European governments by force. He never willed the end of communism nor the end of Soviet influence in the region, but he recognised both as possible outcomes at least from early 1989 when he received intelligence reports to that effect (Garthoff, 1994: 601). Nevertheless, Gorbachev continued to encourage radical reform throughout the region. He was willing to take the risk for a mix of economic and strategic reasons.

First, Eastern Europe had become an economic drain on the Soviet Union.

Immediately after the war, Stalin had exploited the region to rebuild the Soviet Union's shattered economy. It was estimated that Moscow took from Eastern Europe in reparations roughly the equivalent of what the US put into Western Europe in the form of Marshall Aid (Ash, 1994: 91). But this exploitative relationship was reversed after Stalin's death in 1953. By the late 1980s, Professor Karen Dawisha estimated that Soviet subsidies to the region, largely in the form of cheap oil and gas, amounted to as much as two percent of Soviet GNP (Dawisha, 1988: 105).

In the past, Moscow had been willing to pay the cost of its East European empire. Gorbachev, however, came to power eager to review Moscow's position in the region. Traditionally, the region was perceived to be of vital strategic importance to Moscow. It served both as a defensive buffer against the possibility of Western attack and as an offensive bridgehead in case of military action in Western Europe. However, Gorbachev no longer viewed war in Europe as likely. As he shifted Soviet military doctrine away from *blitzkrieg* strategies to defensive defence, he was able to argue for cuts in troops and equipment in the region. Thus, a Warsaw Pact commission reported in 1988 that unilateral cuts in Soviet forces, including total withdrawal from Hungary and Czechoslovakia, could be made without undermining Soviet security (MccGwire, 1991: 359). This report allowed Gorbachev to agree in July 1988 to withdraw all Soviet troops from Hungary (as mentioned earlier) and to announce unilateral force cuts at the UN in December the same year.

Gorbachev also no longer wanted Eastern Europe as a kind of ideological buffer zone which filtered out alien ideas from the West before they could reach and pollute the Soviet Union. On the contrary, Gorbachev sought an end to Moscow's self-imposed isolation and the reintegration of the Soviet Union into the international system. In those circumstances, the East European buffer looked an increasingly costly encumbrance to improved relations with the West. Thus, TASS described the fall of the Berlin Wall on 9 November 1989 as natural and stated Moscow's hope that it would benefit the USSR in terms of its relations with the rest of the world (*Soviet News*, 15 November 1989).

Reluctantly, most hardliners accepted the loss of Soviet influence in the region. Only 'peripheral' figures ever spoke of trying to recapture Eastern Europe (Chernayev, 1994: 166). The International Department, a conservative institution, produced a document which argued that there was no question of trying to restore Moscow's former position in the region (*Frankfurter Allgemeine Zeitung*, 7 June 1991). A secret analysis on the Polish crisis, commissioned by the politburo after Mazowiecki took power, also argued that Moscow had no alternative but to co-operate with the new, non-communist government in Warsaw.[3] New thinkers and old thinkers alike accepted that the world had changed. This was perhaps the most startling revelation of all.

*The role of the West*

The West could claim to have influenced Soviet policy over arms control and the war in Afghanistan. It is difficult to make a similar case for Eastern Europe. From the earliest days of the cold war, the West appeared to accept Soviet dominance in the area. Despite some changes in rhetoric, Western policy remained remarkably consistent throughout the post-war period - it was containment rather than roll-back. Certainly in 1989, no attempt was made to force a Soviet retreat from the region. The Western role in the collapse of communism was, therefore, limited.

This does not mean it was non-existent. Perhaps the simple fact that the West existed as a viable alternative to Soviet communism was its most important role in undermining the system in Eastern Europe. In the USSR, knowledge of the West outside the big European cities was fairly limited, but this was less the case in Eastern Europe where travel was generally easier and communications better. Therefore, as people in the Soviet bloc became more aware of living standards and life-styles in the West, belief in communism dissipated. Many have observed that mass consumerism brought down communism rather than nuclear weapons. Jeans and rock music proved more effective anti-communist weapons than Cruise and Pershing.

At some level this is obviously true. However, NATO was still able to play an important deterrent role in Europe. Documents seized after the cold war showed that the Warsaw Pact was better prepared for invasion than many believed at the time. Military plans for the invasion of West Germany were highly detailed, even down to new street signs and printed money for the occupation government (*International Herald Tribune*, 17 March 1993). Undoubtedly, the US military presence added greatly to the self-confidence of West European countries in the immediate post-war period. The US nuclear umbrella also allowed the countries of Western Europe to spend less on defence and invest more in their civilian economies. This was not a negligible factor in the rapid rise of

---

3 Archives of the general department of the Central Committee of the CPSU, Folio 89, list 9, Document 33, 28 September 1989. Source cited in Steele (1994): 181.

104 RUSSIAN FOREIGN POLICY AND THE END OF THE COLD WAR

West European economies in the post-war period.

A debate has also raged over the possible role of detente in the 1970s in encouraging reform in Eastern Europe (see Ash, 1994). Proponents of detente argued that *Ostpolitik* and the Helsinki Final Act stabilised relations in Europe. In the 1970s, the West formally accepted the division of Europe and the dominance of the Soviet Union in the East. It was hoped this would reduce suspicion and encourage improved relations across the divide. Trade and aid to Eastern Europe would raise living standards whilst the promotion of human rights would make life more tolerable for citizens in the East. Europe, it was argued, would become more interdependent as a result of the detente process and ultimately both the need and the desire for a divided continent would fade and eventually disappear. It was the theory of convergence.

Critics of detente argued that the long-term goals of detente got lost in short-term conveniences. The result was often the opposite of stated intentions. Instead of undermining communism, detente prolonged its existence. Communism, it was argued, was kept afloat in the 1970s through generous Western trade and credit policies. This was most apparent in the case of the GDR. Honecker's government received generous credit terms from Bonn in the 1980s and benefited from being unofficially the thirteenth member of the EC. Most controversial of all, East Germany also earned hard currency through its trade in human beings. Timothy Garton-Ash estimated that 34,000 political prisoners and 250,000 children were bought out of the GDR by Bonn between 1963-89 at a total cost to the FRG of DM 3.5 billion (Ash, 1994: 146). Such trade helped to conceal the real state of the East German economy which, according to politburo member Gunter Mittag, was close to bankruptcy by the time Gorbachev came to power in 1985 (*The Guardian*, 10 September 1991).

Detente was also condemned as immoral. The Helsinki and *Ostpolitik* agreements were described as the Western equivalent of the Brezhnev Doctrine, requiring the people of Eastern Europe to accept Soviet domination of their region for the greater good of stability on the rest of the continent (see Bowker and Williams, 1985). The German Chancellor Helmut Schmidt and the French President Valery Giscard d'Estaing actually supported the Jaruzelski government in the name of European security when martial law was imposed in Poland in December 1981. At such moments, it was hard to escape the unpleasant whiff of appeasement.

The US, however, was less willing to tolerate such blatant violations of human rights. For President Ronald Reagan, the imposition of martial law in Poland showed that nothing fundamental had changed in Eastern Europe since the start of detente in the 1970s. The nature of communism was still totalitarian and the USSR still refused to countenance diversity in its sphere of influence. Therefore, the Reagan administration adopted a more hard-headed attitude to the region. Substantive policy changed remarkably little but the West began to play the human rights card more effectively. The CSCE review conferences after Helsinki were dominated by the issue whilst Western leaders, in contrast to the 1970s, made a point of publicly supporting dissident leaders, such as Vaclav Havel and Lech Walesa. The US also provided aid to Solidarity which helped it survive its eight years as an illegal organisation. During the course of 1989, the West also offered aid and credit to promote reform in the region. Such offers were an incentive for Hungary to open its border to the East Germans in 1989, and the DM 15 billion aid package from Helmut Kohl encouraged Gorbachev to agree to German reunification (Oldenburg, 1994: 110).

Proponents of detente had tended to view both communism and the USSR as omnipresent facts of international life. The USSR was perceived to be a stable state whose great power status was assured for the foreseeable future. Therefore, any attempt to exploit Soviet weaknesses was at best futile and at worst dangerous. In the parlance of detente, a wounded bear was more dangerous than a contented bear. Yet, such thinking overestimated the USSR's ability to control Eastern Europe. Even more importantly, it also ignored the desire of many East Europeans to escape from Soviet domination. The case of Eastern Europe reminds us that there is always a place for morality and justice whenever the issues of international security and order are being discussed.

# Chapter Six

# THIRD WORLD POLICY AND REGIONAL POLITICS

In Lenin's time, the third world did not appear a fruitful area for communist revolution. Countries in the region were predominantly agricultural, often tribal societies, lacking not only a working class but often any form of class structure at all. According to orthodox Marxist theory, the states of the third world were not ready for communist revolution. Lenin, however, recognised the destructive power of nationalism and its potential for overthrowing imperialism. This opened up the possibility of an anti-imperialist alliance between local communists and national liberation movements in the third world. Leninist theory argued that such an alliance would hasten the end of imperialism and provoke the collapse of the international capitalist system. After the revolution, the development of the third world would be promoted and subsidised by the rest of the international socialist community, hence allowing such states to skip capitalism and move straight to socialism. This was the theory of permanent revolution (Lenin, 1916).

Leninist theory on the third world was based on three false assumptions. First, the collapse of imperialism did not lead to the collapse of the international capitalist system. Instead, international capitalism continued to dominate the world economy in the post-imperialist period. Second, permanent revolution proved a fallacy. Those third world states which overthrew colonialism and embraced Marxism-Leninism still found it difficult to escape poverty and political repression. The socialist bloc lacked unity and was unable to provide sufficient aid to substantially effect development patterns. Third, the communists and nationalists rarely formed a natural or stable alliance. Lenin was right in perceiving anti-Western sentiment in much of the third world, but he was wrong in supposing that this would automatically lead to pro-Soviet or pro-communist attitudes. National culture often clashed with the internationalist and materialist principles of Marxism-Leninism. These were problems which all Lenin's successors tried to deal with in different ways. None was able to find a satisfactory solution.

Stalin, always sceptical about the progressive nature of nationalism, found his prejudices confirmed in 1927 when the nationalist Kuomintang in China turned on their coalition partners in the most brutal fashion and destroyed the Communist Party (CCP). Stalin became extremely suspicious of coalition politics, thereafter, and only briefly embraced it again when confronted by the rise of fascism in Europe. When the war was won, he reverted back to what was known after 1947 as the two-camp theory (Zhdanov, 1947). The theory argued that the world was divided into two irreconcilable camps - the capitalist and communist world systems - and within this paradigm, there was no middle ground, no room for compromise or coalition. Therefore, the non-communist nationalists in the third world were perceived to be class enemies of socialism just as much as the imperialists themselves.

The two-camp theory legitimised Stalin's general lack of interest in the third world. In fact, there was little he could have done anyway. The USSR lacked both the economic and military power to act much beyond its own borders. Thus, Stalin concentrated most of his attention on securing control over Eastern Europe. This did not mean that Stalin did not act in the third world when he saw an opportunity. For example, he attempted to maintain a Soviet presence in Iran in 1946 and was only driven out after military threats from the West. Stalin also supported the communist war effort in Korea, 1950-53, secretly deploying Soviet pilots to fight in Chinese colours alongside Mao's forces (see Goncharov, et al, 1995).

Indeed, the most important advance for communism in the third world - the communists taking power in China in 1949 - occurred whilst Stalin was in the Kremlin, albeit with the minimum of support from Moscow. In public, Moscow welcomed the Chinese Revolution, but in private it was greeted without enthusiasm. China was a huge, independent country which could boast a long and proud history. Beijing was never going to be as easily controlled as Moscow's small client states in Eastern Europe. Mao's China clearly posed a potential threat to Moscow's leadership of the international communist movement.

Initially, however, Mao had little choice but to seek an alliance with Stalin. The communist government in Beijing was ostracised by the West and his country needed aid for development. At that time, the USSR looked the only possible source. In fact, the level of aid subsequently offered in the 1950 Sino-Soviet Treaty was a bitter disappointment to Mao. It bred the suspicion in Beijing that Moscow's policies were governed more by traditional concerns of national interest rather than ideological comradeship (see Medvedev, 1986).

After Stalin's death in 1953, Khrushchev favoured a more activist policy in the third world. He abandoned the two-camp theory in 1956 at the 20th CPSU Congress and reverted to a more flexible, Leninist strategy. Khrushchev wanted to exploit the post-war decolonisation movement and favoured support for non-communist, nationalist leaders as long as they adopted an anti-Western policy platform. Khrushchev argued that such leaders (revolutionary democrats) could guide their countries (national democracies) towards socialism on a non-capitalist path of development. As a group, such countries made up, what Khrushchev termed, a 'zone of peace' (Khrushchev, 1956).

Khrushchev embarked on an exhausting diplomatic round from 1955 to promote his new ideas to third world leaders. In 1960, he visited Sukarno's Indonesia, which he praised as a model of nationalist democracy, whilst offering support for its position of neutrality on foreign policy issues. Aid was offered to revolutionary democrats on more generous terms than those available in the West. Most notably, Moscow stepped in to fund the Aswan Dam in Egypt in the late 1950s after the West had decided, on commercial grounds, to pull out.

At first, Khrushchev's initiatives appeared to bear fruit, as a number of third world states in Africa, the Middle East and Asia tilted towards Moscow. By the late 1950s, 14 percent of the world's nations and about a third of the world's population were adjudged to be in the Soviet sphere of influence (The Center for Defense Information, 1986: 706). Soviet optimism was shortlived, however, as familiar problems re-surfaced. The renewed nationalist-communist political coalitions proved unstable. Increasingly, the Kremlin had to turn a blind-eye to nationalist governments, like the one in Egypt, repressing their communist partners. This led to unease in the USSR, especially as China became highly critical of Moscow's third world policy. Furthermore, Soviet aid was unable to prevent the fall of a series of revolutionary democrats in the 1960s, such as Ben Bella in Algeria, Nkrumah in Ghana and Khrushchev's favourite, Sukarno in Indonesia.

Marxism-Leninism survived in China, but the alliance with Moscow did not.

A combination of national rivalry, traditional suspicions and ideological disputes had always created tension between the two communist giants. Mao's contempt for Khrushchev, however, led to an open breach in the early 1960s. The US was unable to exploit this historic split at the time as China turned inward and adopted a policy of neutrality. Beijing criticised both Moscow and Washington for their hegemonic designs and declared that China stood alone as the true representative of third world interests.

When Brezhnev came to power in 1964, the romantic vision of the third world came to an end. Although there was no radical shift in direction, Brezhnev warned that the transition to communism would be long and hard. As a result, three major reforms were introduced (see Golan, 1988). First, generous aid for prestige projects was stopped. Aid was severely cut back and given on more commercial terms. Second, Brezhnev put less faith in the single leader - the revolutionary democrat. Instead, he promoted the Soviet-style vanguard party which was expected to be disciplined, well-organised and better placed to prevent both factionalism at the top and disorder in the country. Neither innovation was particularly successful. Third world debt to the Soviet Union continued to grow and the vanguard parties which were set up in Angola and Ethiopia had little or no effect on conditions in either country.

Third, Brezhnev 'militarised' Soviet third world policy. Soviet arms sales increased massively under his leadership to the extent that the USSR had become the biggest arms supplier to the third world by the early 1980s, accounting for 37 percent of all arms sales (*SIPRI Yearbook*, 1985: 348). The Soviet Union also became a truly global power in this period as it rapidly built up its navy and air force. The Soviet Union was never able to match the US in terms of global reach, but as America turned inward after Vietnam, Moscow was able to flex its muscles in the third world for a brief period without fear of reprisal (see Bowker and Williams, 1988).

America's paranoia was fuelled by a series of leftist revolutions in the third world in the mid to late 1970s. Thus, Angola, Mozambique, Ethiopia, Afghanistan, South Yemen, Nicaragua and Grenada all shifted into the Soviet camp over a brief four year period up to 1979. All revolutions, however, were indigenous affairs and Moscow played little role in their outcome. The one exception was Angola (1975-6), where the Soviet transport of Cuban troops to fight on the side of the MPLA against the US-backed UNITA forces was crucial in the former's ultimate victory. But even in this case, Moscow was successful only after the US had been forced by Congress to pull out of Angola and abandon its military support for UNITA (Bowker and Williams, 1988: 117-131).

But by the early 1980s, the Soviet Union had become more pessimistic once again about the future of socialism in the third world (see, for example, Brutents, 1984). After all the ups and downs of Soviet policy, only about thirteen third world states were still on the non-capitalist path favoured by Moscow. Many of those states proclaimed their Marxist-Leninist credentials simply as a means to get military aid from Moscow. Moreover, the Kremlin soon discovered that the despatch of arms did not necessarily create dependable allies. Egypt, Sudan and Somalia all abandoned Moscow in the 1970s after being close Soviet allies (*Soviet News*, 22 February 1989).

Even more disappointingly from Moscow's perspective, the majority of pro-Soviet states, including Afghanistan, Angola and Nicaragua faced a growing challenge from internal and external insurgency. The priority for Moscow in the 1980s was the retention of existing allies rather than the search for new ones. As Raymond Garthoff has written, the Soviet Union ceased to be an expansionist power in the 1980s and became a counter-revolutionary force, whose main aim appeared to be propping up its collapsing global position (Garthoff, 1994: 717).

Of equal concern to Moscow was the fact that all pro-Soviet states in the third world faced economic crisis. This was a reflection of Moscow's own economic problems. For the Soviet Union had been unsuccessful in its aim of creating an alternative socialist world system centred on the USSR. This was becoming increasingly obvious through the 1970s. It was not just that the Soviet economy was too weak to offer development aid - Brezhnev had recognised this problem back in the mid-1960s - far more worrying was Moscow's weak international trading position. In the early 1980s, only seven percent of all third world trade was with the Soviet Union, and the figure was scarcely any higher for Soviet trade with states of socialist orientation (Valkenier, 1983: 20; Menon, 1986: 61). This was not just a result of Western competition. Increasingly, the Soviet bloc was losing out to third world competition as well. By the 1980s, third world countries could produce better quality goods than the Soviet Union, and at lower prices.

By the early 1980s, the USSR no longer posed a realistic threat to Western economic interests in the third world. This was an important factor in bringing the cold war to an end. Even states of socialist orientation, like Angola and Mozambique, wanted trade with the West. Increasingly, leftist ideas on import substitution were being abandoned. State ownership and central planning were becoming discredited throughout the world. A growing number of Soviet academics, such as Nodari Simoniya (1972) and Karen Brutents (1984) were acknowledging this and writing highly critical accounts of states of socialist orientation.

Hence, the general image in the 1970s of a confident, expansionist Soviet Union was badly mistaken. In fact, Moscow's international position was weaker than it had been in the late 1950s under Khrushchev (The Center for Defense Information, 1986: 706). Soviet gains in the third world in the 1970s were more than balanced out by its losses, which included Chile, Egypt and Somalia. Most important of all, China abandoned its position of neutrality and began in the 1970s to shift into the Western camp. Despite everything, the Soviet Union was still encircled by powerful enemies when Gorbachev came to power in 1985.

## Gorbachev's New Thinking

Gorbachev was highly critical of Brezhnev's third world policies. They had failed according to their own criteria - they had not furthered international communism, and more importantly, from Gorbachev's perspective, they had also failed to enhance Soviet influence around the world. In fact, the Soviet Union in 1985 remained remarkably isolated for a superpower. Of course, Moscow had important third world allies, such as India, Syria and Iraq, but all the major powers - the US, Western Europe, Japan and China - were in opposition to her. Moreover, the majority of influential regional powers, like Israel, Egypt, Brazil and South Africa, were also suspicious of Moscow, fearing a superpower which rejected the international status quo.

Gorbachev's main task in foreign policy was to end Moscow's isolation. The Soviet Union's isolation undermined its credibility as a superpower, it also endangered security and inhibited economic development. Gorbachev intended improving the USSR's international position by rebuilding trust. This he did by abandoning the rhetoric of a revolutionary state. Lenin's ideas on national liberation were deemed no longer relevant in what Gorbachev himself defined as the post-imperial age. Capitalism had not only survived decolonisation, it had strengthened its position (Gorbachev, 1987: 178; Primakov, 1989: 464). Gorbachev refused to view the world in simple bipolar terms. His more positive views of capitalism meant that he no longer defined Moscow's interests as a zero-sum game with the West. He sought a more co-operative relationship with states, irrespective of ideology. The international class struggle was no longer perceived to be the main dynamic of international relations (*Soviet News*, 6 July 1988). Instead, Gorbachev defined Soviet interests in more national terms, with economic and security issues taking precedence.

Gorbachev was reluctant to abandon allies, but he began to distance himself from the most radical states - hence, Moscow's moderate response to the US bombing of Libya in 1986. He also indicated to allies, such as Cuba and Vietnam, an unwillingness to continue an open-ended policy of Soviet aid. Allies were expected to account for money spent and to curb waste in the domestic economy. At the same time, allies involved in civil conflicts were encouraged to seek a negotiated settlement through a policy of national reconciliation. There were, naturally enough, policy variations which depended on a variety of factors, such as the course of Soviet domestic politics; regional and global pressures; as well as economic and strategic advantage. It was not accurate to say, however, that in 1985 Gorbachev sought to unilaterally withdraw from global politics, nor was the USSR forced out of the third world by the Reagan Doctrine or the rising economic cost of its third world interests. On the contrary, Gorbachev hoped Moscow's greater willingness to support international stability would lead to a more influential international role for the Soviet Union at both the regional and global level.

Both Gorbachev and Shevardnadze travelled extensively around the world promoting Moscow's new image. Their charm offensive won over many converts at the diplomatic level. Moscow established diplomatic relations with a range of countries, including Israel, Chile and Saudi Arabia. In practical terms, however, the USSR had little to offer other than raw materials and military equipment. In the past, Soviet influence had often manipulated conflict and regional instability to gain influence in the third world (see Vassiliev, 1993). When Gorbachev demilitarised third world policy, he found Moscow's influence inevitably slipped.

The rest of the chapter is devoted to a consideration of Gorbachev's policy in a number of states and regions. The aim is to reveal the nature of Gorbachev's policy and why he introduced change. Therefore, states and regions have been selected where these factors are most clearly highlighted. The wars in Afghanistan and the Gulf have been left out of the following discussion, but they will be dealt with later in separate chapters.


## The Far East

The Far East had emerged from the 1970s as the most dynamic economic region in the world. Japan overtook Soviet gross GNP in the 1980s; a number of Newly

Industrialising Countries (NICs), such as Singapore, Taiwan and Hong Kong were performing strongly, whilst China could claim the world's highest growth rates in the world after Deng Xiaoping introduced economic reform in 1978. Before Gorbachev's rise to power, however, the USSR was treated with suspicion in most of the region because of its military power and revolutionary ideology.

Moscow had dramatically increased its land and naval power in the region from the early 1960s. By the time Gorbachev became leader, about a quarter of all Soviet troops were deployed in Asia, a third of the navy was in the Pacific and a fifth of all military spending was devoted to the containment of China (Segal, 1990: 89). Moscow was also seen as an expansionist power after its support for Vietnam's invasion of Kampuchea in 1978 and the subsequent acquisition of bases at Da Nang and Cam Ranh Bay.[1]

Gorbachev was partly successful in slowly changing these negative perceptions of the Soviet Union. This process began when Gorbachev made a keynote speech at Vladivostok in July 1986. In it, he offered radical arms cuts and made ambitious proposals for an Asian version of the Helsinki process (*Pravda*, 29 July 1986). After the speech, the navy in the Pacific was cut by three quarters in three years and naval operations were reduced by almost a third (Segal, 1992: 22-23). Gorbachev's UN Speech of December 1988 also led to substantial cuts in troops in Asia, whilst the INF Treaty of 1987 meant all land-based short and medium-range nuclear weapons in Asia were destroyed.

Despite Gorbachev's best efforts, however, detente came to the Far East more slowly than to Europe. In part, this was due to the fact that the region was never as clearly divided as Europe. There was no equivalent of the iron curtain - or bamboo curtain - in the Far East. As a result, local and regional factors played a greater role in international affairs and the superpowers had comparatively less influence.

Relations between the USSR and Japan were slow to thaw despite an apparent complementarity of interests. Tokyo could offer capital investment and advice on how to run a modern, capitalist economy, whilst Moscow had an abundance of energy and raw materials which Japan was so short of. Relations foundered, however, on the issue of the Northern Territories (usually called the Kurile Islands in Russia). The Northern Territories were made up of four islands which Moscow seized from Japan as part of the 1945 Yalta war-time agree-

---

[1] Cambodia was known as Kampuchea from 1976 to 1989.

ment. They served as an important military and naval base in the Pacific and were economically important for fishing and minerals. Since Japan never signed the Yalta agreement, the islands' integration into the Soviet Union was viewed by Tokyo as illegal. Japan wanted the Northern Territories back.

After Gorbachev came to power he indicated a willingness to break the diplomatic log-jam. He seemed ready to revive ideas discussed in the 1950s in which Moscow would return two of the four islands - Shikotan and the Habomai archipelago. Initially, the offer was rebuffed and Tokyo refused to offer aid unless Moscow acknowledged Japanese sovereignty over the other two islands as well. This was an intransigent position. Furthermore, as the USSR began to disintegrate, hardliners in Moscow refused to contemplate giving up any more Soviet territory. So when the Soviet-Japanese summit finally took place in April 1991, Gorbachev had little room for manoeuvre and little progress was made, although Japan did offer some concessions on aid.

Moscow had far greater success with China. In fact, relations were already improving before Gorbachev came to power. There was a recognition on both sides that the standoff had harmed the interests of both sides. Thus, Gorbachev and Vice President Yilin met in July 1985. Diplomatic contacts were increased and a trade pact was signed worth $14 billion over five years. China, however, was unwilling to normalise relations whilst the so-called three obstacles remained. These obstacles were: the Soviet military buildup on the Sino-Soviet border; the Soviet intervention in Afghanistan; and the occupation of Cambodia by Moscow's ally, Vietnam.

In his Vladivostok speech, Gorbachev indicated a willingness to move on all three issues (*Pravda*, 29 July 1986). He reiterated his desire to withdraw from Afghanistan and said he favoured a peaceful settlement in Indochina. He also promised steps to demilitarise the Far East region of the Soviet Union. Progress was slow, but Gorbachev was true to his word. He announced the Soviet pullout from Afghanistan in February 1988; Vietnam had withdrawn from Kampuchea by September 1989; and Soviet troops on the Sino-Soviet border had been halved from the peak mid-1970s to approximately 150,000 by 1991. All Soviet troops were also out of Mongolia by 1992.

Relations improved to such an extent that Gorbachev was able to visit China in May 1989. It was the first summit between the two countries for thirty years. The summit was overshadowed by the public demonstrations in Tiananmen Square, but the meeting was of importance since the two communist giants formally normalised both state and party relations (*Soviet Weekly*, 27 May 1989). The summit also proposed to increase trade, although progress was slowed as the Soviet Union descended into economic and political chaos in the 1990s.

The other main issue for the USSR in the region was the occupation of Kampuchea by Moscow's ally Vietnam. Shortly after Moscow and Hanoi signed a Treaty of Friendship and Co-operation, Vietnam invaded Kampuchea on Christmas Day 1978. Hanoi's military intervention was condemned by the international community and perceived as further evidence of Soviet expansionism. Economic sanctions were imposed on both Vietnam and Kampuchea. The international reaction, however, ignored the fact that the Khmer Rouge was a brutal regime which had made a number of murderous raids on Vietnamese territory prior to Hanoi's intervention. The new government in Phnom Penh was a puppet of Hanoi, but for the majority of Kampucheans it remained far preferable to a return of Pol Pot (see Pilger, 1992: 171-249).

However, the invasion brought China and the US closer together. The rapprochement of the early 1970s was extended as ambassadors were exchanged in 1979. As part of this normalisation process, Deng Xiaoping visited America in January. During his visit, Deng told President Carter that he intended to teach Hanoi a lesson over its occupation of Kampuchea and Carter made no attempt to dissuade him (Medvedev, 1986: 122). The following month, the Chinese launched an attack on Vietnam. In response, large numbers of Soviet divisions in the Far East were put on full alert. Soviet planes repeatedly flew over the Chinese border and unpopulated areas were shelled (Medvedev, 1986: 156). The Vietnamese were able to beat back the Chinese and, fearing Soviet reprisals, Beijing withdrew (Segal, 1990: 112).

A government-in-exile, called the Coalition Government of Democratic Kampuchea (CGDK) was set up in Thailand in 1982. The coalition was headed by Prince Sihanouk, the former monarch of Kampuchea, but it was dominated by the Khmer Rouge. Despite the Khmer Rouge's human rights record, it was the CGDK rather than the Phnom Penh government which gained international recognition, taking up Kampuchea's seat on the UN. The Khmer Rouge military was rebuilt with Chinese aid, whilst the US provided limited aid for the other members of the coalition.

Subsequently, the Khmer Rouge began to launch raids across the border to destabilise the Phnom Penh government. Throughout the conflict, however, the rebels were unable to attain their long-term aim of gaining permanent control over any geographic area of the country (Chanda, 1989-90: 31). The conflict escalated after a government offensive in 1984-85, but thereafter settled down to what William Turley has called a 'stable war' during which the Phnom Penh government was never seriously under threat (Turley, 1990: 438).

Although Hanoi had indicated an interest in withdrawal from 1982, it was only after a change of leadership in 1986 that troop numbers began to be cut back (Leifer, 1992: 71). Moscow welcomed Hanoi's initiatives, but since the politburo at that time had reached no clear policy on Indochina, Gorbachev played a minimal role in the decision to withdraw (Buszynski, 1992: 132). Quite independently of Moscow, Hanoi had become concerned over the growing cost of occupation as the party sought economic reform at home. Hanoi also recognised that its special position as a Soviet ally in the Far East was under threat as Moscow shifted increasingly towards Beijing. The new priority became plain when the USSR offered no support to Vietnam after China took some of the Vietnam-occupied Spratly Islands in March 1988. The Soviet tilt greatly weakened Hanoi's bargaining position.

Vietnam's withdrawal from Kampuchea was completed by September 1989 and a cease-fire between the indigenous forces in Cambodia was agreed in May 1991. Elections were held in Cambodia in spring 1993 under UN supervision. The Khmer Rouge boycotted the election and have since continued to destabilise the country through guerilla attacks.

Moscow effectively abandoned its position in Indochina when most Soviet planes and warships were withdrawn from its base at Cam Ranh Bay by the end of 1989. Such moves promised to unblock relations not only with China but also with the ASEAN states of Indonesia, Malaysia, Philippines, Singapore, Thailand and Brunei. But Moscow's position in the Far East declined markedly after the end of the cold war. More recently, Russia has improved relations with China as Yeltsin seeks to balance American power. Russia has natural links with Asia. It is, after all, both an Asian and a European country. Moscow wishes to remain a player in a region which promises to become the future economic powerhouse of the world.

## Central America and the Caribbean Basin

When Reagan came to power in 1981, Central America and the Caribbean Basin was top of his foreign policy agenda. In the late 1970s, a series of revolutions had scared Washington into believing that Marxism-Leninism was spreading beyond Cuba and on to the Central American mainland. The leftist New Jewel Movement (NJM) seized power on the small island of Grenada in March 1979; and the Sandinistas victoriously marched on Managua in July 1979. Revolutionary politics was on the rise also in Guatemala and El Salvador, where the pro-

American governments were coming under increasing pressure.

Moscow, for its part, played a minimal role in the successful revolutions in Grenada and Nicaragua. However, for a brief period (1979-81), it appeared to adopt a more revolutionary strategy in Central America (Miller, 1988: 54-5). Local Communist Parties began to use language more favourable to the idea of armed insurrection, whilst Moscow increased its aid to the Sandinista government and gave more vigorous backing to the rebel forces (FMLN) in El Salvador.

Moscow provided the FMLN with aid, advice and training, but no direct military aid. After the failure of the so-called 'Final Offensive' by the rebel forces in January 1981, the USSR believed victory was only possible with direct external support (Miller, 1988: 188). This, however, was not forthcoming from Moscow. In fact, all Soviet aid declined after March 1981 and it remained limited until it was cut off altogether in October 1990.

By 1981, the Soviet Union had lost confidence once again in the concept of armed insurrection and reverted back to its more cautious policies of earlier years. Ronald Reagan, however, continued to take a bipolar view of the crisis and argued instability in the region was due to Cuban and Soviet interference. Since the region was perceived to be America's backyard, Reagan came to office committed to a policy of roll-back. Geopolitical realities meant that the US would always dominate the region. And Moscow knew this. An appeal from Cuba to Moscow for further protection after Reagan came into the White House was firmly rejected. A top Soviet official told Castro: 'We cannot go to war over Cuba. You are 11,000 kilometres away. Shall we go there in order to be defeated?' (*Moscow News*, 28 May 1993).

Reagan never attacked Cuba, but he maintained the US embargo against Havana. He also stopped all US aid to the Sandinista government and backed the pro-Western El Salvador with a massive injection of aid. The most dramatic move came, however, when the US invaded Grenada in 1983 to overthrow the Marxist-Leninist government there. Washington said it had intervened to protect about a thousand American citizens whose lives were in danger after the violent overthrow of the NJM leader, Maurice Bishop, by the more pro-Soviet Bernard Coard. However, the coup also presented the US with an ideal opportunity to flex its muscles and show the world that Washington had regained the political will to act overseas. Although Grenada was a tiny island, the action was regarded in some quarters as the final exorcism of the Vietnam syndrome (see, for example, Wiarda, 1991: 113).

The Soviet Union took little interest in Grenada. This was not the case with

Nicaragua. By 1985, it was estimated that Soviet economic aid provided a quarter of Nicaragua's total needs, whilst military aid rose from $12 million in 1979-80 to $600 million in 1986. As a result, Managua developed a formidable army in the context of Central America. However, Moscow insisted throughout that its military aid was for defensive purposes only. Thus, Moscow refused to supply the advanced fighter jets Ortega had asked for because Washington viewed them as offensive.

Reagan, in turn, stepped up aid to opposition groups in Nicaragua. The Contras, largely created and organised by the US, were based mainly in neighbouring Honduras. In 1981, as the armed struggle was beginning, it was estimated the Contras' 'Action Team' only consisted of 500 men. By 1987, this figure had risen sharply to 15,000, but compared to over 100,000 on the government side, it gave the rebels little chance of military victory (Kornbluh, 1988: 7). In fact, their only real chance lay in direct American intervention. Ortega feared this was a possibility after the US invasion of Grenada but Washington appeared deterred by the size of the Nicaraguan army. Instead, covert US action was stepped up. But when these covert activities were discovered in 1984, Congress banned all direct and indirect aid to the Contras. The ban remained in place for two years. However, the ban was circumvented by the White House through the laundering of money from arms sales, including sales to Iran.

Washington found few supporters amongst its allies for its destabilisation policy in Nicaragua. The Contadora group (Colombia, Panama, Venezuela and Mexico), formed in 1983, visited Washington in 1986 and requested an end to American military support for the Contras. The Contadora initiative ran into the ground, but it was soon replaced by the Arias plan in 1987. The main aim of this plan, named after the President of Costa Rica, was to localise the conflict and prevent external intervention, including military aid. Little was expected of the plan until November 1987 when the so-called Irangate scandal broke which laid bare the money laundering scam. The scandal blighted the rest of the Reagan presidency. It also led to a Congressional ban on all military aid to the Contras, which effectively destroyed Reagan's policy in Nicaragua.

The hope for a Contra victory on the battlefield disappeared, but this, in turn, opened up possibilities for a negotiated settlement. The Organisation of American States (OAS) and the UN entered the scene as major players. The Contras' weakened position led to a cease-fire in April 1988, although violence on a lesser scale continued. The OAS met again and the date of February 1990 was set for elections. A repatriation plan for returning Contras was worked out under the aegis of the UN and agreed on 7 August 1989.

The Soviet Union consistently supported both the Contadora initiative and the Arias plan (*Izvestiya*, 26 January 1986), whilst simultaneously increasing military supplies to the Sandinistas. Nicaragua was a useful bargaining chip for Gorbachev at a time when Washington was supplying aid to the mujahideen in Afghanistan. However, in February 1988 (after the Irangate disclosures), Shevardnadze encouraged his Nicaraguan counterpart, Miguel d'Escoto, to enter the talks which resulted a few weeks later in the cease-fire.

George Bush became President in 1989 and he was eager to find a way out of the conflict which had so obsessed his predecessor. His Secretary of State, James Baker, privately acknowledged that US leverage over the whole region had diminished since Irangate (Oberdorfer, 1992: 340). At the Malta summit in December 1989, Gorbachev did not seek unilateral advantage from America's difficulties. Instead, he agreed to Bush's request to stop military aid and pressed the Sandinistas to accept multi-party elections (*International Herald Tribune*, 19 October 1990).

At this point, Soviet policy appeared successful. The Contras had failed to defeat the Sandinistas on the battlefield and US military aid to the rebels had ceased. Moscow had not abandoned its ally, but left it in a strong political position. Almost all the polls pointed to a clear victory for Ortega in the 1990 elections. The polls proved false, however, as the coalition opposition group, United National Opposition (UNO), led by Violeta Chamorro and supported by the US, triumphed - although the Sandinistas remained the largest single party.

The Sandinistas lost the election largely because everyone wanted an end to the civil war which had blighted the country for so long. It had cost perhaps 80,000 lives and grossly distorted the civilian economy. A vote for UNO promised an end to the conflict and a major injection of economic aid from Washington (Vickers and Spence, 1992). The transfer of power from the Sandinistas was achieved peacefully and President Bush publicly thanked Gorbachev for his constructive role in the whole election process (Cox, 1990-91: 282).

The defeat of the Sandinistas also encouraged compromise in El Salvador. Both superpowers were now in support of negotiations to end a war which had become stalemated. The debate in the US Congress in February 1990 indicated that the rich flow of aid ($4 billion by that time) was unlikely to continue at such levels. The USSR had little control over the FMLN, but efforts were made to convince the rebel leadership of the need for national reconciliation. A peace agreement was signed in January 1991 in which promises to demilitarise were made on both sides. A cease-fire was put in place early the following year.

As these events unfolded, Cuba was left isolated in the western hemisphere.

Relations with Moscow had also cooled considerably after Gorbachev's rise to power. The spiralling Cuban debt had made a review of policy in Moscow inevitable (Blasier, 1991: 93). Economic aid had risen from $1-2 billion per year in the 1960s to $4-5 billion in the 1980s (Duncan, 1989: 75). Gorbachev, himself, had allowed the subsidies to rise further when he agreed to $3 billion new credits for the period 1986-90 (Duncan, 1989: 74). But from 1986, the trade in oil and sugar was cut back.

However, there was little sign that Gorbachev wanted a unilateral break with Castro. The Treaty of Friendship and Co-operation, which Castro had long wanted, was finally signed in 1989. But as the Soviet Union collapsed after the August coup, Gorbachev announced the end of all aid to Cuba. Because of Cuba's dependency on the Eastern bloc, the economy contracted over the period 1989-94 by perhaps as much as 45 percent. Soviet troops were also withdrawn, although Moscow kept its intelligence centre at Lourdes.

America made no concessions to Cuba in return. Just the reverse. Washington wished to emphasise that the United States had won the cold war. The US military remained at its base on the island at Guantanamo Bay whilst tightening the embargo which had been in place since the late 1950s. Moscow became keen for the embargo to be lifted but when the issue was first raised at the UN in 1992, at the height of Moscow's pro-Western policy, the Yeltsin administration abstained. By 1995, the US was isolated on the issue, with only Israel supporting Washington's position. To date, Castro has survived but Cuba no longer poses a threat to the American position in Central America and the Caribbean Basin.

## The Arab-Israeli Conflict

The Soviet Union had been one of the first states to recognise Israel in 1948, but thereafter Moscow had thrown its support behind the Arab cause. After the Six-Day War in 1967, the Soviet Union broke diplomatic relations with Israel. Moscow was viewed by Tel Aviv with increasing suspicion as the Soviets gave support to rejectionist Arab states in the region, such as Syria, Libya and Iraq. Israel saw the USSR as a destabilising factor in the Middle East and fully backed Kissinger's diplomacy in the 1970s which marginalised Moscow's influence over the region (Bowker and Williams, 1988: chapter 5).

As Moscow was pushed out of Middle Eastern diplomacy, Brezhnev campaigned for a peace settlement based on UN Resolutions 242 and 338 which proclaimed the right of all states in the region to live within secure and recognised boundaries. Moscow urged Israel to give up territory taken in the 1967 war and to accept the creation of an independent Palestinian state. In return, Moscow called on the Arabs to formally recognise the right of Israel to exist as a state. Moscow also favoured an international conference which would include a place for the USSR as a counter-balance to American power and demanded a comprehensive settlement for the region involving all Arab states.

Moscow hoped to strengthen the Arab position through promoting Arab unity, but this proved impossible. The Arab world continued to splinter. The PLO was divided and in disarray after its flight from Lebanon in 1982. Syria was an enemy of Arafat and his Fatah faction of the PLO, and Asad invaded Lebanon largely to defeat the PLO leader. Egypt was ostracised after its separate peace with Israel in 1978, whilst the Iran-Iraq war (1980-88) was even more divisive.

Moscow's overall aims in the Middle East did not change after Gorbachev came to power but the means of accomplishing them did. Thus, from the mid-1980s, the Soviet Union sought to portray itself as a status quo power. It spoke in favour of improved relations with Israel and argued against a military solution to the Arab-Israeli conflict (Karsh, 1993: 154). Gorbachev also resolved to change practical policy in three vital areas: Jewish emigration; the recognition of Israel; and relations to rejectionist Arab states.

As soon as Gorbachev came to power, contacts between Moscow and Tel Aviv were stepped up. In 1987, Gorbachev eased restrictions on Jewish emigration from the Soviet Union (much to the consternation of the Arab states) and started consular exchanges the same year. By 1989, the consular delegations in each country were acting effectively as embassies, although it was only in October 1991 on the eve of the Madrid Conference that this relationship was formalised. The process of rapprochement was slower than some reformers wanted and they tended to blame residual anti-semitism in leadership circles in Moscow and an abiding reluctance to break ranks with Arab allies. (On this, see Vassiliev, 1993: 295; Ro'i, 1994: 149.)

Although Moscow's influence in the Middle East was limited, Gorbachev did play a role in uniting various factions within the PLO under the leadership of Yasser Arafat. Moscow also welcomed Arafat's recognition of Israel and his renunciation of terrorism in the winter of 1988. The simultaneous declaration of an independent Palestinian state with Jerusalem as its capital was less enthusiastically received in Moscow, but the new Palestinian state was recognised immediately.

Moscow made efforts to improve relations with more moderate, nonrejectionist states in the Middle East whilst relations with old allies, such as Libya and Syria, cooled. Libya, as a significant importer of Soviet arms, had been an important source of hard currency, but Gaddafy's rabid anti-Americanism was unappealing in the new era of superpower co-operation. Relations had turned sour after Moscow provided Gaddafy with no warning of the US air attack in 1986 (Vassiliev, 1993: 289). Although Moscow condemned the strike, the Soviet response was mild, and Gaddafy quietly retired as America's enemy number one.

Asad of Syria remained critical of the PLO acceptance of UNSCR 242, but he recognised the way the wind was blowing and began to moderate his position from the late 1980s. He was well aware of Moscow's shifting position after his visit to Moscow in June 1985 (*Pravda*, 15 April 1987). In the period 1985-90, arms sales to Syria dropped by almost a third (Karsh, 1993: 155). Asad had always paid up on commercial transactions with the Soviet Union, but Moscow had indicated it was no longer willing to tolerate the growing debt accruing on military sales (Vassiliev, 1993: 285).

Change was in the wind, but the real catalyst came with the Gulf War of 1990-91, when Iraq, a leading rejectionist state, was destroyed and Syria, another, joined the Western alliance (see chapter 8). As the USSR collapsed, the region once more fell under American dominance. Even though the US put more pressure on Israel to accept a peace plan, many Arab states were concerned about the Soviet withdrawal, fearing that any peace would have to be on terms dictated by the Washington-Tel Aviv axis (Karsh, 1993: 159).

An international conference was held in Madrid in October 1991. The conference was a long-term goal of Soviet diplomacy, but any feeling of triumph in Moscow was limited. The Soviet Union was visibly in the process of disintegration as the Madrid conference took place and Gorbachev had lost all authority to speak as a world statesman.

When a follow-up conference was held in Moscow in January 1992, Yeltsin did not even bother to turn up. In part, this was due to personal reasons - Yeltsin had noted that many of the radical Arab states supported the August coup in 1991, including the PLO, Saddam Hussein and Colonel Gaddafy - it also appeared, however, that Yeltsin at the time regarded the Middle East as less of a priority for the Kremlin (Vassiliev, 1993: 354). However, Russia has since attempted to re-enter the peace process. Foreign Minister Andrei Kozyrev continued to back the two-state plan, and supported the separate agreements in 1993 between Israel and the PLO, and between Israel and Jordan in 1994.

Ever since Gorbachev came to power, Moscow has argued its interests are best served by stability in the Middle East. War so close to its borders will always be a matter of grave concern, whilst the fear of Islamic fundamentalism spreading to the CIS remains a constant worry. Russia, however, has become peripheral to the Middle East region since the collapse of the USSR. The new Foreign Minister, Yevgeny Primakov, whose particular expertise lies in the politics of the Middle East, will seek to change this and raise Moscow's profile in the region.

## Africa

Moscow had won a number of allies in Africa in the 1970s, including Angola, Mozambique and Ethiopia. These countries were coming under increasing pressure, however, in the early 1980s, as the governments were threatened from internal and external insurrection. Angola was chosen by the Americans as the test case for the Reagan Doctrine.

Reagan convinced Congress that Jonas Savimbi and his UNITA forces were worthy of support, and a ten-year US embargo on arms supplies to UNITA was lifted and deliveries recommenced in 1986. The change in US policy did not fundamentally alter the basic position on the battlefield, however, since aid to the dos Santos MPLA government was correspondingly increased by Moscow and the number of Cuban troops in Angola was doubled to 50,000. As a result, the position of the government forces (FAPLA) remained comparatively strong. By the late 1980s, FAPLA comprised roughly 150,000 troops compared to 60,000 at Savimbi's command (Primakov, 1989: 527). This meant that during the war 'UNITA was restricted to the countryside and limited to sabotage raids and small-scale attacks on military outposts and government installations, and was never able to mount a conventional challenge to government forces' (Somerville, 1993: 81).

South African forces which had intervened in 1987 to protect UNITA had lost lives in a desperate battle over the MPLA city and airport at Cuito Cuanavale in early 1988. These losses became politically sensitive as the political situation in South Africa worsened. Hence, Pretoria became more anxious to find a way out of the impasse (see McFaul, 1989: 126; and O'Neill, 1990-91: 84). In contrast, the political pressure on Moscow to withdraw was minimal. Unlike the Middle East and Central America, Moscow was not perceived as a destabilising influence in the region. On the contrary, the Organisation of African States blamed Pretoria for unrest in southern Africa and many African states saw the Soviet Union as the only means of preventing Pax Pretoria (Kokorev,

1988: 8-9).

Nevertheless, Gorbachev was calling for national reconciliation and an end to the conflict as early as 1986. The war had become a bloody stalemate which neither side could win. It had cost 35,000 lives and devastated the Angolan economy. This meant that Angola had fallen about $2billion into debt with Moscow since 1985 (Somerville, 1993: 81). Since Gorbachev recognised that Moscow had no 'special interests in southern Africa', he was eager to find a settlement to the crisis (Gorbachev, 1987: 187).

Talks were set up in May 1988. It was agreed that the Cubans would withdraw from Angola by 1991 in return for an end to South African military aid to UNITA. Pretoria also agreed to end its illegal occupation of Namibia and the country gained its independence in September 1990 under a pro-Soviet SWAPO government. The agreements, however, failed to end the war in Angola. Finally, in May 1991 a peace treaty was signed between the two warring factions. It stipulated a cease-fire, an end to military supplies from both Moscow and Washington, a merger of MPLA and UNITA forces at much lower levels, and multi-party elections in September 1992 to decide the contours of the future Angola. The treaty was to be monitored by the UN.

Jose de Santos and the MPLA won the subsequent elections, but Jonas Savimbi refused to accept the result. He did not comply with the terms of the peace treaty and relaunched the war. The UN was powerless to prevent the resumption of the conflict which had disastrous consequences for the country. The US was slow to condemn Savimbi, and it was only after President Bush had left office that Washington finally recognised the MPLA as the legitimate government of Angola.

In South Africa, Moscow had close ties with the African National Congress (ANC) and the South African Communist Party. The ANC, banned in 1960, won Soviet support for its armed struggle against the apartheid system (Somerville, 1993: 230). This posture won approval amongst frontline states, but at the expense of East-West relations. The chance of change looked remote until F. W. de Klerk rose to head his party and become State President in 1989. He quickly moved to legalise the ANC in January 1990, released its leader, Nelson Mandela, in February after 26 years in prison, and declared his willingness to negotiate with black leaders on a new constitution. A major step forward was achieved in June 1991, when President de Klerk repealed all racially discriminating laws. Multi-party talks began in April 1993 and elections were scheduled for April 1994, after which a transitionary Government of National Unity would lead the country.

After de Klerk became President, Moscow publicly for the first time called for an end to the armed struggle (Somerville, 1993: 253). Gorbachev's policy of national reconciliation encouraged change in South Africa. The Soviet Union was no longer perceived by the whites as a supporter of anti-South African terrorism and relations between Moscow and Pretoria improved rapidly. Shevardnadze met de Klerk in March 1990 to discuss Moscow's mediation role in the peace process. Consular relations were opened in 1991 and full diplomatic relations were restored early the following year.

Relations between Moscow and the ANC, however, cooled, 1990-91. It became apparent that Gorbachev was more interested in improving economic ties with Pretoria rather than maintaining its principled stance against apartheid. However, the ANC position moderated over time. The armed struggle was abandoned and Nelson Mandela indicated a willingness to accept compromise with other ethnic groups over constitutional arrangements. The ANC won a convincing victory in the 1994 elections and Nelson Mandela was elected President. This followed a trend. Soviet allies in the region, the ANC, SWAPO, MPLA, (in contrast to Central America) won multi-party elections but only, it must be said, after abandoning their former radicalism.

In Ethiopia, the Soviet Union had backed Mengistu Haile Mariam since 1976 to the tune of $12 billion over a fourteen year period. The policies of Mengistu, a quixotic and brutal dictator, led to famine in 1984 and ethnic upheaval in Eritrea and Tigre. After Gorbachev came to power, he encouraged Mengistu to seek a compromise with his opponents, although military aid continued until April 1990. Mengistu was overthrown in May 1991 and fled to Zimbabwe.

The US took no part in the conflict allowing Moscow a relatively free hand. The Horn of Africa was an area of some strategic importance, close to the Red Sea, the Persian Gulf and Indian Ocean. However, in 1989 Moscow withdrew from Ethiopia as the cold war wound down. The cost of its commitment to Addis Ababa was an important factor, at a time when Moscow's support for Mengistu was undermining Soviet credibility as a progressive force. Therefore, the position was very different to that in southern Africa.

## The Reagan Doctrine

Ronald Reagan came to power in 1981 pledged to banish the so-called 'Vietnam syndrome' and reverse Soviet gains in the third world. Reagan denounced the superpower detente of the 1970s which for him symbolised American weakness and decline. His determination to challenge Soviet expansionism in the third world became known as the Reagan Doctrine. It placed emphasis, not on negotiation and compromise, but on military power and a renewed political will to employ it. The aim was to roll back communism in regions where the Soviet hold was weakest.

The Reagan Doctrine was based more on rhetoric than actual action. For direct US military intervention was used just three times during Reagan's term in office: in Grenada, Libya and Lebanon. The overthrow of the Marxist government in Grenada in 1983 and the bombing of Libya in 1986 for state terrorism were low risk operations which gained public support in America, but scarcely affected the East-West relationship. Neither did they abolish the Vietnam syndrome. For the US public remained reluctant to contemplate military intervention if it could involve a significant loss of American life. This was evident in the case of Lebanon, when Reagan was forced to withdraw US troops after 241 marines were killed by a suicide bomber in 1983. As a result, the US tended to offer more indirect support to those fighting communism and Soviet expansionism. Reagan was certainly far more willing than his predecessors to offer large quantities of modern military aid to US allies in the third world. However, not all anti-communist forces received American aid. The opposition in Cambodia received little US support, as did the anti-Marxist forces in Ethiopia. Yet, ambitious claims have been made for the Reagan Doctrine. Some have argued that the renewed challenge from Washington forced the communists to compromise.

It would be absurd to suggest that Reagan's policies had no impact on Soviet third world policy. Since 1945, Western military containment had played an important role in restricting Soviet expansionism. As shown above, Moscow's actions were conditioned by two factors - its own power and the countervailing power of the West. There is no doubt that the USSR was flexing its muscles in the mid to late 1970s, and in those circumstances it was reasonable for Reagan in his first years as President to seek to challenge Soviet activism.

In some regions, it is plausible that his emphasis on military containment and roll-back was influential in forcing concessions from the communists. However, the impact certainly varied from region to region. The case is strongest in Afghanistan, but even there, as will be argued in the next chapter, the argument is less clear-cut than sometimes supposed. In other areas, the case remains largely unconvincing.

In general, Reagan's initiatives did not dramatically change the balance of power on the battlefield, since Moscow responded, as in Angola, by giving more aid to its own client. Thus, the immediate outcome of the Reagan Doctrine tended to be a bloody stalemate rather than a clear victory for any side. As a result, the conflict could only be resolved through an abandonment of absolutist claims on both sides and a willingness to search for reconciliation. Hence, a resolution to the conflict in Nicaragua only came after the Reagan policy had been undermined by the Irangate scandal. In Angola, it was the weakening military position of South Africa which encouraged compromise. Gorbachev's policy of national reconciliation was generally more effective than Reagan's absolutism.

Even after agreement had been reached between the superpowers, it rarely led to peace. Wars continued in Afghanistan and Angola long after Lenin and the cold war had been forgotten. The situation in Cambodia remains highly unstable whilst the Horn of Africa descended into anarchy. Greater optimism, albeit with a great dose of caution, exists in Latin America, the Middle East and much of the Pacific-Asia region. But where peace was secured, however temporarily, it owed more to negotiation and compromise than coercion and competition.

## Economic cost

Another explanation for Soviet new thinking on the third world - sometimes seen as an adjunct, sometimes as an alternative to the Reagan Doctrine - is Paul Kennedy's concept of 'imperial overstretch' (Kennedy, 1987). The argument is that the economic costs of the USSR's third world commitments had become so great that it led to a deterioration in the Soviet Union's domestic economy. As a result, economic costs forced a Soviet withdrawal from the third world. Alexei Kiva, a leading academician, wrote that Moscow's third world policy had exhausted Soviet resources in an 'insane confrontation with the West to find itself bankrupt in the end' (Kiva, 1991: 35; Light, 1991: 266).

There can be no doubt that after coming to power Gorbachev was concerned at the escalating costs of the Soviet Union's commitment to the third world. Martin Walker has estimated the cost of aid, trade credits, subsidies and arms shipments from 1980 to be between $15 and 20 billion per year (Walker, 1993: 280). With the latest information on the size of the Soviet GNP, this amounts to between 1.5 and 2 percent of GNP. This is a considerable sum of money, but not sufficient to explain Soviet withdrawal from the third world (see Spechler, 1989: 39; Menon and Nelson, 1989: 7).

Soviet economic aid to the third world was relatively low. In 1989, third world debt to the Soviet Union was officially recorded at 44 billion rubles by a foreign ministry report, but it continued, the greater part was due back by the year 2000, overdue debts accounted for only 1.4 billion rubles, and the larger part of the debts was owed by countries whose solvency, according to the report, gave no cause for concern (*International Affairs*, Moscow, no. 4, 1991: 47).[2] An official of the Ministry of Defence said of Soviet commitment to

---

2  A more commonly quoted statistic is the *Izvestiya* 1 March 1990 article which estimated a debt almost double that of the Foreign Ministry's report at 85 billion rubles with 57.6 billion owed by socialist allies. If nothing else the great differences in estimates which persisted into the Gorbachev era reveal the difficulty of gathering accurate statistics in the Soviet Union.

Africa: 'The costs to us were less than might have been thought. It was not big money. The military equipment was not first class, and many people from those countries have now received education in our institutions' (Pryce-Jones, 1995: 116).

In fact, the USSR was not suffering from imperial overstretch - not at least in the traditional sense. For Moscow's global position, as stated earlier, was relatively weak when Gorbachev came to power. Possessing few military bases overseas, in 1985 a total of 207,600 Soviet troops were stationed outside the USSR and Eastern Europe - of whom as many as 173,000 were in either Afghanistan or Mongolia. In contrast, the US played a far more active role in the third world than the Soviet Union, with 525,600 of its troops stationed overseas (Military Balance, 1986-87: 19 and 46).

The main problem for Gorbachev was less the total cost of the third world, but that existing Soviet expenditure was wasted. Massive amounts of aid were thrown at a handful of impoverished states which were in no position to repay any debts in the foreseeable future. Cuba received an estimated $4-5bn per year in aid and oil subsidies in the period 1980-86 (roughly equivalent to US aid to Israel); Vietnam received $1bn and Mongolia nearly $1bn (Walker, 1993: 280). In the past, Moscow had given material aid to those countries on the basis of their allegiance to Marxist-Leninist ideology and their pro-Soviet stance in the context of the cold war. When these particular obsessions came to an end and Moscow considered its economic and security interests instead, the logic behind Soviet subsidies fell away.

In sum, Soviet policy was dictated by new thinking. Gorbachev sought an end to costly relations with bankrupt and unstable countries in the third world. Instead, he portrayed the USSR as a status quo power which sought relations on the basis of trade, strategic interest and international status. National interest, rather than ideology, had become the driving force of Soviet foreign policy. Gorbachev hoped this shift in policy would lead to the Soviet Union extending, not reducing, its influence in the third world. The policy failed due mainly to the collapse of communism in the USSR. These issues will be taken up again in more detail in the next chapter on Afghanistan.

# Chapter Seven

# THE WAR IN AFGHANISTAN

Afghanistan was always a state of some strategic interest to Moscow. Sharing a 2,500 km border with the Soviet Union, Afghanistan was wedged between Iran and Pakistan. It was also within range of the Persian Gulf and Indian Ocean - both areas of vital interest to the West. Stalin paid little attention to this impoverished, tribal country, but his successors, Khrushchev and Brezhnev, adopted a different policy. They both made great efforts over the years to build up good relations with Kabul.

To many, it appeared that Moscow's patient diplomacy had finally borne fruit when the Marxist-oriented PDPA (People's Democratic Party of Afghanistan), supported by a small number of disaffected military officers, took power in Kabul in April 1978. This view, however, proved mistaken. For although most of the leaders of the April coup had been trained in Moscow, the Soviet Union played no role in the actual takeover (Kiva, 1991: 38). Indeed, documents later released from the Soviet archives showed that the Soviet Union had sent a message to the PDPA leader, Nur Mohammed Taraki, advising that a coup attempt at that particular time would be 'disastrous' (Dobbs, 1992a: 1; Morozov, 1991a: 37).[1] Nevertheless, after a short delay, Moscow recognised the new Afghan

---

1  Michael Dobbs, a journalist on the *International Herald Tribune*, wrote two articles on Afghanistan, 16 and 17 November 1992, using exclusive material from the Russian archives which were partially opened after the collapse of the USSR. The first article dealt with the Soviet invasion; the second with the withdrawal.

government and in December 1978 signed the Treaty of Friendship and Co-operation.

The PDPA had problems from the start in governing the country. The party, riven by divisions, soon split after taking power into two factions, the Khalq (the masses) and the Parcham (the banner). In a power struggle, the more radical Khalq faction, led by Taraki, won out and proceeded to introduce an ambitious programme of reform. In so doing, the PDPA attacked the most powerful interests in society - the landowners and clergy - whilst simultaneously alienating large sections of the population, especially in the rural areas of the country.

Armed resistance to the Taraki government began in the summer of 1978 and violence had spread to all the provinces of Afghanistan by the end of the year. Seven thousand Soviet advisers were present in March 1979 when a revolt erupted in Afghanistan's second city of Herat. Up to three thousand were killed in the uprising including perhaps as many as 40 Soviet citizens (Cordovez and Harrison, 1995: 36). The same month, Taraki's position as President was further weakened when his more radical rival in the party, Hafizullah Amin, was appointed Prime Minister. The temporary fall of Herat led to doubts in Moscow that the PDPA government could survive. The Soviet politburo held a three-day emergency session on the growing crisis in Afghanistan (Cordovez and Harrison, 1995: 36-37).

On 20 March, Taraki went to Moscow and asked for the Soviet Union to help save the revolution. At that time, the politburo had resolved not to intervene. This view was transmitted to the Afghan President by the Soviet Prime Minister, Alexei Kosygin who told Taraki that military intervention would only compound the problems in Afghanistan with Soviet troops having 'to struggle not only with an external aggressor, but with a significant part of your own people' (Dobbs, 1992a: 7). Nevertheless, Moscow did agree to provide limited aid in the form of helicopter gunships, pilots, technicians and about seven hundred Soviet paratroopers to guard Kabul airport.

By the summer, Moscow recognised that Soviet military aid had not been enough to stabilise the country and the Kremlin began to consider the removal of Amin who was considered a major destabilising force (Morozov, 1991b: 32-35). Taraki's supporters hatched a plot to assassinate Amin on 14 September 1979, but the plan went badly wrong. Amin survived the assassination attempt, but Taraki, who was close to Brezhnev, was executed for his part in the plot (Bradsher, 1985: 112-3). The outcome was a disaster for the Kremlin. Amin took absolute power, replacing Taraki as party leader, whilst Moscow, which was clearly implicated in the assassination attempt, had endangered its close alliance with Kabul (Morozov, 1991: 34). The Soviet leadership became fearful that Amin would turn his country away from Moscow and seek realignment with the West, but although the Afghan leader did, indeed, make a tentative approach to the US around this time, Washington was distracted by the parallel crisis in Iran and failed to respond (Dobbs, 1992a: 7).

It was from this moment that Moscow seriously began to plan for invasion. A KGB report at the time declared that the growing chaos in Afghanistan could only be averted by the removal of Amin from power (Dobbs, 1992a: 7). It argued for the reunification of the PDPA and for the policy of repression to be replaced by a more moderate programme more in line with the wishes of the Afghan people (Morozov, 1991b: 35). In October, Marshal Pavlovsky, head of Soviet ground forces, carried out reconnaissance for the planned intervention. The decision to intervene was taken by a small *ad hoc* group of leaders (Hyman, 1992: 159; Morozov, 1991b: 34), but it was approved at a full politburo meeting on 12 December 1979 (Dobbs, 1992a: 7).

Thus, on the night of 24/25 December 1979, the invasion began as Soviet military planes started landing at Kabul. Two days later, on 27 December, about 1,000 troops, including crack Alpha troops, stormed the Presidential Palace killing both President Amin and his family. Babrak Karmal, earlier expelled from the PDPA leadership by Taraki, was flown back to Kabul by the Soviets to take over. The initial invasionary force numbered about 70,000 rising to a peak in 1985 of approximately 108,000. This represented a fairly small commitment - a limited contingent - as Brezhnev called it at the time (*Pravda*, 13 January 1980). It was, however, the first time since World War Two that the USSR had invaded a third world country, and predictably it led to a worsening of East-West relations.

The Soviets argued their intervention was defensive and in accord with international law (*Pravda*, 31 December 1979). They declared their troops were deployed at the invitation of the legitimate government of a sovereign country and they were simply attempting to restore order in a state which had been destabilised by external forces - most notably by Pakistan, which had territorial claims on the country. Collective action to repel aggression was permitted, Moscow noted, both in the UN Charter and the 1978 Afghan-Soviet Treaty of Friendship and Co-operation. Moscow also announced that Soviet troops would be withdrawn as soon as external interference in Afghanistan ended (*Pravda*, 13 January 1980).

However, the assassination of Amin undermined Moscow's claims. Moreover, the uprising in Afghanistan was largely the result of indigenous forces and clearly represented a popular revolt against the PDPA government and its policies. The UN General Assembly reflected this view when it overwhelmingly condemned the USSR (104-18) and called for its immediate and unconditional withdrawal.

What then were the real reasons for the Soviet invasion? Many world leaders, including President Carter of America and President Zia of Pakistan, believed Moscow's intentions were expansionist. It was argued that the Kremlin was taking advantage of regional instability to make a penetrating strike which ultimately threatened the oil-fields of the Gulf. This was a natural fear for cautious politicians to hold, albeit one that appeared exaggerated even at the time (see Bowker and Williams, 1988: chapter 10). Subsequent information obtained from the Russian archives has corroborated the sceptics by showing that the Soviet Union never had any intention of extending the war beyond the borders of Afghanistan (Dobbs, 1992a).

In fact, the main reason for the invasion was not expansionism but consolidation. Moscow sought to prop up a crumbling allied state strategically placed on its southern border. The Soviet Union wanted to replace Haffizullah Amin with Babrak Karmal, who was perceived in Moscow to be both more moderate and more pro-Soviet. Soviet troops had the limited aim of protecting the new regime over the difficult transitional period after Amin's fall. The coup was to be presented to the world as a local affair -simply another change in leadership within the divided PDPA in a violent, unstable country well known for such tumultuous events. The Soviet intervention was to be portrayed as a police action requested by the legitimate Afghan government in a country already firmly in the Soviet sphere of influence.

The Kremlin believed that the loss of a close ally on its borders would severely undermine its international credibility and allow the US to take advantage. Demchenko, a Soviet commentator, articulated Soviet fears at the time: 'Having lost its bases in Iran ... Washington made no secret of its plans to entrench itself closer to the Soviet-Afghan border by establishing a regime to suit its own interests' (*International Affairs*, June 1980: 116). As detente faded in the late 1970s, Moscow feared the possibility of encirclement by hostile forces - a fear fuelled by international developments, such as an increased US military presence in the Gulf, worsening Sino-Soviet relations, and Amin's westward tilt in autumn 1979.

Contrary to some commentaries, there is little evidence to suggest that Moscow invaded to prevent the spread of Islamic fundamentalism into the Soviet Union. Muslim soldiers were amongst those deployed in the first invasionary force, whilst official documents released since withdrawal also indicate that fears of a religious revival in the USSR did not dominate the minds of the Kremlin leadership at the time of the invasion.[2]  In fact, the Soviets, like the majority in the West, appeared initially, at least, to grossly underestimate the power of Islam in the politics of the region and were surprised by the popular support for the rebels (the mujahideen) and their military strength.  Islam was a rising force in the USSR by the time the Soviets pulled out, it was not of particular significance when they went in.

The final explanation for the Soviet intervention, promoted by Andrei Gromyko in an interview with a British newspaper, argues that the USSR stumbled into war through ignorance and a lack of debate (*The Observer*, 2 April 1989).  This appears largely disingenuous.  The issue of direct intervention had been discussed at least since March 1979 and everyone in the Kremlin seemed aware of the problems of deploying Soviet ground troops (see, for example, Gromov, 1994: 43).  The circle of decision-makers which made the final decision to intervene was small, but it included all the most important figures dealing with foreign policy - General Secretary Brezhnev, Foreign Minister Gromyko, Defence Minister Ustinov and Chairman of the KGB Andropov.  In the spring they had all argued strenuously against military intervention (Gromov, 1994: 43), but by the winter they had reluctantly reached the conclusion that it was unavoidable (Dobbs, 1992a: 7).

It is clearly true, however, that the difficulties of subduing the rebellion were grossly underestimated.  Moscow hoped a limited contingent could restore stability in a relatively short space of time, but Babrak Karmal was perceived in Afghanistan as a Soviet puppet, and the Soviet presence only served to escalate the violence and help unite the opposition.  The government forces, for their part, quickly became demoralised after the Soviet intervention and up to a half of its soldiers deserted in the first months of 1980.

From the outset, the mujahideen set up camps in Pakistan and received Western aid.  They launched attacks from across the border and soon were in control of about three quarters of the country.  The Soviets were unable to seal the border, but they held on to the major cities and supply routes as well as much of the north of the country bordering the USSR.  As a result, the war quickly became bogged down in a stalemate with Soviet aid absolutely vital in propping up the unpopular Kabul government.  After initial optimism, hopes for a quick

---

2  Minutes from selected politburo meetings and conversations between Soviet and Afghan leaders have been published in Gromov, 1994: 22-55; documents are also available in *Voprosy Istorii*, no. 3, March 1993.

resolution to the conflict faded in Moscow.

As early as May 1980, the Soviet government indicated to the UN that it was interested in negotiations and by January 1981, Moscow had pushed Kabul into accepting the UN as an intermediary with Pakistan (Harrison, 1988: 36). Diplomatic efforts did not progress very far, however, until Yuri Andropov replaced Leonid Brezhnev in November 1982. A flurry of diplomatic activity led to Moscow drawing up a timetable for withdrawal in February 1983. The Soviet media began to report more honestly about the war, admitting for the first time that Soviet lives were being lost in the conflict.

Ultimately, however, little came of the initiative. Some have argued that Andropov's illness was significant in scuppering diplomacy (Klass, 1988: 928), but Raymond Garthoff is probably right, to judge from the archive material available, that Andropov was simply unwilling to make the necessary concessions to produce a settlement (Garthoff, 1994: 725). Andropov was determined that a pro-Soviet, communist-dominated government should remain in Kabul. This, however, was simply not acceptable to either the US or the mujahideen (Cordovez and Harrison, 1995: 91-96).

## The Gorbachev period

When Gorbachev came to power in March 1985, he confronted a military and political quagmire in Afghanistan. The government-backed forces did not face the prospect of imminent defeat; on the other hand, a military victory looked unlikely without a major escalation of the Soviet war effort. Victory looked even harder to achieve when the United States increased its military aid to the mujahideen from March 1985. US aid in 1984 was $120 million, by 1987 it had risen to $630 million. In March 1986, Reagan also agreed to supply hand-held Stinger anti-aircraft missiles and other more advanced weaponry. This American commitment boosted morale among the mujahideen at a time when the rebel campaign had been coming under pressure.

In April 1985, Gorbachev who had long been critical of the war in Afghanistan (see Oberdorfer, 1992: 237) set up a secret commission to reassess Soviet policy (*Kommunist*, March 1988: 12). The commission reported back that, with an increased Soviet commitment, military victory was still attainable. As a result, Gorbachev agreed to an escalation in the war but with two important provisos. First, there was no major increase in the deployment of Soviet troops to Afghanistan; and second, the military was given a maximum of two years to turn the tide (Coll, 1992: 2).

As this was agreed, a politburo meeting in October 1985 also took the decision 'in principle' to withdraw from Afghanistan (*International Affairs*, January 1990: 12). The significance of this decision was not immediately apparent. In substance, it seemed to add little to commitments made in the early 1980s, although Gorbachev and other more reformist colleagues saw it as much more than this. Soon after, Gorbachev privately mooted the idea of a Soviet withdrawal to Babrak Karmal when he was visiting Moscow, but Karmal's response was wholly negative: 'If you leave Afghanistan now,' he said, 'next time you'll have to bring in a million soldiers' (*Soviet Weekly*, 8 February 1990). With this rebuff ringing in his ears, Gorbachev needed another year to build up an effective coalition in Moscow in favour of a pull-out.

The war continued to escalate as Gorbachev prepared for the 27th CPSU Congress in February 1986. In his key-note speech, Gorbachev famously described the conflict in Afghanistan as a 'bleeding wound' and indicated Moscow's desire to extricate itself from the conflict. At the same time, Gorbachev emphasised Moscow's vital interests in the country and argued that withdrawal would only be agreed if PDPA members formed part of a transitionary coalition government in Kabul (Gorbachev, 1986: 88-9). Even such caveats were not enough for the majority in the Kremlin and Gorbachev's commitment to withdrawal was deleted from the official, published version of his speech (Shevardnadze, 1991: 47). Yet, the momentum for a peaceful settlement was maintained when Gorbachev made the limited offer of withdrawing 7,000 Soviet troops in July 1986. Then in September, as the Stingers arrived, both Foreign Minister, Shevardnadze and the head of the International Department, Dobrynin, indicated privately to the US that the Soviet Union was ready for a pull-out (Oberdorfer, 1992: 236).

The formal decision on a Soviet pull-out, however, was not made until 13 November 1986. At this fateful meeting, Gorbachev argued that there was no sight of victory and Soviet intervention in Afghanistan should be 'concluded in the swiftest possible time' (Dobbs, 1992b: 7). To make this possible, the politburo decided to dismiss Babrak Karmal and replace him with Dr Najibullah (also known as the more secular, Najib). On a visit to Moscow in December, the new Afghan President was given formal confirmation of the politburo's decision and the following July he was finally given the timetable for withdrawal.

Najibullah was an effective and strong leader who attempted to unite the PDPA and appeal to moderate opinion in the country. Najibullah's background in the secret police (1980-86), however, hindered attempts to portray the new

President as a populist although strenuous efforts were made to improve the image of the Kabul government both at home and abroad. In the domestic arena, Najibullah promoted national reconciliation and Islam was restored as the state religion. In a new constitution drawn up in November 1987, Afghanistan (some two years ahead of Eastern Europe) was proclaimed a multi-party democracy whose economy was based on private property and the market. Elections followed in April 1988 and a coalition government was formed - but it was still dominated by the PDPA and headed by Najibullah. In 1990, after the Soviet pull-out, the PDPA even changed its name and formally renounced Marxism. All these attempts failed to gain popular support for the regime, however, as the opposition continued to call for the removal from government of both Najibullah and the PDPA.

The fate of Najibullah and the PDPA proved to be the stumbling block throughout the period, but many in Moscow, including Shevardnadze, was reluctant to leave their ally in the lurch (Cordovez and Harrison, 1995: 247-252). This was the main reason why the negotiation process dragged on so long. However, Gorbachev indicated a willingness to speed up negotiations at the December 1987 summit with Ronald Reagan. An official commitment to withdraw Soviet troops was made the following February, and on 14 April 1988, the Geneva accords were finally signed under the auspices of the UN. (For the full text of the Geneva accords, see Cordovez and Harrison, 1995: 389-397.)

For most people the most important aspect of the Geneva accords was the Soviet commitment to withdraw within a ten month deadline. In fact, the last troops actually departed on 15 February 1989, a few weeks ahead of schedule. However, this did not, as many hoped, bring the war to an end. The accords had nothing to say about a transition government, and so the bloody power struggle between Kabul and the mujahideen continued. The accords even allowed the two superpowers to continue arms supplies to their respective clients in the war.

Most commentators believed that Najibullah would fall soon after the Soviet pull-out. Shevardnadze himself flew to Kabul to offer the Afghan President a safe haven in the USSR (Shevardnadze, 1991: 69). But Najibullah rejected the offer and stayed in power until April 1992 - a few months longer than Gorbachev. In part, this was due to Najibullah's skill as a politician, but more important was the splintering of the opposition. With the Soviet army gone, the mujahideen lost its unifying focus and tribal loyalties and personal animosities re-emerged. Poor military tactics also lowered morale on the ground.

Nevertheless, Najibullah's position was eroded from early 1990 after a failed coup attempt by his Defence Minister. Increasingly, he was perceived as an impediment to the peace process, encouraging renewed divisions within the government and military. Najibullah's position finally became untenable after the failed Moscow coup of August 1991 when he lost a number of influential supporters in the CPSU, the Soviet military and the KGB.

The Yeltsin administration decided to abandon Najibullah altogether and the Russian President signed an agreement with President Bush in September 1991 to halt all military aid to the warring factions by the New Year. In October 1991, Najibullah's position was weakened further when Moscow accepted, in negotiations with moderate elements of the mujahideen, the prospect of his removal and replacement by an interim Islamic government. As pressure mounted on Najibullah both inside and outside the country, a number of key military officers switched sides to the mujahideen in spring 1992, leaving Najibullah with little option but to resign.

## Reasons for Soviet withdrawal

Why did Gorbachev decide to withdraw his troops from Afghanistan? Were the Soviet troops forced out by military defeat? Were the economic costs of the war becoming too high for the Soviets to bear? What role did public opinion play in the decision to withdraw? And how important was Gorbachev's new political thinking?

### Military costs

The Soviet campaign in Afghanistan had gone badly from the start. What was initially perceived as little more than a police action developed into a desperate and protracted civil war. When Gorbachev came to power, no end was in sight and the Soviet escalation of the war from 1985-86 achieved nothing. After the failure of this initiative, even the more hardline members of the politburo, such as Andrei Gromyko, were satisfied that a military victory over the mujahideen was no longer possible (Gromov, 1994: 234-239).

It would not be correct, however, to infer from this that the Soviet Union was defeated and forced to withdraw. In fact, the Soviet military position was relatively stable and Marshal Akhromeyev was surely right to argue at the politburo meeting in November 1986 that the Soviet army would have been able 'to hold the current position' in Afghanistan 'for the foreseeable future' (Gromov, 1994: 237). Soviet losses appeared sustainable at 13,000 out of a total military force of four million. In comparative terms too, Soviet losses were not so heavy - they ran at five per day, a quarter of the American daily losses in Vietnam (Jukes, 1989: 83). The problem for Gorbachev, however, was that guerilla warfare is not about tanks and territory but hearts and minds, and Moscow and the PDPA had lost that battle long ago. Gorbachev was quick to recognise this fact and realised that the conflict could only end through negotiation and compromise.

The role of American aid in accelerating this process of withdrawal has been a matter of controversy. A number of commentators have argued that Reagan's willingness to support the mujahideen was vital in forcing the Soviets to reassess their position in Afghanistan. Reagan not only increased aid, he was also more willing to supply up-to-date military equipment, most notably Stinger anti-aircraft missiles. In some quarters, this vigorous response was perceived to have been crucial in countering Soviet military initiatives in 1985 (Coll, 1992: 2).

After the delivery of the Stingers, Moscow certainly lost mastery of the skies for a time, which made the supply of towns and military bases more difficult and complicated the whole counter-insurgency campaign. Furthermore, Moscow became more flexible in its negotiating stance after US aid increased and quickly agreed a pull-out - not only in principle (which they had already done in the early 1980s) but also in detail with dates and a timetable (Cogan, 1993: 77; Saikal, 1989: 16; and Isby, 1992: 165). However, the role of the Stingers can easily be exaggerated. Soviet casualties actually decreased after the delivery of Stingers from a peak in 1984 of 2,243, falling to 1,333 in 1987, and 759 in 1988 (*Pravda*, 17 August 1989). Furthermore, aircraft and helicopter losses were scarcely affected. Before the Stingers arrived in 1986, 17 planes and 44 helicopters were downed; afterwards, in 1987, the losses were 19 and 49 respectively; and in 1988, 16 and 14 (Cordovez and Harrison, 1995: 199). The journalist, Mark Urban, earlier revealed that Stingers were far less lethal than sometimes suggested, calculating that they only had a ten percent kill-rate. This was because the Soviet airforce was soon able to counter them by using aircraft that could fly out of their three-mile range, enabling the Soviet and PDPA forces, after initial difficulties, to continue supplies to government-held towns and military bases. Thus, despite the Stingers, government-backed forces were able to finally relieve the besieged town of Khost in one of the biggest battles of the war in December 1987 (Urban, 1990: 296). It is significant too that neither Stingers nor American military aid were discussed at the decisive politburo meeting in November 1986 when the decision to withdraw was made (Garthoff, 1994: 729).

Critics of Ronald Reagan, however, took the argument one stage further and suggested that America's hardline posture actually delayed Soviet withdrawal (see Cordovez and Harrison, 1995; Garthoff, 1994). This analysis concentrated on the delay between the politburo decision in November 1986 to pull-out and the USSR's final withdrawal almost three years later. Cordovez and Harrison argued Reagan's tough stance had made it more difficult for Gorbachev to convince his hawks of the need to withdraw. There may be some truth in this analysis, but it should not be exaggerated. The delay was more likely due to the fact that Moscow was seeking to maintain some political influence in Kabul to prevent anti-Soviet forces moving into the region. However, this was unacceptable, not only to the US, but also, more importantly, to the mujahideen. Reagan's pressure on the Kabul government concentrated minds in the politburo; it also prevented Moscow from dictating peace-terms.

*Economic Factors*

It is always difficult to work out the economic costs of war although many efforts have been made in the case of Afghanistan. SIPRI estimated the annual cost to Moscow to be five billion rubles (*SIPRI Yearbook 1990*: 168), whilst the official Soviet estimate was higher, averaging roughly six billion rubles per year (*Izvestiya*, 17 October 1990). Although economic cost became a reason for withdrawal (see Shevardnadze, 1991: 58), arguably it was not a necessary one. This was so because the war was irrelevant to the overall performance of the Soviet economy. Six billion rubles may sound a lot of money, but it was in fact barely half of one percent of the Soviet GNP in 1985-86. The annual cost was comparable in gross terms to the UK commitment to Northern Ireland over a far longer period, and far less than the cost of Vietnam to the US, which peaked at $25 billion in 1968 (Walker, 1993: 210). There are also grounds for supposing the six billion figure is inflated since much of Soviet military equipment sent to Afghanistan came from obsolete supplies and had already been paid for (Arnold, 1993: 185). Moreover, the potential savings were greatly reduced since military aid continued after withdrawal, with some estimates reckoning it was as high as three billion rubles per year up to August 1991 (Mendelson, 1993: 335).

There is little evidence, therefore, that Moscow's economic commitment to Afghanistan was not sustainable over the medium term. The economic pressures in 1986 when the decision to withdraw was finally made were not great. The Soviet economy looked relatively stable and the Gorbachev administration appeared optimistic at that time over its future performance. It could be argued, however, that the war was beginning to distort Moscow's defence priorities. Over half the Soviet troops stationed outside the Soviet bloc were deployed in Afghanistan. As a result, the war effort was consuming as much as 3-4 percent of the total defence budget. Gorbachev wanted to downgrade Afghanistan as a priority in line with his overall thinking on international relations and the third world generally.

*Domestic Pressure*

Some commentators have also cited public opinion or domestic pressure as a factor in the Soviet decision to withdraw. Ragul Rais, for example, wrote that the Soviet Union pulled out because of 'domestic resentment within the USSR over the loss of Soviet lives in a foreign war of uncertain objectives and of great material cost' (Rais, 1992: 82). It was certainly true that by the time of the pull-out the Afghan war was generally unpopular inside the Soviet Union. All the polls of the glasnost era showed this was so. In the late 1980s, the war had become particularly controversial in Central Asia, where there was a growing identification with the Islamic struggle in Afghanistan.

Nevertheless, the role of public opinion should not be exaggerated. For public opinion in the glasnost period was manipulated rather skilfully by the party leadership through the media with the aim of preparing the people for eventual withdrawal. From 1987, journalists were allowed to report more openly on Afghanistan, and for the first time to refer to the conflict directly as a 'war' (*Moscow News*, 28 August 1988). The people became more aware of the issues in the war, but overall they remained indifferent and there were no major public campaigns to end the conflict. Official statistics showed that few attempted to escape the draft because of the Afghan conflict. In the period 1985-88, there were barely 2,500 draft dodgers - the sharp rise occurred only *after* Soviet withdrawal in 1989 (Arnold, 1993: 144).

The only group in the USSR organised around the issue of Afghanistan was the so-called *Afgantsy*, the war veterans. Approximately half a million Soviet citizens served in Afghanistan, 13,000 died and approximately 30,000 were wounded during the course of the war. Some soldiers who came back from the war found it difficult to fit back into civilian life. Like the Vietnam vets, they were largely forgotten by the public and alienated from the system. However, the *Afgantsy* were divided in their views towards the war, and before the decision was made public, there was no united position on whether the conflict should be brought to a speedy end or conducted more vigorously.[3] As such, they represented a rather inchoate group which was generally disliked in the community and was effectively marginalised by the Soviet elite.

In sum, the country was war-weary, but there was no concerted political

---

[3] For examples of the views of military officers, see *Den'*, 14-20 February 1993; and for the views of the rank and file, see Various Authors, 1989.

pressure in society for withdrawal. Moreover, there were no major political divisions at the top centred around the issue of Afghanistan. In this, there can be no comparison with America and Vietnam. As Isby has written, 'Afghanistan never became an intolerable war for the Soviets, in either its battlefield, internal, financial or diplomatic costs' (Isby, 1992: 177).

*New Political Thinking*

Whilst the military and economic costs of continuing the war were not insubstantial, the argument above is that they were sustainable. Therefore, the crucial new dynamic on Afghanistan came from Gorbachev's new thinking which allowed the Soviet leadership to forget any ideological baggage and act simply in accordance with national interest.

The primary aim of withdrawal was not to promote peace and stability in Afghanistan, although some in Moscow believed that the absence of Soviet troops would encourage it. Most acknowledged, however, that the flaws in the Geneva accords always made peace a most unlikely scenario (Bovin, 1989: 15; and *Moscow News*, 19 February 1989). In simple terms, Gorbachev pulled out because the diplomatic costs of occupation had become too high. There were, however, differences of opinion in the Kremlin over the implications of withdrawal.

The radicals argued that the decision was an historic step and showed that new political thinking was serious. It was also evidence of Soviet goodwill and a desire for radical international change. Others, less optimistic about the prospects for co-operation with the West, preferred to downplay the significance of the Soviet departure from Afghanistan. Thus one Soviet official said, 'Every other major power has lost a war ... Until now that has not happened to us, but now we will be like everyone else' (Hyland, 1990: 182). In this scenario the withdrawal was portrayed as a one-off, a purely pragmatic step which allowed Moscow to extract itself from a difficult situation with the minimum loss of face. Therefore, the Geneva accord was described as a compromise document. Moscow had withdrawn, but Najibullah remained in office and Afghan neutrality had been guaranteed. Gromov and others stressed that the USSR had not been defeated and Najibullah had not been abandoned (*Krasnaya zvezda*, 15 May 1988). This view, therefore, emphasised continued Soviet strength and argued that little had changed since withdrawal.

Finally, it is worth noting that no one in Moscow in 1988 saw the accords as an abandonment of Soviet global pretensions. On the contrary, the Soviet withdrawal was seen as offering Moscow many opportunities to strengthen its position around the world (Shevardnadze, 1991: 47 and 69). The withdrawal led to improved relations with the West and helped reduce tensions. It also produced a thaw with China since Beijing had cited Afghanistan as a major obstacle to normalisation. Thus, as Moscow began the pull-out, a date for the first Sino-Soviet summit since the days of Khrushchev was announced. Moscow also sought to improve relations in the Middle East and the Gulf which had been gravely damaged by its occupation of an Islamic state. Immediately after the withdrawal, Shevardnadze made a high profile trip to the leading countries of the region, including Egypt, Syria, Jordan, Iraq and Iran. Shevardnadze did not visit Tel Aviv, but met the Israeli Foreign Minister, Moshe Arens, in Egypt; he also had talks with Yasser Arafat of the PLO whilst in Cairo.

Such activity clearly indicated that Moscow hoped a reduction in military activism would lead to increased political influence around the world. Gorbachev wanted to embrace a more flexible, multipolar policy toward the developing world, based not on ideology or cold war competition, but on national self-interest. The plan failed because the USSR began its precipitate decline from 1989, and Moscow was no longer able to fulfil the global role Gorbachev had planned out.

## Conclusion

According to cold war psychology, Western policy in Afghanistan was a great success. Under pressure from Washington and the anti-communist mujahideen, the Soviet Union was forced to withdraw and Afghanistan, in turn, renounced Marxism-Leninism. Viewing the war from the perspective of the post-cold war world, however, the victors of the conflict are less easy to identify than the victims. The chief victims of the conflict, of course, have been the Afghan civilians. The country has been completely devastated by the war. Out of a population of roughly sixteen million, one million were killed during the Soviet occupation, two million were wounded, seven million were made homeless and five million became refugees in either Pakistan or Iran. Yet the Soviet departure did not bring peace. Instead, a bloody power struggle among the mujahideen brought further misery to the people of Afghanistan.

Economically bankrupt, the country was awash in modern weaponry. These weapons were being sold to groups in Central Asia, India, Pakistan and the Middle East. Washington became so concerned about Stingers falling into the wrong hands, it offered to buy them back from the mujahideen. The price of the Stingers, however, has been steadily rising and Bush's initial offer of $10 million each was dismissed by the mujahideen as too low (*International Herald Tribune*, 23 July 1993). It has now become clear that the Afghan war has contributed to destabilisation elsewhere in the region. The mujahideen, trained and experienced in war, are blamed by many for the spread of Islamic revolution to secular states, such as Egypt and Algeria. In fact, the rise of Islamic fundamentalism is largely the result of indigenous forces but the Afghans may have played a part in its militarisation and radicalisation. Even Pakistan, which provided a haven for the mujahideen during the Soviet occupation, became concerned over some of their activities, and closed many mujahideen offices and expelled the most radical elements (*International Herald Tribune*, 30 March 1993).

For the USSR, the Afghan war was a complete disaster. The war played a part in fuelling the international phenomenon of Islamic fundamentalism which poses a threat to the stability of Russia and the CIS. War exploded in Tajikistan in 1992 and in Chechnya in 1994. Islam provides only a partial explanation for the conflicts in the former Soviet Union. Nevertheless, the fall-out from the Afghan war continues to haunt Russia.

# Chapter Eight

# THE GULF WAR, 1990-91

The crisis in the Gulf was an unwanted surprise in Moscow. It came at a particularly difficult time for Gorbachev. At home, economic problems were piling up, nationalist unrest was on the rise, whilst his foreign policy was perceived increasingly as a series of one-sided concessions to the West. When the Gulf crisis broke in the summer of 1990, Gorbachev and the radical reformers were clearly in the ascendancy. However, as the crisis developed, the balance of power shifted in favour of the conservatives. This shift was only tangentially a result of the Gulf. Nevertheless, the debate on the crisis was vigorous, with all sides trying to use it to further their cause. This led to some inconsistencies in Soviet policy.

On the issue of the Iraqi invasion and subsequent annexation of Kuwait, however, there was general agreement. The Soviet Union, with its own nationalities' problems, was extremely sensitive on the issue of sovereignty and the forcible change of borders. Therefore, Moscow condemned the Iraqi action and consistently throughout the crisis called for Baghdad's immediate and unconditional withdrawal. Differences of opinion arose, however, over how such a policy aim should be implemented.

There were three basic views in the Kremlin. The first belonged to the new thinkers, led by Shevardnadze, who saw the crisis as a challenge to the post-cold war world. They were most vocal in their condemnation of the Iraqi action and most supportive of the use of military force to reverse it. Shevardnadze stressed the role of international law in maintaining peace and stability and the need in the new world order for the international community to co-operate to punish any transgressors. Shevardnadze put a lot of faith, at least initially, in the United Nations which he hoped could resolve the crisis without resort to war.

The most out-spoken opponents of Shevardnadze, the 'old thinkers', could be found most particularly amongst the military and the nationalist deputies in parliament, centred around the *Soyuz* group. They were far more suspicious than Shevardnadze of American motives in the Gulf. They were dubious that the American response to the Iraqi invasion was based on moral principles, such as respect for international law. In the Middle East, Israel had long defied the UN by holding on to the occupied territories without incurring any international sanctions. 'Old thinkers' argued that the US was simply interested in cheap oil and re-emphasising its dominant world role in the post-cold war era.[1] 'Old thinkers' believed Soviet interests could best be preserved through adopting a position independent of Washington.

Finally, there were the Arabists, led by Yevgeny Primakov, a former academic, a member of Gorbachev's short-lived Presidential Council and, from January 1996, Yeltsin's Russian Foreign Minister. Primakov agreed with many concerns of the 'old thinkers', but in his analysis he emphasised the regional implications of the crisis. He certainly did not support Iraq's expansionism, but he was opposed to the use of force to reverse it. Primakov feared that war would severely destabilise a region of strategic importance to Moscow. He also opposed Shevardnadze's call for a complete break with Baghdad, a traditional ally of the USSR, which Primakov argued would always remain an important player in the region.

## The Crisis

On 2 August 1990, Iraq invaded Kuwait and Iraqi troops gathered menacingly on the Kuwaiti-Saudi border. Six days later, Saddam Hussein announced the annexation of its small neighbour and on 28 August declared Kuwait to be an integral part of Iraq becoming its nineteenth province. Meanwhile, on 17 August, Saddam Hussein had detained foreigners in Iraq as hostages - including

---

[1] Such views were also supported amongst many radicals in the West, see, for example, Brenner (1991), Chomsky (1991) and Pilger (1992).

3,000 Soviets.

Baghdad had been an ally of Moscow since 1958 formalising an ever closer relationship in 1972 when the Treaty of Friendship and Co-operation was signed. Economic and military ties were close, but relations soured from the late 1970s after Saddam's brutal repression of communists and Moscow's rather equivocal stance on the 1980-88 Iran-Iraq War. This deterioration in relations made it rather easier for Gorbachev and Shevardnadze to reach the conclusion in August 1990 that new thinking was more important than old alliances. Saddam had hoped that Moscow would block any anti-Iraqi resolutions in the UN security council, but Moscow refused.

Iraq's act of aggression was blatant and both Gorbachev and Bush perceived Saddam's invasion as a challenge to the post-cold war order (Shevardnadze, 1991: 103; Chernayev, 1993b: 306-7). As a result, Moscow supported the UN Resolution on 2 August (UNSCR 660) which demanded 'the immediate and unconditional withdrawal of Iraqi troops, and the complete restoration and maintenance of the sovereignty, national independence and territorial integrity of Kuwait'. The following day, Secretary of State, James Baker and Eduard Shevardnadze, signed a joint declaration at Moscow airport condemning Iraq. On 6 August, Moscow also agreed to economic sanctions against Baghdad although the Soviet Union supplied about half of all Iraq's military equipment and earned almost a third of its hard currency from its trade with Baghdad (*Soviet Weekly*, 30 August 1990 and 15 November 1990).

Although Moscow backed the UN, the Kremlin hoped an Arab solution to the crisis could be found (*Soviet Weekly*, 6 September 1990). This proved impossible, however, due to the deep divisions amongst Arab states. The leaders of Egypt, Syria and Saudi Arabia saw Saddam's annexation of Kuwait as quite unacceptable and argued it had to be reversed (Freedman and Karsh, 1993: 72). However, Saddam possessed the strongest army in the region, and it was quickly decided by Baghdad's enemies that only the US possessed the military power to eject Iraq. At the emergency session of Arab states on 10 August, the majority agreed, in a highly charged meeting, to the deployment of American troops on Arab soil. At this stage, however, deployment was envisaged to be purely defensive - a Desert Shield - to deter further Iraqi expansionism into Saudi Arabia.

Shevardnadze hoped that American power could be contained through the UN and he made a number of speeches in the summer and autumn of 1990 arguing for the revival of the UN Military Committee. It was always a forlorn hope. The United States was unprepared to allow its soldiers to serve under non-American commanders, and without the Americans, the Military Committee could not work. By December, Shevardnadze had come to accept this was the case (*New Times*, 11-17 December 1990). However, two questions remained. First, could the USSR ever support an American-led war in the Gulf? And second, would Moscow participate in any military action to repel Iraq?

In many ways, Moscow chose the worst of both options. It supported the use of force to maintain sanctions (UNSCR 665) on 25 August, and the use of 'all necessary means' to eject Iraq (UNSCR 678) on 29 November. Yet Moscow refused to participate, even at a symbolic level, in the enforcement of either resolution. This led liberals as well as conservatives to doubt that the USSR was a superpower any longer. For liberals, like the future Russian Foreign Minister, Andrei Kozyrev, non-participation cast doubts on the legitimacy of the USSR to a seat as a permanent member of the Security Council (*New Times*, no. 3, 1991). The conservatives, on the other hand, believed the compliant, passive role of Moscow betrayed an ally and simply emphasised the Soviet Union's loss of superpower status (*Sovetskaya Rossiya*, 12 February 1991).

In early autumn, new thinkers gave hints that Moscow might be willing to consider military participation in the UN effort in the Gulf. At the emergency superpower summit in Helsinki, held on 9 September, Gorbachev in a joint statement with Bush laid out the Soviet position.

'We favour a peaceful settlement of the crisis and will hold a common position in the face of Iraq's aggression ... But we are fully determined to stop the aggression, and should the steps presently taken fail in bringing this about, we are ready to consider the possibility of additional steps being taken in keeping with the UN Charter. We must demonstrate in a most convincing way that aggression cannot and will not benefit anyone' (*International Affairs*, November 1990: 51).

However, at the subsequent press conference, Gorbachev denied this meant direct Soviet involvement (*Vestnik*, October 1990: 28), although Shevardnadze did argue later at the UN that the Soviet Union was willing 'in principle' to take part in an international military force under the flag of the United Nations' (*Soviet Weekly*, 4 October 1990).

Shevardnadze was expressing a minority view in the Soviet Union. So soon after Afghanistan, there was no public support for Soviet involvement in the Gulf. The large Muslim population in the USSR, which had become politicised during glasnost, was particularly concerned at the prospect of Soviet soldiers fighting another foreign war against fellow Muslims. The military, for its part, could tolerate economic sanctions, but there were real problems in contemplating a fight against a former ally under the effective command of the US. Opponents were critical of Shevardnadze's 'on-the-hoof' system of decision-making. They pointed out that vital decisions concerning military action had to be taken by the Supreme Soviet, not the Foreign Minister alone. Shortly before his resignation as Foreign Minister, on 12 December, Shevardnadze made a statement which denied that military participation had ever been seriously considered as an option, except in the case of rescuing the Soviet hostages held in Iraq (*Soviet News*, 19 December 1990). Significantly, all Soviet hostages had been released long before Shevardnadze made this statement.

In any case, Shevardnadze, along with everybody else in Moscow, hoped that Saddam would withdraw without recourse to war. There were differences, however, over how this could be achieved. Primakov believed that the coalition needed to compromise and offer Saddam a way out. He feared that an inflexible negotiating position would only drive Saddam into a corner and make war more likely. Primakov told a Soviet journalist: 'If Saddam faces a dilemma as he sees it - to be eliminated or to go to war - he will go to war' (*Soviet News*, 16 January 1991).[2]

Shevardnadze was of the opposite opinion. He favoured Iraq's unconditional withdrawal from Kuwait and felt that a united front at the UN backed up by a show of massive military force would compel Saddam to abide by UNSCR 660. Therefore, Shevardnadze was opposed to negotiating with the Iraqi leader. He did meet with Tariq Aziz, the Iraqi Foreign Minister, when he visited Moscow but only to impress upon him the urgent need for Iraqi withdrawal and the dreadful consequences for himself and his country if he did not. Shevardnadze feared that any offer of compromise would be misinterpreted in Baghdad as a sign of weakness on the part of the allies (*Soviet News*, 5 December 1990).

The only concession Shevardnadze was willing to contemplate related to a Soviet commitment to kick-start the Middle East peace process in return for Iraq's unconditional withdrawal (Chernayev, 1993b: 307). Bush was not opposed to this in principle, but he was always eager to formally separate out peace moves on the Palestinian issue and the annexation of Kuwait. He was

---

[2] Primakov was attacked by many in the West for a policy described as appeasement. But his position was not very different to that of the US at the time of the Cuban Missile Crisis in 1962 when Kennedy was determined not to humiliate Khrushchev and offered the Soviet leader a dignified way out of the crisis (see Kennedy, 1971).

adamant that there should be no public suggestion that Saddam's act of aggression had been rewarded. However, at the Helsinki summit in September, Bush secretly agreed to an international conference on the Middle East once the Gulf crisis was over (Beschloss and Talbott, 1993: 262).

For his part, Saddam Hussein's tactics were clear. He hoped to keep Kuwait by dividing the alliance and delaying the start of war until Iraq's control over Kuwait was complete. He hoped to do this by offering negotiations which would have appeal to different members of the coalition. The Soviet Union and France were the most important and most vulnerable states in this regard, due to their close ties with Iraq and their status as permanent members of the UN Security Council. He also expected to wean the Arab states away from the anti-Iraqi coalition by linking his withdrawal to a settlement of the Palestinian issue.

His strategy was undermined, however, by inconsistency. He suggested on 12 August that he might pull out of Kuwait if the Israelis withdrew from the occupied territories and Syria from Lebanon. Then, on 23 August, he said he might pull out if he was allowed access to the disputed islands of Warda and Bubiyan and the economic blockade was called off. Yet in other statements right up to the onset of Desert Storm, as will be shown below, Saddam clearly indicated his determination to stay exactly where he was. His aim was prevarication and confusion. Saddam talked a lot, but gave not an inch on the ground.

After it became apparent that the search for an Arab solution had failed, the Soviets stepped up their own diplomatic activity. In October, Gorbachev's special envoy, Yevgeny Primakov, was sent twice to Baghdad to discuss the crisis with Saddam. He was an obvious choice, since he had considerable knowledge of the Arab world and had known Saddam Hussein personally for some time. However, he was also a controversial choice since he openly favoured political compromise. Primakov was adamantly opposed to the annexation of Kuwait, but he expressed sympathy with the idea that Iraq deserved an outlet to the sea and joint access to the disputed oilfields of Rumilia (*Soviet Weekly*, 24 January 1991).

On his first trip to Baghdad on 4-5 October, Primakov took over some Soviet proposals. They called for the unconditional withdrawal of Iraq from Kuwait, but tied this to an international commitment to try to resolve the Arab-Israeli conflict. In addition, Primakov recommended that Iraqi-Kuwaiti territorial claims should be adjudicated by an independent commission of Arab states (Beschloss and Talbott, 1993: 272). Although Saddam Hussein told the Soviet envoy that Kuwait was an integral part of Iraq, he also indicated that he was prepared to consider withdrawal 'under certain circumstances' (Saivetz, 1994: 201). This gave Primakov hope for a political solution and he visited major capitals in the West to argue his case. However, his whole tour was torpedoed by Shevardnadze who privately informed his American guests that the Soviet Foreign Ministry did not support Primakov's position (Beschloss and Talbott, 1993: 274). In the circumstances, it was scarcely surprising that Primakov received a frosty welcome in Washington.

His optimism certainly appeared based on, at best, fragmentary evidence. It was far from clear that Saddam had shifted his position from 23 August when he said he might withdraw if certain conditions - already deemed unacceptable by the coalition - were met. Saddam's intransigence was confirmed when the Iraqi news agency announced on 14 October in the middle of Primakov's diplomatic efforts that 'Kuwait was and will continue to be Iraqi land for ever' (Freedman and Karsh, 1993: 177).

Nevertheless, Primakov went back to Baghdad on 28 October. He reported back that Saddam had seemed more sober and he no longer claimed that Kuwait was Iraq's nineteenth province. This statement did not necessarily mean that Iraq had renounced annexation, but it was a shift in position which both Gorbachev and Primakov thought worth exploring. At the meeting in Baghdad, Saddam said to Primakov, 'I am a realist and I know I will have to go' (*Soviet News*, 16 January 1991). For the coalition, however, such statements looked a long way from accepting UNSCR 660 and unconditional withdrawal, particularly as Saddam was still demanding linkage to the Arab-Israeli dispute and the territorial demand of an outlet to the sea (Beschloss and Talbott, 1993: 279). Later the Soviet government accepted that Primakov's initiatives had not accomplished their objectives (*Izvestiya*, 31 October 1990).

Whilst Primakov sought a political compromise with Baghdad, President Bush came to the conclusion in late October that economic sanctions were not sufficient and Saddam would only be removed by force.[3] Therefore, Bush decided that America needed an offensive rather than defensive force in the Gulf. On 8 November, Bush made an announcement that American troops in the Gulf would be doubled to 500,000. He also began the campaign in the United Nations to gather support for UNSCR 678 and the use of force to eject Iraq.

Views in the USSR polarised on the issue. Conservatives became concerned over the American military buildup in the Gulf which was the biggest since

---

[3]  See Freedman and Karsh (1993): 203-211 and Matthews (1993) for detailed discussion on why Bush took this decision.

Vietnam. The Warsaw Pact's chief of staff, General Lobov, argued that the US deployment formed 'an arch between NATO's eastern wing and Saudi Arabia' and posed a potential threat to the Soviet Union, only 200 kilometres from the Caucasus - already a highly unstable region (*Soviet Weekly*, 6 September 1990). Conservatives sent two diplomatic missions around the Gulf states again calling for a local Arab solution. The division in Moscow was clearly revealed, however, when Shevardnadze flew to Beijing to prevent a Chinese veto in the Security Council on UNSCR 678.

The United States gave two promises to Gorbachev which finally won his personal support for the UN resolution. First, Bush agreed to consult extensively with Moscow at every stage of the crisis; and second, he said that all American troops would be withdrawn from the Gulf after Kuwait had been liberated (Vassiliev, 1993: 351). Moreover, the US accepted for the first time that Moscow should have a role in trying to resolve the Arab-Israeli dispute, and he confirmed his commitment at Helsinki that an international conference on the Middle East would be held at the soonest possible time after the crisis was over. UNSCR 678 was carried on 29 November. China abstained, and only Cuba and Yemen, as non-permanent members of the Security Council, were opposed.

This key resolution accorded the coalition the right to use 'all necessary means', not only to evict Iraq from Kuwait, but also to 'restore peace and stability to the region'. This latter phrase represented an extension of previous resolutions. It was vague in its wording but certainly implied the destruction of Iraq as a major military power in the Middle East. UNSCR 678 also contained the deadline of 15 January 1991 for Iraqi withdrawal. Shevardnadze described the UN resolution, not as a green light for war, but as the last chance for a peaceful settlement. The resolution, he declared, clearly showed the determination of the coalition but it still gave Saddam more than enough time to pack his bags and get out of Kuwait (Vassiliev, 1993: 341).

There followed a period of hectic diplomacy. The day after the UN approved the resolution for military action, President Bush announced he was prepared to go the 'extra mile' for peace and arranged direct talks between Tariq Aziz and James Baker in Geneva for 9 January. Freedman and Karsh described this diplomatic initiative as a 'half mile too far' (Freedman and Karsh, 1993: 235). Arguably, it gave Saddam Hussein reason to believe the coalition feared war and was ready for a climbdown. In fact, the effort was little more than a publicity stunt to convince the American people that everything had been done to seek a peaceful resolution to the crisis. It was scarcely surprising, therefore, that nothing new was offered at Geneva as both sides used the occasion to restate their well-established positions.

Saddam's hopes of division within the coalition may also have risen when Shevardnadze resigned as Foreign Minister on 20 December. Most commentaries detected a more pro-Arabist stance after Shevardnadze's departure. In fact, the shift had begun before Shevardnadze's resignation and it owed less to changes in personnel and rather more to growing worries inside Moscow as the UN deadline for Iraqi withdrawal approached.

On 11 January, Gorbachev phoned Bush again. He declared his continuing support for UNSCR 678 but asked for the deadline to be put back. Gorbachev's proposal was firmly rejected. Bush argued that any postponement would favour Saddam Hussein. It would increase the chances of division within the coalition, allow Saddam more time to consolidate his position in Kuwait, and make the military campaign more difficult for the troops as spring approached. Nevertheless, there was growing nervousness in both the US and the USSR over the prospect of war. In the US Congress, the vote in favour of UNSCR 678 on 12 January was narrow, whilst in Moscow, on the same day, the Supreme Soviet demanded Gorbachev take 'additional steps' to reach a political settlement (*Soviet News*, 16 January 1991).

It was unclear, at this late stage, what Gorbachev could do to arrange a compromise solution. Neither Bush nor Saddam was prepared to lose face at this late stage. Saddam continued to make tempting offers to the coalition but they all fell short of Bush's demand for immediate and unconditional withdrawal. Finally, the UN Secretary General, Perez de Cuellar, visited Baghdad to see if Saddam was serious about compromise. Saddam showed his contempt for the UN mission, however, by keeping the Secretary General waiting for two days before he deigned to meet him on 13 January. The meeting when it came was a disappointment. Saddam made no explicit commitment to withdraw and Perez de Cuellar himself described his trip to Baghdad a failure (Freedman and Karsh, 1993: 269).

France, which had close links with Iraq (supplying approximately 20 percent of its military requirements) was particularly eager, like the Soviets, to avoid conflict if at all possible. On the eve of the air strikes, the French put forward a final peace plan which largely repeated previous attempts to reach a compromise. It proposed Iraqi withdrawal with the guarantee of an international conference on the Middle East to follow. Important details regarding verification and the timing of the withdrawal were not included. The French Foreign Minister, Roland Dumas, met the Iraqi ambassador in Paris about the proposal. He was told that anything was possible if he visited Baghdad and met with Saddam Hussein. The French, however, saw this simply as another delaying tactic and refused to take up the offer (Freedman and Karsh, 1993: 273).

Nevertheless, the French proposal was discussed on 14 January in closed session by the permanent members of the UN Security Council. The US and UK were opposed to the plan, and London put forward a more forcible proposal calling for strict adherence by Iraq to UNSCR 678. The Soviet Union's decision-making process was in disarray at this time as Alexander Bessmertnykh was about to take over from Shevardnadze as Foreign Minister. Initially, Vitaly Vorontsov, the USSR's UN ambassador, followed his own inclination and voted in favour of the British text but after a phone call with Moscow, he later switched in support of Paris. However, in the final analysis, these last-minute wranglings were irrelevant. Both texts were withdrawn as the Prime Minister of France, Michel Rocard, acknowledged that the French initiatives had 'not met with the least response from the Iraqi side' (Freedman and Karsh, 1993: 274).

Bush rang Gorbachev and gave him two hours notice of the start of air strikes against Iraq. Again, the Soviet President asked for a delay of 24 to 48 hours (Gorbachev, 1995b: 246). It was rejected. Any further postponement would have looked like vacillation on the part of the Americans. Therefore, Gorbachev phoned his ambassador in Baghdad to call on Saddam Hussein and demand immediate and unconditional withdrawal (Gorbachev, 1995b: 247). Saddam, however, showed his contempt for Gorbachev and the international community by refusing even to be woken to receive the Soviet President's message (*International Herald Tribune*, 22 February 1991).

### The Air War

On 16 January, 7 pm Washington time, Desert Storm began with massive air strikes against Iraq. Saddam hoped to absorb the initial air attacks, but his integrated air defence was rendered ineffective within a couple of hours (Freedman and Karsh, 1993: 303). The coalition had a virtual monopoly of the air after the first week which proved vital in the eventual defeat of the Iraqi army. The coalition was flying an average of 2,500 sorties per day - or 109,500 sorties throughout the war (Freedman and Karsh, 1993: 313).

After defeat in the air, Saddam had two remaining strategies. First, he hoped to extend the war by firing SCUDs at Saudi Arabia and Israel. The attacks caused more damage than expected, but Saddam's attempts to widen the conflict failed. Israel stayed out of the conflict and the coalition stayed together. Second, Saddam hoped these attacks would provoke the coalition into launching its ground offensive prematurely. If this happened, there was a chance the coalition's war effort would become bogged down in a long and bloody stalemate along the lines of the earlier Gulf War between Iran and Iraq. Such a battle, Saddam thought, would soon become intolerable to the Americans when the 'body-bag count' began to rise. Again, he was unsuccessful as the aerial bombardment went on mercilessly for six weeks.

As war took over from diplomacy, the Soviet Union, with no troops participating, took a back seat. Gorbachev appeared on television on 17 January, regretting the onset of military action. He blamed Saddam Hussein for intransigence, but declared that the Soviet Union had done everything possible to avoid war (*Pravda*, 18 January 1991). In many ways this was true. Gorbachev had felt obliged to make concerted efforts to seek a peaceful settlement, both to appease his more conservative critics and to preserve credibility for his foreign policy line. For war represented a failure for Gorbachev's new political thinking whose central purpose was to seek diplomatic solutions to regional conflicts. Moreover, there was a genuine fear of the implications of war in the Gulf. In this, the Soviet Union was not alone. Most estimates in the Soviet Union reckoned it would be a difficult fight for the coalition forces with thousands of casualties on both sides. Some even predicted defeat for the coalition (Cohen, 1994: 145).

Almost as soon as the air war started, Gorbachev began to call for an end to hostilities. On 18 January, Gorbachev asked Bush for a two to three day cease-fire to allow Saddam Hussein to review his position and withdraw. Once again, Gorbachev was ignored by the allies. Having established supremacy, there was no incentive for the allies to offer any concessions to Iraq. Then, two weeks into the air war, Gorbachev declared a concern over the apparent one-sided nature of the conflict (Gorbachev, 1995b: 248). No longer did Saddam look like a strong dictator in command of a massive and formidable army. Instead, the allies' monopoly of the air gave the conflict the appearance of a superpower wilfully destroying a weak and vulnerable third world state. The Soviets were worried too that the destruction of Iraq could lead to its breakup as an integrated sovereign state and lead to gross instability in the region.

Bessmertnykh took these concerns to Washington and found Baker in sympathetic mood. In another joint US-Soviet statement on 29 January, the two countries offered a cease-fire if Iraq gave an 'unequivocal commitment to withdraw' (Freedman and Karsh: 375). The statement was accompanied with a promise that both Moscow and Washington would make efforts to promote Arab-Israeli peace and stability once the withdrawal was complete. The statement was interpreted in some quarters as a shift from the demand that Saddam observe all twelve UN resolutions in full (*New Times*, 12-18 February 1991). If this had been Baker's intention, then he was out of step with the rest of the White House, and the implications of his joint declaration were repudiated by President Bush within hours of the statement's release.

For Washington, withdrawal was no longer enough. The war aims had shifted towards the destruction of Iraq's offensive capability and the clear defeat of Iraq's military forces, including the Republican Guard (Gordon and Trainer, 1994: 8). Less clearly defined, but also important for America in terms of peace and stability in the region, was the overthrow of Saddam Hussein, which would be most likely to occur after a clear and overwhelming defeat. None of these war aims was desired in Moscow.

The Central Committee passed a resolution on 31 January demanding a new commitment on the part of the Soviet government to seek a political solution. As bystanders in the war, any diplomatic initiative from Moscow was bound to be of limited utility. However, on 8 February, Gorbachev made a key-note statement in which he reiterated his commitment to all UN resolutions relevant to the Gulf crisis, but he continued, 'the logic of the military operations and the character of the military actions are creating a threat going beyond the mandate, defined by those resolutions' (*Soviet News*, 13 February 1991). This was a highly contentious reading of UNSCR 678. But Gorbachev went further and emphasised the need for Arab states to perform a major role in any post-war settlement, with Baghdad as a regional power also holding what the Soviet President called a 'worthy place' in the final settlement. Finally, Gorbachev announced that he was sending his special envoy, Yevgeny Primakov, for a third time to Baghdad to try to secure an Iraqi withdrawal before the onset of the ground offensive (*Soviet News*, 13 February 1991).

By this time, Saddam Hussein faced humiliation and wanted Moscow to extricate him from the mess of his own making. Primakov met Saddam Hussein on 13 February and afterwards declared that he detected 'a glimmer of hope' in the Iraqi President's negotiating position (Freedman, R., 1991: 15). On Friday 15 February, Baghdad radio corroborated Primakov's view when it announced that the Revolutionary Command Council was ready 'to deal with Security Council Resolution 660, with the aim of reaching an honourable and acceptable solution, including withdrawal' (Freedman and Karsh, 1993: 378). Gorbachev asked Bush to hold off the ground offensive until after a visit to Moscow by Tariq Aziz on 18 February when they would explore the peace proposal further (Freedman, 1991: 16). However, there was little incentive at this time for the coalition to give any concessions to Baghdad. Anything other than unconditional surrender by the Iraqi army could be turned around by Saddam to constitute a victory against the Americans. The Soviets, on the other hand, suspected that Bush wanted a complete defeat for Iraq as a personal triumph, a triumph for America and to fulfil American obligations to Israel.

In the meantime, the Americans had grown suspicious of Moscow, believing that they were working to prevent Saddam's defeat (Beschloss and Talbott, 1993: 334). Mitterand, who had been sympathetic in the past to Soviet diplomacy, told Gorbachev that Saddam was probably still playing for time (Freedman and Karsh, 1993: 381). Therefore, Gorbachev's proposal to convene the Security Council to 'register Iraq's acceptance of withdrawal' was rejected (Freedman and Karsh, 1993: 381).

Nevertheless, Gorbachev and his colleagues worked hard on a peace proposal. The first peace proposal was settled on 21 February in which the Iraqis agreed to the complete and unconditional withdrawal from Kuwait. It was a major Iraqi concession, but Bush said the pull-out period of six weeks was too long. So the text was quickly revised with the withdrawal period reduced to three weeks. Aziz accepted UNSCR 660 and declared that withdrawal would begin the day after a cease-fire. In return, it was agreed that all UN resolutions on Iraq would be lifted (*Soviet Weekly*, 28 February 1991). Gorbachev gave a guarantee that Iraq's territorial integrity would be preserved along with its governmental structures and he said that Moscow would oppose any attempt by the allies to punish Saddam Hussein personally (*Soviet Weekly*, 14 February 1991). Aziz went to bed that night apparently believing that his peace plan had prevented the ground offensive against his country.

Although General Schwarzkopf was ready to accept the Soviet plan, President Bush was irritated by Moscow's peace-making efforts and he was unwilling to allow Saddam to dictate the terms of any cease-fire (Cohen, 1994: 146). Thus, in response to Aziz's proposals and to prevent any further Soviet initiatives, Bush put forward his own counter-proposal. It required the withdrawal of Iraqi troops to begin by noon 23 February, with total withdrawal completed in a week, and from the capital, Kuwait City, within 48 hours. It also rejected any Iraqi demands that a cease-fire should be called before withdrawal was completed or that any UN resolutions would be lifted automatically. Bush was simply not prepared to provide Saddam with any face-saving formula.

## The Ground Offensive

On the morning of 24 February, the ground offensive was launched. The coalition forces had expected a clear and convincing victory. They had not expected a rout. The allies cut deep into Iraqi territory to block the Iraqis' retreat as they were driven back by allied forces sweeping across the Saudi-Kuwait border. The absence of any aerial cover gave the Iraqi forces no effective defence, whilst the six week bombardment of Iraqi positions in Iraq and Kuwait had undermined morale. With command, communications and intelligence already destroyed, the backbone of the Iraqi army was defeated within 48 hours (Freedman and Karsh, 1993: 398). As Iraqi troops fled from coalition gunfire, Iraq reluctantly accepted all UN resolutions and a cease-fire was called. The 100 hour ground war was over. Under pressure from Moscow, Iraq formally surrendered and attended the cease-fire talks on 2 March.

The official Soviet response to the launch of the ground offensive was one of regret since the Iraqis had already accepted UNSCR 660. The official release went on to say that the differences between Iraq and the states of the coalition were 'not too wide' and 'lent themselves to resolution within the UN Security Council framework within a day or two' (*Soviet Weekly*, 28 February 1991). Some inside the Soviet Union felt President Bush had shown an unwelcome eagerness to go to war. *Pravda* attacked the United States saying Washington sought 'sole leadership of the world' (*Pravda*, 25 February 1991). Gorbachev declared relations with America had become 'fragile' (Vassiliev, 1993: 344). However, as it soon became apparent that Iraqi forces were being routed, the Soviet position shifted in support of the coalition demands for full adherence to all twelve UN resolutions. At the same time, Moscow pressed for a rapid conclusion to hostilities. Pressure inside America, as well as pressure from countries such as the USSR, led Bush to declare a cease-fire just as coalition forces were closing in on the Republican Guard.

From a military point of view, there were good reasons for continuing the war to finally destroy the Iraqi army. However, the war had become so one-sided a US pilot famously described it as a 'turkey shoot'. Estimates at the time reckoned the Iraqis had suffered as many as 100,000 casualties (later reduced to 20,000) (see Halliday, 1994b: 117) and President Bush believed he would lose public support if the war continued (Gordon and Trainer, 1994: 8). He had secured his main aims of liberating Kuwait and reducing the power of the Iraqi military, although Saddam Hussein survived and the Republican Guard escaped to fight another day.

## The Post-War Period

The Soviet Union attempted to build its bridges with the international community after its failed diplomacy during the Gulf War. Moscow backed the UN cease-fire terms and maintained economic sanctions on Baghdad. Moscow and Washington were agreed about their main post-war aims. They wanted a weakened Iraq which was less of a threat to stability in the region, but also one strong enough to prevent Iranian dominance of the Gulf. This was a delicate balancing act which required considerable diplomatic skill on the part of the international community.

A series of UN resolutions sought to restrict Iraq's military capability and settle the issue of the disputed border between Kuwait and Iraq. UNSCR 687, adopted on 3 April 1991, demanded the removal or destruction of chemical, biological, nuclear weapons and all ballistic missiles over 95 miles. It also set up a special commission (UNSCOM) to implement its decisions and establish monitoring mechanisms to prevent Iraq acquiring such weapons in the future. After a report from an international commission, the border between Iraq and Kuwait was formally redrawn in January 1993, but the new border was rejected by Baghdad since it meant losing the naval base at Umm Qasr and part of the Rumilia oilfield.

The monitoring of Iraq's military capability gave the UN unprecedented rights of access in a sovereign state. This was further extended after the brutal repression by Saddam of opposition groups in the spring of 1991. On 3 April, the UN resolution 688 was passed to allow international humanitarian organisations to visit the troubled areas in the north and south of the country. When this was denied by Baghdad, a safe havens policy, policed by a no-fly zone, was adopted by the US, French and British. This policy was never formally put to the UN for fear it would be voted down by the Chinese or Russians who suspected the safe havens policy would effectively lead to the partitioning of Iraq.

In response to the criticism that the UN was punishing the people of Iraq for the sins of their leaders, two further UN resolutions were introduced in August and September 1991. The resolutions allowed Iraq to export $1.6 billion worth of oil over a six month period so that the government could buy food, medicine and other humanitarian goods. However, Saddam had to accept the supervision of their distribution by the UN, which he rejected as a violation of Iraqi sovereignty.

Saddam had little choice after the war but to formally accept UNSCR 687. However, the Iraqi authorities did little to co-operate in its implementation. The US, in turn, refused to lift economic sanctions until all UN resolutions had been fully implemented. Yeltsin, as the new leader of Russia, backed the American policy and even sent two warships to monitor the embargo in September 1992. However, from 1993 Yeltsin began to adopt a position more independent of the US and called for a progressive easing of sanctions against Baghdad. This was only in part to do with the rise of nationalism in Russia (*Moscow News*, 28 October, 1994). It was also in response to a loss of earnings from one of Russia's most important third world allies. A 1994 report estimated that Russia had lost about $30 billion in the four years since the imposition of sanctions and was owed up to $7 billion (*Moscow News*, 21-27 October 1994). Moreover, Arabists, like Primakov, feared that sanctions could lead to internal instability in Iraq which could have consequences in the rest of the region. Primakov also hoped that an easing of sanctions would be an incentive for Saddam to moderate his policies at home and seek greater accommodation with the international community.

Although France and China, as permanent members of the UN Security Council agreed with the Russian position, the US and UK took the opposite view. They called for vigorous action against any violations of the cease-fire terms and argued that sanctions should only be lifted after Saddam had fully accepted all UN resolutions. Air strikes were used twice in 1993 to emphasise the point.

On 3 October 1994 Saddam Hussein again stirred himself and moved about 10,000 troops close to the Kuwaiti border. The US, however, was able on this occasion to deploy a formidable show of force in rapid time to deter further advances by Saddam. After the Gulf War, the US had negotiated a series of 'ghost bases' in Saudi Arabia and elsewhere which were fully equipped and combat-ready within hours. The Arab leaders had reluctantly come to recognise that the threat of Saddam required an American presence in the region - a fact which was far from welcome, however, among many Arabs in the region.

During Saddam's troop build up, Kozyrev rushed to Baghdad. He claimed credit both for Saddam's demobilisation of Iraqi forces and his formal recognition of the redrawn Kuwaiti border on 10 November 1994. But after Saddam's mobilisation, few trusted Saddam and the US continued to call for the full implementation of all UN resolutions. Kozyrev's action was an attempt to regain Moscow's position in the Middle East, but his diplomacy alienated the US and many of Saddam's Arab neighbours too (*Moscow News*, 3 November 1994).

**Summary**

There were differences of opinion in Moscow over Gorbachev's Gulf policy.

This was inevitable in the more democratic atmosphere that prevailed in the Soviet Union at that time. Differences were visible in the various Soviet newspapers which covered the crisis. However, Anatoly Chernayev, Gorbachev's Presidential aide, who was present at all relevant meetings on the Gulf, has written that the West exaggerated the differences at the top. In the special committee, set up when the air war started to monitor the conflict, Chernayev wrote that not a single member was opposed to the allied use of military force (Chernayev, 1993b: 359). In fact, the centre of disaffection could be found among a relatively small number of deputies in parliament. Yet even there opposition should not be talked up too much. For twice, in September and December, the Supreme Soviet voted approval of Gorbachev's handling of the crisis (Ekedahl and Goodman, 1993: 107). Even as Moscow became worried over the course of the war, there was no attempt by the Soviets to embarrass the Americans when a shelter was bombed on 13 February which contained hundreds of civilians.

Gorbachev later wrote in a Western newspaper that the crisis in the Gulf had been a severe test of new thinking and the New World Order (*The Guardian*, 29 February 1992). The US and the Soviet Union had different interests in the Gulf region but they had been able to co-operate in the enforcement of Iraqi withdrawal. Gorbachev stressed Moscow's positive role in the crisis and claimed credit for persuading the US to gain international legitimacy for their actions by working through the UN. Moscow, for its part, he said, used its links with Baghdad to act as a key mediator in the crisis and made every effort to secure a peaceful resolution to the conflict. But Saddam was intransigent and refused to withdraw. When the war started, Gorbachev said he wanted 'to ensure the military option should remain within the limits determined by the Security Council and that it should not be transformed into total war against Iraq as a state, thus resulting in the destruction of its people' (*The Guardian*, 29 February 1992).

Others, however, were less enthusiastic about Soviet policy. In the West, there were suspicions of Moscow actively supporting Saddam since Soviet advisers remained in Iraq long after the crisis broke (*International Herald Tribune*, 13 February 1991). Although Bush and Baker announced that the new world order survived the Gulf War, Robert O. Freedman, summed up a common American perception when he said that the US-Soviet co-operation had been limited. 'Moscow,' he argued, 'was too closely following its own perceived national interests to be a genuine partner for the United States' (Freedman, R., 1991: 17).

In the USSR, new thinkers agreed that Gorbachev had been too pro-Iraq.

Gorbachev's attempts to prevent war were generally supported, but his attempts to get an immediate cease-fire in the air war were heavily criticised by Shevardnadze and others (Shevardnadze, 1991: 106). For they argued that Moscow's attempt to disassociate itself from the war was aimed, as many in the West had earlier thought, at preventing Saddam's defeat at the hands of the coalition (*New Times*, 12-18 February, 1991).

On the other hand, the Arabists in the Soviet Union were critical of Moscow's abandonment of former allies and feared the war could lead to increased instability in the region (*Soviet Weekly*, 14 February 1991; *New Times*, 27 November 1990). In his autobiography published in 1995, Gorbachev's position had shifted closer to the Arabists. He argued that Bush had thwarted his attempts to find a peaceful solution to the crisis, in large part, for reasons of personal and national prestige. The US, he said, took the opportunity presented by Saddam Hussein to try out its most modern weaponry and emphasise its continued superpower status (Gorbachev, 1995b: 254-58).

Gorbachev's main aim at the time had been to retain relations with the West and improve them as far as possible with the states of the Middle East. This led to strains in relationships but, in general terms, he had some success. Relations with conservative Gulf states were already improving long before the crisis broke but Soviet support for the coalition helped this process along. Most Western leaders recognised the domestic difficulties faced by Gorbachev and acknowledged that his country's support for the coalition against a former ally represented a major shift in Soviet foreign policy thinking. The result, however, was that the Middle East was dominated to a greater extent than ever by the US. This was something the conservatives in Moscow had difficulty coming to terms with.

# Chapter Nine

# YELTSIN AND DOMESTIC POLITICS

Boris Yeltsin was never a natural democrat. Raised as a communist official, he became first secretary in Sverdlovsk (now Yekaterinberg) before being brought to Moscow as party chief in December 1985. In this position, Yeltsin became an enthusiastic supporter of Gorbachev's programme of perestroika and took up a populist position as a staunch opponent of privilege and corruption. He made a point of riding to work on public transport and denounced the life-style of the Russian elite. His blatant publicity-seeking alienated him from colleagues both in the politburo and the Moscow party. Yet, there can be no doubt that Yeltsin's politics struck a chord with the Russian people.

After being promoted to the politburo in early 1986, Yeltsin became disillusioned with the pace of reform. In October 1987, he made an unscheduled speech to the Central Committee which identified Ligachev as the main obstacle to reform and criticised the growing cult surrounding Gorbachev (*Izvestiya TsK KPSS*, 1 1989: 239-41). Shortly afterwards, Yeltsin was taken ill and confined to hospital. Nevertheless, Gorbachev ordered Yeltsin to attend a meeting of the Moscow party on 4 November where he was attacked unmercifully by his colleagues in language uncomfortably similar to that of the Stalinist era. Yeltsin felt deeply humiliated by the whole experience and never forgave Gorbachev for the treatment he received (Yeltsin, 1990: 153-5). Yeltsin was subsequently sacked as Moscow party boss and he also lost his position on the politburo the following February. Yeltsin was demoted to First

Deputy Chairman of *Gosstroi* (state construction), but he did keep his position on the Central Committee.

It appeared that Yeltsin's career was over. However, Yeltsin was not forgotten and when competitive elections were introduced in March 1989, he took the opportunity to resurrect his career. The Russian public saw him as a hero - a man who had risked his career by defying the party apparatus. As a result, he fought successful elections in March 1989 to become a deputy to the Congress of People's Deputies and a year later he was elected by the Sverdlovsk constituency to be a deputy to the Russian parliament. In May 1990, Russian deputies narrowly elected him as chairman of the Russian parliament, and the following year, in June 1991, Yeltsin was elected by the Russian people to the new post of President of Russia. These electoral victories gave Yeltsin a popular legitimacy that Gorbachev always lacked. Yeltsin developed a base of support separate from party and state which allowed him to publicly resign from the party at the 28th CPSU Congress in July 1990.

Yeltsin's defiance during the August coup was his finest hour. After initial doubts, he became identified around the world as a true defender of democracy. Gorbachev had played a pivotal role in bringing down communism, but he no longer had the authority to complete the process of reform. The failed August coup gave Yeltsin his chance to take power in Russia and sweep away the old Soviet system. In an avalanche of events in the autumn and winter of 1991, the CPSU was suspended, the KGB broken up, the USSR abolished and the command economy abandoned. With the old guard defeated or in disarray, Yeltsin seemed uniquely well-placed to supervise the transition to a capitalist, liberal democratic state.

In other respects, however, Yeltsin faced enormous problems. First, the revolution which Gorbachev had started was far from complete. Yeltsin was undoubtedly a popular figure in Russia, but this did not mean general acceptance for his proposed reforms. Most people, in fact, were grossly ignorant of the implications of reform and Yeltsin made the mistake of not encouraging a more wide-ranging debate on the subject. Second, Yeltsin's difficulties were also exacerbated by the situation he inherited from Gorbachev. The economy had been in decline since 1988 and it was in severe crisis by the time Yeltsin took over. The dissolution of the Soviet Union only served to further exacerbate these problems. Finally, there was the problem of power. Yeltsin had authority as Russian President, but his ability to implement policy remained limited. Centrifugal forces combined with weak central institutions reduced substantively his power as President.

Basically, there are two divergent analyses of the Yeltsin period. The first is highly critical of Yeltsin both as a policy-maker and a political leader. This view argues that Yeltsin's liberal economic policies led to economic collapse, whilst his political dogmatism and unwillingness to compromise undermined democracy and strengthened authoritarian tendencies in Russia (see Kagarlitsky, 1992; and Steele, 1994). The second view, in contrast, argues that it was not Yeltsin's intransigence but reactionary opposition which led to crisis. The old elite, made up of nationalists and communists, re-emerged after the collapse of the Soviet Union as a powerful force implacably opposed to the market and liberal democracy. There was no middle ground between the forces of reform and reaction. Therefore, compromise and co-operation with the opposition, it was argued, was never a practical option for the Yeltsin administration (Aslund, 1995; Mau, 1996).

A third view, presented here, emphasises the difficulties of transition, but argues that neither the reformers nor conservatives can escape blame for the series of crises which engulfed post-Soviet Russia. The conservatives in parliament were the worst offenders, but both sides showed a marked reluctance to indulge in the natural give-and-take of democratic politics. After 70 years of Soviet dictatorship, inevitably democratic culture in Russia was weakly developed. As a result, there was little agreement over the rules of the game. Too often the spirit of democracy was forgotten as both sides attempted to manipulate the constitution for political advantage rather than using it as a neutral arbiter of disputes. Both sides were reluctant to accept the legitimacy of the other's point of view. Both sought to destroy the other, rather than engage in rational debate. Thus, the underlying political culture changed very little from the Soviet period. The Leninist maxim, *kto kogo?* (who will crush whom?) remained the principle concept in post-Soviet Russian politics. In the circumstances, it was far from surprising that violence and intrigue remained an integral part of post-communist politics. This will be shown below by first considering Yeltsin's economic reform policy and then moving on to look at the domestic political scene in Russia after the August coup of 1991.

## Economic Reform: Shock therapy

A new government was set up in early November 1991 which was predominantly young and reformist. Gennady Burbulis was Russia's First Deputy Premier and he was fundamental in getting the liberal Yegor Gaidar appointed in charge of economic policy. Other prominent reformers who joined the government included Anatoly Chubais, to deal with privatisation, and Alexander Shokhin, who was made Minister in charge of social affairs.

Inspired by the Polish example, Gaidar favoured a dash to the market - or shock therapy, as it became known. Essentially, shock therapy consisted of three inter-related policies - the freeing of prices; cuts in state spending; and a swift move towards privatisation. The policy was controversial inside Russia from the moment it was announced. Although all serious economists were agreed about the need to introduce market disciplines, doubts remained over Gaidar's strategy. Was he trying to introduce the market too quickly? Were the social costs too high? And what was the ultimate goal of the reform policy? Was it a Keynsian-style social market or a Friedmanite liberal market? (For the debate, see Aslund, 1995: 73-86.)

Yegor Gaidar argued that there was no realistic alternative for Russia but shock therapy. He emphasised the economic crisis he had inherited in the autumn and winter of 1991 and argued that nothing short of radical surgery could revive the Russian economy. Any delay, he said, would only make the situation worse with the state facing the very real possibility of bankruptcy and hyper-inflation (Gaidar, 1995).

There was much truth in Gaidar's argument. No one could seriously doubt that Gaidar faced a crisis situation when he entered office. Any reform policy would have been difficult and painful. In 1991, the Russian GDP had fallen 19 percent over the previous year, the budget deficit had reached the potentially crippling level of perhaps 30 percent of GDP, whilst currency reserves were as low as $100 million (Aslund, 1995: 52). Radicals argued that Gorbachev had already attempted the incrementalist approach in the Soviet period and it had failed. Other Soviet successor states, such as Ukraine, later tried gradualism after the collapse of the USSR, and met with the same result. For all its manifest problems, the Russian economy still emerged as the strongest amongst the Soviet successor states. Gaidar attributed this to his strategy of radical reform.

The Yeltsin government also recognised the political advantages of shock therapy. With the old Soviet elite defeated after the August coup, the autumn of 1991 represented the optimal time to introduce radical change. Furthermore, the Russian people were aware of the crisis in the country and many were prepared to make short-term sacrifices for medium-term gains. Such an attitude, however, as reformists were quick to recognise, was unlikely to last (Mau, 1996: 85-86). Thus, Yeltsin used shock therapy to finally kill off Stalinism in Russia and to emphasise his decisiveness in comparison with Gorbachev's earlier perceived vacillation (Yeltsin, 1994: 147-150).

Therefore, on 28 October 1991, Yeltsin announced the outline of his government's proposed economic reforms and was granted emergency powers by the Russian parliament to push them through (*Rossiiskaya gazeta*, 29 October 1991). The emergency measures were defended by Yeltsin's supporters as necessary to avoid obstructionism and delay, his critics argued they represented an early example of his authoritarian instincts (see Kagarlitsky, 1992: 157-8). At a minimum, the measures revealed that Yeltsin's first priority was economic reform rather than democratisation.

After a delay to allow other republics time to prepare for reform, shock therapy was formally launched in Russia on 2 January 1992. Yeltsin was aware that the transition period would be difficult, but in October he predicted that the Russian public would begin to see improvements by the end of the first year (*Rossiiskaya gazeta*, 29 October 1991). This proved wildly optimistic.

Table 9:1
**Annual Economic Indicators**

| Year | Growth in GDP | Inflation |
|------|---------------|-----------|
| 1991 | -5% | 93% |
| 1992 | -15% | 1353% |
| 1993 | -9% | 896% |
| 1994 | -13% | 303% |
| 1995 | -4% | 190% |

*Sources: Russian Economic Trends*, vol. 4, no. 4, 1995: 112; and *The World Bank Development Report, 1996: 174.*

The immediate impact was dramatic. In the first month of shock therapy, consumer prices rose fourfold and producer prices fivefold. Annual inflation rates never subsequently fell below three figures (see table 9:1). As the table above also shows, the Russian economy entered a period of unprecedented collapse. Industrial and agricultural output was more than halved in the first four years of reform (*Russian Economic Trends*, vol. 4, no. 4, 1995: 113 and 116).

Annual per capita income fell from $4,110 in 1990 to $2,650 in 1994 (World Bank, 1996: 21). The consumption of goods and services dropped 33 percent over the period 1991 to 1995 and capital investment as a percentage of GDP fell from 23.4 percent in 1989 to 15.1 percent in 1995 (*Russian Economic Trends*, vol. 4, no. 4, 1995: 117 and 121). The budget deficit did decline from the heights of 1991, but it remained stubbornly resistant to monetarist policy - at about nine percent of GDP for much of the period (*International Herald Tribune*, 2 December 1994).

Shock therapy had a devastating impact on the majority of Russian citizens. Whilst seven percent of the Russian population were officially registered as dollar millionaires, more than a third were living below the poverty line - a figure that had more than tripled since the launch of Gaidar's reforms (*Russian Review*, 21 February 1994). Official unemployment remained remarkably low throughout the period, but ten percent of the Russian labour force worked part-time and large numbers of workers went unpaid often for months at a time (*Moscow News*, no. 12, 1996). Mortality rates rose by 16 percent and birth rates declined by 14 percent over the period 1992-94 (Arbatov, 1994: 92). Men's life expectancy fell to 59 years in 1994 to become the lowest in Europe (*Moscow News*, no. 12, 1996). Cuts in state spending also led to a crisis in the arts and education. Georgy Arbatov, an adviser to successive Soviet leaders, described this process as the 'de-intellectualisation' of Russian society (Arbatov, 1994: 92).

However, the one issue which seemed to dominate the minds of the Russian people above all others was the explosion in crime. Once one of the safest countries in the world, Russia overtook the US in the mid-1990s in the number of homicides per year (Smiley, 1995: 58). Mafia operations took over large sectors of the market and posed a potential threat to democracy and the economic reform process itself. It was estimated that up to 40 percent of Russia's wealth was controlled by criminal cartels (Lester, 1995: 49).

In the circumstances, it was scarcely surprising that Gaidar's policy met fierce opposition in parliament and certain sections of the Russian media. Yeltsin's own Vice President, Alexander Rutskoi, condemned shock therapy even before it was launched as 'economic genocide' (*Nezavisimaya gazeta*, 19 December 1991), and famously dismissed Gaidar and his colleagues as 'little boys in pink shorts and yellow boots' (*Kommersant*, no. 47, 1991). However, Rutskoi knew little about economics and much of his tirade could be shrugged off by Gaidar as populist rhetoric. More difficult to dismiss, however, was the criticism from other reformist economists, such as the highly respected Grigory Yavlinsky who had earlier drafted the 500-day programme. Yavlinsky had opposed the breakup of the Soviet Union and frequently eexpressed concern over the social effects of shock therapy (see *Moscow News*, nos. 22 and 23 1992). By late 1993, even the Clinton administration began to agree, arguing that the Russian people had seen all shock and no therapy.

No one could deny the difficulties of economic transition. However, reformers claimed the difficulties were not due to too much liberal economics, but to too little. Yegor Gaidar argued that his reform programme had been effectively blocked by the old conservative elite. Gaidar went so far as to argue that shock therapy, for all the rhetoric, had never really been implemented in Russia (Gaidar, 1995: 165). High state spending and continued subsidies to bankrupt enterprises supported by the conservatives, according to Gaidar, distorted the market and led to the problems with inflation and the budget deficit. Viktor Gerashenko, head of the Russian Central Bank since July 1992, was a particular *bete noir* of the reformers and he was accused of conducting a wilfully loose financial policy. Boris Fedorov, Yeltsin's former Finance Minister, summed up this reformist view when he wrote in 1994: 'Last year the average monthly rate of inflation was 20 percent. Registered unemployment was less than 1 percent. Real growth in personal income was 10 percent. Food consumption and retail sales increased. Who in his right mind can call this shock therapy?' (*International Herald Tribune*, 16 February 1994).

Anders Aslund, the Western academic and adviser to Gaidar's team, was the first serious economist to sound optimistic about Russia's prospects. He argued that, despite all the problems, the foundations of a market system had been laid by 1994 (Aslund, 1995: 3). Central to Aslund's analysis was the idea that the state no longer dominated the Russian economy. Investment was increasingly raised by private firms. Private enterprise by 1994 was employing about 60 percent of the workforce and generating about 60 percent of Russian GNP (Aslund, 1995: 266; Hanson, 1994: 37). Retail and services were almost entirely privately owned, whilst prices had been freed on all but a handful of goods and services (Aslund, 1995: 266).

Moreover, Aslund's interpretation of the statistics led him to be more upbeat about Russia's overall economic performance. He accepted that GDP had fallen since 1992, but he showed that official statistics underestimated the growing importance of the private sector in the Russian economy. More importantly, much of this decline, he said, was explicable in terms of essential economic restructuring. Inevitably, it took time for the Russian economy to accommodate market disciplines and for enterprises to respond to consumer demands rather than state orders. However, Russia, he said, had begun to shift away from its earlier, old-fashioned emphasis on iron and steel in favour of services and consumer goods - a balance more typical of a modern developed economy. Aslund also argued that the social costs of shock therapy were bearable. Living standards fell after 1991 but, according to Aslund, whilst real wages dropped 20 percent from 1987 to 1993, real incomes fell over the same period by a rather more modest ten percent (Aslund, 1995: 284). Aslund saw the widening of wage differentials as necessary to raise work incentives and reward risk-taking, and dismissed the idea that they had gone too far. On the contrary, he argued that differentials were similar to those in the UK and somewhat narrower than those in the US (Aslund, 1995: 287). Welfare provisions were basic but education and health were still free for all who wanted it, pensions were index-linked, housing was subsidised and unemployment pay was introduced. In all, welfare consumed some 21 percent of GNP - a not unreasonable figure, Aslund claimed, given the level of Russian development (Aslund, 1995: 287).

Aslund was probably right in suggesting that a market of sorts was safe in Russia, and although he might have exaggerated the strength of the Russian economy, other writers also began to be more optimistic about its prospects. The official journal, *Russian Economic Trends*, accepted that the economic situation had improved since 1994 but argued that economic performance remained patchy. For example, industrial output for 1995 was down by three percent, but the decline, the journal said, was 'concentrated in a few underperforming industries' (*Russian Economic Trends*, vol. 4, no. 4, 1995: 64). Thus, although chemicals and metallurgy experienced 'significant growth', the production of consumer goods had fallen by 12 percent in 1995, and clothing and textiles by 20 percent since 1990. The agricultural sector also showed little sign of recovery since the Soviet era with grain production for 1995 down by almost a third on the *average* since the 1960s (*Russian Economic Trends*, vol. 4, no. 4, 1995: 67 and 75).

At the macro level, however, the economy was performing far more strongly. By the end of 1995, Russia had turned a large trade deficit in 1991 into a healthy trade surplus of $20 billion and the monthly inflation rate was also down to its lowest ever monthly figure of 3.2 percent (*Russian Economic Trends*, vol. 4, no. 4, 1995: 3-6). The OECD predicted that Russia was likely to experience three percent growth in 1996 and ten percent growth thereafter (*International Herald Tribune*, 26 September 1995 and 6 October 1995). This always looked far too optimistic. Nevertheless, Russia was able to attract more foreign investment into the country, including an offer from the IMF of a $10.2 billion loan over a three year period in March 1996. It appeared that some of the estimated $40 billion which had fled the country since 1992, was beginning to trickle back (*Time*, 31 July 1995). However, the economic and legal uncertainties meant that Russia remained a risky and often frustrating place for outside investors. Unfortunately for Yeltsin, improving statistics at the macro-economic level did not lead to improved living standards for the majority of Russian citizens which remained below those of 1985 when Gorbachev first embarked on the process of perestroika.

Boris Raizov, a Russian economic consultant, put these statistics into some kind of context when he wrote in early 1995 that the economic crisis was finally over, but the economic depression had just begun. Economic depression, he went on, was better than crisis, but he predicted that the depression would last at least until the year 2000 (*Russian Review*, 27 January 1995). Raizov was right in emphasising the long-term nature of economic reform in Russia - in that sense, the term shock therapy was always a misnomer.

## The political scene: the struggle for power

Yeltsin neglected the importance of political reform and democratisation when he came to power in 1991-2. Transition theory suggests that a democratic mandate is essential for radical reform to be successful (see Przeworski, 1991; and Lester, 1995). But in the crucial period before the launch of shock therapy, Yeltsin failed to gain approval from the people for his reform programme. He also failed to draw up a new constitution to deal with post-Soviet realities. In other Soviet successor states, referenda or elections were held, but Yeltsin wanted to move ahead quickly. He feared elections could polarise opinion and make radical reform more difficult. Yeltsin argued that there had been too much talk and too little action for far too long. He was determined to change all that and resolved to push through economic reforms with the minimum of consultation.

As a result, Yeltsin was granted emergency powers for twelve months in November 1991. He had the power to rule by decree and appoint his own regional bosses and government ministers (*Rossiiskaya gazeta*, 2 November 1991). In the process, Yeltsin became increasingly unaccountable to those around him. Thus, although he was formally head of the cabinet, he rarely participated in its weekly meetings. He preferred decision-making in small cabals. The remarkable defection of Rutskoi and Khasbulatov from the Yeltsin camp in the autumn of 1991 was, at least in part, attributable to their exclusion from top decision-making groups. Rutskoi always claimed that the first he heard of the *Belovezhsky* agreement, which formally wound up the USSR, was from TV (Kampfner, 1994: 63). On the crucial issue of economic policy, no formal programme for shock therapy was ever published by the government, and it was never formally approved by parliament (Aslund, 1995: 88).

Opposition to Yeltsin's reform programme, led by Rutskoi and Khasbulatov, quickly coalesced around the White House. Congress was already campaigning for an end to the President's emergency powers in spring 1992. At the time, these moves were portrayed by Yeltsin (and Western governments) as a reactionary move by unreconstructed communists and nationalists. It was argued that Congress, which had been elected in March 1990 - more than a year before Yeltsin as Russian President - was no longer representative of public opinion and lacked democratic credentials. There can be no doubt that some deputies in parliament were firmly opposed to reform and took every opportunity to undermine the Yeltsin administration. However, any blanket condemnation of Congress would be unfair. It neglected the variety of views within parliament and seemed to forget that parliament only eight months earlier had been the centre of opposition to the August coup. Yeltsin could claim to have the backing of the majority in Russia on most issues - at least up to the parliamentary elections of December 1993 - but this could not gainsay the fact that the opposition still represented a significant minority of the Russian people who were genuinely concerned over the direction of government policy.

However, Yeltsin did acknowledge the dislocation caused by shock therapy, and brought more conservative figures into his administration in the spring of 1992. Thus, Gennady Burbulis, the *eminence grise* behind the reforms, was dropped as First Deputy Premier and the more conservative figure of Yuri Skokov was elevated to head the newly created Security Council. Yeltsin claimed he wanted more of a balanced ticket. But there was no movement on either side on what had become the central issue in Russian politics. Who rules Russia? The President or parliament? Yeltsin argued executive power lay with the President since he had been directly elected by the people in June 1991. The constitution, on the other hand, seemed to grant overwhelming power to Congress. According to the constitution, the President had no right to appeal over the head of parliament and demand a referendum. He had no right to dissolve parliament and call new elections. And only Congress could amend the constitution - a prerogative it chose to exercise on no less than 300 occasions.

It would always have been difficult for Yeltsin to build a coalition with parliament, but he can be criticised for making so little effort. Yeltsin could never have won over the recalcitrant hardliners, but his real failure lay in losing the support of other more moderate and pragmatic deputies. Anatoly Chubais, Minister of Privatisation, said 65 percent of deputies supported Yeltsin in April 1992, but by October that figure had been almost halved (*The Guardian*, 19 October 1992).

By the end of 1992, relations between parliament and the President had worsened considerably. In December, Congress rejected Yeltsin's appeal to extend his emergency rule and also refused his call for a referendum to decide the issue of executive power. However, in a late compromise between Khasbulatov and Yeltsin, it was agreed that a referendum could be held in the spring in return for further concessions from Yeltsin. Thus, Yeltsin accepted the right of parliament to ratify the appointment of key ministers and he agreed to drop Yegor Gaidar in December 1992 as acting Prime Minister (although he stayed on as economic adviser) and replaced him with the more centrist figure of Viktor Chernomyrdin, the former boss of the Russian gas industry, *gazprom*. At the same time, Burbulis was dropped from the presidential entourage altogether. Commentators read the changes as a defeat for Yeltsin but market reform continued, albeit at a rather slower pace than originally envisaged by Gaidar.

However, this compromise agreement was overturned by Congress in March 1993 when it rescinded its earlier agreement to hold a referendum. There followed further amendments to the constitution which were interpreted by Yeltsin as an attempt to reduce his role to a ceremonial figure-head. The amendments proposed that the government could present draft laws to parliament without presidential approval and parliament also denied the President the right to issue decrees or dissolve any popularly elected body. In response, Yeltsin went on TV on 20 March 1993 to announce a referendum for 25 April and in the interim the imposition of 'special rule'.

Valery Zorkin, chairman of the Constitutional Court, immediately ruled Yeltsin's decree unconstitutional and so Congress began impeachment proceedings against the President. However, the decree, when finally published on 24 March, was more moderate than Yeltsin's TV address. Why this occurred is not entirely clear. It is most likely that Yeltsin feared he did not have sufficient support at that time to defy Congress, but others have argued that his TV address was deliberately provocative to draw out and embarrass his opponents (Clark, 1995: 214-215). If the latter were true, it was largely successful as the public rallied behind the President. The impeachment motion still went ahead, but it failed by 70 votes to get the required two-thirds majority in Congress.

After this moral victory, Yeltsin got his way and the deputies agreed to a referendum. However, Congress still insisted on setting the questions. As a result, the referendum ended up essentially as a vote of confidence in Yeltsin and his economic reforms. The desperate state of the Russian economy in the spring of 1993 gave parliament every reason to believe the vote would go against the President. However, the Russian electorate once again surprised a lot of people. A respectable 64 percent of the electorate voted. Of those, 58 percent supported Yeltsin as President and as many as 53 percent backed the continuation of economic reform (*Rossiiskaya gazeta*, 6 May 1993). Even though Yeltsin failed to get the absolute majority required to call new parliamentary elections, the referendum still represented a remarkable victory for the President. Unquestionably, the result gravely weakened the position of the conservatives whose claim to be speaking on behalf of the vast majority of ordinary Russian people was seriously undermined.

In the wake of the referendum result, Yeltsin called for a new constitution to resolve the issue of executive power in Russia. When Congress continued to block his initiatives, Yeltsin resolved once more to take decisive action. On this occasion, he made sure that he was backed by his ministers and military officers before announcing emergency measures on 21 September 1993. In a seventeen point decree, Yeltsin dissolved Congress, announced fresh parliamentary elections and called a referendum on the new constitution. Both votes were to be held on 12 December. Yeltsin made it clear that he fully expected the people to back him and vote for a more reform-minded parliament (*Rossiiskie vesti*, 22 September 1993). In anticipation of a great electoral victory, Yeltsin brought Gaidar back into the government as First Deputy President on 28 September, indicating a determination to return to his earlier more radical policies.

Both Rutskoi and Khasbulatov denounced the President's decree as an effective coup d'etat and called an emergency session of parliament (*Moscow Times*, 22 September 1993). As the official reason for the dispute with Yeltsin was over the constitution, it would have strengthened their democratic credentials had they fought for their ideals at the ballot box. Instead, they decided to occupy the White House in a conscious replay of the August coup. Nevertheless, there can be no doubt that the rebels had a strong case for arguing Yeltsin's actions were unconstitutional. Yeltsin admitted as much but argued, with some truth, that the constitution, written in 1978 in the days of Brezhnev, was an inadequate document on which to base political actions in the post-Soviet period. Yeltsin also pointed out that the most vociferous defenders of the constitution - a red-brown alliance, as he called it - had poor liberal credentials themselves (Yeltsin, 1994: 242).

Clearly, Yeltsin took the initiative when he closed down parliament and suspended the constitution, but conspiracy theorists have gone further in suggesting
that Yeltsin consciously provoked the violent climax on 3-4 October. There are
two versions of what happened. The official view is that the leaders in the White
House made a bid for power and were close to victory before the rebels were
beaten back at *Ostankino*, Moscow's TV centre (Yeltsin, 1994). The second
argues that Yeltsin encouraged the rebel uprising on Sunday 3 October as a means
of legitimising the assault on the White House and the ultimate destruction of his
opponents (Steele, 1994: 377-382; Clark, 1995: 246-264). What is the evidence?
To provide any answers it is necessary to give a brief outline of the events surrounding the attempted coup of October 1993.

After the announcement of emergency measures, the Constitutional Court sat
on 22 September and found Yeltsin's decree to be unlawful. In the light of this
ruling, Congress stripped Yeltsin of his powers as President and swore in Alexander Rutskoi as acting President (*Rossiiskaya gazeta*, 23 September 1993). In
response, Yeltsin decided to isolate the rebels inside the White House and cut
off all telephone communications. Two days later, after two people died as a
result of an armed attack by rebels on a military building, the White House was
placed under seige. Electricity and heat were turned off and razor wire was
placed around the building. People could still leave the building but entry was
barred by interior police.

Rutskoi, as self-proclaimed President, set up a parallel government in the
hope of undermining Yeltsin's authority. In this, Rutskoi had in mind the role
Yeltsin had played in the August coup as an alternative focus of legitimacy to
the Emergency Committee. As acting President, Rutskoi made appeals to the
military, but only an estimated one to two hundred officers actually came over
to the White House (Taylor, B., 1994: 10). Rutskoi appointed Vladislav Achalov
as a rival Defence Minister, but it was a poor choice. Achalov was not a very
popular figure and Rutskoi's tactic of trying to split the military seemed to
alienate many officers. The majority, including Defence Minister, Pavel Grachev,
remained loyal to Yeltsin throughout the crisis and other key government figures,
such as the Prime Minister, Viktor Chernomyrdin, also came out forcefully behind Yeltsin's emergency measures (*Moscow Times*, 22 September 1993).

Overall, relatively few supported the rebels. There were several thousand
outside the White House most days and around 15,000 on the final day, but a
poll taken on 23 September found 62 percent supported Yeltsin's emergency
measures and only six percent recognised Rutskoi as *de facto* President (*International Herald Tribune*, 6 October 1993). However, the rebels took comfort

from the fact that the majority of regional soviets backed the White House and opposed parliament's dissolution. Support for the rebels in the regions only added to fears in the Kremlin that if the crisis were allowed to drag on for any length of time, the country might actually fall apart (Yeltsin, 1994: 266).

The siege lasted almost two weeks. As it dragged on, Rutskoi and Khasbulatov, holed up in the White House, became dominated by extremist figures, such as General Albert Makashov and the self-styled Stalinist Viktor Anpilov (*Moscow Times*, 29 September 1993). Many of the more pragmatic deputies left the White House - some after receiving monetary inducements from Yeltsin, others simply to avoid bloodshed. On the first day of the crisis, 658 delegates out of a total of 1,033 were in the White House to attend the emergency session of Congress. By the end, there were only about one hundred.

After a week, an uneasy and sometimes violent stalemate was reached. In an attempt to break it, Yeltsin, on 29 September, ordered all weaponry in the White House to be handed over within twenty-four hours (*Moscow Times*, 30 September 1993). Fears grew of a violent end to the seige. However, the deadline was allowed to pass after the intervention of the Russian Orthodox Church. Finally, an agreement was hammered out early Friday morning, 1 October, stating that weapons would be placed under the joint guard of government and rebels. In return, electricity was turned on, with the promise of a withdrawal of the interior police from around the White House.

After Yeltsin's concession, the rebel leadership appeared to believe they had gained the upper hand in the power struggle. As a result, they reneged on their earlier agreement and restated their absolutist demand that everything should return to the position before 21 September. This would mean no parliamentary elections and no new constitution. Clearly the demand was unacceptable to Yeltsin. So he issued a second ultimatum on 2 October, demanding that everyone in the White House leave the building within forty-eight hours. Once more, the crisis appeared to heading towards a violent climax.

Next day, Sunday 3 October, about 15,000 rebel supporters overwhelmed 5,000 interior troops to gain access to the White House. The seige was finally broken. The guards around the parliament building under instruction from the Interior Minister, General Viktor Yerin, put up no opposition (Steele, 1994: 378). Believing that the security forces had deserted the government, Rutskoi and Khasbulatov thought the critical moment had arrived. They addressed their supporters from the White House balcony and called for insurrection. Rutskoi called on his supporters to take the mayor's office and then the *Ostankino* TV centre (Kutsyllo, 1993: 112). Both institutions had been unabashedly pro-Yeltsin during the seige and a source of particular anger to the rebels.

The mayor's office was close to the White House and had been heavily guarded throughout the emergency. On 3 October, however, the troops had disappeared and the buildings were taken with ease early on Sunday afternoon (Kutsyllo, 1993: 115). At 7.30 p.m., the attack on the TV centre began when a grenade was thrown killing a guard. Reinforcements were sent to *Ostankino* to secure its defence against a mob of about 4,000. 62 died in the subsequent battle on the streets of Moscow (*Moscow Times*, 5 October 1994). Radio and TV broadcasting from *Ostankino* was closed down until midnight. This led Khasbulatov to believe that victory was at hand. He declared that the TV centre had been seized, and went on, 'Today we must seize the Kremlin' (*International Herald Tribune*, 9-10 October 1993).

Yeltsin returned from his dacha at 6 p.m. on the evening of 3 October to direct operations against the rebels. Rutskoi still refused to negotiate unless parliament was reopened. Defence Minister Grachev told Yeltsin that the military was ready to aid interior forces around strategic institutions in Moscow, but troops were slow to arrive and fighting continued around *Ostankino* into the small hours (Yeltsin, 1994: 273). It was only after Yeltsin gave guarantees that he would take responsibility for military action that Grachev finally agreed to storm the White House the following morning, Monday 4 October (Yeltsin, 1994: 278). Even then, the crack Alpha troops refused to act until one of their members was killed by a sniper (Yeltsin, 1994: 12).

At 7 a.m., the assault on the White House began and lasted ten hours. From various positions around the building, tanks shelled the White House without any response. The rebel leaders tried to negotiate their surrender as soon as the assault began. Finally, in early evening the rebels came out of the burning building and gave themselves up. Rutskoi and Khasbulatov were both arrested. According to the official figures, the casualty list during the course of the emergency was 187 dead and 437 wounded - a massive increase on the three that died during the August coup of 1991.

But what of the two theories on the crisis? There was some truth in both of them. Yeltsin acted provocatively in suspending the constitution, but the rebels undeniably made a bid for power on 3 October and tried to violently overthrow a democratically elected President. Many of those supporting Rutskoi and Khasbulatov were extremists with no interest in democracy or compromise. Moreover, the evidence suggests that all the violence was initiated by the rebels or their supporters. An officer was killed by the rebels as they marched on the White House on the morning of 3 October, and the death of a guard outside

*Ostankino* appeared to precipitate the violence there too. The conspiracy theory, however, rests on two main factors. First, why were the rebels allowed such easy entry into the White House? It was obvious the crisis was reaching a climax on that weekend of 3-4 October, yet the interior troops around the White House put up no defence. Furthermore, the guards which had been standing outside the mayor's office and TV centre throughout the crisis were nowhere to be seen when the rebel assault began. Where had they gone? No one seemed to know (Kutsyllo, 1993: 115). Second, conspiracy theorists were sceptical that the state, to use Yeltsin's own words, was 'hanging by a thread' (Yeltsin, 1994: 274). Despite the rhetoric of rebel leaders, the Kremlin was never under threat during the violence of Sunday night. The mob around *Ostankino* was easily beaten away, only about a hundred rebels were armed and the Yeltsin side suffered only one casualty during the seige (Clark, 1995: 247). In fact, many eyewitnesses reported that most of the shooting on the night of the 3-4 October was carried out by government forces. It is also doubted that TV and radio had to be closed down. The *Ostankino* director, Vyacheslav Bragin, under orders from Chernomyrdin, forbade any filming of the fighting around the TV centre which might have revealed the one-sided nature of the battle (Clark, 1995: 247). The blank TV screens, however, all added to the impression of impending civil war and revolution which became the ultimate justification for the subsequent attack on the White House.

Yeltsin supporters, however, argued that civil war had been a real possibility. It was feared that some military officers might defect to the rebel camp once the fighting broke out (*Moscow News*, no. 4, 1994). The hesitations of military officers on the Sunday night and the long delay in troops reaching Moscow city centre are cited as proof of the possible dangers. Yeltsin had to go personally to the military high command in the early hours of Monday morning and give his Defence Minister, Grachev, a written order before he agreed to strike against the White House.

It may be that the conspiracy theory stretches the facts a little, but at a minimum Yeltsin used the opportunity to out-manoeuvre his most recalcitrant opponents. The West supported the action in the hope that it represented the final death throes of the communist system and would facilitate reform. Yeltsin, for his part, hoped the storming of the White House would restore his prestige as the right man for a crisis (Yeltsin, 1994: 6). Yeltsin and his supporters, however, were disappointed. Unlike August 1991, Yeltsin was not perceived in Russia as the hero of the hour. The former Soviet President, Mikhail Gorbachev, articulated a common view when he said that the assault on the White House on

Monday morning had been unnecessary since the danger of revolution had already passed (*Moscow News*, 7-13 October 1993).

The events of October heralded neither a more democratic state nor a more workable one. Reformers were greatly concerned that once again the military had moved centre stage in Russian politics. It was an uncomfortable thought that the process of reform had become increasingly reliant on the support of a powerful but disillusioned military.

## Yeltsin's fall in popularity

After the defeat of Rutskoi and Khasbulatov in October 1993, Yeltsin drew up a new constitution with the aim of giving the President far greater executive powers at the expense of parliament and the republics. It may have been necessary to have a strong President given the lack of viable political parties in Russia, but inevitably it also increased the fears of the emergence of a personal dictatorship.

The new constitution abolished the two-tier system of the Supreme Soviet and the Congress of People's Deputies in favour of a bicameral parliament. The 178-seat upper house was called the Federation Council and the 450-seat lower house, the State Duma. The President had the right to veto parliamentary legislation and in contrast to the pre-October version of the constitution, he was allowed to dissolve parliament and declare a state of emergency. The President also had the right to issue decrees which the new Federal Assembly could not cancel. Any changes to the constitution required a two-thirds majority in both the Federal Council and the State Duma. Democrats feared that the Duma would resemble the parliament of Tsarist days (from which it took its name) and be little more than a talking shop.

Before the election, Yeltsin closed down the Constitutional Court, reduced the power of local government and suspended publication of some newspapers. Furthermore, Yeltsin reneged on a promise during the seige of the White House to hold early presidential elections and said he would serve the full term through to June 1996. The speaker of the upper house, Vladimir Shumeiko, supported by Yeltsin aides, even floated the idea in the summer of 1994 that presidential elections should be delayed beyond the five-year term (*Moscow News*, 8-14 July 1994). With the media in Yeltsin's pocket and his main opponents behind bars, commentators openly wondered whether the December elections could ever be called free.

However, Yeltsin did make concessions as the election drew nearer. Parties and blocs were allowed to contest the election if they accepted the principles of democracy and received 100,000 signatures. Thirteen parties - including Zyuganov's Communist Party, Zhirinovsky's ultra-nationalist LDPR and Gaidar's pro-government Russia's Choice - were successful and registered for the elections. All the registered parties were accorded time on television to debate the issues. However, in a clear breach with democratic values, Yeltsin forbade any discussion of the new constitution which accorded so much power to the President.

Russia's Choice was backed by Yeltsin, although he refused to campaign on its behalf. Yeltsin wanted to stay above the political fray. However, his apparent lack of enthusiasm for the party was mirrored more generally in the country as a whole. Gaidar's party looked like yet another *ad hoc* creation with no roots outside Moscow - and precious few roots, for that matter, outside the walls of the Kremlin itself. The reformers also fatally weakened their position prior to the election by being unable to offer a unified front. Instead, the reformers split into three parties - Russia's Choice, Shakhrai's Unity party and Yavlinsky's Yabloko.[1]

Nevertheless, all the polls pointed to a comfortable victory for the reformers. But once again the polls proved wrong. According to the new constitution, electors had two votes - one for the party or bloc, and the other for individual candidates in constituencies. On the party slate, Zhirinovsky's Liberal Democratic Party of Russia (LDPR) recorded the highest vote with 23 percent; and Russia's Choice led by Gaidar got only 15 percent. The reformers did better in the constituencies, however, and as a result, Russia's Choice won the most seats in the Duma with 70, but out of a total of 450, this was still a disappointing result and fell well short of the expected parliamentary majority. The LDPR won 64 seats; the communists 48 seats and their close allies, the Agrarian Party 33 (*Byulleten' tsentral'noi izbiratel'noi kommissii Rossiiskoi Federatsii*, no. 12, 1994: 67).

No party or bloc won a majority in parliament. But the result was a boost to Zhirinovsky and Zyuganov, and gave them both a legitimate voice in Russian politics. In contrast, Gaidar's position was gravely weakened as leader of Russia's Choice and he resigned as deputy Prime Minister in January 1994. The West was as shocked as Yeltsin by the result. Not only was Zhirinovsky seen as

---

[1] In Russian, *yabloko* means apple, but here it is also meant as a rough acronym for the three leading members of the party: Yavlinsky, Boldyrev and Lukin.

a threat to peace and stability, but the vote indicated that since the April referendum the Russian people had turned against reform. No longer could nationalist and communist deputies be dismissed as unrepresentative of public opinion. For the first time, Yeltsin had effectively lost an election.

Yeltsin had two choices - to tough it out in the name of reform or shift to a more nationalist position in line with public opinion. If he chose to fight, Yeltsin could take comfort from the fact that constitutional changes had rendered parliament far weaker than before. However, it soon became clear that the Duma was not going to be totally subservient to the President. One of its first acts in February 1994 was to grant an amnesty to all those involved in both the August coup and the seige of the White House. The result of this decision was to allow Yeltsin's bitterest enemies to re-enter the political fray.

Table 9:2
**Fall in Yeltsin's popularity**

| | | |
|---|---|---|
| December 1992: | 37.0% | (Gaidar removed) |
| July 1993: | 28.0% | (After the April referendum) |
| October 1994: | 13.0% | (Black Tuesday: the collapse of the ruble) |
| December 1994: | 11.8% | (After the start of the war in Chechnya) |
| June 1995: | 6.0% | (After the Budyonnovsk hostage crisis) |

*Source: Moscow News*, 30 June-6 July 1995: 2.

Yeltsin's reputation continued to slip as he was unable to reassert his position after the elections. The President who had criticised Gorbachev's lurch to the right in the winter of 1990, now began to surround himself with a small group of more hardline advisers, such as his bodyguard Alexander Korzhakov and the chief of the Interior Ministry Mikhail Barsukov. As Yeltsin's popularity declined dramatically in 1994 (see table 9:2), his maverick behaviour became a matter of embarrassment.

In October 1994, the Duma finally stirred itself. On Black Tuesday, the ruble lost 25 percent of its value in one day. Most of its value was later restored, but the Duma argued the fall of the ruble was due to ministerial incompetence and held a vote of no confidence in the government on 11 October 1994. Although only 54 deputies supported the government, the motion failed because the constitution required an absolute majority. Less than a year later, in June 1995, after Chechen rebels took hostages in the Russian town of Budyonnovsk, a second no-confidence vote was held. On this occasion, the government was defeated when 243 backed the motion. However, the action was little more than an indication of growing unease in the Duma over the direction of policy. For, according to article 93 (1) of the new constitution, the Duma had no power to overthrow the President except through impeachment, and article 117 stated that an absolute majority vote of no-confidence by the Duma in the government could be accepted or rejected by the President. If rejected, the Duma could vote again and if an absolute majority was again in favour of the no-confidence motion, the President was obliged to announce the resignation of the government and dissolve the Duma. In July, the Duma voted against committing suicide when only 193 voted against the government, thus falling 33 below the necessary absolute majority.

This showed the executive power of the President. However, Yeltsin found himself increasingly unable to wield it. Two debilitating heart attacks in 1995 weakened his position further whilst parliamentary elections at the end of the year confirmed the decline of the reformers. Russia's Democratic Choice, led by Gaidar, gained only nine seats, Yabloko got 45, and Chernomyrdin's new centrist party, Our Home Is Russia, picked up 55.[2] The vote for Zhirinovsky's Liberal Party fell, but he still held on to 51 seats. But the main winner in December was clearly the Communist Party and its close ally, the Agrarian Party, which together won 187 seats (Sakwa, 1996: 392-3). The Communist Party fought a good campaign. It was one of the few parties in Russia which was well-organised, could boast a mass membership of about a half million and branches in most areas of the country. The communists appeared particularly well-placed for the upcoming presidential election in June 1996.

## The presidential election

The communist candidate, Gennady Zyuganov, was well ahead of Yeltsin in all opinion polls as the campaign process began in early 1996. However, Yeltsin surprised a lot of people with the vigour of his election campaign - at least in the first round. Yeltsin argued that a vote for Zyuganov would reverse all his

---

2  Gaidar changed the name of his party leading up to the parliamentary elections in 1995 from Russia's Choice to Russia's Democratic Choice.

reforms and plunge the country back into the dark ages of neo-Stalinism. Whether such an interpretation of Zyuganov's policies was fair was hotly debated inside Russia. Zyuganov's statements on the issue were ambiguous, whilst he surrounded himself with unrepentant Stalinists who, many feared, would pull the strings behind the scenes if the communists were to win. By the spring, Yeltsin began to get his message across and he moved ahead of Zyuganov in most opinion polls. The final result in the first round, however, was close. Yeltsin won 35 percent of the vote, with Zyuganov trailing by only three percent (Sakwa, 1996: 393).

The surprise result, however, was that of Alexander Lebed who came in third with almost 15 percent. Lebed is an authoritarian Russian nationalist but his campaign against crime and corruption hit a chord with the public, especially amongst that section of the electorate which might otherwise have voted communist. After Lebed's strong first round performance, he was brought briefly into the Yeltsin administration, until his dismissal in October 1996, as head of the powerful Security Council. Lebed's support for Yeltsin appeared important in Yeltsin's final victory when he received 53 percent of the vote - a decisive 13 percent ahead of Zyuganov (*Political Calendar*, 4 July 1996: 5). The balance of power in the Kremlin began to shift as Yeltsin sacked a number of his closest advisers, including Defence Minister Pavel Grachev, Interior Minister Mikhail Barsukov and his personal bodyguard Alexander Korzhakov. The new powerbrokers who emerged were Yeltsin's own daughter, Tatyana Dyachenko, and the former Minister of Privatisation, Anatoly Chubais.

The West was relieved when Yeltsin won the election. Despite his health problems, his maverick behaviour and instinctual authoritarianism, Yeltsin was still seen as the best man to continue the reform process. However, democracy in Russia is still far from secure. Russia has still not witnessed a constitutional transfer of power. Until this happens, final judgement on the fate of Russian democracy must be withheld. This is not just an academic point. Both before and during the election campaign, influential figures in the Yeltsin camp, fearing a communist victory, routinely spoke to the press about postponing or cancelling the presidential election. Doubts were also frequently expressed in the Russian media that Yeltsin would ever voluntarily give up power to Zyuganov (*Moscow News*, 13-19 June 1996 and 20-26 June 1996). It was such talk that led commentators to fear that a communist victory might lead to civil war.

Yet despite all the rumours, the presidential election did go ahead on schedule, and despite Yeltsin's control over much of the media, international monitors declared the election free and fair (*Political Calendar*, 4 July 1996: 2).

Furthermore, 69 and 67 percent respectively voted in the two rounds of voting - rather more than typically vote in presidential elections in the United States (*Political Calendar*, 4 July 1996: 7). It is still true, however, that the Russian people are generally bored with the process of politics. They crave order and stability. They have frequently voted in significant numbers for populist and anti-democratic candidates, like Zhirinovsky, and 40 percent still voted for Zyuganov in the second round of the presidential election.

Nevertheless, democracy in Russia has survived - despite an economic crash worse than that experienced by Weimar Germany in the inter-war years. For that, the Russian people deserve much credit. It is time now, however, for the politicians to act more responsibly. They need to escape the Leninist mind-set and be more prepared to compromise and abide by the democratic spirit of the constitution. Storming the White House has got to be a thing of the past. More than anything, Russia needs a viable and responsible opposition which can offer the Russian people a credible alternative government. As yet, there is no sign of such a party or bloc. Until this happens, the elections in Russia will never take on the routine nature of their equivalents in the more mature democracies of the West.

# Chapter Ten

# REGIONAL CONFLICTS IN THE CIS

As chapter three showed, few in Russia actively willed the end of the Soviet Union. The USSR was brought down by a combination of nationalists in the non-Russian republics and a relatively small band of pro-Western, reformist politicians centred around Yeltsin. Gorbachev's supporters argued that the formation of the CIS in December 1991 was nothing less than a second coup against the Soviet President in little more than three months. No referendum nor presidential election was held in Russia to ratify the abolition of the union. Gorbachev accepted the end of the USSR and resigned on Christmas Day 1991, not because he supported the creation of the CIS, but because he recognised that he had little alternative. Effective power in the USSR had already shifted to the republics and Yeltsin's Russia. Both Gorbachev and the communist hardliners were defeated.

Post-Soviet Russia remained a huge country, but it had been reduced to roughly the borders of the seventeenth century. From being a mighty superpower, Russia now had a population and an economy slightly smaller than that of Brazil (*International Herald Tribune*, 5 March 1996). Since Russian nationalism had been so closely tied to concepts of empire and messianism, the people had grave difficulties getting used to their country's much reduced international status. A poll conducted in March 1992 found that roughly 70 percent of the Russian population favoured the restoration of the Soviet Union (Lester, 1995: 283).

The end of the cold war appeared to leave Russia without a purpose and without a clearly defined national identity. However, for liberal reformers, such as Burbulis, Gaidar, Kozyrev and Shakhrai, who devised the *Belovezhsky* agreement, union institutions were seen as the main repository of reaction (*Moscow News*, 15-21 February 1996). The centre had to be abolished to finally kill off communism. Radical reform would no longer be constrained by more backward political cultures in Central Asia. It was thought an independent Russia would prosper since Moscow would no longer need to subsidise other republics or police their ethnic conflicts. Russia would finally release itself from the burdens of empire and be able to develop as a truly democratic state (see Grachev, 1995: 66). Russian reformers called for a policy which amounted to the benign neglect of the other Soviet successor states.

However, such a policy did not last long. By 1993, the Yeltsin administration was adamantly stating in both its Foreign Policy Concept and its new Military Doctrine that the CIS (or the 'near abroad' as the Russians sometimes called it) was now Moscow's top foreign policy priority (see *International Affairs*, January 1993; and *Rossiiskie vesti*, 18 November 1993). This shift occurred in part because of the rise of nationalism in the country, but even more important was the realisation amongst officials of every political stripe, that a policy of benign neglect was simply not tenable. As a land-based empire, Russia found it far more difficult to shed its 'colonies' than earlier European imperial powers. The links between Moscow and Soviet successor states remained close after the collapse of the USSR. There were three main reasons for this.

First, there was the issue of the Russian diaspora. An estimated 25 million Russians lived in the fourteen other Soviet successor states and whilst many nationalists exaggerated the discrimination against the Russian minorities, Moscow had an undoubted obligation to defend their interests. This was not only a matter of basic human rights but of practical politics too. For if discrimination led to mass migration, it would put untold economic and social pressure on the Russian Federation at a time of uncertain transition. Fears of discrimination also led to war in Moldova and the threat of war elsewhere in the CIS. Second, Russia retained economic interests in the near abroad. The severing of economic ties after the breakup of the Soviet Union had been a major factor in the subsequent economic crisis in all Soviet successor states. The economies of the former Soviet Union were highly interdependent and inter-republic trade collapsed by 50 percent in the first two years after the formation of the CIS (Webber, 1996: 292). It was estimated that 20 percent of the economic slump in Russia was due to the breakup of the USSR; 40 percent in Ukraine; and 70 percent in

Central Asia (*Russian Review*, 12 December 1994). This basic fact was increasingly acknowledged by all sides leading to gradual moves towards closer economic integration in the CIS.

Finally, Russia became increasingly concerned over the rise in ethnic conflict on its periphery. The abolition of the USSR had not led, as many had expected, to the end of ethnic conflict. On the contrary, instability and violence escalated and Moscow became increasingly involved as an external power in these areas. Moscow presented itself as a stabilising force in the region and always denied any imperialist intent. Moscow had to act, it was claimed, because the Soviet successor states were too weak to defend themselves and the rest of the international community was unwilling to contribute its own peacekeeping troops. Moreover, Moscow argued that Russia's peacekeeping efforts should be supported by the UN since they accorded with international law and the CIS collective security agreement of March 1992 (see *New Times*, no. 4, January 1994; and Kreikemeyer and Zagorski, 1996). Thus, Moscow, it was claimed, intervened only by invitation and always respected the sovereignty and territorial integrity of the state concerned. Furthermore, Moscow also sought, wherever possible, to act not unilaterally but as part of a multi-national CIS force.

The American analyst, Raymond Garthoff, generally accepted Moscow's claim. He pointed out that in the five principle conflicts in the former Soviet Union - Nagorno-Karabakh, South Ossetia, Abkhazia, Trans-Dniester and Tajikistan - none were instigated by Moscow. Furthermore, no attempt had been made to redraw boundaries by force or take back regions, such as the Crimea, South Ossetia or Abkhazia, which had expressed a desire to be reintegrated into the Russian Federation (Garthoff, 1994: 787). This remains true. However, Garthoff was writing in 1993, and there is little doubt that Moscow has since adopted a more interventionist policy in the CIS (see Allison, 1996). In particular, Moscow was determined to maintain its influence in the Caucasus where it had important strategic and economic interests.

The events in Chechnya were important in this context too. For although Moscow attempted to differentiate its activities in Chechnya from those outside the Russian Federation, the brutal war waged by the Russians in Chechnya seemed symptomatic of a renewed national assertiveness. It also seemed symptomatic of Yeltsin's inability to resolve problems in Russia without resort to violence. This was unfortunate, for in most cases Russia acted in the CIS - as Garthoff suggested - with moderation and reasonable goodwill. Moscow recognised it had little to gain from instability on its periphery and much to lose. This will be shown below, with the case studies arranged in ascending order of

Russian interventionism. First, however, it is important to say a few words about the CIS.


## The CIS

As stated in chapter three, the CIS was formed on 8 December 1991 by the three slavic states of the USSR - Russia, Ukraine and Belorus. It was extended on 21 December to include eight other Soviet successor states. Only Georgia and the three Baltic Republics - Latvia, Lithuania and Estonia - refused to join, although the national parliaments in both Azerbaijan and Moldova temporarily refused to ratify the agreement. By 1993, however, only the Baltic Republics remained outside the CIS framework.

The CIS was never perceived by its members to be the successor to the Soviet Union. It was not a state, it had no central decision-making bodies and it had no authority in international law. The CIS was a loose organisation which simply provided the leaders of Soviet successor states with a forum to discuss issues of mutual interest. Its future, however, remained in doubt. Was the CIS a purely transitional organisation whose main duty was the management of the breakup of the USSR? Or could the CIS survive and play a role similar to the EU? All members had different conceptions of the CIS. Some republics - like Ukraine, Moldova and Azerbaijan - were most opposed to the development of any supranational institutions. Others, however, hoped such moves could help stimulate trade and provide collective security against the threat of internal violence and external aggression.

Obviously, the destiny of the CIS lay with Russia. Russia was the dominant country in the region in terms of size, natural resources, economic strength and military power. Russia comprised 50 percent of the USSR's population and produced 60 percent of its GDP (Aslund, 1995: 104). After the breakup of the Soviet Union, Russian military forces numbered 2.8 million and according to the commander of the CIS, Yevgeny Shaposhnikov, Russia inherited 70 percent of the Soviet Union's nuclear arsenal and 80 percent of its air force and navy (Webber, 1996: 175).

Initially, Yeltsin appeared to take relatively little interest in the CIS, but this soon changed as Moscow began to recognise the near abroad as a top priority. The Foreign Ministry set up a department to deal with the CIS countries in the autumn of 1992, and in January 1994 a separate Ministry for the CIS was created with a high ranking minister appointed the following November (Webber,

1996: 100). Three matters were of greatest concern to Russia in the CIS. First, the future of the Soviet military; second, the issue of peacekeeping, which is the focus of this chapter; and third, economic policy. All three will be briefly discussed below.

The possible disintegration of the Soviet military had been one of the biggest concerns as the USSR collapsed. The formation of the CIS had been perceived as a means of getting military acceptance for the breakup, for it offered the prospect of some kind of unified military in the post-Soviet era. However, it was agreed in December 1991 that states could form their own national armies, and in spring 1992, Russia decided to form its own military and Ministry of Defence. The failure to create a unified military force was finally recognised by the CIS when the heads of state formally agreed to abolish the joint command of forces in September 1993. Although some co-ordinating structures continued to exist, the abolition effectively served to emphasise Russian military dominance on the territory of the former Soviet Union.

Nevertheless, a Collective Security Treaty was agreed in May 1992. Article four sanctioned the use of military assistance by participating states should one of their number be subject to an act of aggression (*Krasnaya zvezda*, 23 May 1993). Like most other CIS agreements, however, it flattered to deceive. First, only six states signed up. Second, there was no guarantee equivalent to article 5 of NATO's Washington Treaty which committed all members to come to the aid of another in the event of aggression. Azerbaijan was keen to have such security guarantees since it would then require the CIS to take some action against Armenia (see below). Russia, however, was not prepared to give such broad commitments. Russian troops were ill-trained for peacekeeping duties and the cost of any such role was thought to be prohibitive. Ukraine, for its part, refused to sign the Collective Security Treaty fearing it would give Moscow a free hand to further its national interest by force (see Webber, 1996: 193-4).

In economic relations a similarly mixed pattern evolved. Logic suggested that the years of economic interdependence within the USSR should encourage the maintenance of close links between the Soviet successor states. However, more short-term nationalist interests predominated. Russia was unwilling to allow other more conservative states to dictate the speed and direction of economic reform. It, therefore, cut subsidies to other republics through raising the prices of its exports closer to world prices. Since Russia was one of the most radical republics, it was unprepared to allow other states to stall reform. As a result, it effectively abandoned the ruble zone over the period 1992-3 to prevent other republics from undermining Moscow's more monetarist policies through profligate spending and credit policies.

In the circumstances, it was scarcely surprising that proposals for an economic union in October 1993 were not taken up. As time went on, the growing differences between the economic structures and performances of CIS states made integration all the more difficult to achieve. Moscow was dubious about the prospects of integration fearing the costs would fall predominantly on Russia. Some other republics also were wary fearing that integration would only lead to their further subordination to Russian national interests. Non-Russian nationalists may have exaggerated the dangers, but Moscow's increasing willingness to use its economic power as a bargaining lever for unilateral advantage fuelled suspicions.

The moves towards integration appeared to get a big boost in March 1996 when the Duma passed a non-binding resolution which abrogated the original *Belovezhsky* agreement. On 29 March, leaders of Russia, Belorus, Kazakhstan and Kyrgyzstan met in the Kremlin and formed the club of four. The group favoured further integration in the fields of economics, culture and education. The meeting also set up an Interstate Council and an Integration Committee. Four days later, the process of integration seemed to take another leap forward when Moscow and Minsk decided to set up a Community of Sovereign Republics. Initially, only Belorus and Russia signed up although others were invited to join. The treaty called for a common constitution, a common budget, common currency, the co-ordination of foreign policy and the integration of military forces.

20,000 people demonstrated in Minsk against the treaty which many saw as a prelude to a full merger with Moscow. Yeltsin denied this was the aim although Alexander Lukashenko, the authoritarian leader in Minsk, was openly supportive of the idea. The reason was not too difficult to discern. The Belorussian economy was in severe crisis - annual per capita income had fallen from $5,000 before the breakup of the USSR to only $996 in 1995 (*Time*, 15 April 1996). Lukashenko is looking towards Moscow to pay off Belorussian debts and kick start his economy. Kazakhstan and Kyrgyzstan are less in need of Russian subsidies, but they feel that closer ties with Moscow will help stabilise the position in their countries.

It is far from clear whether Yeltsin's moves towards re-integration represent much more than a populist attempt to curry favour amongst Russian nationalists. There is certainly little enthusiasm in Moscow to underwrite the bankrupt economies of fellow CIS states. By 1994, Russian subsidies to other CIS states had already reached an estimated $18 billion per year (*Russian Review*, 12

December 1994). There appeared to be little incentive for Moscow to maintain such subsidies in the longer term.

Thus, despite the rise of the empire builders as a political force in Russian politics, we can still expect leaders in the Kremlin to drag their feet over the issue of reintegration. For there are few obvious advantages for Moscow in pursuing political reintegration. In fact, Yeltsin has pursued a highly successful policy since 1993 which has seen him increase Russian influence throughout the CIS without the incubus of empire. A mix of diplomacy and sabre-rattling has proved sufficient to bring reluctant states, like Georgia, Azerbaijan and Moldova, back into the fold as full members of the CIS. Others like the club of four recognise the economic benefits of closer ties. Any attempt to reimpose a Russian empire, on the other hand, is likely to lead to the brutality and economic devastation the world has witnessed in Chechnya since December 1994.

### Ukraine and the Crimea

Relations between Ukraine and Russia were vital for the future of the CIS. They were the largest republics and economically the most important. Ukraine had claims to being a regional power. With a population of 52 million, it had produced about 20 percent of the Soviet Union's consumer goods and was commonly referred to as the country's bread basket. Yet Ukraine felt very vulnerable as a nation-state. For Russia was seen as a constant threat to its independence and sovereignty. This was due to a combination of tangible and less tangible factors. Most obviously, Russia was a huge country with a population almost three times the size of Ukraine. Russia retained a massive army and a richness of natural resources, especially energy resources, which gave Moscow leverage in its relations with Kiev. Russia could also claim an interest in Ukrainian affairs since more than a fifth of the population was Russian.

Leonid Kravchuk, the first President of independent Ukraine, had the difficult task of seeking legitimacy through appeals to nationalism, whilst at the same time trying not to offend the Russian minority. He was not altogether successful. For tensions were high between Moscow and Kiev in the first few years after the collapse of the Soviet Union. This tension found expression in the tussle over nuclear weapons and the Black Sea Fleet. As the next chapter shows, the question of nuclear weapons had largely been resolved by 1994, but how the Black Sea Fleet was to be divided between the two republics remained a live issue. The dispute added to the tension between the two states whilst also undermining the effectiveness of the fleet through the uncertainty over its future. Discipline suffered and there were problems over financing (Webber, 1996: 187-8).

What made resolving the issue of the Black Sea Fleet so difficult was the fact that it was based at Sevastopol in the Crimea - a region in Ukraine which was seeking reunification with Russia. The Crimea had been a part of Ukraine only since 1954 when Khrushchev presented it to Kiev as a gift to mark the 300th anniversary of Ukrainian liberation from Polish-Lithuanian rule. Khrushchev's gift was of little significance as long as both Russia and Ukraine were a part of the USSR. However, as the USSR broke up, the ethnic Russians, who made up sixty percent of the population of 2.7 million, formed the Republican Movement of the Crimea and began to press for secession from Ukraine.

These moves were actively encouraged by nationalists in the Russian parliament which in May 1992 declared illegal the 1954 transfer of the Crimea to Ukrainian jurisdiction. Yeltsin quickly acted to soothe frayed nerves in Kiev and denounced the declaration at the June summit between the two republics. However, this did not stop parliament voting unanimously in July 1993 both to reclaim control over the city of Sevastopol and to bring the entire Black Sea Fleet under Russian control. This declaration, however, was rendered null and void when Yeltsin forcibly dissolved parliament in September 1993.

In the Crimea, meanwhile, it appeared that moves towards secession were gaining pace. In the Crimea's first presidential elections in January 1994, 70 percent voted for Yuri Meshkov, a Russian nationalist who campaigned on a programme of independence for the Crimea. Two months later, Meshkov's party won a landslide victory in elections to the Crimean parliament. A non-binding plebiscite gave an overwhelming majority for greater autonomy for Crimea and closer ties to Russia. The local parliament passed constitutional amendments raising the status of Crimea to that of a republic providing it with the consequent right to raise a militia and establish Crimean citizenship (Webber, 1996: 103).

The crisis in the Crimea appeared to be moving towards a climax until the more pro-Russian Leonid Kuchma replaced Kravchuk as President in July. Relations between the two states improved, and this greatly affected politics in the Crimea itself. In March 1995, Kuchma moved decisively and sacked Meshkov. Crimea's constitution was annulled and new elections called for June. The mood in the Crimea had changed. This time, the pro-Russian nationalists lost heavily and Yevhen Suprunyuk was voted Prime Minister, a man who favoured closer co-operation with Kiev.

The Yeltsin administration played an important role in defusing the tension in the Crimea. Despite parliament's provocative actions, Yeltsin consistently promoted a negotiated settlement and refused to contemplate any alteration of borders. Instead, Moscow called for greater autonomy for the Crimea and the respect of minority rights in the whole of Ukraine. This was undoubtedly a sensible policy and one that appeared to be successful after Kuchma showed a willingness to co-operate more with Russia over issues such as the Non-Proliferation Treaty and the division of the Black Sea Fleet.

## Nagorno-Karabakh

The conflict in Nagorno-Karabakh between Armenia and Azerbaijan had been going on since 1988 (see chapter 3), but it was only after the collapse of the Soviet Union that all-out war was unleashed. As Russia withdrew from its garrison in the autonomous republic, pro-Yerevan forces in Nagorno-Karabakh took advantage in May 1992 to drill a land corridor seven miles wide through to Armenia. The following year, pro-Armenian forces launched a second major offensive which was successful in taking up to a fifth of Azeri territory. This humiliating defeat led to political chaos in Baku and ultimately, in the summer of 1993, to the remarkable return to power of the old Brezhnevite politburo member, Gaidar Aliyev.

The war over Nagorno-Karabakh bore resemblance to the struggle in Bosnia. Both featured conflict between Muslims and Christians, and in both cases the Christians were armed and supported by their fellow nationals in a neighbouring state. However, the Armenian government - also like the Serbs in Belgrade - was eager to emphasise its non-participation in the conflict, but the claim had no more credence than that made by Milosevic. The fully mechanised and partially air-borne attacks on Azerbaijan in spring 1992 was evidence enough of Yerevan's active participation in the war.

Although both the UN and the CSCE have been brought in to broker a settlement, Russia retained its role as the key external force in the conflict. No Russian troops were deployed in the region and Moscow claimed neutrality throughout the conflict. In practice, however, Moscow tilted towards Armenia until their land-grab in 1993. As Russian diplomacy shifted back more in the direction of Baku, Aliyev - whose instincts were far more pro-Russian than those of his predecessor - was enticed back into the structures of the CIS and Moscow increased its military presence in the republic. However, Aliyev was not prepared to be seen by his people as a puppet of Moscow and he resisted pressure to allow Russian troops to patrol the Azeri-Iranian border.

Azerbaijan launched an offensive to try to take back its occupied territory, but when it was quickly beaten back by the Armenians, a cease-fire agreement was signed in May 1994. However, the agreement did not provide any basis for a long-term settlement. The Armenians in Nagorno-Karabakh still wanted reunification with Yerevan, and as a guarantee of its security they further demanded that the land corridors to Armenia remain open. The Azeris, for their part, were unwilling to accept any settlement which could freeze Armenian military gains.

Moscow continued to seek a settlement similar to that in the Crimea where Nagorno-Karabakh would gain considerable autonomy but formally remain a part of Azerbaijan (*Moscow News*, 7-13 March 1996). If such an agreement could be found, all sides would benefit. Armenia is close to bankruptcy due to the economic blockade imposed by Baku, whilst Azerbaijan's very status as a nation-state is under threat due to its losses in the war. Azerbaijan, however, retains the potential to become a wealthy country because of the rich oil fields beneath the Caspian Sea. Russia is eager for peace and stability in the region so it too can benefit from oil and safer transport routes through the Caucasus region. In the meantime, the two republics have become more dependent on Moscow both in economic and military terms (see Furman and Asenius, 1996: 151).

## Moldova

Moldova (formerly Moldavia), is a relatively small republic of 4.3 million people in the south west of the former Soviet Union, with its capital at Chisinau. The republic had been taken from Romania and integrated into the USSR in 1940. The majority population in Moldova was of Romanian extraction, although about 27 percent was slav. The slavs congregated mainly on the left bank of the Dniester river - an area of some economic importance to the republic as a whole.

As nationalism gathered force in Moldavia in the late 1980s, pressure began to grow in some quarters for unification with Romania. The slavs were opposed to any such unification and, to protect their own position, they began to establish authority over the territory of Trans-Dniester. As the USSR collapsed, the slavic minority declared independence in December 1991 for the republic of Trans-Dniester. Since about 40 percent of Trans-Dniester was made up of ethnic

Moldovans, it was scarcely surprising when the declaration met with fierce opposition. As the slav leadership extended its control over the region by force, Chisinau attacked the slavs at the town of Bendery. The crisis exploded into war in May and June 1992 and hundreds died in the subsequent fighting.

The Russian 14th army, stationed in Trans-Dniester, came to the support of the slav rebels. The army beat back the Moldovan forces and consolidated slav control over Trans-Dniester. General Alexander Lebed was rushed to the region to become commander of the 14th army. He gave open support to the separatists, but Moscow moved swiftly to broker a compromise. On 7 July, a cease-fire agreement was signed which recognised the territorial integrity of the Moldovan republic, but accorded Trans-Dniester considerable autonomy and the right of secession if Moldova were ever to reunite with Romania. Russian and Moldovan troops were delegated to monitor the cease-fire agreement.

The region remained tense, but slowly the situation began to stabilise. Both sides showed a willingness to compromise. The people of Trans-Dniester came to realise that Moscow would not recognise their region as an independent state, whilst nationalist fervour abated amongst the Romanian population. As a result, pro-Romanian nationalists lost their position in government after elections in February 1994, and in a referendum shortly afterwards, 95 percent backed the concept of a fully independent Moldova merged neither with Romania nor Russia. In response, the Chisinau government introduced a new constitution in July which backed up the earlier cease-fire agreement and guaranteed minority rights to all people in Moldova.

Tension eased in Trans-Dniester and opened the way in October 1994 for an agreement between Moscow and Chisinau for the full withdrawal of Russian troops (with certain important provisos) over a four year period. General Lebed opposed the move, warning that Russian withdrawal would lead to a resumption of the war. Many slavs agreed with him, but Moscow dismissed Lebed as commander of the 14th army in June 1995. In response, Lebed resigned from the military and entered politics. He presented himself to the electorate as a tough-minded military officer who had been able to both defend the interests of the Russian minority and bring peace to Trans-Dniester.

The Moldovan economy suffered from the Trans-Dniester conflict, but after the cease-fire the republic began to perform more strongly. In 1995, Moldova was the first CIS state since the collapse of the USSR to record positive economic growth, albeit from a low base and only a modest 1.5 percent (*Time*, 30 October 1995). Moldova was also performing rather better on the political front too. For whilst most other CIS states began to slide back into authoritarianism, Chisinau's new constitution showed a willingness to continue on the difficult path towards democracy. The prospects for Moldova look reasonably bright (*New Times*, January 1996: 11). Moscow, along with the new government in Chisinau, can claim some credit for that fact.


## Tajikistan

A dreadful bloody war broke out in September 1992 in the Central Asian Republic of Tajikistan. The catalyst for war was the overthrow of the communist leader, Rakhman Nabiyev. The nature of the conflict, however, was controversial. Rebels portrayed it as a struggle between old-style Stalinists and progressive democrats. Dushanbe, on the other hand, argued it was an Islamic uprising against a democratically elected government. It was easy, however, to overestimate the importance of ideology - whether Islamic or communist - when in fact, clan and regional rivalries, exacerbated by economic collapse, appeared to be the main reasons for the conflict (*Nezavisimaya gazeta*, 21 January 1993).

Moscow paid little attention to the problems in Central Asia until Nabiyev was overthrown. With the exception of Kazakhstan (the only state in Central Asia which bordered Russia), Moscow had few strategic or economic interests in the region. However, as the war reached the Tajik capital of Dushanbe, Moscow felt it had little alternative but to intervene. Russia felt obliged to protect the 300,000 Russians living in Tajikistan at the time; and also feared the spread of the conflict to neighbouring muslim states where significant numbers of Tajiks lived. Russian tanks of the 201st division moved in and were supported by Uzbek airpower. The small Tajik army played only a minor role in the battle. This was because many soldiers were unwilling to fight and those that were willing were often poorly trained for such a conflict (*Nezavisimaya gazeta*, 29 April 1993). Nevertheless, the external intervention proved decisive, and by December 1992, the communist government had been reinstated, albeit under the new leadership of Emomali Rakhmonov.

It proved to be a brutal regime. After victory, Rakhmonov began the bloody elimination of his opponents. By the end of 1993, it was estimated that up to 80,000 had died, 800,000 had emigrated to other CIS countries, and a further 100,000 had fled across the border to northern Afghanistan where many fellow Tajiks lived (*Izvestiya*, 21 December 1993). Tajikistan was placed under emergency rule. Its economy was in ruins and totally dependent on Moscow. It was estimated that subsidies from Moscow accounted for as much as 70 percent of government expenditures (Rubin, 1993-94: 81).

Russian commentators started talking about a new Afghanistan (*Izvestiya*, 24 February 1993). Russian troops were once again propping up an unpopular and repressive regime in the face of Muslim and nationalist opposition. There was also a danger of the internationalisation of the conflict when cross border raids from Afghanistan began in the summer of 1993. In July, 24 Russian border guards were killed in one such assault, and as a result, the 2,000 kilometre Tajik-Afghan border was heavily guarded by 15,000 troops - mainly from Russia. The rebels have said they will only negotiate after the removal of Rakhmonov and the complete withdrawal of Russian troops (*Izvestiya*, 21 December 1993). Neither eventuality is at all likely in the near future. In contrast to the Russian intervention in Afghanistan, however, Moscow received Western sympathy for its actions in Tajikistan. It was generally accepted that Moscow had acted in the interests of stability by supporting the legitimate government in Dushanbe and by acting against Islamic extremism in the region. Moscow consistently found that it was more likely to get Western sympathy for its military interventionism in the post-cold war world when it was suppressing Muslims - whether in Chechnya or Azerbaijan - than any other single group in the former Soviet Union. However, the problem was that Russia's military intervention against the insurgents could, like in Afghanistan, make the perceived threat of Islamic fundamentalism little more than a self-fulfilling prophecy.

## Georgia

Georgia is a small but strategically important country in the Caucasus. Georgia was at the forefront of the nationalist movement which gripped the USSR in the late 1980s (see chapter 3). The Georgian leader, Zviad Gamsakhurdia, was a radical nationalist who declared independence in April 1991. However, after the collapse of the USSR, Gamsakhurdia's extreme nationalism and increasingly dictatorial leadership destabilised the country and encouraged two of the three autonomous republics - South Ossetia and Abkhazia - to secede from Georgia. Gamsakhurdia lost the support of his colleagues in Tbilisi and he was ousted in a political coup, which was supported in Moscow, in December 1991. Shevardnadze returned to Georgia as leader in March 1992 and he was elected President in October.

It was clear to Shevardnadze that he had to end the conflict with the rebellious regions in Georgia if the economy was ever to be rebuilt. He started by focusing his attention on South Ossetia. South Ossetia had wanted to reunite with North Ossetia and, like its northern partner, officially become a part of the Russian Federation. Again, Russia indicated it was unwilling to see borders changed. This allowed Shevardnadze to conclude an agreement in which South Ossetia's autonomy, which had been denied by Gamsakhurdia, was formally recognised by Tbilisi. At the same time, Shevardnadze signed an agreement with Russia in July 1992 in which joint forces acted as peacekeepers and patrolled the border with North Ossetia. The two republics, therefore, remained separate, but an uneasy calm was restored to the area.

The conflict in Abkhazia proved more difficult to settle. Although only about 18 percent of the population was ethnic Abkhazian, separatists declared independence from Georgia in August 1992. As tensions rose, Shevardnadze sent Georgian troops to the republic in the expectation of a quick victory. When Georgia failed to put down the uprising, Shevardnadze blamed Russian support for the separatists. As the conflict escalated in early 1993, Shevardnadze declared Russia and Georgia to be effectively at war (*Izvestiya*, 17 March 1993). In February, he reported that Russian aircraft had bombed residential quarters in the capital of Sukhumi killing sixty people (*Izvestiya*, 25 February 1993). Reports from deserters suggested that the rebels were getting large amounts of fuel and modern tanks from the Russian military in Abkhazia (*Izvestiya*, 17 March 1993).

Officially, Moscow was neutral, but Abkhazia was of considerable strategic importance to Russia. It was tempting for Moscow, after the problems in Sevastopol, to maintain its position in Abkhazia, on its southern border. This was acknowledged in unusually honest language by the Russian Defence Minister, Pavel Grachev, who said in February that 'Russian troops should not leave Abkhazia because that would mean losing the Black Sea' (*The Observer*, 11 July 1993). Soon afterwards, Yeltsin made two speeches confirming the strategic importance of the region and the need for Russia to establish Russian bases in the Caucasus (Dale, 1996: 127). As stated earlier, Russia was simply not willing to withdraw from the Caucasus region and risk the political vacuum being filled by forces antagonistic towards Moscow.

A cease-fire, brokered by Russia and the UN, was finally agreed at Sochi on 27 July 1993. However, the Abkhazians violated the cease-fire and took advantage of the Georgian withdrawal to take the capital, Sukhumi, in September. Neither Russia nor the UN acted to prevent this. It was a humiliation for

Shevardnadze who had personally sponsored the cease-fire.

As Abkhazia fell to the separatists, Gamsakhurdia returned from exile in a bid to overthrow the Shevardnadze government which he saw as illegitimate. He rallied his forces, the Zviadists, in his home region of Zugdidi and quickly seized nine towns, including the Black Sea port of Poti, a major supply point for the whole country. By mid-October, the Zviadists had captured up to a third of the country.

With the prospect of the total collapse of his country, Shevardnadze on 18 October 1993 made an appeal to Moscow to come to his rescue. Having played a part in destabilising Georgia, Moscow now came to the support of the government against the violently anti-Russian Zviadists. In November, eight warships were moved up from Sevastopol to a position off the Georgian coast, and troops were deployed to free the port of Poti and to guard the main roads leading to the Georgian capital of Tbilisi. The supply of advanced Russian weaponry to government forces was decisive and the Zviadists were quickly defeated. Zviad Gamsakhurdia, who was already terminally ill, committed suicide on New Year's Eve 1993.

The support of the Russians had its price, however. Shevardnadze was compelled to bring Georgia into the structures of the CIS, and in February 1994 he allowed Russia the right to military bases in his country. He had little choice. The Georgian economy had been devastated by civil war and Tbilisi depended on Moscow even to the extent of paying wages to its state employees. The Georgian journalist, Melor Sturua, of *Izvestiya* wrote at the time that Georgia had effectively ceased to exist as an independent state. The autonomous republics of Abkhazia and South Ossetia, he went on, were mere protectorates of Russia and Shevardnadze had become the equivalent of a Russian consul (*International Herald Tribune*, 30-31 October 1993).

## Russia and Chechnya

After the collapse of the USSR, analysts were divided over the likelihood of Russia following suit. Jessica Stern, for example, argued that the Russian Federation was 'not sustainable as a state' (Taylor, T., 1994: 54). She noted that Russia was a huge country which traversed eleven time zones. It was divided, like the USSR, along ethnic lines into 21 autonomous republics and 68 regions. The politics of Moscow often seemed far away and irrelevant to those outside the metropolis. As a result, the process of decentralisation continued after the collapse of the Soviet Union as the republics grabbed power and increasingly declared sovereignty from Moscow. Disintegration looked possible as the Russian economy foundered.

However, collapse was unlikely unless central authority in Moscow broke down completely (see Galeotti, 1995: 190). The main reason was that the ethnic mix in Russia did not parallel that in the former Soviet Union. Thus, the regions and republics of Russia were ethnically mixed, but only in Chechnya, Chuvashaya, North Ossetia and Tyva did the titular group make up a majority of the population. Russians, on the other hand, made up 82 percent of the Russian Federation. Therefore, most non-Russian ethnic groups were too small, too isolated or too poor to be sustainable as independent entities outside Russia. This basic fact was recognised by most ethnic leaders who signed the Russian Federation Treaty in March 1992. However, the war in Chechnya was a brutal reminder of the continued existence of centrifugal forces in Russia.

The war in Chechnya erupted suddenly and came as a surprise to the people of Russia and the outside world. Generally, Yeltsin had sought diplomatic solutions to ethnic problems inside Russia. Tatarstan was a good example of this. Like Chechnya, Tatarstan was a predominantly Muslim republic which had refused to sign the Russian Federation Treaty. Like Chechnya, it was economically important to Moscow - Tatarstan had large reserves of oil. Nevertheless, a treaty was signed with Moscow in February 1994, which committed Tatarstan to remain in Russia, but allowed the republic considerable autonomy over its own affairs. Such an arrangement was typical of agreements made with Trans-Dniester and the Crimea. Most commentators expected that a similar compromise could be worked out with Chechnya. However, this proved mistaken.

Chechnya was a small republic on Russia's southern border in the northern Caucasus. Strategically, it was of vital importance to Moscow. It was oil rich, and vital rail links and pipe-lines from the Caspian to the Black Sea ran across the republic. In 1989, its population was 1.2 million. The majority was Muslim, but about 25 percent was of ethnic Russian descent. The region was first absorbed into Tsarist Russia in 1860, but the Chechens retained a strong sense of their national identity. In 1944, Stalin exiled half a million to Kazakhstan for, it was said, collaborating with the Nazis. They were only allowed to return to their homeland from 1957. This concession did nothing, however, to dilute Chechen nationalism.

Indeed, Chechnya took part in the general nationalist upsurge which gripped all of the Caucasus region in the Gorbachev period. Thus, in November 1990, the Chechen parliament declared its intention to secede from the USSR and a month after the August coup in 1991, Dzhokhar Dudayev, a General in the Soviet military, seized power. In October 1991, over 90 percent of the Chechen electorate ratified Dudayev's presidency amidst Russian claims of ballot rigging. Yeltsin refused to recognise the election result and the Russian Congress declared it constitutionally null and void (*Delovoi Mir*, 25 February 1995). Nevertheless, Dudayev still went ahead and declared Chechen independence in November 1991. In response, Yeltsin, on 8 November, announced a state of emergency in Chechnya and moved interior troops to the border. On this occasion, however, no violence took place. The Supreme Soviet, so often criticised for its nationalism, voted against military action and the troops were withdrawn after three days.

However, Dudayev made no effort to compromise. Instead, after refusing to sign the Russian Federation Treaty in March 1992, he began to deport the remaining Russian troops from the republic and seized much of their military equipment. Ingushetia, which had merged with Chechnya in 1936, was so concerned over Dudayev's actions, it seceded from Chechnya in July and unilaterally signed the Russian Federation Treaty. Ingushetia boasted most of the oil, and the economic situation in Chechnya proper worsened markedly. An estimated 60 percent of the Chechen population soon found themselves without a job (*Moscow News*, no. 3, 1996). Opposition to Dudayev, funded partly from Moscow, appeared to be growing.

In response, Dudayev closed down parliament in June 1993, sparking clashes between government and rebel forces. As small-scale guerilla warfare broke out in the autumn, Moscow saw an opportunity to reassert its influence in the republic and formally bring Chechnya back into the Russian Federation. In June 1994, an alternative Chechen government was set up, with strong backing from Moscow, called the Provisional Council. It was led by Umar Avturkhanov. In August, Avturkhanov called for the armed overthrow of the Chechen President. Moscow promptly sent armoured vehicles and 40 billion rubles to help the Provisional Council in its bid for power (*Moscow News*, 16-22 December 1994). Avturkhanov's rebel forces launched their attack in the autumn and attempted to take the Chechen capital, Grozny, on 26 November. However, the rebels were routed and Russian personnel involved in the attack were captured.

Yeltsin felt his authority had been severely damaged by Avturkhanov's defeat. He argued that the conflict could spread beyond Chechnya and destabilise the rest of the Caucasus region if Moscow retreated. Therefore, Yeltsin and a few close colleagues decided to use force to unseat Dudayev and capture Grozny (*Moscow News*, 13-19 January 1995). On 11 December 1994, 40,000 Russian troops (later increased to almost 60,000) - the biggest deployment since Afghanistan - were ordered into Chechnya. Two weeks passed before Yeltsin explained his decision to the Russian public. In a TV broadcast, Yeltsin declared that Chechnya was a totalitarian state which was used as a base for terrorism, drugs and arms running. The Dudayev clique, he went on, was well-armed and posed a threat to the territorial integrity of the Russian Federation (*Nezavisimaya gazeta*, 28 December 1994).

Although the Russian people generally had little time for the people of the Caucasus - the blacks (*chornye*), as they called them - few supported military action in Chechnya. In an opinion poll of Russians in early 1995, two-thirds condemned the military action, although only 11 percent supported the Chechens in the war (*Moscow News*, 24 February-2 March 1995). Both the Duma and Federation Council condemned the military intervention. The war in Chechnya was the cause of a decisive breach between Yeltsin and many of his former reformist colleagues, including Yegor Gaidar, leader of Russia's Choice. The invasion also split the military, with conservative figures, such as Lebed and Gromov, both coming out publicly against Yeltsin's decision to use force. In fact, one of the few influential figures outside the government who came out firmly in support of the Russian President was the ultra-nationalist, Vladimir Zhirinovsky - an uncomfortable bedfellow for Yeltsin.

Of course, government figures supported Yeltsin, but many were still surprised when Andrei Kozyrev, the archetypal Westerniser, backed military action in Chechnya. Kozyrev argued that the intervention was justifiable in international law since Chechnya was formally a part of the Russian Federation, and therefore Moscow had the right to move into the republic and disarm military forces not accountable to the legitimate authorities of state (*RIA Novosti*, 2 February 1995). Kozyrev did, however, support negotiations to resolve the dispute as quickly as possible (Poptsov, 1995: 464). The West generally accepted the logic of Kozyrev's position and reluctantly backed Russia's military action. It was only when the war dragged on that doubts were raised over proportionality.

Before the intervention began, Russian Defence Minister, Pavel Grachev, had told Yeltsin that Grozny could be captured in two hours by a single regiment of paratroopers (*The Guardian*, 11 January 1995). This proved to be a hopelessly optimistic prediction. In practice, the Russian action had the effect of raising morale amongst the Chechens and uniting them once again around their President, Dzhokhar Dudayev. In contrast, the Russian military was badly organised and badly led. Despite a massive technological advantage and complete mastery of the skies, the first Russian attack on Grozny was easily driven back by the Chechen rebels.

On New Year's Eve, Moscow tried again and a second assault was launched. The Chechens, with only about 15,000 regular soldiers, fought bravely but were eventually overwhelmed by the might of the Russian military. The Presidential Palace was taken in mid-January and Grozny fell soon after. But the war continued until the last stronghold of the rebels, Samashky, was overrun in April 1995. Even then, the Dudayev supporters simply retired to the mountains to prepare for the next phase of the campaign against Moscow.

In the course of the war, Chechnya had been devastated. Russian tanks and indiscriminate air strikes had terrorised a whole people. By the summer of 1995, at least 20,000 had died in the conflict and 200,000 more were either homeless or refugees (Poptsov, 1995: 463).[1] Grozny, itself, had been reduced to rubble with little sign of reconstruction more than a year later. It seemed, however, that by the spring of 1995 Moscow, albeit at huge cost in terms of money and lives, had won the war in Chechnya. This, however, was a bad misreading of the situation, for Dudayev and his colleagues had not given up the struggle against the Russians.

Thus, after a period of relative calm, the Chechens launched their terrorist campaign against Moscow. In June 1995, a group of Chechen rebels, led by Shamil Basayev, took a thousand people hostage in a hospital in the small town of Budyonnovsk in southern Russia. The crisis only ended when Chernomyrdin agreed to a cease-fire, negotiations over a political settlement and the safe passage of the rebels back to Chechnya. However, neither side abided by the terms of the cease-fire and by the autumn it was already showing signs of unravelling. Talks were finally suspended by Yeltsin in October 1995 after rebels attempted to assassinate the Russian military commander in Chechnya, Lieutenant General Anatoly Romanov. Renewed terrorism climaxed in a second hostage crisis in January 1996 in the small town of Pervomaiskoye on the Dagestan-Chechen border which ended with the rebel leaders escaping despite the bombardment of their positions by the Russian military and airforce.

In the spring of 1996, the crisis in Chechnya escalated once again into all-out war. Dzhokhar Dudayev was killed on 21 April and replaced as leader by his Vice President, Zelimkhan Yandarbiyev. Although Yandarbiyev was perceived as a hardliner, he met with Yeltsin on 27 May and hammered out another cease-fire agreement. Yeltsin was desperate for some kind of progress in the lead-up

---

[1]   The number of deaths had risen to at least 30,000 by the summer of 1996.

to the presidential election in June 1996. Yandarbiyev, for his part, was eager for a cease-fire after heavy losses in the spring fighting and recognised that the election offered the Chechens a chance of getting concessions from Moscow. At that time, however, on the crucial issue of Chechnya's status, neither side seemed willing to compromise. The Chechens wanted full independence, whilst Moscow was only offering autonomy within the Russian Federation (*Moscow News*, 6-12 June 1996). As a result, the war continued almost without a break throughout the summer.

However, Lebed, Yeltsin's newly appointed special envoy, managed to secure a peace agreement on 31 August 1996, which involved greater concessions on the part of Moscow. Although Yeltsin appeared unenthusiastic about the settlement, he signed a decree on 23 November which built on Lebed's earlier efforts. The decree called for the withdrawal of all Russian troops from Chechnya, the holding of local elections in early 1997 with a final decision over Chechnya's status delayed until the year 2001.

The agreement appeared to be the best chance for peace since the beginning of the war in December 1994. There were worries, however. First, Yeltsin's decree appeared to signal a defeat for Moscow. Hardliners were unwilling to accept such a humiliation and argued that it could set a dangerous precedent for other Russian republics which might also want to secede from the Russian Federation. Second, it was unclear whether Russian withdrawal would herald long-term peace in the region. The nascent civil war which was brewing before the Russian invasion could flare up again. If this did happen, it would be difficult for any government in Moscow to remain indifferent to conflict in an area of such strategic importance. Furthermore, the ethnic mix in the Caucasus region would always make the spread of the conflict a dangerous possibility for Moscow. The constant fear, therefore, is that the present ceasefire is little more than a suspension of a conflict between the Russians and Chechens which has been going on in one form or another for over a hundred years.

## Conclusion

Before the tragedy of Chechnya, Yeltsin could claim with some justification to have played a stabilising role in the CIS. However, Chechnya was a fiasco waiting to happen. Under pressure from nationalists, Yeltsin had adopted from 1993 an increasingly brash policy towards the near abroad. He had the tendency to enter negotiations with unsigned treaties in one hand and a kalashnikov in the other. It was a remarkably successful policy for a while, as Moldova, Azerbaijan and Georgia were all cajoled into joining the CIS. However, as Moscow's dominance grew within the CIS, Yeltsin became over-confident. Independently-minded Chechnya, it was argued, could be subdued in a matter of hours. This ignored the history of Chechnya, the determination of the Chechen leaders and the weakness of the Russian army after years of decline.

Nevertheless, the events in Chechnya should not obscure the fact that Yeltsin has acted with reasonable consistency in the near abroad. He has opposed border changes whilst favouring autonomy for ethnic regions and civil rights for minorities. This was a sensible policy. However, it also became the justification for the war in Chechnya which so badly undermined Yeltsin's reputation as a democrat.

# Chapter Eleven

# RUSSIAN POLICY TOWARDS THE WEST

The West held a constantly changing attitude towards Boris Yeltsin. In the days of his struggle with Gorbachev, Yeltsin was treated with considerable suspicion. He was seen as a maverick whose attacks on Gorbachev risked the entire reform process in the Soviet Union. Such misgivings were never fully cast aside, but when Yeltsin defied the hardliners in August 1991 he was recast as the hero who had defeated communism. In June 1992, Yeltsin went to America and addressed a joint session of the US Congress and delighted his audience by announcing the death of communism with the promise that it would never rise again in his country (*International Herald Tribune*, 18 June 1992). Yeltsin reached out to the West and called for partnership to replace cold war enmity. For the next two years, he had some success in forging an alliance with Washington on a number of important issues. START II was signed in January 1993; the final Russian troops left Eastern Europe on schedule in August 1994; and Moscow distanced itself from a number of its more radical allies in the third world, such as Cuba and Afghanistan.

However, the partnership began to fray from early 1993. Relations cooled on a whole series of issues from NATO enlargement to the war in Bosnia. By the time of the CSCE conference in Budapest in December 1994, relations had deteriorated so far that Yeltsin warned that the cold war could be replaced by a 'cold peace' (*International Herald Tribune*, 6 December 1994). Why was there a reversal to chillier East-West relations?

The most common view places responsibility on Russia. Leszek Buszynski put this case when he wrote: 'Russia's relationship with the West has altered because of a change in the power balance between opinion groups within Moscow' (Buszynski, 1995: 112). As shown in the previous chapter, the Yeltsin administration did shift to the right over the period and undoubtedly its more nationalist rhetoric was to some extent determined by domestic pressure. However, as will be shown below, not all blame should rest with Moscow for the downturn in relations. The West must also take its share of responsibility for acting at times with considerable insensitivity towards Moscow.

After the collapse of the Soviet Union, Russia had to try to come to terms with its much reduced status in the world. Some Westernisers, like Foreign Minister Andrei Kozyrev, were ready to accept that Russia was no longer a superpower. For others this was more difficult, particularly since its cold war enemy had emerged more powerful than ever. With the end of the USSR, it appeared to many that the last restraint on US international hegemony had been removed. Moscow was keen to claim that the end of the cold war did not represent a defeat for Russia, but the West seemed keen to take advantage of Russian weakness.

The traditional concern of encirclement resurfaced in the post-cold war world. To the west, NATO pressed for enlargement. To the east, China continued its military buildup whilst the Japanese remained highly suspicious of Moscow because of the Northern Territories dispute. To the south, Turkey and Iran seemed eager to increase their influence in the muslim-dominated Soviet successor states in the Caucasus and Central Asia.

Initially, Kozyrev had hoped to manage Russian decline through partnership with the West, but it often appeared that Moscow's tougher more nationalist line gained Russia more international respect. For a while, the West almost took Russian support for granted. Moscow needed economic aid and, so the argument went, it could ill afford to antagonise the West. But no partnership could last for any length of time based on such an unequal relationship. Increasingly, it became clear that Russia had some interests different to those of the West. Calls intensified inside Russia for Moscow to be more assertive in its foreign policy. This was reflected in a debate over foreign policy which took place in 1992 inside Yeltsin's own administration. This will be outlined below.

**The foreign policy debate**

Boris Yeltsin had little interest in foreign policy. He wrote virtually nothing about the topic in either of his two volumes of autobiography. Therefore, when Yeltsin became Russian President he gave his Foreign Minister, Andrei Kozyrev, a fairly free hand to devise a strategy for the post-Soviet world. At least in his early days, Kozyrev was a strong Westerniser. In many respects, the strategy he devised was a continuation of Gorbachev's new thinking, but he rejected the Soviet leader's more idealistic notions of a New World Order in favour of a policy based more firmly on Russian national interest. The problem, however, was determining the nature of Russian national interest in the post-cold war world.

Kozyrev argued that Russian foreign policy should be subservient to domestic politics - everything should be dedicated to economic reconstruction (Kozyrev, 1992). For Kozyrev, this meant a policy of integration into the international capitalist economy, for two main reasons - first, because of the long-term benefit of increased trade; and second, because of the short-term expectation of attracting more aid to help Russia over the difficult transition period (*Izvestiya*, 2 January 1992; *Nezavisimaya gazeta*, 1 April 1992). Gorbachev had pursued a similar strategy without eliciting large sums of Western money, but Kozyrev believed he would have more success. Gorbachev had only tried to reform communism, he argued, whilst Yeltsin had overthrown it. Therefore, the West had no need to fear that its aid would be used to prop up a failed and repressive communist system (Kozyrev, 1992: 14).

Kozyrev's ideas dominated the foreign policy debate in Russia until the spring of 1992. Thereafter, Kozyrev's position came under serious threat as the Foreign Ministry lost its virtual monopoly over Russian foreign policy decision-making. In March, the Russian Ministry of Defence was created, followed by the Security Council in May. Both institutions became the repository of more conservative and less pro-Western views. At the same time, Yeltsin's foreign policy adviser, Sergei Stankevich, published an article in a Russian newspaper critical of Kozyrev's overall strategy (*Nezavisimaya gazeta*, 28 March 1992; see also, Stankevich, 1992).

Stankevich criticised Kozyrev for his prioritisation of the US. Instead, Stankevich argued for a greater emphasis on the near abroad and third world countries, especially the Middle East, South-West Asia and the Pacific Rim. Stankevich described his views as Eurasianist and Kozyrev's as Atlanticist. In many ways, Stankevich was reviving the centuries old debate between Westernisers and Slavophiles. It was different, however, in one important respect. Stankevich was a centrist in Russian politics. He was not advocating a return to expansionist policies or the complete rejection of Western culture. On the contrary, he supported reform and recognised it was not in Russia's interest to ignore the West. Stankevich's critique of Kozyrev was important because it came from a reformer and a potential ally of the Russian Foreign Minister.

Kozyrev also faced less sympathetic opposition from a growing number of influential nationalists, including Yeltsin's Vice President, Alexander Rutskoi, and the chairman of Congress, Ruslan Khasbulatov. The nationalists were more anti-Western than Stankevich in outlook and highly suspicious of Western motives in its dealings with Russia. They argued that the West had deliberately undermined the Russian economy to take advantage of temporary Russian weakness and reimpose its global dominance. Russia, it was argued, should seek to reassert its international status and rebuild Russian military power (see Webber, 1996: 123-4).

Kozyrev and the Foreign Ministry began to shift to the right to accommodate the increasing popularity of nationalist and Eurasianist thought. This was most clearly revealed when the Russian Foreign Policy Concept was published in January 1993 followed by the new Military Doctrine in the autumn (see *International Affairs*, January 1993; *Moscow News*, no. 25, 1993). The Foreign Policy Concept continued to advocate co-operation with the West and argued in favour of partnership with the US on certain issues, such as nuclear proliferation and the mediation of regional conflicts, but emphasis was now firmly placed on the need to retain the status of Russia as a great power. The document also formally acknowledged that the near abroad was Russia's top foreign policy priority. Therefore, it emphasised Moscow's obligation to protect Russian nationals in the near abroad, to defend the territorial integrity of the CIS and to patrol its external borders (*International Affairs*, January 1993). The Military Doctrine which followed later in the year, extended this idea and argued that Russia had the right to use military force in the defence of Russian nationals on the territory of the former Soviet Union (*Rossiiskie vesti*, 18 November 1993).

As the last chapter showed, Moscow did indeed pursue a more interventionist policy over time in areas of strategic importance in the near abroad - most notably in the Caucasus - but in the case of the far abroad, the shift was more one of rhetoric than substance. It was true, however, that Russia wanted to be treated by the outside world as a great power - it wished to be consulted on issues of strategic interest and have its views taken into account. Such demands did not, however, involve a reversal of policy. Raymond Garthoff summed up Moscow's policy shift by arguing that it was a corrective to 'somewhat naive expectations of an American embrace and partnership on the basis of new thinking' (Garthoff, 1994: 786).

However, little is predictable or certain in Yeltsin's Russia. The so-called Weimar scenario has many close parallels in Russia today - the loss of status, the national humiliation, the economic deprivation. Even the myth of the stab in the back has strong resonance in certain quarters in Russia - including the revived Communist Party - with Gorbachev and Yeltsin perceived as Western agents who deliberately engineered the fall of the mighty Soviet Union. The existence of a multi-party system in Russia is not in itself enough to ensure against fascism. After all, Adolf Hitler was voted into power by the Germans, a highly developed country with a longer history of democracy than Russia. For a time, at least, Vladimir Zhirinovsky looked ready to become a Russian Hitler.

The hope for Russia is that history rarely repeats itself. Indeed, one important lesson of history is that Nazism did not save Germany. Nazism would not save Russia either. The Russian military has increased its political influence since the storming of the White House in October 1993, but there is little evidence to suggest that militarism is on the rise. The military action in Chechnya was largely condemned by the Russian public, and there was little eagerness amongst Russians to fight in Yugoslavia or take back Eastern Europe. Zhirinovsky's pledge to have Russian soldiers wash their boots in the warm waters of the Indian Ocean had little resonance even amongst his own supporters. Democracy in Russia may be a fragile growth, but it remains the best hope for Russia. It is also the best hope for peace in Europe and the world.

In the meantime, relations with the West have proved difficult and this is likely to continue for some time into the future. Problems include: the issue of nuclear weapons, the CFE Treaty, NATO enlargement, and Western aid. These matters will be taken up below. The war in Yugoslavia has been given a separate chapter.


## Nuclear Issues

As the cold war ended, the West's main concern related to the future of the Soviet nuclear arsenal. Initially, the CIS was set up in large part to deal with such worries. It was agreed that there would be a 'single command' over nuclear weapons on the territory of the former Soviet Union, and on 30 December, a Joint Command of Strategic Forces was set up with Yevgeny Shaposhnikov as its commander-in-chief. However, the decision to launch nuclear weapons rested with the Russian President, albeit in consultation and co-ordination with other CIS states. Therefore, the exact role of the CIS was unclear. When Russia assumed overall command of nuclear weapons on the territory of the former Soviet Union, the Joint Command was formally abandoned in the summer of 1993.

In the meantime, the CIS also committed itself to honour arms control treaties signed by the Soviet Union.[1] As the Soviet Union broke up, this proved more difficult to accomplish than some had initially believed. However, Yeltsin was eager to press ahead with new arms control agreements which would reduce the risk of nuclear war and emphasise the break with the old cold war world. Yeltsin recognised that America's main concern related to strategic missiles and proceeded to negotiate START II which was formally signed in January 1993. As chapter four stated, START II represented a radical departure in arms control policy. The treaty targeted modern weaponry and sought to significantly reduce first strike capability by limiting ICBMs and banning land-based MIRVs. The Russian military was generally opposed to the treaty because it left the core of the US naval and air force in place whilst the abolition of Russia's SS18s struck at the heart of Russian nuclear strategy.

START II would provide for a significant cut in the nuclear arsenals on both sides, but it would not rid the world of the threat of nuclear armageddon. The US and Russia would still retain more than enough nuclear weapons to blow the world up many times over. For all that, START II represented an important breakthrough in arms control agreements. The threat of a premeditated first-strike which so preoccupied military strategists both sides of the iron curtain during the cold war, has by common consent disappeared. START II, however, faced problems over ratification, due to the rise in Russian nationalism and a renewed American interest in BMDs and NATO enlargement. Sergei Solodovnik from the Moscow State Institute of International Relations, wrote: '... START II was conceived as an element of peace and partnership with America, but we have been betrayed, as there is neither partnership, nor security, nor peace' (*Moscow News*, 22-28 February 1996).

Worries have also arisen over other related issues, such as nuclear proliferation, and the maintenance and safety of nuclear weapons. Thus, as the Soviet Union broke up, the most immediate question was what would happen to the approximately 27,000 nuclear warheads deployed on its territory. The vast

---

[1] For details, see *Agreements on the Creation of the Commonwealth of Independent States signed in December 1991/January 1992* (1992), Russian Information Agency/Novosti Press, London.

majority of nuclear missiles were deployed in Russia, but tactical missiles were scattered throughout the former Soviet Union. Many tactical weapons had already been transferred to Russia in Gorbachev's time, but it was agreed in December 1991, that the remainder would be transferred by the following July. Since nationalist leaders feared the theft and unauthorised launch of these smaller weapons, the transfer was relatively trouble-free and completed two months early.

Initially, it seemed similar agreements could be struck between Russia, Ukraine, Belorus and Kazakhstan over strategic nuclear weapons. In May 1992, all four states signed the Lisbon protocol agreeing to abide by the original START I treaty. Article five of the protocol stated that Russia would retain its status as a nuclear power, but the other three states would give up their nuclear weapons within a seven-year period and sign the Non-Proliferation Treaty as non-nuclear states (see *Arms Control Today*, June 1992: 34-37). In the interim, nuclear weapons were formally placed under the central control of the CIS.

Problems arose, however, over Ukrainian compliance with the START I protocol. Almost as soon as the protocol was signed, Kiev began to drag its feet on the issue. Nuclear weapons were seen as a symbol of its great power pretensions and an effective deterrent against any future attack from Russia. However, it slowly began to dawn on leaders in Kiev that its nuclear status served no defensive or strategic purpose. Despite the strategic weapons being formally placed under CIS control, in reality, positive operational control - the ability to launch the missiles - remained in Moscow. Kiev did argue at one time that negative operational control should be retained - that is, the ability to prevent the launch of missiles from Ukrainian territory - but this was generally seen as a negotiating ploy since the best way to ensure no nuclear weapons were launched from Ukrainian territory was to dismantle the weapons concerned in accordance with treaties already signed. Moreover, abolition looked more and more attractive as the Ukrainian economy teetered ever closer to bankruptcy in 1993 and the cost of maintaining the missiles was estimated to be $40 billion per year (*Nezavisimaya gazeta*, 27 April 1993).

Thus, in January 1994, Ukraine finally agreed at a trilateral summit in Moscow, involving Clinton, Yeltsin and Kravchuk, to transfer all its strategic weapons to Russia over a seven year period. In return, Kiev was promised $1 billion worth of aid from Washington and Moscow (SIPRI, 1994: 677-8). Kiev signed the Non-Proliferation Treaty in November 1994, by which time all other Soviet successor states were also signatories. The Non-Proliferation Treaty got an important boost the following year when its duration was extended indefinitely at a conference in New York.

The fear of proliferation amongst Soviet successor states faded, but proliferation beyond the borders of the former Soviet Union through the illegal transfer of nuclear material or expertise remained a problem. The Soviet nuclear complex had been extensive. Approximately 900,000 Soviet citizens had worked with nuclear weapons, 2,500 had detailed knowledge of weapons design, and 3,500 worked with uranium enrichment or plutonium production (Norris, 1992). Given the desperate state of the Russian economy, the temptation was great for individuals to sell their knowledge abroad or smuggle nuclear technology or fissile material out of the country. It was, therefore, scarcely unexpected when a scandal broke in the spring and summer of 1994 over the smuggling of a record amount of highly toxic weapon-grade material from Russia through Germany. These were not the first seizures in Germany and many feared they represented just the tip of the iceberg.

Moscow downplayed the dangers at the time and argued that the whole affair was a set-up. A Russian journalist wrote: 'the amount of plutonium confiscated by the German special services is so small that one cannot seriously speak about an impending nuclear threat. Any country that wants the bomb can get plutonium more easily and cheaply from spent reactor rods in any one of the many nuclear power plants in the Asian region'. He concluded, why smuggle the material through Germany instead of through the far more porous borders to the south (*Moscow News*, 19-25 August 1994)? Russia's Minister for Atomic Energy, Viktor Mikhailov, agreed. He declared that weapon-grade materials in Russia were perfectly safe, and claimed that the well-publicised scandals were an excuse by the West to muscle in on the Russian nuclear industry in the name of safety and security (*Moscow News*, 10-16 February 1995).

Although Russians are very prone to conspiracy theories, later revelations showed that the German secret services had acted in this case as *agents provocateurs* (*The Guardian*, 10 April 1995). This was not to say that smuggling did not exist. Illegal transfers remained a potential danger. However, Hans Blix, the chief of the International Atomic Energy Agency (IAEA), was keen not to sensationalise the problem. In an interview with a Moscow-based newspaper, he said much of the smuggling was of natural uranium, low intensity uranium or depleted uranium which could not be made into bombs. Most smuggling, he went on, came from civilian units where controls had been lax in the past, but they had been greatly improved since (*Moscow Tribune*, 4 July 1995).

Nevertheless, worrying reports continued to be published relating to the maintenance and control of fissile material in Russia. There is certainly no room for complacency, but the nightmare scenarios predicted by many commentators back in 1991 have not as yet come to pass (see Bluth, 1994). In part, this is due to the aid and technical expertise of the West. Indeed, this has been perhaps the most successful aspect of Western assistance to Russia. However, such aid needs to be kept up to reduce risks in the future.

## Conventional forces

The main treaty dealing with conventional forces was the CFE treaty signed in 1990. The treaty committed both sides to major cuts in equipment and troops, and also demanded the remaining forces be subject to certain zonal limits. The treaty was drawn up on the basis of parity between NATO and Warsaw Pact forces to prevent any future blitzkrieg-style attack. However, the treaty seemed out-dated when the cold war came to an end and both the Warsaw Pact and the USSR were abolished in 1991. Yet in the spirit of the times, the CFE was not abandoned but amended at Tashkent in May 1992 with troops and equipment reallocated to the newly independent states of Eastern Europe and the former Soviet Union (for details, see *Military Balance*, 1992-1993: 237-41). Agreements were also reached over personnel levels in what became known as CFE 1A. Both came into effect in July 1992.

However, a growing number of defence specialists in Moscow argued that the amended CFE treaty did not take sufficient account of Russia's changed security interests after the collapse of the USSR. In particular, the military argued that the CFE reduced Moscow's ability to deploy troops on its southern and north-western borders. The urgent need for greater flexibility was amply illustrated in Russian eyes by the war in Chechnya when Russia deployed more tanks and armoured combat vehicles (ACVs) in the early assaults than allowed in the CFE treaty for the whole of the Northern Caucasus region (*Moscow Times*, 21 September 1995).

Generally, the West accepted that Moscow had a genuine grievance over its 'flank limits' in the treaty. A framework agreement was quickly devised when Western diplomats became concerned that Russia would be unable to fulfil its treaty obligations by the final date of 17 November 1995. Although neighbouring countries, in particular, declared themselves concerned over the agreement, the amendments demanded by Moscow were insignificant in terms of the overall treaty (*International Herald Tribune*, 30 October 1995). 50,000 items of military equipment were destroyed in accordance with the treaty at a ratio of two to one in favour of the NATO states. The US ambassador to the 1996 CFE review conference declared himself satisfied with the treaty and said Moscow had successfully 'complied with the overall limits applicable to Russia' (*Arms Control Today*, April 1996: 4).

However, Russia's hardening position on the CFE treaty was seen by some as indicative of the growing influence of the military in Russian politics. After the storming of the White House in October 1993, the new Military Doctrine was published which appeared to reflect the more conservative views in the Defence Ministry (see *Rossiiskie Vesti*, 18 November 1993). The document jettisoned Gorbachev's ideas on non-nuclear defence and defensive defence along with Brezhnev's earlier commitment to no-first use of nuclear weapons. Although the document did reflect changing views in the Yeltsin administration, in many respects the new military doctrine was simply an attempt to come to terms with the new international reality facing Russia. Thus, the re-emphasis on nuclear deterrence did not necessarily signify a return to a more aggressive posture vis-a-vis the West, but more a recognition of Russia's dramatic decline in conventional military power (*Krasnaya zvezda*, 14 December 1993). Vladimir Lukin, chairman of the Duma's Foreign Affairs Committee, said, '... When we had three times as much conventional weaponry as NATO, NATO deployed tactical nuclear weapons near the borders of the Warsaw Pact. Now NATO has a three-fold conventional superiority over us. What are we supposed to do?' (*The Guardian*, 22 March 1996).

The once formidable Soviet military is in disarray. Cuts in the military have been based on financial prerogatives rather than security needs. Defence spending was slashed to about 2.9 percent of GDP in 1995 as the Russian economy collapsed (*Russian Economic Trends*, vol. 4, no. 4, 1995: 11). Furthermore, in 1994, the military received only 46 percent of its capital allocation; in 1995, just 50 percent; and in 1996, an estimated 70 percent. The result has been grossly undermanned, under-equipped and under-trained units (*Moscow News*, 13-19 June 1996). The Western defence journal, *Jane's*, reported that 51 of 81 land divisions in early 1996 were not combat-ready. It went on to argue that Russia would be unable to mount military operations outside the CIS well into the next century (see *International Herald Tribune*, 17-18 February 1996). Official Russian sources state that the number of ships in the navy has dropped by more than half, with the Russian navy becoming little more than a coastal force (*Moscow News*, 13-19 June 1996). Morale in the Russian army is very low. This was exemplified by the military operation in Chechnya which was badly planned and badly organised. The Russian military might want more influence, but it is very conscious of its current weakness.

## Eastern Europe and NATO enlargement

After the dissolution of the Warsaw Pact in 1991, a power vacuum opened up in Eastern Europe. The states making up this region were small and felt vulnerable during the period of transition. Economic crisis throughout the region added to a feeling of paranoia. Although the macro-economic situation in the northern states improved dramatically from 1993, this rarely contributed to greater political stability. This was not difficult to understand. Unemployment remained high in most countries and average living standards remained below those of 1989. The general feeling of disillusionment was evidenced by the return to power of reform communists in Poland, Hungary, Bulgaria and Lithuania. Three states in Eastern Europe - the USSR, Yugoslavia and Czechoslovakia - split up under nationalist pressure. Only Czechoslovakia emerged without war and only the Czech Republic without severe economic decline. In Prague, the velvet revolution was followed by the velvet divorce. In Yugoslavia and the southern rim of the former Soviet Union, however, the breakup led to conflict. Nationalism in the rest of the region is on the rise but it has been contained so far - the threat of conflict spreading beyond the current war zones, however, remains a possibility.

Although Russia was geographically further from its Warsaw Pact allies after the end of the cold war - the newly independent states of Ukraine, Belorus, the Baltic Republics and Moldova provided a new buffer - Moscow was still seen potentially as a destabilising force. Russian support for the Serbs in Bosnia was viewed in much of Eastern Europe as a clear sign that Moscow had changed very little since the end of the cold war. As a result, much of Eastern Europe looked west - to NATO and the EC - for security and aid.

After the end of the cold war, NATO was looking for a new role. Since the communist threat had been defeated, it appeared to many that NATO should follow the Warsaw Pact's example and disband. West European leaders, however, were desperate to preserve the Atlantic Alliance if at all possible. For NATO had other roles which had outlived the fall of the Berlin Wall. Most important of all, Western Europe recognised the need for American leadership and military participation in European security. If nothing else, the wars in Yugoslavia had proved Europe's inability to deal with major crises without Washington.

President Clinton, for his part, was an enthusiastic supporter of NATO enlargement. It looked good policy from a moral point of view - the US could be seen to be responding to the wishes of small countries which had recently thrown off the yoke of communist dictatorship. It was good domestic politics too, since it bolstered America's image as a leader both at home and abroad. Finally, it also legitimised NATO's continued existence and the US presence in Europe.

Unfortunately, however, there was little discussion in Washington over the implications and practicalities of enlargement (Lieven, 1996: 178-9). The greatest problem to overcome was Russia and Russian attitudes. Russia was too big to be included in NATO, but it was also too big to be excluded from the security debate in Europe (see Worner, 1994). Initially, Yeltsin indicated a desire for Russia to join NATO, but this was later acknowledged in Moscow as unrealistic (see *Moscow News*, 15-21 February 1996). As a result, Moscow came out in opposition to NATO enlargement. It was not difficult to see why. NATO was a military organisation with a clear conventional superiority over Russia. It was dominated by the US and armed with nuclear weapons. Instead of NATO being abolished as Moscow had hoped, it was looking to further strengthen its position. Moscow had agreed to a reunified Germany joining NATO on the understanding that the West would not seek further expansion eastward (*Moscow Times*, 31 August 1995). It appeared to many in Moscow that the West had reneged on this agreement. If NATO absorbed Poland and the Czech Republic, what was to stop it taking in former Soviet republics like Ukraine or the Baltic States? Moscow favoured blocking enlargement before such questions could begin to be asked (*NATO Review*, February 1994: 22).

However, on a visit to Warsaw in September 1993, it seemed that there might have been a change of heart in Moscow. In a joint declaration with Lech Walesa, Boris Yeltsin stated that Polish membership of NATO 'does not go against the interests of other states, including the interests of Russia' (*Moscow News*, 3 September 1993). No doubt rumours in Moscow that Yeltsin had agreed to this whilst drunk were scurrilous. Nevertheless, he was quick to retract his statement when he returned home. At a press conference, Yevgeny Primakov, the chief of the Russian Foreign Intelligence Service (and from January 1996, Russian Foreign Minister), refuted his President's words and said that enlargement 'would bring the biggest military grouping in the world, with its colossal offensive potential, directly to the borders of Russia. If this happens', he went on, 'the need would arise for a fundamental reappraisal of all defence concepts on our side, a redeployment of armed forces and changes in operational plans' (*International Herald Tribune*, 26 November 1993). Any such reappraisal was likely to include further revisions to the START and CFE treaties or even expansion into areas not covered by NATO enlargement - most probably, Soviet successor states, such as Ukraine and possibly even the Baltic States (see *Nezavisimaya gazeta*, 14 March 1995). It was even suggested that if NATO membership was offered to the Baltic States, it would mean war (*The Guardian*, 3 February 1996). Therefore, the irony of NATO enlargement was that it could encourage the very actions it was designed to deter.

It appeared, however, that a compromise had been reached in November 1991, when NATO formed the North Atlantic Co-operative Council (NACC). The NACC was open to all NATO members and countries of Eastern Europe and the former Soviet Union. Its actual role was simply to introduce the workings of NATO to East European countries and to act as a general consultative body on security issues. The long-term aim of the NACC, however, was disputed. East Europeans tended to see NACC as a prelude to full membership, whilst Moscow saw it as a substitute for enlargement.

After the election of President Clinton, the US sided with the East Europeans and pressed for further progress on NATO enlargement. Thus, at the NATO summit in January 1994, the concept of Partnership for Peace (PFP) was formally adopted by the Atlantic Alliance. The PFP had three main objectives: first, to encourage democratic control over the military; second, to develop military co-operation between partners; and third, to 'consult with any active participant in the Partnership, if that partner perceived a direct threat to its territorial integrity, political independence, or security' (FCO, 1994: A2; and PFP Framework Document, January 1994). All ex-Warsaw Pact countries signed up for PFP, but Russia resisted and only joined in June 1994 after receiving guarantees of its rather ill-defined 'special status' in the Partnership.

No sooner had the Russians signed up for PFP than NATO set up a commission in December 1994 to study the implications of full membership for East European states. The formation of the commission surprised many members of NATO and outraged Moscow. The motivation for the sudden urgency appeared to be Washington's growing concern over the rise of nationalism in Russia and Moscow's perceived intransigence over Bosnia. In response, Kozyrev refused to sign a series of agreements relating to Russia's PFP membership and Yeltsin went to the CSCE summit in Budapest and warned of the possibility of a 'cold peace' (*The Guardian*, 6 December 1994).

In September 1995, the commission reported back and declared in favour of full NATO membership for all East European states that wanted it. The document also stated that new members should be given the basic collective security guarantee outlined in article 5 of the 1949 Washington Treaty. This stated that an attack against one member was deemed an attack against all. The commission, however, side-stepped a number of critical issues, including a time-table for recruiting new members and the deployment of nuclear weapons in those states. The document was seen as something of a compromise in the West, but it failed to comfort Moscow and led to some disappointment in Eastern Europe. Although the US continued to press for enlargement, a growing number of officials were recognising the possible dangers, practical difficulties and financial costs of bringing Eastern Europe into the integrated military command of NATO.

Moscow, for its part, continued to argue for NATO's abolition. Andrei Kozyrev said in a series of interviews that NATO was ill-suited to deal with the main problems of the region - migration, economic dislocation and nationalism. Kozyrev favoured more inclusive organisations, such as the Organisation on Security and Co-operation in Europe (OSCE) (see *Moscow News*, 30 June-6 July 1995). As the only truly pan-European body which existed during the cold war, the OSCE did not carry the ideological baggage of other organisations like NATO. Set up in 1975 by the Helsinki Final Act, all European states, plus the US and Canada as NATO states, were members.[2]

The main attraction of the OSCE for Moscow lay in the fact that Russia was a member and could play a full part in the decision-making process. The OSCE was indeed able to play a useful role in Eastern Europe through the monitoring of human rights and elections, and through acting as a mediator in ethnic conflicts in areas such as Trans-Dniester in Moldova. However, the OSCE was encumbered by two severe limitations. First, it was not a military organisation and, therefore, could not implement agreements. Second, the OSCE comprised over fifty sovereign states, including all the Soviet successor states, which made consensus decision-making extremely difficult. Thus, the West was not opposed to expanding the role of the OSCE but viewed the organisation more as a useful adjunct to existing organisations, rather than as a possible replacement for NATO. A fact Kozyrev's successor, Yevgeny Primakov, appeared to accept as he adopted a less confrontational stance on NATO enlargement.

The final European institution of importance in security matters was the Eu-

---

[2]  The Conference on Security in Europe (CSCE) changed its name in January 1995 to the Organisation on Security and Co-operation (OSCE). Albania was the only European country not to sign the Helsinki Final Act in 1975, but Tirana signed up after the end of the cold war. All fifteen Soviet successor states became members of the CSCE after the breakup of the USSR in 1991.

ropean Union (EU). Many believed that the EU was better placed than NATO or the OSCE to encourage the integration of Eastern Europe into the West. The EU was generally viewed by the European public as a remarkable success in reducing nationalism after World War II and sponsoring prosperity across the member states. The EU was primarily an economic organisation and one that was exclusively European. It was, therefore, viewed in Moscow much more positively than the US-dominated, defence organisation, NATO.

Even so, it was accepted in Europe after the cold war that the EU, like NATO, had to reform to adapt to new international realities. There were, however, divisions over how this should be achieved. France favoured deeper integration as envisaged by the Maastrict Treaty to offer a unified front to confront the destabilising effects of East European transition. Britain argued that a smooth transition would best be achieved through the expansion of the EU to take in new East European members. Germany favoured both options. The question was whether the EU could accommodate both deeper integration and a wider membership. There were reasons to doubt it.

A wider membership would almost certainly require radical structural changes to the EU. In particular, its agricultural and regional policies would suffer. Greece, one of the EU's poorest member, receives $780 per capita annually in regional aid, which amounts to between five and six percent of its total GNP. If such a policy were kept in place after enlargement, EU pay-outs would come to seven percent of GNP for Slovenia; 13 percent for the Czech Republic; and 34 percent for Bulgaria (*International Herald Tribune*, 1 November 1995). It is difficult to see how the EU budget could stand the strain. The unification of Germany, which is a good indicator of the possible costs of EU expansion, cost the Federal Republic 5 percent of GNP annually plus a 7.5 percent solidarity tax on income after 1990, but the process of integration was deemed only half complete by 1995 (*International Herald Tribune*, 1 November 1995). This policy was sustainable only because of the strength of political will in Germany. It is far from clear that the same political will exists in the case of other East European states.

Meanwhile, a core of EU members attempt to further integrate their political and economic policies. Although there are doubts over the time-table, a single currency looks like going ahead before too long. Such moves may make a lot of economic sense for current EU members, but it would make future membership for East European states more difficult. The feeling persists that the EU is bent on becoming a rather exclusive rich man's club. The image of first and second class membership, or concentric circles as it is sometimes referred to, only serves to deepen that suspicion.

However, Russia became a full member of the European Council in February 1996. Although fourteen other ex-communist states were already members, it was a controversial decision. For the Council was set up in 1949 to promote democracy and human rights throughout Europe. In the light of the Russian offensive against Chechnya, many believed that Moscow had foresworn the right to join. However, the vote was conclusively in favour of Russia joining - 165 for and only 35 against. Presumably, Europe was willing to turn a blind eye to Russian atrocities since membership of the European Council cost Western Europe nothing in terms of trade or lost business.

## Aid and trade

Kozyrev hoped that Western aid would be sufficient to subsidise Russia's difficult transition process towards a liberal democracy and a market economy. Russia lacked capital and was forced to look outside for investment. Although the response from the West disappointed many (see Aslund, 1995: 215-220), there can be no doubt that Moscow achieved much in a relatively short period. Russia became a member of the IMF and the World Bank in April 1992. In July 1992, at Munich the G7 offered $24 billion to the CIS, including an $18 billion package to Russia. At Tokyo, the following year, the sum had gone up to $43 billion. In May 1990, the European Bank of Reconstruction and Development (EBRD) was set up to provide much-needed capital for East European economies. By 1994, the bank was funding about 43 investment projects in Russia at a total cost of $1.5 billion (*Moscow Times*, 4 July, 1995). Moscow also benefited from other aid packages, involving technical expertise, money to ensure the safety of nuclear weapons, as well as a series of bilateral schemes from a number of Western countries.

Despite all this, Moscow soon became disillusioned with the West. Even though the sums of money were huge, it would have taken much more to make a substantial difference to the performance of the Russian economy. The US gave approximately $10 billion in Marshall Aid to the countries of Western Europe in the period 1948-50. This amounted to 2 percent of the receiving nations' GNP. If the equivalent of Marshall Aid had been offered to Moscow (as some suggested at the time), then $30 to $50 billion were required annually for the countries of the former Soviet Union (Utagawa, 1992: 52). In the best of times, such amounts were unlikely to be available over the medium-term, but as the Western world entered a long period of recession after the cold war, even Germany (which provided about half of all aid to the former Soviet Union) was unwilling to continue its generous contributions to any region of Eastern Europe other than the former GDR. In any case, the desire to invest in Russia fell away when it seemed so much investment was wasted due to corruption, crime and the seemingly intractable problems over economic transition.

Russians also became sceptical over the reasons for Western aid (see, for example, *Izvestiya*, 22 April 1993). Much aid was tied to Russian compliance with IMF directives over inflation and the budget deficit. The Russian government, however, was often unable to sustain such policies due to the social costs. Rutskoi was no doubt wildly exaggerating when he declared that the West was pursuing purposeful policies to weaken Russia, but the West could be accused of hypocrisy in advocating austerity packages that would never have been tolerated at home. Nevertheless, the West, as lender, had some justification in laying down certain economic terms for the granting of aid. More difficult to stomach for many Russians, however, was the linkage of aid to issues of domestic politics, and particularly policy in the near abroad. For example, the US Senate passed an amendment in September 1993 linking aid to the withdrawal of Russian troops from the Baltic Republics (Webber, 1996: 299).

A further cause of resentment related to the nature of aid. Little aid was offered in the form of grants; most was tied to the purchase of Western products which offered limited long-term gains for the Russian economy. A Western report on US aid to Russia noted that 'the largest chunk is earmarked for the salaries and travel expenses of US consultants ... to supervise the various assistance programmes' (*International Herald Tribune*, 12 May 1995). A Russian survey discovered that 75-80 percent of all Western aid was given for financing the Russian debt (*Russian Review*, no. 3, 1994: 10). Thus, in the muddled world of international economics, in the first three years after the fall of the USSR, more money was leaving Russia than arriving from the West in the form of aid. In the single year of 1993, as much as $20 billion fled Russia for Western banks, although some did begin to trickle back from 1994 (*Russian Review*, no. 4, 1994).

If aid was not the panacea the Yeltsin administration had hoped for, trade to the West was a problem too. Progress was made in some important areas. The US accorded Russia 'Most Favoured Nation' (MFN) status in 1992 which essentially meant the reduction of tariffs - something the US had already offered the Soviet Union back in 1972 before Moscow pulled out due to highly restrictive amendments imposed by Congress (see Bowker and Williams, 1988). In 1994, the COCOM arrangement was abolished which imposed restrictions on advanced technological goods which could be used for military purposes. The EU also reduced tariffs on certain goods, although they often remained in place on goods Eastern Europe was best placed to export, such as coal, steel, textiles and most agricultural products. As a result, a growing trade imbalance between the two parts of Europe emerged. An EU deficit in trade of $1 billion in 1990 was turned round into a $5 billion surplus in 1993 (*International Herald Tribune*, 18 April 1994).

Whilst Moscow suffered from trade restrictions in Western Europe, it also faced economic embargoes on many of its former allies, such as Cuba, Libya, Iraq and Serbia. It was estimated that sanctions up to 1993 cost the Russian treasurer anything from $20 to $30 billion (*Moscow News*, 21 May 1993). It made sense, therefore, for Russia to make up this loss elsewhere. Increasingly, Moscow turned to the arms trade. In the 1980s, Russia was one of the world's leading arms exporters with a trade averaging $20 billion annually (*Nezavisimaya gazeta*, 29 September 92). By 1993, this trade had collapsed to $2.5 billion (*Moscow News*, 21 May 1993). Russia was determined to turn this around and began to compete far more effectively in the arms market from 1995. The US, however, remained the market leader with a 70 percent market share in the mid-1990s (*Time*, 19 December 1994).

However, the US became concerned over Russian high technology sales to countries such as China and Iran. There were grounds for America's unease - obviously such sales could destabilise unsettled parts of the world. Nevertheless, it was also true that the American position was suffused with hypocrisy. Many Russian military experts believed it simply reflected an American desire to keep out effective competition (*Russian Review*, 31 October 1994). Thus, the US objected to Moscow's plan to sell nuclear reactors to Iran. The IAEA had approved the sale, but Washington objected on the grounds that it would aid Tehran's quest for nuclear weapons. The irony was all the greater since Clinton had done a deal to provide similar reactors to Pyongyang free of charge in what was presented to the world by Washington as a plan to *prevent* nuclear proliferation in North Korea.

The US stance made little sense and simply fuelled nationalist resentment in Moscow. In any case, Washington had lost its leverage over Moscow since its aid to Russia had fallen dramatically over the years. There was little incentive for Moscow to compromise. The deal with Iran was worth $1 billion whilst American aid slated for 1996 came to $260 million.

## Conclusion

The Russian romance with the US has come to an end. As stated earlier, this was not unexpected. Russia remains a country that is very different from the US. There is little natural cultural affinity between America and Russia. Therefore, there is little reason to expect a long-term partnership between the two countries. Co-operation can be expected only when interests coincide. And even though relations have cooled considerably, areas of mutual interest still exist on issues such as nuclear proliferation and nuclear safety. There are also grounds to hope that Russia and the US can co-operate to maintain peace and stability in Europe and the CIS.

However, relations with the West will be more difficult in future. Since 1993, Russia adopted a more independent and nationalist line. Andrei Kozyrev was having increasing difficulty accommodating this new shift with his earlier Westernism. His departure from government was often predicted, but it finally came after the 1995 parliamentary elections. His successor as Foreign Minister, Yevgeny Primakov, was a rarity in the Yeltsin administration being a man who had been a prominent official in the Gorbachev era. He had come to international prominence during the Gulf War when he won the reputation in Washington of being a 'trouble-maker' (*The Guardian*, 13 January 1996).

Primakov can certainly be characterised as a Eurasianist. At a press conference, he argued that Russia was still a great power and relations with the West would be put on a par with India, Japan, the Middle East and the Near East (*The Guardian*, 13 January 1996). He rejected the idea of a return to the cold war, but repeated his opposition to NATO enlargement and said START 2 would not be ratified if Washington sought to amend the 1972 ABM treaty. He also declared that the sovereignty of the twelve Soviet successor states 'cannot negate the need for economic integration' (*International Herald Tribune*, 13-14 January 1996). Such policy statements, however, were less a sign of a shift in policy and more a confirmation of policies already enacted. Primakov, however, had the advantage of being more convinced than his predecessor of their necessity.

# Chapter Twelve

# THE WARS IN YUGOSLAVIA

As Yugoslavia collapsed into war in 1991-2, Russia had its own problems nearer home and paid relatively little attention to events in the Balkans. Initially, Moscow was prepared to play a largely passive role in support of Western diplomatic efforts, but from 1993 Moscow showed a greater willingness to adopt a more independent line - a development not universally welcomed in the West, particularly as it coincided with a revival of Russian nationalism at home. As Russia tilted towards the Serbs, critics argued that it was encouraging Serb aggression in Bosnia and making a just settlement more difficult to achieve (see, for example, *International Herald Tribune*, 8 December 1994). This view, however, was rather simplistic for two main reasons.

First, Moscow's influence over Serb actions was exaggerated - not least by the Russians themselves. National interest in both Moscow and Belgrade proved stronger than pan-slavism. Both sides used the other for their own self-interested purposes. Serbia sought Russian support because of its influence in international forums - most notably as a permanent member of the UN Security Council. Moscow, for its part, saw the Yugoslav crisis as an opportunity to present itself still as a great power whose influence was required to resolve problems in the Balkans and elsewhere around the world. However, this essentially instrumental relationship was abandoned whenever it proved inconvenient to either party.

Second, Russian policy, despite its pro-Serb tilt from 1993, remained within the international consensus throughout the Yugoslav crisis. In fact, it was the Western powers of Germany and the United States which were more prepared - for good or ill - to break that consensus. The Germans swept aside EC policy and unilaterally recognised Slovenia and Croatia in December 1991; whilst the United States used its powerful position to undermine the Vance-Owen Peace Plan in 1993 and after November 1994 refused to monitor the arms embargo.

The main criticism of Russian policy related to its opposition to peace enforcement operations but, in fact, this was fully in line with all nations who had UN troops on the ground in the former Yugoslavia. The EC envoy, Lord Owen, derided the US for advocating a policy which, he said, comprised of peacekeeping on the ground and peace enforcement in the air (Owen, 1995). Reasons for international caution varied across the nations, but none relished the idea of becoming involved in another Balkans war. No nation, including the US, was prepared to commit the many thousands of ground troops needed to fight an effective war against the Serbs (Freedman, L., 1994-5: 61).

This central fact meant that the international community had two basic options - to allow the different ethnic groups to fight it out amongst themselves or to mediate a diplomatic solution to the conflict. Those that favoured diplomacy recognised that Russia's links to the Serbs could prove useful. For no lasting solution to the problems in the former Yugoslavia was possible without Serb agreement. However, Washington claimed credit for its more interventionist stance from the summer of 1995 which led to the peace agreement the following November. It was clear that US pressure on the Serbs was decisive, but Moscow's earlier diplomatic initiatives in Belgrade should not be ignored. Moscow was quick to appreciate in 1993 that Milosevic had changed his colours and was willing to work for peace. This shift was the single most important factor in ending the war in Bosnia two years later.

## The fall of Yugoslavia

Yugoslavia was created as a state out of the ruins of World War I. The country was always an uneasy alliance of different ethnic groups in a region of historic instability. A short and tortured existence was finally brought to an end in 1941 when Yugoslavia collapsed as a state and the country descended into the most brutal civil war. (See table 12:1 for the distribution of ethnic groups in Yugoslavia when the country began to break up.)

Table 12:1
The Distribution of Ethnic Groups in the Republics of Yugoslavia*

| Republic | Capital | Pop (millions) | Major national groups |
|---|---|---|---|
| Serbia | Belgrade | 9.3 | Serb (66%), Albanian (14%) |
| Croatia | Zagreb | 4.5 | Croat (80%), Serb (12%) |
| Bosnia | Sarajevo | 4.0 | Muslim (39.5%), Serb (32%), Croat (17%) |
| Slovenia | Lublijana | 2.0 | Slovenian (90%) |
| Montenegro | Titograd | 0.5 | Montenegrin (68%), Muslim (13%) |
| Macedonia | Skopje | 2.0 | Macedonian (67%), Albanian (20%) |
| **Total** | | **22.3** | |

NB. *Serbia includes the provinces of:*

| | | |
|---|---|---|
| Kosovo | *1.9* | *Albanian (77%); Serb (13%)* |
| Vojvodina | *2.0* | *Serb (54%); Hungarian (19%)* |

* Statistics for the column on the population in republics from the 1989 census; and for the provinces from 1991. On the distribution of national groups in each republic from the 1981 census. Collated from various sources, including *Eastern Europe and the CIS,* Europa Publications, London, 1992: 277.

In the post-war period, Tito managed to stitch the country back together and achieved political stability through a combination of charisma, communist dictatorship, and the disciplines of the cold war. Tito's main aim was to give Serbia, the largest republic, a major stake in the future of Yugoslavia whilst preventing it from dominating the new federation. He achieved this delicate balancing act by creating a decentralised state in which the six republics (and after constitutional changes in 1974, also the two Serb provinces of Kosovo and Vojvodina) were accorded real power, whilst the Serbs were allowed to dominate the federal institutions of the party, state and military.

Such a set-up was sustainable whilst Tito lived, but after his death in May

1980 the whole system began to unravel. Central authority became paralysed by the complex system of collective decision-making which Tito had devised to allow all ethnic groups to be heard. Thus, when the country began to suffer from economic decline in the 1980s, the government found itself unable to respond effectively. As a result, by the time Gorbachev came to power in 1985, none of the ethnic groups in Yugoslavia was satisfied with the status quo (Cviic, 1991: 60-63).

The wealthier republics of Slovenia and Croatia sought further decentralisation. They favoured radical economic reform and they believed this was being blocked by the poorer republics. Serbia wanted the opposite. Serbia wanted to increase the powers of the centre and control the centrifugal forces in the country. The Serbs feared the radical economic reforms, advocated by Lublijana and Zagreb, would undermine the weaker Serb economy, whilst greater autonomy for the republics could be seen as the further abandonment of the estimated 2.5 million Serbs living outside the republic.

Slobodan Milosevic became leader of the Serb Communist Party in 1986. The following year, he went to the autonomous province of Kosovo where Serb nationalists were claiming discrimination by the Albanian majority. After facing mass demonstrations, Milosevic came out firmly in support of the Serb minority and launched his career as a Serb nationalist. Later in 1987, Milosevic used the issue of Serb nationalism to oust his former patron, Ivan Stambolic as Serb President, and proceeded to shift power in Yugoslavia towards the Serbs. By 1990, he had undermined the autonomy of the two Serb provinces, Kosovo and Vojvodina, and brought the republic of Montenegro under Serb control. The dictatorial methods employed by Milosevic to achieve these ends alienated non-Serbs and contributed materially to the final collapse of Yugoslavia a year later.

The polarisation of opinion amongst the different ethnic groups in Yugoslavia was starkly revealed in the multi-party elections which were held at various times in 1990 in all the republics. The communists generally performed well in Orthodox Christian areas - most notably in Serbia, whilst in Catholic Slovenia and Croatia, they were defeated by democrats or nationalists - or a combination of both.

After the elections, Slovenia held a referendum in December 1990 and the people voted overwhelmingly for independence. This was a turning point in the history of Yugoslavia. If Slovenia were to secede from the federation, it would leave Zagreb without an ally, and Serbia in an even more dominant position within a truncated Yugoslavia. After the idea of a confederation was rejected by

Belgrade the following spring, Slovenia and Croatia issued a joint statement declaring independence on 25 June 1991. The move was condemned by the international community which opposed the redrawing of borders in a region with a history of ethnic conflict. The Soviet Foreign Minister, Alexander Bessmertnykh, was only reflecting the general international view, when he declared in an official statement that a single, independent Yugoslavia was 'an important element of stability in the Balkans and in Europe as a whole' (*Pravda*, 29 June 1991).

## War in Slovenia and Croatia

International diplomacy failed both to maintain the federation and to prevent the ensuing conflict. War flared in Slovenia as the Yugoslav National Army (JNA), dominated by the Serbs, moved against Lublijana after its declaration of independence. However, the JNA action was not successful in forcing Slovenia back into the federation. The war only lasted ten days and a cease-fire agreement, brokered by the EC (with Russia playing no role), was signed on 7 July 1991 at Brioni.

Hopes that similar agreements would be possible elsewhere in Yugoslavia, however, proved misplaced. Slovenia was, in many ways, a unique case, being ethnically homogenous and united in its desire for independence. This fact afforded the JNA less justification for action than in the cases of Bosnia or Croatia where significant minorities opposed secession. Moreover, militarily the Slovenes proved to be far better organised than the JNA had ever imagined and, since the war in Croatia was already under way, the JNA was reluctant to fight on two fronts. Slovenia was perceived in Belgrade to be less important than Croatia, so a cease-fire was quickly arranged.

As the JNA withdrew from Slovenia, the Serb aim of a united federal Yugoslavia dominated from Belgrade had to be abandoned, but this did not mean an end to the conflict in Yugoslavia. On the contrary, Milosevic had long since made it absolutely clear that if Yugoslavia were to break up, he would seek the redrawing of borders (which he described as purely administrative) to more accurately reflect ethnic divisions in the region (Bebler, 1993: 82). Since the majority of the Serb diaspora lived in Croatia and Bosnia, inevitably Belgrade's attention shifted to those republics.

Franjo Tudjman had been elected President of Croatia on a nationalist ticket in April 1990. The 600,000 Serbs living in Croatia soon became worried by the policies of his new government and Milosevic had little difficulty in whipping up Serb nationalism against Zagreb. Tudjman glorified the independent state of Croatia which had existed during World War II and re-introduced many of the national symbols of that time, including the red and white checkerboard flag. Such references to the war-time *Ustashe* state only reminded Serbs of the brutal racist attacks perpetrated against their nation during that period. Fears of history repeating itself were intensified when some Serbs in state posts were dismissed, and the local police force in some Serb areas was disarmed.

The Serbs reacted by setting up the autonomous Serb province of Krajina on Croatian territory in August 1990 and declaring independence in the spring of 1991. Although the Serbs formed the majority population in Krajina, it was also important to Croats both as a cultural centre and a strategic trading route to the Adriatic. The dispute led to fighting from autumn 1990, escalating into war after the declaration of Croatian independence in June 1991 with the JNA supporting the rebels. The conflict quickly became far more destructive than anything seen in Slovenia. In the summer and autumn of 1991, the ancient city of Dubrovnik was shelled repeatedly by the Serbs whilst Vukovar to the east was levelled to the ground.

At the Moscow summit in July, Bush and Gorbachev issued a joint statement condemning the violence and demanding respect for human rights. Gorbachev's more conservative opponents in the Kremlin, however, took a less neutral line. Dmitri Yazov, the Soviet Defence Minister, agreed on 10-11 August to a secret $2 billion arms deal with Serbia. The deal included helicopter gunships, rocket launchers and tanks (Glenny, 1993: 61). The weaponry, however, was never delivered because of the fall of the conservatives in Moscow after the failed August coup.

However, the defeat of the Moscow putschists did not appear to have any direct impact on the course of the war. The fighting continued as a series of cease-fire agreements was negotiated in the conference hall but ignored on the battlefield. In the hope of containing the conflict, the UN decided to impose an arms embargo on all of Yugoslavia in September 1991. Moscow supported the UN resolution (UNSCR 713) whilst also indulging in some bilateral negotiation itself. Both Milosevic and Tudjman visited Moscow in October and hammered out a cease-fire agreement with Gorbachev. But the agreement, like others negotiated earlier by the EC, was not honoured. Gorbachev, much weakened politically after the August coup, found (like Yeltsin, his successor) that Russian influence over his fellow slavs was limited.

As the war escalated, the West debated the merits of formally recognising the independence of the two breakaway republics. It became a source of great tension within the Western alliance. The Germans favoured recognition on both moral and pragmatic grounds. Bonn argued that the EC should not oppose the democratic wish of the people of Croatia and Slovenia for self-determination. European support for the central authorities of Yugoslavia was having the effect of legitimising the use of force against the breakaway republics. Other states in the EC - most notably Britain - argued that recognition would encourage the complete disintegration of Yugoslavia and imply, erroneously, a readiness on the part of the international community to defend the sovereignty of the newly independent states.

International law is a muddle on the issue. For it accords no absolute right to minorities to secede, yet it simultaneously argues that the central authority has no right to use force to prevent this happening (Higgins, 1993: 468). The EC, therefore, chose a compromise position, arguing that recognition was only possible in the context of an overall settlement to the Yugoslav problem. Recognition was denied Croatia since it was not in full control of its territory and was not in a position to grant full civil rights to its ethnic minorities.

However, Bonn broke ranks in December 1991 and decided unilaterally to recognise both Slovenia and Croatia. This was, at best, an insensitive move. It evoked fears in Serbia that a newly reunified Germany was once again flexing its muscles and seeking to extend its influence into the Balkans. The decision by Bonn was generally condemned, yet the EC quickly reversed its policy and formally recognised the two breakaway republics on 15 January 1992. The reason for the sudden U-turn is still not entirely clear. However, it appeared to have more to do with alliance management within the EC rather than the real interests of Yugoslav citizens. At the same time, it was important to note that recognition had become more acceptable to the international community since the collapse of the USSR. Russian President Boris Yeltsin favoured self-determination for the Soviet Union, and he had little time personally for Slobodan Milosevic who had supported the conspirators in the August coup. Therefore, Yeltsin followed the EC's lead and recognised both Slovenia and Croatia in February - some two months before Washington.

Bonn's argument that recognition would encourage a settlement appeared vindicated when a cease-fire was signed in January 1992. A UN Protection Force (UNPROFOR) was set up and 14,000 troops were sent in June to Krajina to monitor the agreement. No US troops were deployed, but Yeltsin, for the first time, accepted a UN peacekeeping role for Russia and agreed to deploy 1,000 soldiers. The deployment provided a useful opportunity for Yeltsin to emphasise Russia's break with the past and its willingness to play a more positive and co-operative role in the future of European security. It was the height of Moscow's pro-Western foreign policy.

The truce in Croatia was unstable, however, since it failed to settle any of the outstanding issues between the Serbs and Croats. The agreement was reached only after the Serbs were in occupation of Krajina (made up of West Slavonia, East Slavonia and Krajina itself) which comprised approximately thirty percent of the republic. Zagreb remained committed to taking back territory lost in war and, with the help of the US and Germany, began to build up its military strength to that end.

## The war in Bosnia

The cease-fire of January 1992 in Croatia left the Republic of Bosnia Hercegovina dangling in a disintegrating Yugoslavia. In the circumstances, the Bosnian government, elected in November 1990 and led by Alija Izetbegovic, had two basic options - to remain in rump Yugoslavia dominated by an increasingly nationalistic Serbia; or to declare independence. Izetbegovic was well aware that secession was a move fraught with risk. Both Zagreb and Belgrade perceived Bosnia, not as a potential bona fide nation-state, but as little more than an administrative area of Yugoslavia. Thus, before the outbreak of war, Milosevic and Tudjman made well-publicised plans to partition the republic between themselves (Glenny, 1993: 143-44).

In an attempt to resolve the issue, President Izetbegovic, at the recommendation of the EC, called a referendum for March 1992. The overwhelming majority of Muslims and Croats voted for independence but most Serbs, who made up a third of the Bosnian population, boycotted the election. The Bosnian Serbs refused to recognise Bosnian independence and instead set up a parallel government at Pale with Radovan Karadzic as leader.

In Croatia before the war, the Tudjman government acted provocatively towards the Serbs. The same can scarcely be said of the Izetbegovic government, which included Croats and Serbs amongst its ranks and advocated a multi-cultural, pluralist and secular state. Despite this, many Serbs feared that Bosnia would become an Islamic state which would seek to repress the Serb nation and culture. Historically, the Serbs had perceived themselves on the front-line fighting against the expansion of Islam in Europe. The Ottoman empire had disintegrated long ago, but in the 1990s, it seemed, Islam was once again on the rise.

The majority of Serbs were simply not prepared to live under the leadership of Alija Izetbegovic, a devout Muslim, who had written an academic work in the 1970s promoting the idea of an Islamic state in Bosnia (see Glenny, 1993: 154).

Such worries were rejected by Izetbegovic as scare-mongering. He said his views in the book were misrepresented by Serb nationalists, and in any case they had changed since the book was published. Izetbegovic said that he hoped the divisions in Bosnian society would not lead to war, as they had in Croatia, because his country had a reputation for ethnic tolerance. He also felt that Western recognition of his country after the referendum in April 1992, provided some kind of guarantee against Serb aggression. Sadly, his optimism was misplaced and Bosnia descended into violence and the most bloody war in Europe since 1945.

The headquarters of the JNA were located in Bosnia, and the republic was, therefore, awash in weaponry. As Bosnia moved towards independence, military bases and military equipment were taken over almost exclusively by the Serbs. The Bosnian government, in contrast, had little military equipment and in the early stages of the war was incapable of defending itself against the heavily armed Serbs.

From the spring of 1992, the Serb army launched a vicious war against the Muslims (or the Bosniacs, as they were also known). By Christmas, the Serbs were in occupation of about 70 percent of the country. As they swept through Bosnia, the Serbs terrorised Muslim civilians and forced them to flee their homes. This barbaric policy became known as ethnic cleansing. The aim of the policy was to carve out a sustainable and ethnically pure Serbian state out of Bosnia Hercegovina.[1]

It appeared the only way Bosnia could survive as a state in the winter of 1992 was through Western military intervention. Yet, the international community stood back and wrung its hands in despair. Military intervention was always a risky option, but if any international action were to be taken, then spring 1992 appeared the optimal time. In the first phase of the war, the Muslims and Croats were in an uneasy alliance and the Serbs had not yet achieved all their war aims. By the end of the year, this had all changed with the Serbs in occupation of seventy percent of the country and the Croats abandoning their alliance with the Muslims and about to launch their own land-grab (Freedman, L., 1994-5: 61).

---

[1] For details on the policy and effects of ethnic cleansing, see Glenny, 1993; Almond, 1994; Rieff, 1995; and Silber and Little, 1995.

At this point, the war became a more complex three-way fight with the Muslims being squeezed out to only about ten percent of the Bosnian land mass. From this moment, any attempt to reverse war gains by external intervention would have been both costly and extremely difficult. Was NATO to fight only the Serbs or the Croats as well? It was estimated that about 400,000 ground troops would have been needed to enforce a peace in Bosnia, and almost as many to maintain it over a prolonged period of time (Freedman, L.,1994-5: 61). No state was prepared to deploy anything like that number of troops on behalf of the beleaguered Bosniacs.

Instead, the international community sought to bring the war to a speedy conclusion through diplomatic means. The prospects for co-operation between East and West made mediators more hopeful that a compromise solution could be reached. In this early phase of the war through to the end of 1992, Moscow acknowledged that Belgrade bore the heaviest responsibility for the Bosnian conflict. Therefore, Moscow supported economic sanctions against Belgrade in May; approved the extension of UNPROFOR to Bosnia to deliver humanitarian aid in September; and backed a No-Fly Zone for all military aircraft over Bosnia in October. Moscow even accepted a role for NATO in policing the No-Fly Zone, as long as any military action was approved by the UN - a process that became known as the 'dual key' approach.

In January 1993, the EC and UN unveiled the Vance-Owen Peace Plan (VOPP). The plan was strongly backed by Russia and all the EC states. The VOPP aimed to retain Bosnia as a sovereign state within its current boundaries but, recognising the ethnic divisions within the country, called for the state to be divided into ten cantons: three for the Muslims; three for the Serbs; three for the Croats; and the tenth, Sarajevo, to remain a multi-ethnic city. The plan required the Serbs to give up over thirty percent of its territorial war gains, and it was estimated that up to 75,000 UN troops would be needed to police the agreement.

However, Bill Clinton, inaugurated as President in January 1993, was lukewarm towards the proposal. The reasons for his opposition changed over time. At first, the US argued that the VOPP was unfair to the Muslims. The VOPP, it was said, appeased Serb aggression, ratified ethnic cleansing, and worst of all did not even offer the prospect of a long-term solution. This was because the plan was unjust and therefore the Muslims would, at some future date, rise up against the imposed settlement. By the spring, the US position had turned 180 degrees. The US now suggested that the plan was too radical (Owen, 1995: 170). It was now recognised in Washington that the VOPP required a major Serb withdrawal and Clinton had become concerned over the deployment of US ground troops to force the Serbs back. Thus, in February 1993, Warren Christopher declared the US was not prepared to impose a settlement on the parties in Bosnia (Owen, 1995: 282). According to David Owen, this lack of will on the part of the US scuppered the VOPP and the last chance of a peace which was committed to the reversal of ethnic cleansing (Owen, 1995: chapter 4).

The alternative proposal from the Clinton administration which was floated in February 1993 was the so-called 'lift and strike' option. The idea was to lift the arms embargo on the Muslims and support their war effort through NATO air strikes. In effect, this meant giving air support for the Muslims to fight their own war. The US argued the merits of the case in two ways. First, the arms embargo did not apply to Bosnia since it had been imposed on all of Yugoslavia in September 1991 before Bosnia had been recognised as an independent sovereign state. Second, every sovereign state had the absolute right in international law to self-defence as stated in article 51 of the UN Charter. If the international community was not prepared to defend Bosnia, then the US declared a moral duty to give the Bosniacs the means to do so themselves.

The Clinton initiative was greeted unenthusiastically by his allies when Warren Christopher, the Secretary of State, tried to sell it on a round trip of European capitals in early 1993. The implicit aim of 'lift and strike' was the escalation of the conflict in Bosnia. This ran directly counter to the aims of Britain, France and Russia. After the collapse of the VOPP, these countries favoured the speediest possible termination of hostilities in Bosnia - almost at any price. Whilst Clinton was encouraging the Muslims to fight on to get a fairer deal, London, Paris and Moscow were arguing that the Muslims had effectively lost the war and should sue for peace. They argued that the longer the war went on, the greater the danger of the conflict sucking in other Balkan states. Thus, the containment of the war became an end in itself. If this involved the surrender of the Muslims, so be it. Justice would have to give way, as so often in the Balkans, to *realpolitik*.

In the face of such fierce opposition, the 'lift and strike' strategy was dropped, although it was never formally abandoned by Christopher. Instead, containment, a rather vague and indeterminate concept, became official policy in Washington too. However, as part of this new overall strategy, the UN approved a safe area policy, first in Srebrenica in April, and then extended in May to Sarajevo, Gorazde, Zepa, Bihac and Tuzla. The ostensible aim was to defend the Muslim populations in the six designated areas from Serb attack. However, the declaration was based on bluff since the areas were not demilitarised and only 7,500 extra troops were deployed instead of the estimated 35,000 required. As a result, the Serbs continued to beseige safe areas and the Muslims used them as military bases to launch attacks against their enemies (Owen, 1995: 355).

Hopes for peace were low in the autumn and winter of 1993. It was also a difficult year in Moscow. Parliament was critical of Yeltsin's servility towards the West on Bosnia at the expense of Serbia - Moscow's traditional ally. Yeltsin's critics were vilified in the West as extreme Slavophiles. It was true that many statements made in parliament were ill-considered and blindly pro-Serb. It was also true that many statements were made simply to embarrass the Russian President as part of the ongoing domestic power struggle in Moscow. This did not mean, however, that all criticism was without merit. The timing of the criticism was also not wholly related to the rise of nationalism in Moscow. In fact, the nature of the war in Bosnia changed fundamentally in 1993 when the Croats broke their alliance with the Muslims and began to attack their former allies. The conduct of the Croats in the war was little better than the Serbs, as they too pursued a policy of ethnic cleansing. This did not exculpate the Serbs as some Russian parliamentarians claimed, but it did demolish the common perception of the Serbs as the sole villain of the piece. It also left the international strategy of singling out Belgrade for retribution without any logical rationale. If Belgrade suffered from economic sanctions, why not Zagreb?

The Russian parliament called for an end to the embargo on Belgrade which was costing Moscow at least $3.5 bilion, and for recognition of rump Yugoslavia which comprised Serbia and Montenegro (*Izvestiya*, 29 June 1993). Although Yeltsin refused to shift from the common international position on these specific points, the divisions in the West over policy encouraged his administration to take a more active diplomatic role in the Yugoslav crisis (*New Times*, no. 28, 1993). The Russian government favoured improved relations with Belgrade as a means of bringing the war to an end. It was argued that the historical and cultural ties between the two nations provided opportunities for Moscow to exert its influence over the Serbs.

However, the US position towards the Serbs toughened after a bomb killed 69 civilians and wounded over 200 in the Sarajevo central market on 5 February 1994. TV cameras were there to capture the event and the horror galvanised Western public opinion. Clinton argued for decisive action against the Serbs and threatened NATO air strikes to remove the heavy weaponry around Sarajevo. When Russia rejected the proposal at the UN Security Council, only China supported Moscow. Moscow was heavily criticised for failing to keep in step with the West (see Crow, 1993), but the decision to threaten air strikes represented a sudden and dramatic shift in NATO's position. The concept of air strikes had been rejected back in the spring of 1993 and the reasons for this decision seemed as relevant in February 1994. The attack on the Sarajevo market was a dreadful event, but it was only one among a series of atrocities which had resulted in almost 10,000 deaths since the start of the seige in 1992 (Silber and Little, 1995: 345).

As the Bosnian Serbs refused to move their heavy weaponry from around Sarajevo, Vitaly Churkin, Russia's special envoy, conducted some bilateral diplomacy with Pale. Ratko Mladic, commander of the Bosnian Serb army, feared that if he withdrew the weaponry, the Muslims would move in and take advantage. But Churkin got agreement after negotiating the redeployment of four hundred Russians from Krajina to Sarajevo. They were welcomed by the Serbs as conquering heroes. The Russian deal with the Serbs was described in Moscow as a political triumph for Yeltsin. The Russian army newspaper, *Krasnaya zvezda* (not a traditional Yeltsin supporter), proudly declared that the settlement showed that Russia was still a great power. Only Russia, it announced, was trusted by the Bosnian Serbs and was able to negotiate a deal (*Krasnaya zvezda*, 19 February 1994).

Whilst many Western governments were relieved that NATO air strikes had been avoided, many commentators in the US viewed the Russian initiative with some alarm. Although the guns fell silent and life in Sarajevo became more tolerable at least for a while, the removal of the heavy weapons did not end the seige of the city. Western critics argued that the position of the Serbs around Sarajevo had actually strengthened since the presence of Russian troops made any further threat of air strikes less convincing. American newspapers were full of warnings that Russian foreign policy was reverting to cold war attitudes. Moscow, once again, it was said, was supporting the aggressor in a regional conflict against an American ally (*International Herald Tribune*, 4 March 1994).

To show American resolve, NATO, just a few days after the Sarajevo deal, on 28 February, in its first military action since its creation in 1949, intercepted Serb jets over the No-Fly Zone in Bosnia. This was one of any number of violations, so the timing of the NATO strike created deep suspicion in Moscow. Nevertheless, the Yeltsin administration came out in reluctant support of the NATO action since the violation was blatant and undisputed.

However, the following April, when NATO planes attacked Serb positions around Gorazde, this time on the ground, it caused greater ructions in Moscow. The Serbs had moved their heavy artillery from Sarajevo to Gorazde after the Russian-brokered deal and had begun the bombardment of another safe area.

The NATO air strike was justified under UNSCR 824, which authorised 'close air support' for the UN peacekeeping troops under seige. In the case of Gorazde, this involved twelve UN military observers in the area. However, as an American newspaper wrote, UNSCR 824 was little more than a convenient fig-leaf as America sought to up the stakes and shift to a more partisan position in the Bosnian conflict (*International Herald Tribune*, 13 April 1994). It was recognised that NATO air strikes were risky since they endangered UN troops on the ground who were lightly armed and vulnerable to attack.

Yeltsin expressed outrage at NATO's actions which, he said, could mean 'eternal war' in the Balkans (*Pravda*, 13 April 1994). He clearly felt that the lack of consultation over NATO plans showed a contempt for Russian sensitivities. Nationalists, as well as more moderate figures, such as Ambartsumov and Lukin, saw the attack as further evidence that the US wanted to throw its weight about and threaten Russian strategic interests (*Moscow News*, 15-21 April 1994 and 22-28 April 1994).

However, the furore slowly died down, for two main reasons. First, the air strikes were light and ineffective and had no impact on the ground. Second, the Serbs embarrassed the Russians by defying their diplomatic initiatives to defuse the crisis and end the bombardment of Gorazde (*Moscow News*, 29 July - 4 August 1994). Vitaly Churkin, the hero of Sarajevo, expressed outrage when his diplomatic efforts over Gorazde were ignored. His failure barely two months after the triumph at Sarajevo weakened the Russian claim to have effective leverage over the Bosnian Serbs. As a result, Moscow's objections to a second round of air strikes against Serb positions around Gorazde were lifted. Ultimately, Karadzic climbed down in the face of NATO threats, indicating to many that air strikes should have been used earlier to undermine, if not defeat, the Serb military (see Rieff, 1995: 156-57).

By early 1994, the US was playing a more active role in Bosnian diplomacy. Thus in March, Washington sponsored a deal between the Muslims and Croats to end their war and create in Bosnia a bi-national entity confederated to Croatia. Tudjman signed up for the Muslim-Croat Federation after getting offers of US aid to develop his economy and rebuild Croat military power. This agreement immediately shifted the balance of power on the battlefield in Bosnia against the Serbs.

In April, the Contact Group was formed with just five members - the US, Russia, Britain, France and Germany - to streamline the decision-making process. In the process, the EU and UN were both effectively sidelined. The following month, the group put forward a new peace proposal which gave 51 percent of Bosnia to the new Muslim-Croat confederation and 49 percent to the Bosnian Serbs. The proposal was again rejected by Karadzic who was unhappy with the details of the map. However, this decision led to the complete isolation of the Bosnian Serbs.

Slobodan Milosevic had been working for peace since 1993 and he came out firmly in favour of the Contact Group plan. When it was thrown out by Pale, he finally disassociated himself from his compatriots across the Drina river, and in August 1994 cut economic and political ties with the Bosnian Serbs. Russia used the Milosevic-Karadzic split to freeze relations with the Bosnian Serbs and curtail its dealings with Radovan Karadzic (*Sevodnya*, 4 August 1994). At the same time, Moscow moved closer to Milosevic in the hope that he could mediate a peace settlement. Kozyrev went so far as to describe Milosevic as 'the leader of the peace party', and pressed for the lifting of economic sanctions on Belgrade once a cease-fire had been agreed (*Izvestiya*, 3 August 1994).

In these new conditions, Russia responded with restraint after NATO air strikes hit Bosnian Serb targets in early August in the area of Sarajevo. Karadzic called for 'total war', but without response from Moscow. The independent Russian newspaper, *Izvestiya*, wrote, 'One gets the impression that the Bosnian Serb leaders have utterly discredited themselves in the eyes of Russian foreign policy-makers, and that henceforth the Kremlin intends to deal only with Slobodan Milosevic' (*Izvestiya*, 9 August 1994).

Even though the former US President, Jimmy Carter, was able to negotiate a four-month cease-fire over the winter of 1994-95, few supposed that it heralded a stable peace. Pessimism proved well-founded when the war started up again in the spring of 1995. For a while, the conflict followed a familiar course. The Serbs resumed the seige of Sarajevo and continued to humiliate the international community. In May 1995, 300 UN troops (including 13 Russians) were taken hostage in response to NATO air strikes against Serb positions. It appeared the international effort in Bosnia was collapsing altogether.

However, the international community, galvanised by the new French President, Jacques Chirac, resolved to take action at the London conference in July. The delegates were determined to seek greater protection for the UN peacekeepers. This was achieved in two ways. First, it was decided to deploy a rapid reaction force in Bosnia; and second, the peacekeepers already there were redeployed to less vulnerable positions outside Serb-held areas. The UN role was also marginalised as the dual key - the need for UN approval for all NATO military action - was effectively abandoned. The US also elbowed aside the Contact Group, which had been unable to get an agreement for its plan, and

Richard Holbrooke was delegated by Clinton to get a peace settlement. The immediate effect of relocating UN forces was the fall to the Serbs of two further safe areas - Srebrenica in July and Zepa in August. However, the Croats had used the winter cease-fire to rebuild their military forces and were now in a position to challenge Serb supremacy. In May 1995, Croatian forces took back West Slavonia and swept through Krajina the following August. The ease with which the Croats expelled the Serbs suggested that a deal of some sort might have been done by Zagreb and Belgrade. This seemed all the more likely later in November when Milosevic also agreed at Dayton to hand over the remaining Serb possession on Croatian territory, East Slavonia, over a period of one to two years. For the Serb population, however, the Croat advances represented a humiliating defeat as they were forced to abandon their homes and decamp to Serbia. The Croats pursued a policy of ethnic cleansing that in scale, if not in brutality, matched anything perpetrated by the Serbs in Bosnia (*Time*, 11 March 1996).

Meanwhile, the US strategy in Bosnia was to back up its more forceful negotiating strategy with military power. Thus, from 30 August, NATO's operation 'Deliberate Force' was launched with a two-week campaign of air raids and artillery strikes against Bosnian Serb positions. Russia was outraged that it was again being excluded from the peace process in Bosnia and Yeltsin described the NATO air strikes, in a moment of grotesque hyperbole, as 'genocide' (*International Herald Tribune*, 13 September 1995). The air strikes were finally suspended after the Serbs withdrew their heavy weaponry from around Sarajevo and lifted the seige of the Bosnian capital on 14 September.

The Muslim-Croat confederation took advantage of the bombing raids to push back the Serbs roughly to the 49 percent of territory stipulated by the Contact Group plan. The ethnic cleansing that continued meant that Croatia was almost free of all Serbs and Bosnia was effectively partitioned into three ethnic areas. Once again, it was unclear whether the Serbs were being routed or in the process of withdrawing. The NATO bombing was on a different scale to the earlier pin-pricks against Serb positions, but it still remained limited - the two-week bombing amounted to the equivalent of one active day in the Gulf War (Atkinson, 1995). However, NATO explained the sudden change in fortune for the Muslims and Croats in terms of precision bombing which, it was claimed, succeeded in breaking Serb command and communications on the battlefield (Atkinson, 1995).

In August, Milosevic was delegated by the Pale parliament to negotiate on behalf of the Bosnian Serbs. Progress was rapid. A cease-fire was signed on 5

October which came into effect a week later. After three weeks of hard negotiating in Dayton, Ohio, a peace agreement was finally signed on 22 November. It contained five main elements. 1. Bosnia was recognised as a sovereign state within its present borders. 2. Bosnia would contain two other mini-states, the Muslim-Croat Federation and the Bosnian Serb Republic. Both of these mini-states would have their own presidents, parliaments and military. 3. Sarajevo would be a united city under Bosniac control. 4. People charged with war crimes would be excluded from public office in Bosnia. 5. NATO would police the agreement with support from other states. 60,000 troops would be deployed, including 20,000 Americans and 1,400 Russians.

The Croats emerged as the main victors from the Yugoslav wars. They had created an ethnically pure Croatia which was confederated to half of Bosnia. The other ethnic groups were less happy. Many Serb nationalists were dismayed by the loss of Krajina and Sarajevo, the capital of Bosnia. Radovan Karadzic predicted that Sarajevo would become the Beirut of Europe. The Serbs could claim to have created a larger Serbia, but not the Greater Serbia they had been fighting for. The Muslims lost most of all. They have to put faith in the Muslim-Croat Federation as a means of maintaining their independence. However, both the Bosnian Serb state and the Muslim-Croat Federation are permitted close ties with their bigger neighbours in Belgrade and Zagreb. If these ties are allowed to develop, it could lead to the *de facto* partition of Bosnia along the lines Milosevic and Tudjman had discussed before the war broke out in 1992.

The US tried to claim all the credit for the moves towards peace, but this was a rather simplistic view. There can be little doubt that the US intervention on the side of the Croat and Bosnian governments from 1994 shifted the balance of power on the battlefield away from the Serbs. The arming of the Croats allowed Zagreb to take back Krajina, and the NATO air strikes in August and September 1995 weakened the Serb position in Bosnia and led to the Muslim-Croat advance. However, the deal brokered by Richard Holbrooke was arguably less favourable to the Bosnian government than the earlier Vance-Owen Peace Plan which the US administration had done so much to undermine. The Dayton deal was signed in 1995 because the US backed it, but two years had passed since the demise of VOPP and in the interim thousands had died and thousands more had become refugees.

In fact, the key to peace lay, as the Russians had argued much earlier, in Belgrade. Milosevic abandoned his nationalism almost as quickly as he had discovered it. Thus, Milosevic consistently supported a negotiated settlement in Bosnia from 1993, and from the summer of the following year he was even prepared to abandon his co-nationals in Bosnia and Croatia to this end. Without this dramatic policy shift, there would have been no Dayton accord. The United States and Germany were slow to recognise Milosevic's metamorphosis. Indeed, if Russia's initiatives had been taken up earlier, peace might have come to Bosnia before 1995. David Owen has argued that allowing the war to drag on so long not only meant more misery for the people of Bosnia, it also weakened the position of the Muslims. Under the current agreement, the Muslims are reliant on the Croats and the UN troops which have no obligation to remain after a twelve month period. The *de facto* partition of Bosnia between the Croats and Serbs still seems the most likely outcomes of the Dayton accord. A resumption of war after the withdrawal of the UN troops remains a tragic possibility especially since the Bosnians are being trained and armed by the US in anticipation of righting by force some of the wrongs of Dayton.

## Conclusion

Moscow was criticised for its pro-Serb stance in Yugoslavia. The opposition to air strikes and the lifting of the arms embargo was said to encourage the Serbs in their expansionist policy in Bosnia. However, Russian policy only had an impact at the margins at most. In fact, the Serbs made their biggest land-grab in Croatia and Bosnia at a time when Moscow was most willing to passively follow the Western lead. The Russian opposition to the escalation of the war simply reflected majority opinion in most of the capitals of the world. Even after the rise of nationalist thinking in Russia, Moscow backed both the main international peace proposals on Bosnia - the VOPP in 1993 and the Contact Group Plan from 1994.

The main cause of division between Russia and the West related to Russian pride. Yeltsin wanted Moscow to be treated as an equal partner in the international decisions over Yugoslavia. Yeltsin became concerned when the US and NATO began to assert themselves in the region and failed to consult with Moscow over such important issues as air strikes. There was never any chance of direct Russian military intervention, however. Vitaly Churkin said in spring 1993 that Russia 'will never get into a confrontation with the world community over the map of Bosnia' (*Izvestiya*, 21 April 1993), and the Defence Ministry warned against over-stretching the military in areas no longer of vital strategic interest to Moscow (*Moscow News*, 7 September 1993; *International Herald Tribune*, 16 February 1994). After the debacle in Chechnya, enthusiasm for a

Russian military adventure in the far abroad declined even further (*Nezavisimaya gazeta*, 4 February 1995).

Although the Russian parliament articulated a more pro-Serb stance than the government, public pressure for a more activist stance was also limited. Most people in Russia had a natural empathy with the Serbs, but the appeal of pan-slavism was often exaggerated. There was little public interest in the Yugoslav conflict, and Vladimir Zhirinovsky's efforts to whip up support for the Serbs fell largely on stony ground (*Izvestiya*, 5 February 1994). The former Russian Premier, Nikolai Ryzhkov, went so far as to complain over the apathy of the Russian people in the face of the NATO air strikes against Bosnian Serbs at Gorazde in spring 1994 (*The Observer*, 17 April 1994). In 1993, Western intelligence reckoned that there were only about 500 Russian volunteers fighting in the former Yugoslavia, and not all of these were fighting on the side of the Serbs.[2] This latter fact was not altogether surprising since all the belligerents in Bosnia, including the Muslims, were slav. The prospect of slavic unity was further undercut when Milosevic formally split from Karadzic and the Bosnian Serbs in August 1994. After that, it was difficult for Russian nationalists to demand a more pro-Serb stance when Belgrade and Pale were divided over the fundamentals of policy.

Nevertheless, Moscow came out of the Yugoslav crisis badly. The image of Yeltsin's Russia took a battering as Moscow was commonly seen as supporting the aggressor. Although Russian rhetoric could be criticised, in practice Moscow performed a positive service in maintaining links with the Serbs. For the US-German strategy of isolating Belgrade had obviously failed by the summer of 1995. Russian participation in the post-Dayton peacekeeping force (IFOR) was also important to help reassure the Serbs that their interests would not be ignored.

---

[2]   Interview with personnel at the British Foreign and Commonwealth Office.

# Chapter Thirteen

# THEORIES OF THE COLD WAR

This book has been mainly concerned with practical politics during the period 1985-96. This chapter attempts to place these issues into some kind of broader, more theoretical perspective. Five main questions are discussed below. What were the origins of the cold war? What was the nature of the cold war? Why did it come to an end in the period 1989-91? Who won the cold war? What will the post-cold war world look like, and what is the future role of Russia within it?

## Origins of the cold war

The first two decades of the cold war were dominated by a debate between traditional and revisionist scholars. Amongst the leading traditionalists were George Kennan (1947) and Richard Pipes (1981); whilst the leading revisionists included William Appleman Williams (1962) and Thomas Paterson (1979). The two schools differed over why the cold war started but they shared an underlying purpose - both sought to attribute responsibility for the cold war (see Cumings, 1993: 542). The traditionalists placed most of the blame on the USSR; the revisionists on the USA.

Traditionalists saw the USSR as a militant, aggressive state which called for international revolution and the overthrow of the Western way of life. In the inter-war years, the USSR was militarily too weak to effectively challenge the

West, but after 1945 Moscow gained both the military power and the political will to export revolution - first to Eastern Europe and then to an increasing number of states in the developing world. The West responded by adopting a policy, its author, George Kennan, called containment (Kennan, 1947: 575). This was portrayed by traditionalists as a minimalist response to a very real Soviet threat. Although Washington sometimes used the rhetoric of roll-back, Kennan's original concept of containment never envisaged the violent over-throw of communism in the USSR or Eastern Europe. The essential message of containment was - thus far, but no further.

The revisionists challenged the orthodox vision of the Soviet Union as a preda-tory state and the US as a passive and rather reluctant superpower. After all, it was the US, not the USSR, which was in a position to dominate the post-war international system. Whilst the Soviet economy lay shattered by war, the mighty dollar bestrode the world. Alone amongst the combatant countries, the US ex-perienced economic growth during World War II and emerged in 1945 account-ing for over 50 percent of total world output. No other country could even boast a third of America's GNP in the immediate post-war period (see Ra'anan, 1990: 68). In the military field, however, US dominance was less absolute. The USSR had a massive land army in 1945 which had just proved itself in tank warfare against the Nazis, but the US possessed a far greater global reach with its formi-dable navy and air force. Most important of all, the US had the monopoly of the atomic bomb for the first four years of the cold war up to 1949, whilst the Ameri-can mainland remained invulnerable to a Soviet nuclear strike until the mid-1950s at the earliest. As one revisionist expressed it - the world turned upside down after the war and the Americans found themselves on top (Paterson, 1979: 18-19).

The US, according to the revisionists, used this dominance to create a world in its own image. An international economic system was created based on Ameri-can principles of free enterprise and free trade, underpinned by international institutions dominated by the US, such as the World Bank and the IMF. Stalin, who perceived such a system inimical to Soviet interests, tightened his grip over Eastern Europe and formed an autarkic Soviet bloc. Revisionists, in contrast to traditionalists, portrayed this self-imposed isolationism as a defensive, rather than offensive, move - a sign of weakness rather than strength.

However, from the 1970s both orthodoxy and revisionism came under chal-lenge from a third school, known as post-revisionism. Two of the leading scholars in this school were John Lewis Gaddis and Daniel Yergin (Yergin, 1980; Gaddis, 1983). The essential call of the post-revisionist was for a more objective and nuanced vision of the cold war. Most importantly, the attempt of the tradition-alist and revisionist to apportion blame for the cold war was rejected. This, they argued, was not what academic research should be about - such accounts tended to reveal more about the author's prejudices than the origins of the cold war. Post-revisionists saw East-West tension as being the result of a complex pattern of actions and interactions in which domestic politics, leaders' personalities, misperceptions and misunderstandings all played a part in producing the tangle of relations which later became known as the cold war.

Many revisionists saw post-revisionism as an attempt to revive orthodoxy rather than provide a more objective reading of the cold war, and one of Gaddis' critics famously dismissed his theory as 'orthodoxy plus archives' (Kimball, 1983: 198). Nevertheless, post-revisionists were successful in de-politicising the debate over the cold war. Although there were always dissenters, post-revisionism became the new orthodoxy in cold war scholarship. The vast majority accepted that the search for blame in the cold war was futile. It would never be possible to definitively argue that one or other side started it. This general consensus allowed the debate to move on to other, albeit related, issues. One of these issues, taken up below, relates to the nature of the cold war. What was the cold war all about? What were its defining characteristics?

## The nature of the cold war

The debate on the nature of the cold war can be subdivided into two central questions. First, what was the central dynamic of the cold war? Was it an ideological contest, a great power struggle or a domestically generated pseudo-conflict? Second, was the cold war a uniquely dangerous period in history or was it, as a growing number of scholars argued from the 1970s, a time of remarkable peace and stability? - 'a golden age', as the Marxist historian, Eric Hobsbawm, later called it (Hobsbawm, 1994).

### The Central Dynamic of the Cold War

Fred Halliday, a leading British scholar on the cold war, argued that ideological difference was the central dynamic of post-war East-West relations - the cold war, he said, was an inter-systemic conflict (Halliday, 1993). Unlike revisionist and traditionalist scholars, Halliday was not arguing that either capitalism or communism was to blame for the cold war; he was simply saying that the very existence of the two social systems made tension inevitable. This was so, he argued, for two main reasons. First, capitalism and communism were inherently incompatible social systems; and second, they were doomed to competition since they both  possessed a universalist drive to recreate themselves on a global scale (Halliday, 1994a: 181). Capitalism needed growth and constantly expanding markets; Soviet communism needed to expand to legitimise the revolution. This universalist drive was not only inherent in either system, it was also justified by its leading proponents and propagandists as universally beneficial. Only the final global victory of communism or capitalism, depending on one's perspective, could bring prosperity, justice, and world peace. Thus, the elimination of alien systems became a moral imperative as well as a practical necessity. (On this discussion, see Lenin, 1916; Kant, 1950; Doyle, 1986; and Fukuyama, 1989.)

Few would wish to deny the importance of ideology in understanding the cold war but, as Fred Halliday himself would accept, the clash of ideologies can only ever provide a partial explanation. For if ideological differences were the sole cause of the cold war, then why did the cold war begin in 1945, and not in 1917 at the time of the Bolshevik Revolution? And why was the cold war directed against the USSR and not against communist China? Such apparent anomalies could best be understood, many argued, in terms of great power politics or realist international relations theory.

According to the realist, state behaviour is not determined by ideology or domestic politics but by human nature and/or the anarchical nature of the international system. Anarchy in this sense does not imply perpetual chaos, but simply that there is no legitimate authority above the sovereign state. In this respect, the international system is crucially different from the domestic system in which the citizen grants the state the power and the authority to govern and maintain order for the wider collective good. International law and international institutions do exist, but in realist theory they lack the means to implement decisions. Therefore, no state can ever rely on a higher authority to come to its aid in times of need. A state might be lucky, like Kuwait; it might not, like East Timor. The world, according to a realist, is a self-help system in which states act in their own perceived national interest. To defend and extend those interests a state must seek to maximise its own power. Although realists recognise that power is made up of a number of factors, the military factor is generally viewed as the most important - it is, after all, the ultimate means for a state to impose its will on another. Of course, states can co-operate in certain circumstances. For example, military alliances are formed, but these are seen as purely temporary and instrumental arrangements to deter a commonly perceived threat; once the threat has gone, the alliance is likely to break up. The world, therefore, is characterised in  realist theory by conflict, arms races and the division of the world into power blocs. The realist world is cynical and amoral, and hence the term, *realpolitik*.

The realist, therefore, viewed the cold war as a typical great power struggle. Great powers, irrespective of ideology, are doomed, in the realist scenario, to a military struggle for pre-eminence. Therefore, after the collapse of the old European order at the end of World War II, it was inevitable that the two new global powers would come into conflict. Only the US and the USSR had global pretensions at that time, and posed a credible challenge to the other's security and global power. This was the difference after World War II. This was why the cold war began in 1945. The USSR now had sufficient military strength to be perceived as a threat to Western interests. Therefore, Western Europe formed NATO to balance the growing Soviet military strength in the East. According to the realist, the alliance had nothing to do with cultural or ideological ties. For the US also formed an albeit far looser political alliance in the 1970s with the People's Republic of China. In this case, ideology was irrelevant. It was, as the realist said, all a matter of power politics, as Washington attempted to improve its global position vis-a-vis Moscow.

Although scholars would differ over emphases, most adopted some kind of synthesis of the realist and inter-systemic explanation (see, for example, Zwick, 1990: 113; Miller, 1991: 2-8; and Garthoff, 1994: 752). In practice, there seemed little reason to try to separate out the two theories, especially when leading theorists, such as Morgenthau and Halliday, were reluctant to offer mono-causal explanations (see Morgenthau, 1978: 86-87; and Halliday, 1994a: 170). A synthesis also afforded the advantage of allowing, in the spirit of post-revisionist scholarship, a more nuanced understanding of superpower behaviour. Thus, Halliday was certainly right in identifying ideological heterogeneity in the international system as a cause of tension, but its importance varied over time and across regions. For example, communism posed a threat to stability in Western Europe after the war because of the strength of the Communist Party in a number of countries - most notably France, Italy and Greece. However, by the 1970s, this threat had faded. Leftist politics remained a strong influence in Western Europe, but the Soviet alternative seemed increasingly irrelevant to the new issues of the European Left, which tended to focus more on human rights, feminism and green issues. In the Middle East, on the other hand, great power rivalry *always* seemed a better explanation of superpower behaviour. Whilst capitalist economics dominated the region, neither the Western nor the Soviet way of life held much attraction for the vast majority of inhabitants in most Arab countries.

Realists and inter-systemic theorists could also agree that the cold war was a result of a basic clash of interests - of whatever kind. This remained the majority view for all students of the cold war, but it is important to briefly consider two other explanations - idealism and internalism - which sought to challenge, in the former case, aspects, and in the latter, the entirety of this core assumption.

Idealism is a liberal and normative theory of international relations. It accepts the realist argument that anarchy can lead to war, but suggests this is a reason to change, rather than accept, existing international structures. Idealists further argue that the realist conception of international anarchy is simplistic. State behaviour on issues as disparate as trade and war is highly regulated by a panoply of international institutions, international law and inter-state agreements. Hedley Bull, not an idealist himself, argued that states are 'conscious of certain common interests and common values' and believe themselves to be 'bound by a common set of rules and institutions' (Bull, 1977: 13). A world government may be a distant, and perhaps an undesirable, prospect but some kind of international society has already emerged to temper the effects of anarchy.

Few writing within the idealist framework would wish to deny the existence of a clash of interest between the superpowers in the post-war period. However, they would reject Halliday's claim that these interests were irreconcilable and argue that the two superpowers had some interests in common which were often concealed by the propaganda of the cold war. Perhaps the most obvious was the mutual desire to avoid direct superpower conflict and nuclear war. Thus, whilst idealists largely accepted the consensus view on the origins of the cold war, they were more optimistic about the future. Realists and inter-systemic theorists could only envisage the end of the cold war as one state or social system prevailing over the other. As this seemed highly unlikely at least until the late 1980s, most observers expected the cold war to continue for the foreseeable future. Idealists, however, believed that at least the extremes of the cold war could be tempered through negotiation and summitry. Arms control and *Ostpolitik* were examples of what might be achieved. The more romantic idealist believed that such agreements could help bring the two sides together and ultimately lead to the end of the cold war.

Internalists held a more radical view of the cold war than the idealist. Internalists denied that a basic clash of interest existed between the two power blocs. They argued the opposite - that a coincidence of interest existed between the elites of the two superpowers (Kaldor, 1990b: 35). The cold war, they said, was internally rather than externally generated; essentially, it was the result of domestic politics. The external threat was invented rather than real. Mary Kaldor called the East-West conflict an 'imaginary war' (Kaldor, 1990a). The cold war, internalists suggested, served the interests of the arms industry and buttressed the power of the elite both sides of the iron curtain. It legitimised high defence spending, the control of domestic populations, and ultimately the superpower status of both the US and the USSR (see Cox, 1986). The real division in international politics was North-South, not East-West (Chomsky, 1992). The implication of the internalist analysis was that the cold war itself was remarkably stable and unlikely to end without radical change in one or other bloc.[1]

The notion of the manipulation of an external threat for domestic purposes was not controversial in the case of the Soviet Union (see, for example, Kennan, 1947: 570). Internalists, in the tradition of post-revisionist scholarship, however, sought to extend the idea to include the Western powers. In this regard, the internalist saw the McCarthyite phenomenon in the US less as an aberration of American history, and more as an extreme example of state control in the West. Most scholars rejected the idea of a coincidence of interests between superpowers, but were ready to accept the importance of domestic politics in any explanation of the cold war. Even First Secretary Nikita Khrushchev and US President Dwight Eisenhower, at various times in the 1950s, warned against the growing influence of the military-industrial lobby in their respective countries.

*Stability Theory*

The second debate on the nature of the cold war centred around the question of stability. Traditionally, analysts had viewed the cold war as a uniquely dangerous period. This was because of the existence of nuclear weapons and their destructive capability. For the first time in human history, the world had to contemplate the possibility of its total destruction. Therefore, much of cold war historiography concerned itself with the possibility of the cold war going hot. Books on the period were filled with discussions of the nuclear arms race and the possibility of escalation in a series of regional crises, which included Berlin, Korea, Cuba and the Middle East. From the 1960s, however, a growing number of writers began to comment on the stabilising features of the cold war. John Lewis Gaddis, captured this idea best when he described the post-war period, not as the cold war, but as the 'long peace' (Gaddis, 1986 and 1987). How far was it true to say that the cold war was stable?

Stability in this sense did not imply world peace or an end to the underlying rivalry between the superpowers. Wars continued, especially in the third world,

---

[1] Internalist was a term used by Fred Halliday (1994a: 173) to refer to a group of radical and Marxist writers, which included Michael Cox (1986), Mary Kaldor (1990a) and Noam Chomsky (1992).

throughout the cold war period, killing an estimated 21 million people (LaFeber, 1992: 13). Nor did stability imply justice. Much of Eastern Europe remained, against its will, under Soviet domination, whilst the gap between the rich and the poor nations of the world continued to widen. No, stability was meant in a far more limited way - many argued far too limited a way - to mean simply the durability of the international system and the absence of a major war between the great powers (see Deutsch and Singer, 1964: 390).

The internalist theory was able to explain cold war stability within its central concept of the existance of a coincidence of interests between the superpowers. For the other theories, however, the existence of stability appeared more problematic. The realist, Kenneth Waltz, tried to explain it in terms of the bipolar structure of the cold war and the existence of nuclear weapons (Waltz, 1964; 1979; and 1982). Traditionally, bipolarity was perceived to be destabilising since it fuelled a confrontational atmosphere between great powers. Waltz, however, turned these conventional ideas on their head. He argued that bipolarity aided international stability, essentially because of its simplicity. As he pointed out, 'in the great power politics of a bipolar world, who is a danger to whom is never in doubt' (Waltz, 1979: 170). Instead of this leading to tension, Waltz argued it allowed leaders to gauge threats more accurately and construct military strategies to counter them (Waltz, 1979: 170-2). In the anarchical international system, factors such as certainty and predictability were believed to be the best guarantees against conflict.

Bipolarity also aided stability because it was felt to accurately reflect the distribution of power in the post-war international system. Thus, the US and USSR were recognised internationally as superpowers and their status was not under threat from third parties. As evidence, Waltz referred to the switch of allegiance by China in the 1970s. In a multipolar system, he argued, the defection of such a major power would have caused intolerable dislocation in the international system, possibly leading to great power conflict. But in the post-war bipolar system, the switch proved manageable without any serious threat to stability or the dominant positions of the two superpowers (Waltz, 1979: 169).

Waltz also challenged the view that nuclear weapons were destabilising. On the contrary, Waltz argued that nuclear deterrence worked. The destructive capability of nuclear weapons which so concerned some other writers was, according to Waltz, a factor for stability. In the era of MAD, no leader could think in terms of winning a nuclear war. Therefore, military strategists no longer planned for victory, but for the avoidance of war. The fear of escalation, Waltz argued, also encouraged political leaders to act with greater caution (see Waltz,

1982). Although many would dispute it (see, for example, Thompson, 1982), it was probably true that nuclear weapons and bipolarity, aided stability. But neither phenomenon could fully explain it.

Bipolarity was only ever an approximate description of reality (see Lebow, 1995: 28-33). As the revisionists pointed out, the world was dominated by the US in the early period of the cold war; and when the USSR could claim rough strategic parity in the mid-1970s, it was at the expense of its economic competitiveness. The USSR was always an incomplete superpower (Dibb, 1988). Bipolarity as a concept only made sense so long as the military was emphasised over and above other factors of power. This was a mistake especially when so much of the superpower rivalry was about ideology.

It was also true that the fear of nuclear war was a factor in moderating the behaviour of the superpowers, but MAD remained a highly risky strategy. The result of any breakdown in nuclear deterrence would have been, quite literally, catastrophic. Moreover, it was not self-evident that nuclear weapons were necessary to deter superpower aggression. It was certainly arguable that conventional weapons had been enough to deter a major conflict in Europe. For example, during the Berlin Blockade of 1948-49, the US had the monopoly of nuclear weapons, yet refused to escalate the crisis despite Stalin's highly provocative land blockade. Instead of driving through the blockade, the West chose to supply Berlin for almost a year by air.

Realists, therefore, argued that stability emerged from the division of the world into roughly balancing, and hugely destructive, power blocs. Idealists, on the other hand, argued that rapprochement rather than division aided stability. The cold war standoff of the Stalinist years was later replaced by negotiation and summitry. Nuclear brinkmanship was replaced by general agreements over the management of the arms race and the management of a divided world. Thus, a Hot Line was set up in 1963 to improve communications between the Kremlin and the White House, the Non-Proliferation Treaty was signed in 1968, and in the 1970s the SALT treaties were signed along with a whole series of other agreements on crisis management and prevention. Arguably, however, the most important agreements of the detente period were those concerning Europe. The division of Europe had been accepted as a geo-political reality, at least since the construction of the Berlin Wall in 1961 and this was formalised (although not at a *de jure* level) through Brandt's *Ostpolitik* of the early 1970s and the Helsinki Final Act of 1975. Although the agreements had certain subversive aims (see chapter 5), the overriding purpose was the stabilisation of Europe through the formal recognition of the status quo. To this extent, detente in Europe was largely successful. It was in regions of the third world where no such agreements were reached that conflicts continued and the danger of escalation remained a possibility.


## The End of the Cold War

The relationship between the superpowers had become regularised in the detente period of the 1970s. However, stability theory had exaggerated the process and misled the world into supposing that the cold war was a durable feature of the international landscape. It was generally believed that the bipolar system was immutable and that the only way the cold war was likely to end was through a major systemic war. In the circumstances, the cold war was not ideal but to many it seemed the lesser of two evils. Why then did the cold war end in the 1980s? Why did it end so comparatively peacefully?

The realist, whose emphasis was always on external and military factors, could argue that America's containment policy finally wore the Soviet Union down and forced Moscow to dismantle the cold war (Kissinger, 1995: 802). It was certainly true that Western military containment in Europe had been remarkably robust. The US commitment to West European defence through NATO had proved to be an effective deterrent against possible Soviet expansionism. Elsewhere, however, with the important exception of Japan, the history of containment policy was less happy. Indeed, the policy all but collapsed in the mid-1970s with America's defeat in Vietnam. Reagan came to power in 1981 with the express aim of trying to reinvigorate American containment policy through a massive military buildup and a greater willingness to support anti-Soviet forces in the third world. Reagan's supporters argued this change in policy was a major factor in ending the cold war (see Kissinger, 1995: 764; and Shultz, 1993: 371).

Reagan was successful in changing the public mood in America but, as this book has shown, his actual programme changed very little on the ground and certainly was not sufficient to explain the radical change in Soviet foreign policy in the late 1980s. As chapter four showed, the Reagan military buildup did not affect the military balance between the superpowers and certainly did not threaten Soviet security. The Soviet Union lost no wars, it lost no territory, and it did not even lose the arms race. Post-Soviet Russia, for all its obvious weaknesses in other respects, retained a massive nuclear capability which could still destroy the world several times over. It was true that the USSR was coming under pressure in the third world in the 1980s, but this had more to do with the failing international communist system rather than US containment policy (see chapter 6). In Afghanistan, the US support for the mujahideen reduced the options for Moscow, but even there it was not the main reason for Soviet withdrawal (see chapter 7). In Eastern Europe, where the cold war effectively ended, the role of the US in undermining Soviet dominance was minimal (see chapter 5).

The most that could be said was that the Soviet Union was suffering from 'imperial overstretch' (see Kennedy, 1987). Although there are problems with Kennedy's concept of imperial overstretch when applied to the USSR, it was nevertheless true that Moscow's eagerness to maintain its superpower status was undermining its overall economic performance. In particular, Moscow's attempt to keep pace in the arms race with the US proved debilitating. When Reagan came to power, it became obvious to the leaders in the Kremlin that there was little sign of the arms race slowing. At a minimum, this put pressure on the politburo to seek a way out of the logic of the cold war. However, it is important to note that it was only after Gorbachev came to power in 1985 that progress was made and the structures of the cold war began to be dismantled.

Fred Halliday also rejected the realist emphasis on military containment and argued the end of the cold war revealed the central importance of the inter-systemic contest (Halliday, 1993 and 1994a). When communism fell, the cold war simultaneously came to an end. According to Halliday, however, communism did not fall because of America's advantage in smart weaponry or SDI, as Reagan's supporters suggested, but simply because Western society existed as a viable, alternative social system (see also Kennan, 1947 and Fukuyama, 1989). At least from the late 1960s, the West's political freedoms, consumer society and youth culture were envied by an increasing number of people in the East. The Soviet Union appeared dull and colourless in comparison. In Halliday's own words, it was the T-shirt rather than the gun-boat that forced communism's ultimate surrender (Halliday, 1995: 215).

There can be little doubt that the collapse of communism was crucial in bringing the cold war to an end. However, this coincidence of events did not prove that capitalism and communism were irreconcilable. The cold war was plainly winding down before the final collapse of the Soviet Union in 1991. Partnership between the two social systems might have been difficult but the two superpowers had effectively worked out a relationship of peaceful co-existence by the 1970s. By this time, the USSR had ceased to be an anti-status quo power and communism was no longer perceived in the West as an economic threat to the dominant international capitalist system (Lynch, 1992). The cold war had become more a military, rather than an ideological, struggle for ascendancy.

The internalist, perhaps of all the cold war theorists, had the biggest problem in explaining its demise. If the cold war had been functional for the elites in Moscow and Washington, why had they allowed it to end? Mary Kaldor argued that pressure from below *forced* the rulers to dismantle the cold war system (Kaldor, 1990-91: 181). In the West, mass protest was directed against the arms race; in Eastern Europe against the Soviet system itself. Although it is difficult to find explicit evidence that the people precipitated change, there is little doubt that the mass protests of the 1980s reflected the prevailing *zeitgeist* on both sides of the iron curtain. The levels of nuclear overkill possessed by both superpowers had patently become absurd; whilst the Soviet system was patently failing alongside its Western counterpart. At the same time, the process of globalisation rendered the political barriers between Eastern and Western Europe increasingly untenable. The cold war structures were looking more and more archaic.

It was also interesting to note that Gorbachev took up some of the ideas of Western peace campaigners. His new thinking rejected realist notions of bloc politics and the arms race. Instead, he offered unilateral and asymmetrical arms cuts, and on-site verification to monitor all arms agreements. As idealists might have predicted, such initiatives built up trust and won over the public and even the more hard-bitten political leaders in the West. All the memoirs of the protagonists indicate that personal relations were vital in making rapprochement possible and bringing the cold war to a speedy and peaceful conclusion (see Shevardnadze, 1991; Gorbachev, 1995b; Reagan, 1990; and Shultz, 1993). As Gorbachev contemplated the end of the cold war, even the Soviet military recognised that war with the West in the era of MAD was never an option. Thus, when the Soviet empire suddenly crumbled, there was little option but to peacefully accept its demise (Waltz, 1993).

### Who won the cold war?

The cold war was over. Who had won? Gorbachev argued that we were all winners. Stalinism had been defeated in Europe and the impending threat of nuclear devastation had been averted. Furthermore, the end of the cold war opened up unprecedented opportunities for international co-operation and a New World Order. Although the initial euphoria soon dissipated, Gorbachev's optimism was not wholly misplaced. The attempt by Iraq to annex Kuwait in 1990 was thwarted by co-ordinated international action, whilst rapprochement between the superpowers also provided an impetus for peace in areas as far apart as Central America, the Middle East, South Africa and Indochina.

Although many acknowledged some truth in Gorbachev's arguments, the majority viewed the end of the cold war as a victory for the West (see Fukuyama, 1989; Halliday, 1993; and Kissinger, 1995). As one American official said at the time: 'the cold war is over and the West has won'. The Soviet Union had collapsed. Communism in Europe had been defeated. Western ideas seemed triumphant. Francis Fukuyama's article, 'The End of History' was controversial, not because it claimed victory for Western capitalism and the liberal democratic order, but because it claimed this victory was permanent and irreversible (Fukuyama, 1989).

The West might have won the cold war, but what of the US? Martin Walker argued in his book, *The Cold War,* that both superpowers had been gravely weakened by their efforts in the cold war, and he went so far as to describe them as 'superlosers' (Walker, 1993: chapter 14). The real victors of the cold war, he said, were Japan and Western Europe which had prospered whilst sheltering under the US security umbrella. The US security umbrella allowed America's allies to spend less on defence and invest more in their civilian economies. They had also benefited from the American sponsorship of the post-war liberal democratic order which had promoted free trade and free enterprise within an internationally regulated economic system (see Ikenberry, 1996). Western Europe and Japan were now challenging American economic hegemony.

Even if Walker's attempt to compare the plight of the Soviet Union and the United States is dismissed as a gross exaggeration, many agreed with his overall analysis that Washington had emerged from the cold war in a much weakened position. Declinist literature argued that the US no longer had the economic power or the political will to continue its global role in the post-cold war world. (For the debate on this, see Kennedy, 1987; and Nye, 1990.) In this respect, the Gulf War was perceived as the last hurrah of the old world rather than the dawn of a New World Order. The Gulf War showed that the US retained the military power to act on the world's stage, but for many scholars more significant was the fact that the US war effort was effectively bankrolled by Germany and Japan.

However, the view of the US as a fatally weakened superpower no longer stands up to serious scrutiny. In fact, the US has emerged from the cold war stronger than ever. As Martin Walker has since acknowledged, the US has begun 'to enjoy a global hegemony which may be unique in history. Its military power recreates the global reach of the Royal Navy in the days of Pax Britannica with the military punch of the Romans. The collapse of the Soviet Union has removed the last force on the planet capable of imposing serious restraint upon America's strategic will' (*The Guardian,* 7 August 1996). Washington currently spends more than the next ten military powers combined. Yet the fear of imperial overstretch has retreated. The US spends a massive $250 billion annually on defence, but this amounts to just over three percent of its current GDP - the lowest percentage figure since 1940 and a fraction of the 15 percent spent during the Korean War (*The Guardian,* 7 August 1996). The US economy may no longer dominate as it did in the 1950s, but it remains by far the world's largest economy with a GDP roughly a third greater than that of its nearest rival, Japan (World Bank, 1996: 211). Furthermore, the US shows no sign of relinquishing its leading position in the near future. Indeed, from the late 1980s, the US improved its economic position against its main rivals, Western Europe and Japan - in large part due to its lead in information technology. According to Martin Walker, the US is, in fact, more of a global economic leader in the Clinton era than it has been for twenty years (*The Guardian,* 7 August 1996).

Nor has the US been a reluctant superpower, as sometimes portrayed; on the contrary, it has actively sought its current hegemonic position (see Cox, 1995). Secretary of State, Warren Christopher, stated clearly on a number of occasions that the US was determined to continue its global role as long as it was not restrained in its actions by other states or international organisations, like the UN (*New York Times,* 28 May 1993). This was seen most clearly in Bosnia, when the US pushed aside the EU, the UN and even the Contact Group, in its unilateral push for a settlement. Later, Washington refused to provide troops in Bosnia to police the Dayton accord it had sponsored unless the peacekeeping force (IFOR) was NATO-led, and therefore US-dominated. Problems remain over the definition of American national interest in the post-cold war world, and the memory of Vietnam continues to hang like a cloud over all American foreign policy decision-making. Nevertheless, few believe that major problems in the world can be resolved without US participation. If nothing else, this seemed to be proved by the European experience in Bosnia.

However, Kenneth Waltz has argued that Pax Americana is unlikely to last. Waltz views unipolarity as unstable. He has argued that other states will emerge sooner or later to challenge the hegemon and create new divisions in the world (Waltz, 1993). So far, however, there is little sign of any challenge. In fact, the most powerful states in Europe and the Pacific region generally welcome US hegemony and perceive it to be the best guarantee of continued stability and security in their region. The number of US troops in Europe may have fallen dramatically since 1991, but NATO has not collapsed as many expected. On the contrary, it seeks to enlarge its membership and enlarge its role in the world.

## The post-cold war world

There are three basic views on how the post-cold war world will turn out. The optimistic view, the pessimistic view, and the view that argues little has changed. Francis Fukuyama, a liberal theorist, counts as an optimist. He argued that the end of the cold war altered the basis of the international system for the better (Fukuyama, 1994; see also Ikenberry, 1996). Post-cold war changes, he said, had encouraged the spread of the market and liberal democracy which would bring prosperity and make war less likely. War was less likely, it was claimed, because 'democracies do not fight each other'. Therefore, the spread of democracies in the post-cold war world would improve the chances of peace and enlarge the so-called 'pacific union' (see Doyle, 1986).

Although politicians tend to be highly sceptical of academic theories, this is one liberal politicians seemed eager to embrace. Why democracies should be more peace-loving is disputed, however - even among liberals. A number of possible reasons suggest themseves: the political constraints on the leadership through popular control and constitutional checks and balances; the commitment in democracies to uphold the law, incuding international law; and finally, the notion that,war in the modern age is increasingly perceived to be irrational. MAD and nuclear weapons only served to emphasise this latter fact. War disrupts economic activity and endangers free trade. Furthermore, in the more interdependent contemporary world, the traditional goals of war - the capture of territory, population and natural resources - no longer appeared so relevant for modern, post-industrial economies. Democracies seemed well-placed to take account of these changing circumstances. For decision-making in democracies was felt to be less arbitrary and more rational. Democracies, therefore, only contemplated war in the most extreme cases. Nevertheless, democracies clearly do fight wars - in Vietnam, the Falklands, the Gulf - and often for reasons familiar to international relations scholars, namely national interest. Therefore, democracy is no guarantee of peace. It remains, however, just about the best predictor of international behaviour that we have got.

Idealists, unlike realists, are sympathetic to such theories. They are more open to the idea that the international system can change and is changing. They were not alone in perceiving a world less dominated by inter-state war and conflict. In modern democracies, the military-industrial complex is less important. They spend less on defence as a percentage of GNP than in the past - a trend which quickened after the end of the cold war, with NATO countries cutting their defence spending by 18 percent between the years 1985 and 1995 (Taylor, T., 1996: 151). Fewer people are employed in defence and defence-related industries. Armies tend to be smaller and more professional. High technology weaponry requires well-trained recruits rather than a mass, conscripted army typical of the industrial age. The Western post-industrial states seem to be moving, in the words of the sociologist, Martin Shaw, towards a post-military society (Shaw, 1991). This offered hope for the future, although a non-violent world clearly still remained a distant prospect. Wars continue in the post-cold war period, but war between the developed democracies has become virtually unthinkable.

Sceptics, however, argued either that nothing had changed or that things had become worse since the end of the cold war. Realists argued that the end of the cold war had not altered the basic fact that states act, and will continue to act, according to their own perceived national interest and not for the common good. The lack of international action in Bosnia would be just one example of such behaviour. Realists were always sceptical about the longevity of the New World Order. They all expected new divisions to emerge, the ony debate was over what those divisions would be. Some believed that nationalist tension would rise (Mearsheimer, 1990). Others that there would be a clash of civilisations or cultures (Huntington, 1993). Yet others foresaw a division along economic lines with new power blocs being centred around the US, Germany and Japan. On one thing, however, there was general agreement - the end of bipolarity bred uncertainty and tension. States could no longer rely on their erstwhile superpower ally for security, therefore, they would have to provide more for their own defence. Democracy, economics and global interdependence, identified as so important by idealists, were perceived by realists to be of second order importance in international relations (see, for example, Mearsheimer, 1990). The realist predicted the post-cold war world would be as brutal as any other in human history. The realists' pessimism about the New World Order proved prescient, but Mearsheimer's bleak scenario of a Europe dividing once more into military blocs has, as yet, not transpired. Nor is it likely to. For the world has changed, and Europe has changed more than most.

Radical theorists tended to dismiss realist thinking on future structures of the international system as unimportant, and largely accepted Fukuyama's argument that the central feature of the international system was the dominance of capitalism or the liberal democratic order. However, in contrast to liberals, radicals, such as Noam Chomsky and Eric Hobsbawm, viewed the prospect with alarm (Chomsky, 1992; Hobsbawm, 1994). Indeed, Eric Hobsbawm argued that the defeat of the USSR had unleashed a new, brutalised capitalism on the world - a capitalism which no longer feared the prospect of socialist revolution (Hobsbawm, 1994: 27). Capitalism remained, in the eyes of radicals, a highly exploitative system. In the post-communist world, capitalism produced a growing gap between winners and losers. Welfare was cut, job security faded, income differentials rose. Yet, the state appeared increasingly unable - or unwilling - to control these global forces and defend the interests of its working people. Thus, at the very moment the West was proclaiming victory over the forces of dictatorship, a growing number of its people were left feeling vulnerable and unrepresented. The state was not carrying out what was considered to be its traditional role. Power seemed as unaccountable as ever.

The radicals might have exaggerated the mood of impending doom, but Russians were quick to discover the downside of the new liberal democratic order. Since Yeltsin embarked on the path of marketisation, Russia has faced economic decline and political chaos. Nevertheless, the majority in Russia seemed to accept that there could be no return to neo-Stalinism when they voted for Yeltsin in the 1996 presidential election. However, Russian culture, based on a collectivist ethic and a strong state, means that Russia is unlikely ever to become a democracy on the model of either the US or UK. This is not necessarily a matter of concern. There are many possible models of liberal democracy. *Pace* Huntington, differences in culture do not *ipso facto* pose a threat to Western interests. It is certainly not obvious that Orthodox Christianity is something to be feared or condemned (Huntington, 1993).

This book has adopted an attitude which has been generally sympathetic to many of the ideas of idealist international relations theory. Accepting all the problems of the post-cold war world identified by realists and radical theorists, it still seems that the best hope for a peaceful future rests with a Russia which overcomes its present troubles and becomes a well-ordered, prosperous, pluralist, trading nation-state. If nothing else, the end of the cold war has shown that domestic politics does influence foreign policy. The realists were wrong during the cold war to concentrate so much on external factors and balance-of-power politics. The same mistake should not be repeated now. Instead of seeking to exclude Moscow, the West should try to integrate Russia into the international community. After the war, both Germany and Japan were successfully absorbed into the liberal democratic order. With the right encouragement, there is little reason to suppose that Russia could not follow suit. If successful, it would certainly represent a huge stride towards the ultimate idealist goal of world peace. The stakes for Russia and the world could scarcely be higher.

# FURTHER READING

Sources have been cited throughout the book, but this general review provides a guide to the books which have been particularly useful both as background and more detailed texts.

## Soviet and Russian foreign policy

On Soviet foreign policy, a very good history is provided by Joseph L. Nogee and Robert H. Donaldson, *Soviet Foreign Policy Since World War II* (Pergamon, 1988). One of the few books dealing with foreign policy in the Gorbachev period is: Robert F. Miller, *Soviet Foreign Policy Today: Gorbachev and the New Political Thinking* (Unwin and Hyman, 1991). The two most comprehensive volumes on foreign policy since the end of the USSR are: Peter J. Shearman, ed, *Russian Foreign Policy Since 1990* (Westview, 1995); and Mark Webber, *The International Politics of Russia and the Successor States* (Manchester University Press, 1996).

## US-Soviet relations

On US-Soviet relations, Peter G. Boyle, *American-Soviet Relations: From the Russian Revolution to the Fall of Communism* (Routledge, 1993) provides the best introduction to the topic, and is also unusual in dealing with the whole

Soviet period. There are rather more books looking at the post-war period. A good general introduction is offered by Richard Crockatt, *The Fifty Years War: The United States and the Soviet Union in World Politics, 1941-1991* (Routledge, 1995). Other useful texts include Walter LaFeber's more revisionist (and often up-dated), *America, Russia and the Cold War* (McGraw-Hill, 1993). Martin Walker's *The Cold War and the Making of the Modern World* (4th Estate, 1993) is an excellent supplement to the two above books. Its particular strength is showing the impact of international economics on the course of the cold war.

There are many fine books providing a more theoretical account of the cold war and the post-cold war world. Amongst those, are: John Lewis Gaddis, *The United States and the End of the Cold War* (Oxford University Press, 1994); David Armstrong and Erik Goldstein, eds, *The End of the Cold War* (Frank Cass, 1990); and Richard Ned Lebow and Thomas Risse-Kappen, eds, *International Relations and the End of the Cold War* (Columbia University Press, 1995).

**The End of the Cold War**

The best and most comprehensive account of the end of the cold war can be found in: Raymond L. Garthoff, *The Great Transition: American-Soviet Relations and the End of the Cold War* (Brookings Institution, 1994). Two excellent insider accounts of how the cold war ended are: Don Oberdorfer, *The Turn: How the Cold War Came to an End, 1983-90* (Cape, 1992); and Michael R. Beschloss and Strobe Talbott, *At the Highest Level: The Inside Story of the End of the Cold War* (Little Brown, 1993). David Pryce-Jones in *The War That Never Was: The Fall of the Soviet Empire, 1985-1991* (Weidenfeld and Nicolson, 1995) has also provided many new insights into the collapse of communism through a series of interviews with leading officials and dissident figures in the former Soviet Union and Eastern Europe.

**Russian texts**

In the Soviet period, Russian texts were generally of limited value due to restrictions placed on scholars by the state. On the issue of East-West relations, the vast majority of texts provided a propagandistic view of Soviet foreign policy. A good example of this type of history could be found in the two-volume official account edited by Andrei A. Gromyko and Boris N. Ponomarev, *Russian*

*Foreign Policy, 1917-45* and *Russian Foreign Policy 1945-80* (Progress, 1981). Interestingly, the second volume makes no reference to the Soviet intervention in Afghanistan. It is worth noting that in certain areas of policy, the academic world was able to write more freely. For example, some lively writing was published in the late 1970s and early 1980s on Soviet policy towards the third world. For a review of such scholarship, see Jerry F. Hough, *The Struggle for the Third World* (Brookings Institution, 1986); and Elizabeth Kridl Valkenier, *The Soviet Union and the Third World: An Economic Bind* (Praeger, 1983). As writers tried to come to terms with glasnost, more instructive volumes appeared, albeit usually suffused with orthodox thinking, see, for example, Henry (Genrikh) Trofimenko and Pavel Podlesny, *USSR-USA: Lessons of Peaceful Coexistence* (Novosti, 1988).

A growing number of fascinating books were also published by political participants and officials which have been used extensively in this work. Gorbachev's own *Perestroika: New Thinking for our Country and the World* (Collins, 1987) is a kind of manifesto for perestroika, whilst his later two volume work, *Zhizn i reformi* (Novosti, 1995) is a detailed autobiography which provides a review of his thinking and adds useful details to the period up to the collapse of the Soviet Union. For critical views of perestroika, see Yeltsin's *Against The Grain: An Autobiography* (Cape, 1990) which takes the reader up to his victory in the 1989 elections, and *The View From The Kremlin* (HarperCollins, 1994) which includes material on the August coup and the storming of the White House in October 1993. Two of the best accounts by conservatives within the Gorbachev entourage are: Yegor Ligachev, *Inside Gorbachev's Kremlin* (Pantheon, 1993); and Valery Boldin, *Ten Years That Shook The World* (HarperCollins, 1994).

On foreign policy, Shevardnadze's, *The Future Belongs to Freedom* (Free Press, 1991) is largely a review of new thinking. Anatoly C. Chernayev, Gorbachev's foreign policy adviser, has published his diaries of the period in *Shest' let c Gorbachevym* (Progress Kultura, 1993). Russia's Foreign Minister, Andrei Kozyrev, has also written a book on the period, *Preobrazhenie* (Mezhdunarodnye otnosheniya, 1995).

### Domestic issues

The most comprehensive text on politics in the Gorbachev era is Stephen White's *Gorbachev in Power* (Cambridge University Press, 1990) which went through many revisions and names before ending up as *After Gorbachev* (Cambridge University Press, 1993). Archie Brown has also written a detailed book evaluating the importance of Gorbachev's leadership in the period 1985-91 in *The Gorbachev Factor* (Oxford University Press, 1996). On democratic reform, the book by Michael E. Urban provides a mass of interesting information on the first elections to the Congress of People's Deputies in 1989 in *More Power to the Soviets: The Democratic Revolution in the USSR* (Elgar, 1990). For the Yeltsin period, the fullest account remains Richard Sakwa's, *Russian Politics and Society*, (2nd edition: Routledge, 1996). On economics, Alec Nove's classic text, *An Economic History of the USSR* (Penguin, 1992) is still the most informative and readable. For a more detailed summary of economic perestroika, see either Anders Aslund, *Gorbachev's Struggle for Reform* (Cornell, 1989); or Marshall Goldman, *What Went Wrong With Perestroika?* (Norton, 1991). On the current situation, see Yegor Gaidar, *Gosudarstvo i evolyutsiya* (Evrasiya, 1995); and Anders Aslund, *How Russia Became A Market Economy* (Brookings Institution, 1995).

There is a growing literature on the nationalities question. The classic text on the Gorbachev period is Helene Carrere d'Encausse, *The End of the Empire* (Basic Books, 1991). Karen Dawisha and Bruce Parrott, *Russia and the New States of Eurasia: The Politics of Upheaval* (Cambridge University Press, 1994); and Ian Bremmer and Ray Taras, eds, *Nations and Politics in the Soviet Successor States* (Cambridge University Press, 1993) also look at the post-Soviet period.

**Foreign policy**

On defence matters, Michael MccGwire has written a brilliant and controversial book, *Perestroika and Soviet National Security* (Brookings Institution, 1991). It was one of the first explanations for the change in Russian thinking and argued that Reagan's policies slowed down the process of reform in the Soviet Union. On Eastern Europe, the fullest account of Soviet relations with the region can be found in Alex Pravda, ed, *The End of the Outer Empire: Soviet-East European Relations in Transition* (Sage, 1992). The most insightful book on the internal aspects of change can be found in Ivo Banac, ed, *Eastern Europe in Revolution* (Cornell, 1992). A fascinating account of East German-Soviet relations can be found in Jeffrey Gedmin, *The Hidden Hand: Gorbachev and the Collapse of East Germany* (AEI, 1992).

On the third world, a good overall text is Mark N. Katz, *The USSR and Marxist Revolutions in the Third World* (Cambridge University Press, 1990). On the current scene, see various chapters in Peter J. Shearman, ed, *Russian Foreign Policy Since 1990* (Westview, 1995). On the Far East, Gerald Segal is one of the most authoritative writers in the West and one of his more recent books on the subject is: *The Soviet Union and the Pacific* (Unwin Hyman, 1990). On Africa, see Keith Somerville, *Southern Africa and the Soviet Union* (Macmillan, 1993). On the Middle East, Galia Golan has written a number of excellent books, and one of her more recent is *Soviet Policy in the Middle East: From World War II to Gorbachev* (Cambridge University Press, 1990). On Central America and Latin America, see Nicola Miller, *Soviet Relations with Latin America, 1959-87* (Cambridge University Press, 1989).

For the case studies, the most comprehensive account on Afghanistan is Diego Cordovez and Selig S. Harrison, *Out of Aghanistan: The Inside Story of the Soviet Withdrawal* (Oxford University Press, 1995). It argues that the Reagan Doctrine had little to do with the subsequent Soviet withdrawal. An earlier account which reached the same conclusions is Mark Urban's, *War In Afghanistan* (Macmillan, 1990). As yet, there is nothing as detailed regarding Soviet policy during the Gulf War, although a number of articles and chapters have been published on the subject. The most comprehensive work looking at the political as well as military aspects of the war is: Lawrence Freedman and Efraim Karsh, *The Gulf War, 1990-1991: Diplomacy and War in the New World Order* (Faber, 1993). A mass of books has been published on the wars in the former Yugoslavia. Most are concerned with the western peacekeeping effort. For a balanced overview of the conflict, see Misha Glenny's, *The Fall of Yugoslavia* (Penguin, 1993) or Laura Silber and Allan Little, *The Death of Yugoslavia* (Penguin, 1995). For an insider's account of the negotiating process, see David Owen, *Balkan Odyssey* (Gollancz, 1995).

# BIBLIOGRAPHY

(ACA) Arms Control Association (1989), *Arms Control and National Security*, Arms Control Association, Washington.

Adomeit, Hans (1995), 'Russia as a Great Power in World Affairs: Image and Reality', *International Affairs* (London), vol. 71, no. 1.

Allison, Roy (1996), 'The Military Background and Context to Russian Peacekeeping', in Jonson and Archer, eds, *op cit.*

Almond, Mark (1994), *Europe's Backyard War: The War in the Balkans*, Heinemann, London.

Alperovitz, Gar (1995), *The Decision To Use The Bomb*, HarperCollins, London.

Arbatov, Alexei (1989a), 'How Much Defence is Sufficient?', *International Affairs* (Moscow), April, no. 4.

Arbatov, Alexei (1989b), 'Space-Based ABM Weapons and the ABM Treaty', in Primakov, ed, *op cit.*

Arbatov, Alexei (1993), 'Russia's Foreign Policy Alternatives', *International Security*, vol. 18, no. 2, Fall.

Arbatov, Georgi (1992), *The System: An Insider's Life in Soviet Politics*, Random House, New York.

Arbatov, Georgy (1994), 'Eurasia Letter: A New Cold War', *Foreign Policy*, no. 95, Summer.

Armstrong, David and Erik Goldstein, eds (1990), *The End of the Cold War*, Frank Cass, London.

Arnold, Anthony (1993), *The Fateful Pebble: Afghanistan's Role in the Fall of the Soviet Empire*, Presidio Press, Novato, California.

Ash, Timothy Garton (1990), *We, The People: The Revolution of 1989 Witnessed in Warsaw, Budapest, Berlin and Prague*, Granta, Cambridge.

Ash, Timothy Garton (1994), *In Europe's Name: Germany and the Divided Continent*, Vintage, London.

Aslund, Anders (1989), *Gorbachev's Struggle for Reform*, Cornell University Press, Ithaca, New York.

Aslund, Anders (1995), *How Russia Became a Market Economy*, Brookings Institution, Washington DC.

Atkinson, Rick (1995), 'The Anatomy of NATO's Decision To Bomb Bosnia', *International Herald Tribune*, 17 November.

Banac, Ivo (1992), ''Post-Communism as Post-Yugoslavism: The Yugoslav Non-Revolutions of 1989-90', in Banac, ed, *op cit*.

Banac, Ivo, ed (1992), *Eastern Europe in Revolution*, Cornell University Press, Ithaca and London.

BBC (1994a), 'Tales From Berlin: The Fall of the Wall', 30 October.

BBC (1994b), 'The Fatal Error: The Fall of the Wall', 6 November.

Bebler, Anton (1993), 'Yugoslavia's Variety of Communist Federalism and Her Demise', *Communist and Post-Communist Studies*, vol. 26, no. 1, March.

Bell, Coral (1995), 'Why An Expanded NATO Must Include Russia', in Ted Galen Carpenter, ed, *The Future of NATO*, Frank Cass, London.

Beschloss, Michael R. and Strobe Talbott (1993), *At the Highest Levels: The Inside Story of the Cold War*, Little Brown and Co, London.

Blasier, Cole (1991), 'Moscow's Retreat From Cuba', *Problems of Communism*, vol. XL, no. 6, November-December.

Bluth, Christoph (1994), 'Strategic Nuclear Weapons and US-Russian Relations: From Confrontation to Co-operative Denuclearization', *Contemporary Security Policy*, vol. 15, no. 1, April.

Boldin, Valery (1994), *Ten Years That Shook the World: The Gorbachev Era As Witnessed By His Chief of Staff*, Basic Books, London.

Bovin, Alexander (1989), 'Ten Hard Years in Afghanistan', *Soviet Weekly*, 21 January.

Bowker, Mike and Phil Williams (1985), 'Helsinki and West European Security', *International Affairs* (London), vol. 61, no. 4, Autumn.

Bowker, Mike and Phil Williams (1988), *Superpower Detente: A Reappraisal*, Sage, London.

Bowker, Mike and Robin Brown, eds (1993), *From Cold War To Collapse: Theory and World Politics in the 1980s*, Cambridge University Press, Cambridge.

Boyle, Peter (1993), *American-Soviet Relations: From the Russian Revolution to the Fall of Communism*, Routledge, London and New York.

Bradsher, H. S. (1985), *Afghanistan and the Soviet Union*, Duke University Press, Durham N.C.

Bremmer, Ian and Ray Taras, eds, (1993), *Nations and Politics in the Soviet Successor States*, Cambridge University Press, Cambridge.

Brenner, Robert (1991), 'Why is the United States at War with Iraq?', *New Left Review*, no. 185.

Brezhnev, Leonid, (1974), *Leninskii kurs* (Lenin's path), vol. 4, Moscow.

Brown, A. H. (1974), *Soviet Politics and Political Science*, Macmillan, London.

Brown, Archie (1996), *The Gorbachev Factor*, Oxford University Press, Oxford and New York.

Brown, Chris (1984), 'Regional Conflict in Southern African Strategy' *African Affairs*, vol. 83, no. 320, January.

Bruszt, Laszlo and David Stark (1992), 'Remaking the Political Field in Hungary: From the Politics of Confrontation to the Politics of Competition', in Banac, ed, *op cit.*

Brutents, Karen (1984), 'Osvobodivshiesya strany v nachale 80-kh godov' (Liberated countries at the beginning of the 1980s), *Kommunist*, no. 3.

Brzezinski, Zbigniew (1989), *The Grand Failure: The Birth and Death of Communism in the Twentieth Century*, Macdonald, London.

Bull, Hedley (1977), *The Anarchical Society: A Study of Order in World Politics*, Macmillan, London.

Buszynski, Leszek (1992), *Gorbachev and South East Asia*, Routledge, London and New York.

Buszynski, Leszek (1995), 'Russia and the West: Towards Renewed Geopolitical Rivalry?', *Survival*, vol. 37, no. 3, Autumn.

Carr, E. H. (1939), *The Twenty Year Crisis*, Macmillan, London.

Carrere d'Encausse, Helene (1991), *The End of the Empire*, Basic Books, New York.

Center for Defense Information (1986), 'Soviet Geopolitical Momentum: Myth and Menace', in Robbin F. Laird and Erik P. Hoffmann, eds, *Soviet Foreign Policy in a Changing World*, Aldine Publishing Co., New York.

Chanda, Nayan (1989-90), 'Civil War in Cambodia', *Foreign Policy*, no. 76.

Chernayev, Anatoly C. (1993a), *Shest' let c Gorbachevym: po dnevnikovym zapisyam* (Six Years With Gorbachev: A Diary), Progress Kultura, Moscow.

268 RUSSIAN FOREIGN POLICY AND THE END OF THE COLD WAR

Chernayev, Anatoli (1993b), *Die letzten Jahre einer Weltmacht: Der Kreml von innen* (The Last Years of a Superpower: Inside the Kremlin), Deutsche Verlags-Anstalt, Stuttgart.

Chernayev, Anatoly (1993c), 'The Phenomenon of Gorbachev in the Context of Leadership', *International Affairs* (Moscow), June.

Chernayev, Anatoly (1994), 'Gorbachev and the Reunification of Germany: Personal Perspectives', in Gorodetsky, ed, *op cit.*

Chernoff, F. (1991), 'Ending The Cold War: The Soviet Retreat and the US Military Buildup', *International Affairs* (London), vol. 67, no. 1.

Chomsky, Noam (1991), 'The US and the Gulf Crisis', in Bresheeth, Naim and Yuval-Davis, Nira, eds, *The Gulf War and the New World Order*, Zed Books, London and New Jersey.

Chomsky, Noam (1992), *Deterring Democracy*, Vintage, London.

Clark, Bruce (1995), *An Empire's New Clothes: The End of Russia's Liberal Dream*, Vintage, London.

Cogan, Charles G. (1993), 'Partners in Time: The CIA and Afghanistan since 1979', *World Policy Journal*, vol. X, no. 2.

Cohen, Eliot A (1994), 'Tales of the Desert', *Foreign Affairs*, vol. 73, no. 3, May-June.

Cohen, Stephen and Katrina vanden Heuvel (1989), *Voices of Glasnost: Interviews with Gorbachev's Reformers*, W. W. Norton, London and New York.

Coll, Steve (1992), 'Secret CIA Escalation in '85 Tipped Afghan Balance', *International Herald Tribune*, July 21.

Cordovez, Diego and Selig S. Harrison (1995), *Out of Afghanistan: The Inside Story of the Soviet Withdrawal*, Oxford University Press, Oxford and New York.

Cox, Michael (1986), 'The Cold War and Stalinism in the Age of Capitalist Decline', *Critique*, no. 17.

Cox, Michael (1990-91), 'From Superpower Detente to Entente Cordiale? Soviet-US Relations, 1989-1990, in Bruce George, ed, *Jane's NATO Handbook, 1990-1991*, 3rd edition: NATO, Brussels.

Cox, Michael (1995), *US Foreign Policy After the Cold War: Superpower Without A Mission?*, Pinter/RIIA, London.

Crampton, R.J. (1994), *Eastern Europe in the Twentieth Century*, Routledge, London and New York.

Crawshaw, Steve (1992), *Goodbye to the USSR: The Collapse of Soviet Power*, Bloomsbury, London.

Crockatt, Richard (1995), *The Fifty Years War: The United States and the Soviet*

*Union in World Politics, 1941-1991*, Routledge, London and New York.

Crow, Suzanne (1993), 'Russia Adopts a More Active Policy', *Radio Free Europe/Radio Liberty Research Report*, vol. 2, no. 12, 19 March.

Cumings, Bruce (1993), 'Revising Postrevisionism or the Poverty of Theory in Diplomatic History', *Diplomatic History*, vol. 17, no. 4, Fall.

Cviic, Christopher (1991), *Remaking the Balkans*, Pinter/RIIA, London.

Dale, Catherine (1996), 'The Case of Abkhazia (Georgia)', in Jonson and Archer, eds, *op cit.*

Dashichev, Vyacheslav (1994), 'On the Road to German Reunification: The View From Moscow', in Gorodetsky, ed, *op cit.*

Davis, Christopher M. (1990), 'Economic Influences on the Decline of the Soviet Union as a Great Power: Continuity Despite Change', in Goldstein and Armstrong, eds, *op cit.*

Davis, Lynn E (1988), 'Lessons of the INF Treaty', *Foreign Affairs*, vol. 66, no. 4, Spring.

Dawisha, Karen (1988), *Eastern Europe, Gorbachev and Reform: The Great Challenge*: Cambridge University Press, Cambridge.

Dawisha, Karen and Bruce Parrott (1994), *Russia and the New States of Eurasia: The Politics of Upheaval*, Cambridge University Press, Cambridge.

Deudney, Daniel and G. John Ikenberry (1991), 'Soviet Reform and the End of the Cold War: Explaining Large-Scale Historical Change', *Review of International Studies*, vol. 17, Summer.

Deutsch, Karl W. and John D. Singer (1964), 'Multipolar Systems and International Stability', *World Politics*, vol. 16, no. 3, April.

Dibb, Paul (1988), *The Soviet Union: The Incomplete Superpower*, 2nd edition: Macmillan/IISS, and London.

Diuk, Nadia and Adrian Karatnycky (1993), *New Nations Rising: The Fall of the Soviets and the Challenge of Independence*, John Wiley, New York and Chichester.

Dobbs, Michael (1992a), 'Secret Memos Trace Kremlin's March To War', *International Herald Tribune*, 16 November.

Dobbs, Michael (1992b), 'With Kabul Falling, Soviet Slide Began', *International Herald Tribune*, 17 November.

Doyle, Michael (1986), 'Liberalism and World Politics', *American Political Science Review*, vol. 80, no. 4, December.

Duncan, W. Raymond (1989), 'Cuban-Soviet Relations: Directions of Influence' in Edward A. Kolodziej and Roger E. Kanet, eds (1989), *The Limits of*

*Soviet Power in the Developing World*, Macmillan, London.
Dunmore, Timothy (1980), *The Stalinist Command Economy: The Soviet State Apparatus and Economic Policy, 1945-53*, Macmillan, London.

Ekedahl, Carolyn and Melvin Goodman (1993), 'The Soviet Union and the Invasion of Kuwait', Hollis, ed, *The Soviets, Their Successors and the Middle East*, London, RUSI, St Martin's Press.
Ellman, Michael and Vladimir Kontorovich, eds (1992), *The Disintegration of the Soviet Economic System*, Routledge, London and New York.
Eyal, Jonathan (1992), 'Giving Up Illusions and Unravelling Ties', in Pravda, ed, *op cit.*

FCO (1994), 'Partnership For Peace: A NATO Initiative', *Background Briefing*, Foreign and Commonwealth Office, London, March.
Frankland, Mark (1990), *The Patriots' Revolutions: How East Europe Won Its Freedom*, Sinclair Stevenson, London.
Freedman, Lawrence and Efraim Karsh (1993), *The Gulf Conflict, 1990-1991*, Faber, London.
Freedman, Lawrence (1994-5), 'Why the West Failed', *Foreign Policy*, no. 94, Winter.
Freedman, Robert O. (1991), 'Moscow and the Gulf War', *Problems of Communism*, vol. XL, no. 4.
Friedrich, Carl J. and Zbigniew K. Brzezinski (1956), *Totalitarian Dictatorship and Autocracy*, Harvard University Press, Cambridge, Mass.
Fukuyama, Francis (1989), 'The End of History?', *National Interest*, no. 16, Summer 1989.
Fukuyama, Francis (1994), 'Against the New Pessimism', *Commentary*, vol. 97, no. 2, February.
Fuller, Graham (1991), 'Moscow and the Gulf', *Foreign Affairs*, vol. 70, no. 3, Summer.
Furman, Dimitry and Carl Johan Asenius (1996), 'The Case of Nagorno-Karabakh (Azerbaijan), in Jonson and Archer, eds, *op cit.*

Gaddis, John Lewis (1983), 'The Emerging Post-Revisionist Synthesis on the Origins of the Cold War', *Diplomatic History*, vol. 7, Summer.
Gaddis, John Lewis (1986), 'The Long Peace: Elements of Stability in the Postwar International System', *International Security*, vol. 10, no. 3.
Gaddis, John Lewis (1987), *The Long Peace: Inquiries into the History of the*

*Cold War*, Oxford University Press, Oxford.

Gaddis, John Lewis (1994), *The United States and the End of the Cold War: Implications, Reconsiderations, Provocations*, Oxford University Press, Oxford.

Gaidar, Yegor (1995), *Gosudartsvo i evolyutsiya* (State and Evolution), Evraziya, Moscow.

Galeotti, Mark (1995), *The Age of Anxiety: Security and Politics in Soviet and Post-Soviet Russia*, Longman, London and New York.

Garthoff, Raymond L. (1994), *The Great Transition: American-Soviet Relations and the End of the Cold War*, Brookings Institution, Washington DC.

Gati, Charles (1990), *The Bloc That Failed: Soviet-East European Relations in Transition*, Indiana University Press, Bloomington.

Gedmin, Jeffrey (1992), *The Hidden Hand: Gorbachev and the Collapse of Eastern Germany*, AEI Press, Washington.

Geron, Leonard (1990), *Soviet Foreign Economic Policy Under Perestroika*, Pinter/RIIA, London.

Glenny, Misha (1993), *The Fall of Yugoslavia*, Revised edition: Penguin, Harmondsworth.

Glynn, Patrick (1992), *Closing Pandora's Box: Arms Control and the History of the Cold War*, Basic Books, New York.

Golan, Galia (1988), *The Soviet Union and National Liberation Movements in the Third World*, Unwin and Hyman, London.

Golan, Galia (1990), *Soviet Policy in the Middle East: From World War II to Gorbachev*, Cambridge University Press, Cambridge.

Goldman, Marshall (1991), *What Went Wrong With Perestroika?*, W. W. Norton, London and New York.

Goncharov, Sergei, John W. Lewis, Litai Xue (1995), *Uncertain Partners: Stalin, Mao and the Korean War*, Cambridge University Press, Cambridge.

Gorbachev, Mikhail S. (1984), *Zhivoe tvorchestvo naroda* (The Living Creativity of the People), Politizdat, Moscow.

Gorbachev, Mikhail S. (1986), *Political Report of the CPSU Central Committee to the 27th Party Congress*, Novosti, Moscow.

Gorbachev, Mikhail S. (1987), *Perestroika: New Thinking For Our Country and the World*, Collins, London.

Gorbachev, Mikhail S. (1988), 'Report by Mikhail Gorbachev, General Secretary of the CPSU Central Committee', *Documents and Materials*, Novosti, Moscow.

Gorbachev, Mikhail S. (1991), *The August Coup: The Truth and the Lessons*,

HarperCollins, London.

Gorbachev, Mikhail S. (1995a), *Zhizn' i Reformy* (Life and Reforms) (volume one), Novosti, Moscow.

Gorbachev, Mikhail S. (1995b), *Zhizn' i Reformy* (Life and Reforms) (volume two), Novosti, Moscow.

Gordon, Michael R. and Bernard E. Trainer (1994), 'Inside Story: Why the Gulf War Ended When It Did', *International Herald Tribune*, 24 October.

Gorodetsky, Gabriel, ed (1994), *Soviet Foreign Policy, 1917-91: A Retrospective*, Frank Cass, London.

Grachev, Andrei S. (1995), *Final Days: The Inside Story of the Collapse of the Soviet Union*, Westview, Boulder, Co.

Gray, Colin (1984), 'Moscow is Cheating', *Foreign Policy*, no. 56, Fall.

Gromyko, Andrei A. and Boris N. Ponomarev (1981), *Russian Foreign Policy, 1917-45* (volume 1), Progress, Moscow.

Gromyko, Andrei A. and Boris N. Ponomarev (1981), *Russian Foreign Policy 1945-80* (volume 2), Progress, Moscow.

Gromyko, Andrei (1989), *Memories*, Hutchinson, London.

Gromov, Boris, B (1994), *Ogranichennyi kontingent* (Limited Contingent), Progress, Moscow.

Gross, Jan T. (1992), 'Poland: From Civil Society to Political Nation', in Banac, ed, *op cit.*


Halle, Louis J. (1967), *The Cold War As History*, Chatto and Windus, London.

Halliday, Fred (1993), 'The Cold War as Inter-Systemic Conflict: Initial Theses', in Bowker and Brown, eds, *op cit.*

Halliday, Fred (1994a), *Rethinking International Relations*, Macmillan, London.

Halliday, Fred (1994b), 'The Gulf War, 1990-1991 and the Study of International Relations', vol. 20, no. 2, April.

Hanson, Philip (1994), 'The Future of Russian Economic Reform', *Survival*, vol. 36, no. 3, Autumn.

Harrison, Mark (1993), 'Soviet Economic Growth Since 1928: The Alternative Statistics of G. I. Khanin', *Europe-Asia Studies*, vol. 45, no. 1.

Harrison, Selig (1988), 'Inside the Afghan Talks', *Foreign Policy*, no. 72, Fall.

Hayek, F. K. (1944), *The Road To Serfdom*, Routledge, London.

Higgins, Rosalyn (1993), 'The New United Nations and Former Yugoslavia', *International Affairs* (London), vol. 69, no. 3, 1993.

Hobsbawm, Eric (1994), *Age of Extremes: The Short Twentieth Century, 1914-*

*1991*, Michael Joseph, London.

Hogan, Michael, ed (1992), *The End of the Cold War: Its Meaning and Implications*, Cambridge University Press, Cambridge.

Holloway David (1983), *The Soviet Union and the Arms Race*, Yale University Press, New Haven.

Hosking, Geoffrey (1985), *A History of the Soviet Union*, Fontana, London.

Hosking, Geoffrey (1990), *The Awakening of the Soviet Union*, Heinemann, London.

Hough, Jerry F. (1980), *Soviet Leadership in Transition*, Brookings Institution, Washington D.C.

Hough Jerry F. (1986), *The Struggle For The Third World*, Brookings Institution, Washington DC.

Hough, Jerry F. (1988), *Opening Up the Soviet Economy*, Brookings Institution, Washington DC.

Huntington, Samuel P. 'The Clash of Civilizations?', *Foreign Affairs*, vol. 72, no.3, Summer 1993.

Hyland, William G. (1990), *The Cold War Is Over*, Random House, New York and Canada.

Hyman, Anthony (1992), *Afghanistan under Soviet Domination, 1964-1991*, 3rd edition: Macmillan, London.

Ikenberry, G. John (1996), 'The Myth of Post-Cold War Chaos', *Foreign Affairs*, vol. 75, no. 3, May-June.

Isby, David (1992), 'Counter-Insurgency and the Lessons of Afghanistan' in Derek Leebaert and Timothy Dickinson, eds (1992), *Soviet Strategy and New Military Thinking*, Cambridge University Press, Cambridge.

Jacobsen, Carl G. (1990), 'Soviet Strategic Policy Since 1945', in Carl G. Jacobsen, ed, *Strategic Power: USA/USSR*, Macmillan, London.

Jonson, Lena and Clive Archer, eds (1996), *Peacekeeping and the Role of Russia in Eurasia*, Westview, Boulder Co. and Oxford.

Jukes, Geoffrey (1989), 'The Soviet Armed Forces and the Afghan War', in Saikal and Maley, eds, *op cit.*

Kagarlitsky, Boris (1992), *The Disintegration of the Monolith*, Verso, London.

Kaldor, Mary (1990a), *The Imaginary War: Understanding the East-West Conflict*, Basil Blackwell, Oxford.

Kaldor, Mary (1990b), 'After the Cold War', *New Left Review*, no. 180, March-

April.
Kaldor, Mary (1990-91), 'Avoiding a Division in Europe', *World Policy Journal*, vol. 81, no. 1, Winter.
Kampfner, John (1994), *Inside Yeltsin's Russia*, Cassell, London.
Kant, Immanuel (1950)[1795], *Perpetual Peace*, Merrill, New York.
Karsh, Efraim (1993), 'Soviet-Syrian Relations: The Troubled Partnership', in Light, ed, *op cit.*
Katz, Mark N., ed (1990), *The USSR and Marxist Revolutions in the Third World*, Cambridge University Press, Cambridge.
Kennan, George (X) (1947), 'Sources of Soviet Conduct', *Foreign Affairs*, vol. 25, no. 4, July.
Kennedy, Paul M. (1987), *The Rise and Fall of Great Powers: Economic Change and Military Conflict From 1500 to 2000*, Random House, New York.
Kennedy, Robert F. (1971), *Thirteen Days: A Memoir of the Cuban Missile Crisis*, W. W. Norton, New York.
Khasbulatov, Ruslan (1993), *The Struggle for Russia: Power and Change in the Democratic Revolution*, Routledge, London and New York.
Khrushchev, Nikita S. (1956), *Report of the Central Committee of the CPSU to the Twentieth Party Congress*, Foreign Languages Publishing House, Moscow.
Kimball, Warren F. (1983), 'Responses to John Lewis Gaddis: "The Emerging Postrevisionist Synthesis on the Origins of the Cold War"', *Diplomatic History*, vol. 7, no. 3, Summer.
King, Charles (1995), *Post-Soviet Moldova: A Borderland in Transition*, RIIA Post-Soviet Business Forum, London.
Kirkpatrick, Jeanne (1989), 'Dictatorships and Double Standards', *Commentary*, November.
Kissinger, Henry (1995), *Diplomacy*, Simon and Schuster, London.
Kiva, Alexei (1991), 'The Third World's Illusions and Realities', *International Affairs* (Moscow), October.
Kiva, Alexei (1992), 'The Superpower Which Ruined Itself', *International Affairs* (Moscow), no. 2, February.
Klass, Rosanne (1988), 'Afghanistan: The Accords', *Foreign Affairs*, vol. 66, Summer.
Kokorev, Vladimir and Anatoli Reznikovsky (1988), *Southern Africa: The Essence of the Conflict*, Moscow, Novosti.
Kornbluh, Peter (1988), 'Test Case for the Reagan Doctrine: The Covert "Contra" War', *Third World Quarterly*, vol. 10, no. 1.
Kozlova, Alla (1989), 'Ratification of the INF Treaty: Debates in the USSR and

USA', in Primakov, ed, *op cit.*

Kozyrev, Andrei (1992), 'Russia: A Chance For Survival', *Foreign Affairs*, vol. 71, no. 2.

Kozyrev, Andrei (1995), *Preobrazhenie* (Transfiguration), Mezhdunarodnye otnosheniya, Moscow.

Kreikemeyer, Anna and Andrei V. Zagorski (1996), 'The Commonwealth of Independent States', in Jonson and Archer, eds, *op cit.*

Kulikov, V. G. (1988), *Doktrina zashchity mira i sozializma* (Doctrine for the Defence of Peace and Socialism), Moscow.

Kutsyllo, Veronika (1993), *Zapiski iz belogo doma: 21 sentyabrya - 4 oktyabrya* (Notes from the White House, 21 September to 4 October), Kommersant, Moscow.

LaFeber, Walter (1992), 'An End To Which Cold War?', in Michael J. Hogan, ed, *op cit.*

LaFeber, Walter (1993), *America, Russia and the Cold War, 1945-90*, 6th edition: McGraw-Hill, New York.

Lapidus, Gail W., Victor Zaslavsky and Philip Goldman, eds (1992), *From Union To Commonwealth: Nationalism and Separation in the Soviet Union*, Cambridge University Press, Cambridge.

Larson, Deborah W. (1985), *Origins of Containment: A Psychological Explanation*, Princeton University Press, Princeton.

Lebow, Richard Ned (1995), 'The Long Peace, the End of the Cold War and the Failure of Realism', in Lebow and Risse-Kappen, eds, *op cit.*

Lebow, Richard Ned and Thomas Risse-Kappen, eds (1995), *International Relations Theory and the End of the Cold War*, Columbia University Press, New York.

Leifer, Michael (1992), 'Cambodia in Conflict', in Leslie Palmier, ed, *op cit.*

Lenin, Vladimir I. (1978)[1902], *What's To Be Done?*, Progress, Moscow.

Lenin, Vladimir I. (1986)[1916], *Imperialism: The Highest Stage of Capitalism*, Progress, Moscow.

Lester, Jeremy (1995), *Modern Tsars and Princes: The Struggle For Hegemony in Russia*, Verso, London.

Lewin, Moshe (1988), *The Gorbachev Phenomenon*, Radius Hutchinson, London.

Lieven, Anatol (1996), 'Baltic Iceberg Dead Ahead: NATO Beware', *The World Today*, vol. 52, no. 7, June.

Ligachev, Yegor (1993), *Inside Gorbachev's Kremlin: The Memoirs of Yegor Ligachev*, Pantheon, New York.

Light, Margot (1991), 'Soviet Policy in the Third World', *International Affairs* (London), vol. 67, no. 2, April.

Light, Margot, ed (1993), *Troubled Friendships: Moscow's Third World Ventures*, British Academic Press, London and New York.

Limberg, Wayne, (1990), 'Soviet Military Support for Third World Marxist Regimes', in Katz, Mark N., ed, *op cit.*

Lynch, Allen (1992), *The Cold War Is Over - Again*, Westview, Boulder, Co.

McAuley, Mary (1984), 'Nationalism and the Multi-ethnic State', in Harding, Neil, ed, *The State and Socialist Society*, Macmillan, London.

McElvoy, Anne (1992), *The Saddled Cow: East Germany's Life and Legacy*, Faber, London.

McFaul, Michael (1989-90), 'Rethinking the "Reagan Doctrine" in Angola', *International Security*, vol. 14, no. 3.

MccGwire, Michael (1991), *Perestroika and Soviet National Security*, Brookings Institution, Washington DC.

Malcolm, Neil, ed (1994), *Russia and Europe: An End to Confrontation?*, Pinter, London.

Maley, William and Amin Saikal, eds (1995), *Russia In Search Of Its Future*, Cambridge University Press, Cambridge.

Malia, Martin (Z) (1990), 'To the Stalin Mausoleum', *Daedalus*, vol. 119, no. 1.

Matthews, Ken (1993), *The Gulf Conflict and International Relations*, Routledge, London and New York.

Mau, Vladimir (1996), *The Political History of Economic Reform in Russia, 1985-1994*, Centre for Research into Communist Economies, London.

Mearsheimer, John J. (1990), 'Back to the Future: Instability in Europe after the Cold War', *International Security*, vol. 15, no. 1, Summer.

Medvedev, Roy (1980), *On Soviet Dissent*, Columbia, New York.

Medvedev, Roy (1986), *China and the Superpowers*, Basil Blackwell, Oxford and New York.

Medvedev, Zhores (1983), *Andropov*, Basil Blackwell, Oxford and New York.

Medvedev, Zhores (1986), *Gorbachev*, Basil Blackwell, Oxford and New York.

Melvin, Neil (1995), *Russians Beyond Russia: The Politics of National Identity*, Pinter/RIIA, London.

Mendelson, Sarah, E. (1993), 'Internal Battles and External Wars: Politics, Learning, and the Soviet Withdrawal From Afghanistan', *World Politics*, vol. 45, no. 3, April.

Menon, Rajan (1986), *Soviet Power and the Third World*, Yale University Press,

New Haven and London.

Menon, Rajan and Daniel N. Nelson, eds (1989), *Limits to Soviet Power*, Lexington Books, Lexington, Mass.

Meyer, S. M (1985), 'Soviet Strategic Programmes and the US SDI', *Survival*, vol. 27, no. 6.

*Military Balance* (Various years), IISS/Brassey's, London.

Miller John (1993), *Mikhail Gorbachev and the End of Soviet Power*, St. Martin's, London.

Miller, Nicola (1988), *Soviet Relations with Latin America, 1959-87*, Cambridge University Press, Cambridge.

Miller, Robert F. (1991), *Soviet Foreign Policy Today: Gorbachev and the New Political Thinking*, Unwin Hyman.

Morgenthau, Hans (1978) [1948], *Politics Among Nations*, Fifth edition: Knopf, New York.

Morrison, John (1992), *Boris Yeltsin*, Penguin, Harmondsworth.

Morozov, Alexander (1991a), 'Our Man in Kabul: Between Amin and Karmal', *New Times*, 38, 24-30 September.

Morozov, Alexander (1991b), 'Our Man in Kabul: Shots Fired in the House of the Nation', *New Times*, 41, 8-14 October.

Nogee, Joseph L. and Robert H. Donaldson (1988), *Soviet Foreign Policy Since World War II*, 3rd edition, Pergamon Press, New York, Oxford.

Norris, R. S. (1992), 'Soviet Nuclear Archipelago', *Arms Control Today*, January-February.

Nove, Alec (1992), *An Economic History of the USSR, 1917-1991*, Final edition: Penguin, Harmondsworth.

Nye, Joseph S. (1990), *Bound To Lead: The Changing Nature of American Power*, Basic Books, New York.

Oberdorfer, Don (1992), *The Turn - How The Cold War Came To An End: The United States and the Soviet Union, 1983-90*, Cape, London.

Oldenburg, Fred (1994), 'The Settlement in Germany', in Malcolm, ed, *op cit*.

O'Neill, Kathryn and Barry Munslow (1990-91), 'Ending the Cold War in Southern Africa', *Third World Quarterly*, vol. 12, nos. 3-4.

Owen, David (1995), *Balkan Odyssey*, Victor Gollancz, London.

Palmier, ed (1992), *Detente in Asia?*, Macmillan, London.

Partos, Gabriel (1993), *The World That Came In From The Cold*, RIIA/BBC

World Service, London.

Paterson, Thomas (1979), *On Every Front: The Making of the Cold War*, W. W. Norton, New York and London.

Pavlov, Valentin (1983), *Gorbachev-putch: Avgust iznutri* (The Gorbachev Putsch: The August Events From The Inside), Delovoi Mir, Moscow.

Pilger, John (1992), *Distant Voices*, Vintage, London.

Pipes, Richard (1977), 'Why the Soviet Union Thinks It Can Fight and Win a Nuclear War', *Commentary*, July.

Pipes, Richard (1981), *US-Soviet Relations in the Era of Detente*, Westview, Boulder, Co.

*Political Calendar* (Various issues), Russian Information Agency, Novosti, London.

Poptsov, Oleg (1995), *Khronika vrmen 'Tsarya Borisa': Rossiya, Kreml', 1991-1995* (Chronicles of Tsar Boris: Russia, the Kremlin, 1991-1995), Sovershenno Sekretno/Edition Q, Moscow and Berlin.

Pravda, Alex, ed (1992), *The End of Outer Empire: Soviet-East European Relations in Transition*, Sage, London.

Primakov, Yevgeny, et al, eds (1989), *Disarmament and Security Yearbook,1988-89*, Novosti Press, Moscow.

Pryce-Jones, David (1995), *The War That Never Was: The Fall of the Soviet Empire, 1985-1991*, Weidenfeld and Nicolson, London.

Przeworski, Adam (1991), *Democracy and the Market: Political and Economic Reforms in Eastern Europe and Latin America*, Cambridge University Press, Cambridge.

Puschel, K. (1989), 'Can Moscow Live With SDI?', *Survival*, vol. 31, no. 1, January-February.

Ra'anan, Uri (1990), 'Is The Cold War Over?', in Armstrong and Goldstein, eds, *op cit.*

Rais, Ragul B. (1992), 'Afghanistan and Regional Security after the Cold War,' *Problems of Communism*, May-June.

Reagan, Ronald (1990), *An American Life*, Simon and Schuster, London and New York.

Reddaway, Peter (1989), 'The Helsinki Process and Human Rights in the USSR', in Dilys M. Hill, ed, *Human Rights and Foreign Policy*, Macmillan, London.

Regan, Donald T. (1988), *For The Record: From Wall Street to Washington*, Harcourt Brace Jovanovich, New York.

Remnick, David (1993), *Lenin's Tomb: The Last Days of the Soviet Empire*, Viking, London.

Rieff, David (1995), *Slaughterhouse: Bosnia and the Failure of the West*, Vintage, London.

Risse-Kappen, T. (1991), 'Did Peace Through Strength End The Cold War? Lessons From INF', *International Security*, vol. 16, no. 1.

Rogov, Sergei (1995), 'Russia and the United States: A Partnership or Another Disengagement?', *International Affairs* (Moscow), no. 7.

Ro'i, Yaacov (1994), 'The Problematics of the Soviet-Israeli Relationship', in Gorodetsky, ed, *op cit*.

Roucek, Libor (1992), *After the Bloc: The New International Relations in Eastern Europe*, RIIA, Discussion Paper, 40, London.

Rubin, Barnett R. (1993-94), 'The Fragmentation of Tajikistan', *Survival*, vol. 35, no. 4, Winter.

Ruhl, L. (1991), 'Offensive Defence in the Warsaw Pact', *Survival*, vol. 33, no. 5, September-October.

*Russian Economics Trends*, (Various editions), Whurr Publishers, London.

Sagdeev, Roald (1994), *The Making of a Soviet Scientist: My Adventures in Nuclear Fusion and Space From Stalin to Star Wars*, John Wiley, New York.

Saikal, Amin and William Maley, eds (1989), *The Soviet Withdrawal From Afghanistan*, Cambridge University Press, Cambridge.

Saivetz, Carol R. (1994), 'Moscow and the Gulf War: The Policies of a Collapsing Superpower', in Gorodetsky, ed, *op cit*.

Sakharov, Andrei D. (1990), *Trevoga i Nadezhda* (Worries and Hopes), Interverso, Moscow.

Sakwa, Richard (1989), *Soviet Politics: An Introduction*, Routledge, London and New York.

Sakwa, Richard (1990), *Gorbachev and His Reforms, 1985-1990*, Philip Allan, Hemel Hempstead.

Sakwa, Richard (1993), *Russian Politics and Society*, Routledge, London and New York.

Sakwa, Richard (1996), *Russian Politics and Society*, 2nd edition: Routledge, London and New York.

Sanders, David (1985), *Lawmaking and Co-operating in International Politics: The Idealist Case Re-examined*, Macmillan, London.

Segal, Gerald (1990), *The Soviet Union and the Pacific*, Unwin Hyman, Boston and London.

Segal, Gerald (1992), 'Soviet Perspectives', in Palmier, ed, *op cit.*

Shaw, Martin (1991), *Post-Military Society: Militarism, Demilitarization and War at the End of the Twentieth Century*, Polity, Cambridge.

Shearman, Peter J. (1993), 'New Political Thinking Reassessed', *Review of International Studies*, vol. 19, no. 2.

Shearman, Peter J., ed (1995), *Russian Foreign Policy Since 1990*, Westview, Boulder, Co.

Sheehan, Michael (1992), 'Security and International Relations in Eastern Europe', in *Eastern Europe and the Commonwealth of Independent States, 1992*, Europa, London.

Shenfield, Stephen (1985), 'Star Wars: A Soviet Account', *Detente*, no. 3, May.

Shevardnadze, Eduard (1991), *The Future Belongs To Freedom*, Free Press, New York.

Shevtsova, Lilia (1992), 'The August Coup and the Soviet Collapse', *Survival*, Spring.

Shlapentokh, Vladimir (1990), *Soviet Intellectuals and Political Power: The Post-Stalin Era*, Princeton University Press, Princeton.

Shultz, George P. (1993), *Turmoil and Triumph: My Years as Secretary of State*, Scribner's, New York.

Silber, Laura and Allan Little (1995), *The Death of Yugoslavia*, Penguin, Harmondsworth.

Simoniya, Nodari (1972), 'Natsionalizm: politicheskaya bor'ba v osvobodivshikhsya stranakh' (Nationalism: the political struggle in liberated countries), *MEMO (Mirovaya ekonomika i mezhdunarodnye otnosheniya)* (World Economics and International Relations), no 1.

*SIPRI Yearbook: World Armaments and Disarmament*, (Various years), OUP/ SIPRI, Oxford.

Sivachev, Nikolai and Nikolai Yakovlev (1979), *Russia and the United States*, Chicago University Press, Chicago.

Smiley, Xan (1995), 'Murder Most Common', *The World In 1996*, The Economist Publications, London.

Smith, Anthony D. (1991), *National Identity*, Penguin, Harmondsworth.

Smith, Hedrick (1990), *The New Russians*, Hutchinson, London.

Somerville, Keith (1993), *Southern Africa and the Soviet Union*, Macmillan, London.

Spechler, Diana R. and Martin C. Spechler (1989), 'The Economic Burden of the Soviet Empire: Estimates and Reestimates', in Rajan Menon and Daniel

N. Nelson, eds, *Limits to Soviet Power*, Lexington Books, Lexington and Toronto.

Stankevich, Sergei (1992), 'Russia in Search of Itself', *National Interest*, no. 28, Summer.

Stepankov, Valentin and Yevgeny Lisov (1992), *Kremlevskii zagovor* (The Kremlin Conspiracy), Ogonek, Moscow.

Steele, Jonathan (1994), *Eternal Russia: Yeltsin, Gorbachev and the Mirage of Democracy*, Faber and Faber, London and Boston.

Talbott, Strobe (1984), *Reagan and the Russians*, Vintage Books, New York.

Taylor, Brian (1994), 'Russian Civil-Military Relations After the October Uprising', *Survival*, vol. 36, no. 1.

Taylor, Trevor, ed (1992), *The Collapse of the Soviet Empire: Managing the Regional Fall-Out*, RIIA and IIGP, London.

Taylor, Trevor (1994), *European Security and the Former Soviet Union*, Royal Institute of International Affairs, London.

Taylor, Trevor (1996), 'Cashing in the Dividend - Quietly', *The World Today*, vol. 52, no. 6, June.

Thatcher, Margaret (1993), *The Downing Street Years*, HarperCollins, London.

Thompson, E. P. (1982), *Beyond the Cold War*, Merlin, London.

Thompson, E. P., Fred Halliday and Rudolph Bahro, eds (1982), *Exterminism and Cold War*, Verso, London.

Trofimenko, Henry (1988), 'Ending the Cold War, Not History', *Washington Quarterly*, vol. 13, no. 2.

Trofimenko, Henry and Pavel Podlesnyi (1988), *USSR-USA: Lessons of Peaceful Coexistence*, Novosti, Moscow.

Turley, William S. (1990), 'The Khmer War: Cambodia after Paris', *Survival*, vol. 32, no. 5, September-October.

Uhlig, M. A. (1993-94), 'The Karabakh War', *World Policy Journal*, vol. X, no. 4, Winter.

Urban, Mark (1990), *War in Afghanistan*, 2nd edition: Macmillan, London.

Urban, Michael, E. (1990), *More Power To The Soviets: The Democratic Revolution in the USSR*, Elgar, Aldershot.

Utagawa, Reizo (1992), 'Economic Implications of Change in the Former Soviet Union', in Taylor, T., ed, *op cit*.

Valkenier, Elizabeth Kridl (1983), *The Soviet Union and the Third World: An Economic Bind*, Praeger, New York.

Various Authors (1989), *Afghanistan In Our Lives*, Novosti, Moscow.

Vassiliev, Alexei (1993), *Russian Policy in the Middle East: From Messianism To Pragmatism*, Ithaca Press, Reading.

Velikhov, Y. (1986), *Weaponry in Space: The Dilemma of Security*, Mir, Moscow.

Vickers, George R. and Jack Spence (1992), 'Nicaragua's Balancing Act', *World Policy Journal*, vol. 9, no. 3, Summer.

Vigor, P. H. (1986), *The Soviet View of Disarmament*, Macmillan, London.

Walker, Martin (1987), *The Waking Giant: The Soviet Union Under Gorbachev*, Abacus, London.

Walker, Martin (1993), *The Cold War and the Making of the Modern World*, 4th Estate, London.

Waltz, Kenneth J. (1964), 'The Stability of the Bipolar World', *Daedalus*, vol. 93, no. 3.

Waltz, Kenneth J. (1979), *Theory of International Politics*, Random House, New York.

Waltz, Kenneth J. (1982), *The Spread of Nuclear Weapons: More May Be Better*, Adelphi Paper, no. 171, IISS, London.

Waltz, Kenneth J. (1993), 'The New World Order', *Millennium*, vol. 22, no. 2, Summer.

Webber, Mark (1996), *The International Politics of Russia and the Successor States*, Manchester University Press, Manchester and New York.

Wettig, Gerhard (1993), 'Moscow's Acceptance of NATO: The Catalytic Role of German Unification', *Europe-Asia Studies*, vol. 45, no. 6, 1993.

White, Stephen (1990), *Gorbachev in Power*, Cambridge University Press, Cambridge.

White, Stephen (1993), *After Gorbachev*, Cambridge University Press, Cambridge.

Wiarda, Howard J. (1991), 'Is Cuba Next?', *Problems of Communism*, vol. XL, no. 1, January-April.

Williams, William A. (1962), *The Tragedy of American Diplomacy*, Delta, New York.

World Bank (1996), *From Plan To Market: World Bank Development Report1996*, Oxford University Press, Oxford.

Worner, Manfred (1994), 'Partnership with NATO: The Political Dimension', in *NATO's Sixteen Nations*, vol. 39, no.2.

Yeltsin, Boris N. (1990), *Against the Grain: An Autobiography*, Cape, London.
Yeltsin, Boris N. (1994), *The View From the Kremlin*, HarperCollins, London.
Yergin, Daniel (1980), *Shattered Peace: The Origins of the Cold War and the National Security State*, Penguin, Harmondsworth.
Zaslavskaya, Tatyana (1984), 'The Novosibirsk Report', *Survival*, vol. 28, no. 1, Spring.
Zhdanov, Andrei (1991)[1947], 'Two-Camp Theory', in Gale Stokes, ed, *From Stalinism to Pluralism: A Documentary History of Eastern Europe since 1945*, Oxford University Press, Oxford and New York.
Zic, Zoran (1992), 'Eastern Europe', in Mary Hawkesworth and Maurice Kogan, eds, *Encyclopedia of Government and Politics*, vol. 2, Routledge, London and New York.
Zwick, Peter (1990), *Soviet Foreign Policy: Process and Policy*, Prentice Hall, New Jersey.

# INDEX